de Gruyter Studies in Organization 37
Kono: Long-Range Planning of Japanese Corporations

de Gruyter Studies in Organization

International Management, Organization and Policy Analysis

A new international and interdisciplinary book series from de Gruyter presenting comprehensive research on aspects of international management, organization studies and comparative public policy.
It will cover cross-cultural and cross-national studies of topics such as:
— management; organizations; public policy, and/or their inter-relation
— industry and regulatory policies
— business-government relations
— international organizations
— comparative institutional frameworks.

While each book in the series ideally will have a comparative empirical focus, specific national studies of a general theoretical, substantive or regional interest which relate to the development of cross-cultural and comparative theory will also be encouraged.
The series is designed to stimulate and encourage the exchange of ideas across linguistic, national and cultural traditions of analysis, between academic researchers, practitioners and policy makers, and between disciplinary specialisms.
The volume will present theoretical work, empirical studies, translations and 'state-of-the art' surveys. The *international* aspects of the series will be uppermost: there will be a strong commitment to work which crosses and opens boundaries.

Editor:

Prof. Stewart R. Clegg, University of St. Andrews, Dept. of Management, St. Andrews, Scotland, U.K.

Advisory Board:

Prof. Nancy J. Adler, McGill University, Dept. of Management, Montreal, Quebec, Canada
Prof. Richard Hall, State University of New York at Albany, Dept. of Sociology, Albany, New York, USA
Prof. Gary Hamilton, University of California, Dept. of Sociology, Davis, California, USA
Prof. Geert Hofstede, University of Limburg, Maastricht, The Netherlands
Prof. Pradip N. Khandwalla, Indian Institute of Management, Vastrapur, Ahmedabad, India
Prof. Surenda Munshi, Sociology Group, Indian Institute of Management, Calcutta, India
Prof. Gordon Redding, University of Hong Kong, Dept. of Management Studies, Hong Kong

Toyohiro Kono

Long-Range Planning of Japanese Corporations

Walter de Gruyter · Berlin · New York 1992

Dr. *Toyohiro Kono* is Professor of Business Administration at the
Faculty of Economics, Gakushuin University, Tokyo

∞ Printed on acid-free paper which falls within the guidelines
of the ANSI to ensure permanence and durability.

Library of Congress Cataloging-in-Publication Data

Kono, Toyohiro.
    Long-range planning of Japanese corporations / Toyo-
hiro Kono.
    (De Gruyter studies in organization ; 37)
    ISBN 3-11-012914-0 (alk. paper)
        3-11-013793-3 (pbk.)
    1. Corporate planning—Japan. 2. Strategic plan-
ning—Japan. 3. Decision-making—Japan. 4. Corporations,
Japanese. I. Title. II. Series.
HD30.28.K66   1992
658.4'012—dc20   92-18407
                                    CIP

Die Deutsche Bibliothek — Cataloging-in-Publication Data

Kono, Toyohiro:
Long-range planning of Japanese corporations / Toyohiro
Kono. — Berlin ; New York : de Gruyter, 1992
    (De Gruyter studies in organization ; 37 : International
    management, organization and policy analysis)
    ISBN 3-11-012914-0 (geb.)
        3-11-013793-3 (brosch.)
NE: GT

Typesetting: converted by Knipp Textverarbeitungen. Wetter. — Printing: Ratzlow-Druck,
Berlin. — Binding: D. Mikolai. Berlin. — Cover Design: Johannes Rother, Berlin. —
Printed in Germany.

Preface

This book tries to describe the formal long-range planning process of Japanese corporations, to analyze the formal strategic decision making process and to find theories through this analysis.

There are many other books dealing with strategic decisions, but there are few books which deal with formal long-range planning. It is one of the strengths of Japanese corporations to use formal long-range planning to carry out innovative, analytical strategic decisions.

Long-range planning practices are very popular among large corporations, and successful companies such as Hitachi, Toshiba, Canon, Bridgestone Tire and Eizai Pharmaceuticals have been using formal long-range planning systems for more than thirty years to make innovative strategic decisions. Successful Japanese corporations have been making challenging innovative decisions, not incremental decisions and have been using internal development and not acquisitions. Large capital investment in the steel industry and aggressive new product development in electronics products industries are typical cases. To initiate and integrate these decisions formal long-range planning has been useful.

The author does not neglect the importance of informal, emergent decision making, the relations between informal decisions and formal decisions are studied in this book. Simply speaking, emergent or ad hoc decisions are properly evaluated and positioned by the formal long-range strategy. Without long-range visions, ad hoc decisions will not be successful and the resources will not be allocated properly.

The features of this book are as follows:

(1) It is not just a description of the practices of Japanese corporations, but it tries to find out principles of formal strategic decisions through the study of long-range planning. It tries to find out the typologies, cause-effect relationships and numerical relationships.
(2) As was already mentioned, it is a study of formal, analytical strategic decisions, which are important in Japanese corporations in arriving at a consensus. However, the author tries to find out the relationship between informal or intuitive decisions and formal analytical decisions.
(3) One of the goals of formal long-range planning is to vitalize corporate culture. Many Japanese corporations use long-range planning for changing corporate culture.
(4) The formation of corporate resources are important contents of the long-range plan. This book has devoted many pages to it because it takes a long lead time to formulate strong resource structures, which are the basis for producing outstanding product market strategies.

(5) This book deals with quantitative computations to some extent, particularly in capital investment, personnel planning and profit planning. There has been too much neglect regarding this aspect of planning in recent literature.

(6) The author has conducted many surveys, visited many companies and collected many materials; this book is based on empirical analysis.

The need for a formal, written strategic plan can be explained by two groups of factors.

(1.1) The increased speed of change in the environment activated by technological advancement and the change of the internal environment calls for changes of the strategy of corporations. The formal long-range plan is useful to regularly scan the environment and to regularly investigate the strategic issues of the corporation. Without long-range planning, it is hard to create an opportunity to raise basic issues which affect the corporation.

(1.2) As competition in the world market is becoming more severe, companies need to make better decisions by analytical processes. The formation of regular comprehensive plans stimulates creative strategic thought in various departments. It can mobilize the ideas of people in many departments and in many levels of the hierarchy of the organization. These ideas should be better than sudden orders from top management, often with hidden intentions. The formal long-range planning can be useful in formally soliciting ideas to restructure the company. Without formal planning, the ideas will flow anyway.

(1.3) The lead time of decisions, or the time span from the conception of ideas to their implementation and profitable operation is becoming longer, hence companies need to forecast the long-range future and have to make investment well in advance, when the company has enough resources. Reactive decisions are too late.

(2.1) The large corporation has many projects and resources are limited. Human resources and physical resources have to be allocated among many projects so that the timing of investment and the effectiveness of investment are appropriate. For this purpose, comprehensive planning is useful. Without formal long-range planning, it is hard to concentrate resource allocation on key projects. It may be hard for the company to construct a strong resource structure to implement innovative product-market strategies.

(2.2) Strategic decisions are learning processes in many respects, and knowledge is accumulated through making decisions. For learning purposes, written plans are more useful than 'invisible' decisions, because written plans are seen by many decision makers.

(2.3) The long-range plan can be used to motivate people, because it shows the future of the company and it can visualize the future image of the company.

The author has been studying long-range planning for more than thirty years, and has written many books in this area. This book is based on extensive surveys. Data was collected from (a) mail questionnaire surveys, responses being usually from more then three hundred companies, (b) interviews with corporate planners, (c) case presentations and discussions in study groups of corporate planners, (d) cases published in business journals and in newspapers, (e) cases published as books. In Particular the author has had bimonthly meetings with corporate planners for more than twenty years. Case presentations and discussions in the meetings have been extremely useful in understanding the practices and issues in planning.

The outline of this book is as follows:
Chapter one through chapter four deals with the purposes and limitations of long-range planning, the processes of planning and organizations for planning. Several types of planning are identified.

Chapter five through chapter eight analyzes the information collection, the finding of strategic issues and the generation of strategic ideas.

Chapter nine through chapter ten studies the formation of resource structure, the evaluation of strategies and resource allocation. Many pages are devoted to the analysis of the accumulation and strengthening of corporate resources.

Chapter eleven and chapter twelve study the integration and coordination of projects, and the profit planning which is planning useful for coordination. Some computation methods are presented.

Chapter thirteen through chapter fifteen explains decision-making under uncertainty, the implementation of the plan, and problems and success factors of planning.

Acknowledgments

I am grateful to the members of the study groups of corporate planners at the Japan Productivity Center and at the Business Research Center. The presentation of cases and discussions there were extremely informative and enlightening. From Gakushuin University, I owe many thoughts to my colleagues, whom I had frequent discussions with. My assistants at Gakushuin University, Ms. T. Yoshino and Ms. A. Yanagida cheerfully helped to arrange survey material and typed many pages of work. Dr. Bianka Ralle, of Walter de Gruyter encouraged me to publish this book and Mr. Robert Ramsay, of Edinburgh, conducted the English editing of the manuscript. I wish to extend my hearty gratitude to all of them.

January 1992   Toyohiro Kono

Table of Contents

Chapter 1 The concept and role of long-range planning

1.1 The concept of long-range planning

The management process starts with planning. The whole management process is comprised of planning, organizing, staffing, motivating and controlling. If planning is not appropriate, then the following processes are not effective.

The organization has four sub-systems, as the table 1.1 shows, namely, (1) organizational goals and philosophies, (2) product-market strategies, (3) resource structures and (4) operations. These four sub-systems become the subjects of planning. The area of long-range planning is mostly focused on the first three, the subjects of short-range planning are mostly concentrated on operations. Operations are based on the strategy and the structure, so long-range planning is a plan based on the premises of the short-range planning. This means that long-range planning is construct on the premises of daily operations.

Excellent Japanese companies such as Canon, Bridgestone (tire manufacturing), Hitachi and Eisai (pharmaceutical products) have been constantly using long-range planning for more than twenty years.

1.1.1 The characteristics of long-range planning are as follows

(a) The Subjects of plans.

As has been mentioned already, the subject of long-range plans are corporate strategy and structure. These are conceptually indicated on Table 1.1. The long-range plan can be divided into two parts: a long-range strategy and a medium-range plan. The long-range strategy (A) stipulates any major changes in long-range goals, product-market strategy and the structure of the company. The medium-range plan (B) covers the improvement of these areas, namely, the competition strategy, personnel plan and capital investment plan.

The administrative plan (F), contains the policies and rules which govern repetitive production and marketing activities. It makes possible the application of Fredrick Taylor's "one best method" (Taylor, 1911).

Budgeting (G), states decisions on the quantity and timing of production and marketing, and on the enhancement of productivity and profitability. (F) and (G) are not part of the long-range plan; they are created after the long-range plan. The long-range

Table 1.1 Subjects of long-range planning

Subjects \ Change	(1) Innovation	(2) Improvement	(3) Maintenance or repetition
(a) Goals	Large change of business philosophy	Change of business philosophy	Business creed
(b) Product-market strategy	New product development Vertical integration Multinational management	Competitive strategy	
(c) Structure	New capital investment Acquisition of other companies Agreement and joint ventures	Recruitment of personnel and training Improvement of facilities Improvement of rules and standards	Wage and salary system Maintenance of facilities Rules and standards for production and sales
(d) Operation			Material purchasing plan Production plan Sales plan Profit plan

A · · · Long-range strategy }
B · · · Medium-range plan   } Long-range plan

F · · · Administrative plan

G · · · Budgeting

plan is a prerequisite for the administrative plan and the short-range plan. If there is no long-range plan, the budget will be built based either on the implicit strategy of some managers, which is not well thought out or it might be based on the past experience and it might thus be conservative.

(b) Comprehensiveness.

A long-range plan is a comprehensive plan or a "period plan". Systematic information collection and extensive idea-gathering are stated and many alternatives are raised. These are then evaluated, selected and ranked by priorities, and resources are allocated in the most profitable way. By this comprehensive approach, the company can save the cost of information collection by reducing the duplication of collection, and can have the right ranking of projects by conducting simultaneous comparisons. If an individual corporate strategy is decided upon independently, particular information is gathered and then the project is evaluated and upon decided separately from the formal comprehensive plan. This approach does not result in the best allocation of resources.

Such sudden strategic decision happens, however, even in a company which has well established long-range plans. If these are prohibited the planning system will lose flexibility. In particular, when the timing of a decision is important, for example, when opportunities for company acquisitions or for joint-venture appear unexpectedly, then they are decided on separately. As Mintzberg states, strategic decisions are conducted in the following way (Quinn, Mintzberg & James, 1988).

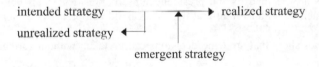

However, these emergent strategies can be appropriately evaluated if the long-range strategy is decided on beforehand. Here again the need for long-range planning is clear.

(c) Formally written plan.

The long-range plan is a written plan and is formally authorized plan. It is not a hidden conception in the brain of the president or C.E.O., which is not visible by other persons and is the source of spontaneous commands. The long-range plan is the result of formal decision-making and is a consensus of the top management team and of the divisions concerned. The consensus is particularly important in Japan. The long-range planning is used as a tool for decision-making by consensus. The planning functions as a tool for coordinating the activities of several departments.

It is a written document and is made public to members above certain levels. By sharing in the goals and strategies they come to know what they should do now in preparation for tomorrow. The outline of the long-range plan is usually made public to all employees by some means, and by knowing the long-range goals, people can understand the meaning of the jobs they are performing today.

1.2 Effects of long-range planning

The subject of long-range planning is corporate strategies, although not all corporate strategies are plan in long-range plan. More than that, some companies do not even use formal long-range planning. Kyocera, for example has grown rapidly as a manufacturer of ceramic package for semiconductor since its establishment in 1959, with a sales of ¥311 billion in 1988, selling products all over the world and having many production plants in the U.S. and in other countries. It has a clear philosophy and strategy, the philosophy being "Respect heaven and love your people". It has clear strategic policies on quality, product development, on organizational structure and on personnel management. However, it has never used formal long-range plans to date, most of its strategic decisions are taken by the president & C.E.O. Inamori.

Nintendo, originally a playing card manufacturer, entered into the toy business using electronics technology and is now selling gaming system called "Family computer" to 10 million families all over the world. It has a clear strategy, putting an emphasis on the application of electronics technology and related software to toys. It sells hardware at a relatively cheap price to promote the sales of the software, which is the major source of profit. It does not have a long-range planning system. Important strategies are decided by the president himself. President Yamauchi states that the environment is so uncertain that he cannot build comprehensive long-range plans.

These two cases show that strategic decisions can be taken without formal long-range planning.

However, many surveys show that the majority of large corporations in Japan have long-range plans. A survey by MITI (Ministry of International Trade and Industry) on a variety of management practices shows that, in 1983, 69% companies (out of 480 manufacturing companies) and in 1986, 75% companies (out of 598 manufacturing companies) have long-range plans. The ten year average was about 70 percent, and the overall performances measured by growth rate and return on total investment of the companies which had long-range plans were better than those which did not have long-range plan. The differences were statistically significant at 5 percent risk every year. (MITI, 1984, 1987)

Many companies have also had the long-range plans for many years. According to our survey of 249 corporations with long-range plans in 1989, 49 percent of companies had had long-range plans for more than 10 years, 21 percent had had then for more than 5 years and 22 percent had had for less than 5 years.

It may not be appropriate to estimate of general effects of long-range planning; instead, we should identify what sort of planning has had what sort of effects. Here, we

Table 1.2 A model of the cause-effect ralationship of long-range planning systems

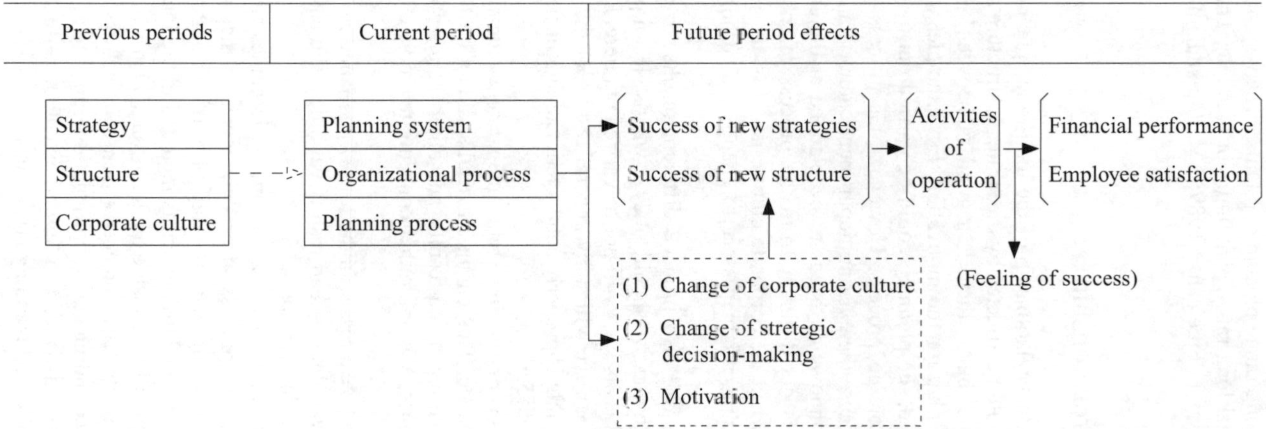

(note) (1) - - -▷ indicates discontinous ralations

(2) ☐ indicates causal variables

(3) ⬚ indicates direct effects (intervening variables)

(4) [ ] indicates indirect effects (intervening and end-results variables)

will examine the general effects of long-range planning systems. (There are many research papers on the effects of formal long-range planning. For example, Thune and House, 1970; W. R. King, 1983; E. Freeman, 1989; V. Ramanujam, 1987; A. Langley; 1988)

1.2.1 Model of cause-effect relationship

Table 1.2 is a model of the cause-effect relationship of the long-range planning system. The present planning system could be affected by the strategy, structure and corporate culture of the previous period, but if there is a good fit between them, the long-range plan will not be able to plan for the innovation. For example, when the company's product mix is diversified, the planning could be carried out by either a decentralized process or by a bottom-up process. However, this process will not bring about innovative planning because the existing department cannot plan a completely new business. This sort of innovation needs to be planned at the corporate level, where the planning process is not different from the process of specialized companies. In the similar manner, when the corporate culture is not lively, planning could be superficial so before planning, it is necessary to change the corporate culture first.

The different styles of planning will also produce different results. In order to identify the results of long-range planning, we should analyze what styles of planning bring about what kinds of results. This analysis will not be carried out here, it will be done in the last chapter. In this chapter, we will study general results, or the average values of results, assuming that planning is properly conducted. Conditions necessary for success will be studied in Chapter 15.

Long-range planning affects decision-making style and strategy contents, and eventually affects financial performance. This chains of results cannot be fully followed, because it takes a long time to reach end-results, and other factors will intervene to influence financial performance. We will rather concentrate on the effects influenced directly.

This cause-effect relationship can be expressed in the following manner;

Causal variables → intervening variables → end-results variables. We have to be satisfied here with finding the intervening variables.

Of the intervening variables, change to decision-making style comes first. This means that the formal decision-making process affects the decision-making style both inside and outside long-range planning or in the daily life of the organization. Formal planning itself changes decision-making, which is included in the long-range planning process. This is the meaning of being inside the long-range plan.

The next intervening variables are strategy contents, resource structures and operations. The change of product mix and change of production equipments are examples of these. These changes will be analyzed to a limited extent, because it is hard to notice whether they are a result of formal planning processes or not.

1.2.2 Effects on decision-making processes

The long-range plan is a formal decision-making process, and it affects the other parts of the decision-making process. Table 1.1.b at the end of this chapter shows the survey results of the effects of long-range planning as perceived by the corporate planner.

(1)   Innovation effects
(1.1)   Perception of strategic issues
The long-range plan helps the company identify problems and thus it helps the company to scrutinize the past strategy, and to reflect on this past pattern. By planning, the company is forced to do this regularly every year. This is useful in changing the strategy formulation pattern and in changing the strategy itself. Strategic issues include both threats and opportunities. Strategic issues are studied by the planning department, top management and by other departments, after which temporary goals are set. This becomes the starting point of formulating a number of strategies. Long-range goals indicate the future direction of the company.

Organizations tend towards inertia. One sugar company, for example, did not see related business opportunities other than those in the sugar industry, and naturally has had low performance for many years.

People do not like change. The reasons are two-fold. Those who run risks will be afraid of failure in new trials, and those who are outside the project will be afraid of loosing opportunities for promotion, be afraid of changes in their status.

However, as the environment, both external and internal, evolves, the company has to cope with changes in order to survive and has to change the product-market strategy. Long-range planning systems make it necessary to regularly self-examine past strategy, to find out problems and new opportunities. This is an 'unfreezing' effect. The survey results in Table 1.1.b show that this effect is considered as important.

(1.2) Enhancing the sensitivity to environmental change, and changing the orientation of members to strategy.

Perception is selective, and is oriented by the structure of understanding. Both an individual and a company look for things which they want to see and based upon the patterns that they are accustomed to see. There are too many things to see in the environment, so they see and understand things through a sort of spectacles, by a certain cognitive structure, by a schema, by a map. This perceptual pattern is changed by experience. The long-range planning system forces a company to see new things, to change glasses, to see the future changes in the environment and to find out opportunities and threats.

People like to do the daily operations. This is called "Gresham's law on decision" (Simon, 1977). Daily operation have little uncertainty, feed back is fast and the results tend to be reflected in rewards. Gresham's law is a kind of schema, and this has to be changed.

Canon, for example, entered into the copying machine business, a decision which was done as a part of the formal long-range planning process. Predictions for the demand of cameras, at the time, were not very bright, and among a number of opportunities for business machines, the copier was selected as the most hopeful opportunity for Canon.

Long-range planning can also change decision-making patterns. People can become more strategy oriented. People learn how to think strategically, through the experience of building the long-range plan. Thus, the marketing department will try to find out what are the long-term future needs of consumers, the production department will figure out what should be the future pattern of factory automation and the personnel department will try to investigate future gaps in the human resources.

(1.3)   Increasing strategic options
The lead time for decision has become much longer. Research and development, for example, takes long time before it bears the fruits. Owning to these of long lead times, the new product development, changes to the product mix, research and development, enhancement of quality of personnel, changes in production facilities and changes in the location of production lots, large scale cost reductions cannot be carried out in short periods of time. The longer the time horizon, the more that can be controlled, and thus the strategic options can be increased.

Decision are changed from a response to past stimulus (St $- 1 \rightarrow$ Rt), to a response to future prospect (Rt $\leftarrow$ St $+ 1$).

Long-range planning does not deny the role of emergent strategic or ad hoc decision, but the companies cannot totally rely on the emergent strategies or boot-legs. Hitachi and Tokyo Power Supply have had long-range plans for years, and this approach is quite necessary for those companies, who undertake a large amount of long-term commitment.

Planning for the future does not mean to decide upon everything now. The future is uncertain, and where there is a high uncertainty. The broad policies, or strategic issues, are identified. These broad directions can show what information is needed and what ideas are important. This orientation towards information collection and idea generation is one of the important functions of long-range planning.

(2)   Co-ordination effect
(2.1)   Co-ordination of departmental activities
The long-range plan is a comprehensive plan or a period plan. It can function as a co-ordinating tool. It avoids piece-meal decisions. Piece-meal decisions are a first-in first-out decision procedure. Under this system, important projects will not be able to have resource allocation. When earlier commitments do not leave resources available. Sometimes the louder the voice of some department heads, the more resources they will obtain, and formal comprehensive plans will help the company assign better priorities to important projects.

Co-ordination in general can be conducted by (a) hierarchy of organizations, (b) rules and procedures, (c) self-coordination, (d) planning and, (e) the sharing of common goals. Co-ordination for long-range plans is carried out through the last two.

(2.2)   Better resource allocation

The companies may commit resources now in preparation for tomorrow, at the sacrifice of short-term projects. Long-range planning tries to allocate resources on a longer time horizon.

With formal planning, a company can prepare their resource structures in order to carry out future product-market strategies. New products, for example, needs to have capable personnel, appropriate equipment, sales channels and information systems for operations. By using comprehensive planning new product-market strategies can have enough resources and financial balance, or liquidity, will also be maintained.

Fuji Window Frame Manufacturing Company which was the largest manufacturer in that business at one stage, but went to bankrupt because of an overly aggressive strategy, overproduction and overcapacity without having enough sales channels and services. It did not use formal long-range planning to attain a balance of resource allocations.

(3)   Motivation effect

(3.1)   Providing members with future dreams

The long-range plan shows the future vision of the company and enables employees to have the future dreams of their own. The growth of the company will give them more opportunities for promotion and provide them with improved treatment. Japanese employees tend to work in the same company for a life time, they identify themselves with the company, and the future vision of the company gives them dreams of their own.

One local gas supply company used long-range planning for motivation. The company let young managers build the long-range strategy of the company and thus the company tried to let young managers build future dreams of the company and dreams of their own.

Recently, being close to the end of this century, many companies have started "21st century committee's" which are expected to formulate the vision and basic direction of their company at the beginning of the next century. Membership of the committee consists of the young managers, and they are selected from among many applicants. Through this method, the company expect to have good ideas and also to motivate young people.

Some people will not be motivated by the long-range plan, when they do not like the suggested change, when they think that the new strategy will threaten their positions, when they do not participate in planning process. These problems have to be solved. This will be studied in the following sections.

1.3 Limitations and problems of long-range planning

The long-range planning system has some limitations and problems. These problems are analyzed in chapter 14, but we will have a quick look at the issues, in order to establish the right conception of long-range planning.

There are a number of criticisms against formally-written long-range plans. For example, the G Pharmaceutical Company raised the following problems: (a) Anxiety over uncertainty, because the premises or assumptions change after the plan is formulated. (b) Collecting strategic information is time consuming and costly. (c) It is difficult to arrive at a consensus because line managers are more involved with short-range operations and planners tend to depend on numbers. (d) The plan may be formulated, but it is not implemented for several reasons. These problems reflect typical criticisms against a formal comprehensive plan. The survey data also indicates that the above are common problems.

Firstly, there is the difficulty of prediction or uncertainty. How to cope with uncertainty will be studied in Chapter 13, but here we will state the problem. When the environment is uncertain and changing, prediction becomes difficult, but the necessity of forecasting is that much greater. While the environment is stable, the company can only continue with the present strategy. Under a changing environment, a change of strategy is necessary after taking into considerations the risks involved in the new strategy.

As the lead-time becomes longer, the company cannot dispense with long-term predictions. It takes more than ten years to develop new pharmaceutical products, for example. In order to develop these new products, long term forecasting has to be done.

Long-range plans do not intend to make decision on details in the future. When prediction is uncertain, the direction or policy will be decided, but detailed decision will be taken as the situation becomes clearer. Incremental decisions or sequential decisions are also used.

Secondly, a large amount of strategic information has to be collected in order to build a long-range plan. This is essential for analytical decisions. However, we have to consider the cost-efficiency of collecting the information. The efficiency of expenditure for information is determined by the following formula:

The improvement of decision making – expenditure for information = efficiency of expenditure for information.

The efficiency of the expenditure for information can be improved by avoiding a simple enumeration of numbers or an all-inclusive plan, and instead by concentrating on important issues. Long-range plans over two time-spans are also useful in simplifying the planning.

Thirdly, the necessity of a long-range plan may not be recognized by line departments. This comes from an insufficient perception of planning by line departments and the adverse attitude of those departments concerned. In this case, planning by line departments is not strategic and does not include an appropriate evaluation of strengths and weaknesses. Decision making is in effect sometimes distorted by short-term orientation.

When the performance of a line department is evaluated by short-range results, then these departments are not interested in strategic planning. The method of performance evaluation matters here.

Many strategic projects prove to be a failure if performance is evaluated by a minus-point, or negative reinforcement system. The department may lose motivation towards planning and implementing strategic plans. Minus-point systems mean only failures are taken into consideration.

This problem can be considered from a different angle. Some strategic planning cannot be shaped by a bottom-up approach. In order to adapt and make use of opportunities in the environment, discontinuous innovation is needed. Discontinuous innovation can be planned by top management, the corporate planning department and the development department. Also, project teams can be made use of. These strategic planning departments should be reinforced in addition to line departments.

The sensitivity of line departments towards changes in the environment has to be enhanced. Each department should be encouraged to improve its sensitivity towards changes in the outside environment. Motivation towards using a strategic mind is important. The merit rating system should reflect risk-taking behavior.

On the other hand, the long-range planning system itself changes the attitude of operating units, if it is successful. This is a chicken-and-egg problem, but to start from a small-scale long-range project is one approach.

Participation is one element for success in long-range planning. Operating units can learn through experience, and in order to make them willing to participate, long-range planning should start from small-scale planning.

Top management commitment can change the attitude of operating departments. It can suggest the importance of long-range planning and suggest that merit-rating will reflect the quality of planning and its implementation.

The above three means – the sanction system, learning through experience and top management leadership – are a general model of affecting an attitude change in a group of people. The importance of these approaches is evidenced by the survey on the recent changes of planning systems.

As one of organizational problems, there is a difficulty of coordination. There are a number of requests from many departments, but evaluations of these projects are difficult, and prioritization is hard to give. The resources are limited. Each departments will be more concerned with their own interests rather than those of the corporation as a whole, A hockey stick style request for capital investment is one such case.

The result may be too many projects, or "too many flowers" in flower arrangement. For the strategic plan to be successful, it is necessary to concentrate resources onto the key projects. How can this be done? This problem will be studied in chapters 10 and 11, but one or two solutions are suggested here. Clear goals will provide evaluation criteria for the ranking of projects. Top management and the planning department should properly identify the strategic issues and should reach the consensus on the future vision of the company.

The top management and the planning department have to be strong enough to make objective judgments on the evaluation. The louder the voice, the more the resource allocation – this has to be avoided.

Some projects should be allowed to proceed without evaluation. These projects are in the early stages of development, and might become hopeful products, experiments are allowed.

Fourthly, plans may not be carried out because of the lack of top management commitment and lack of interest of operating departments. This problem is studied in chapter 14, but we will suggest brief comments on it. If the assumption of plan is not appropriate because of changes in the situation, then the plan is not realistic. The plan needs to be flexible and needs to be updated from time to time.

The follow-up of implementation should be conducted. Top management's concern with implementation, frequent referred to the long-range plan, frequent checking of the results of the plan with respect to the progress and performance are necessary.

1.4   Individual project plans
and the comprehensive long-range plan

The relationship between individual project planning and long-range planning is important for recognizing the merits of and limitations of long-range planning. We asked whether strategic projects were formulated in the process of long-range planning, and the answers are shown in Table 1.2.b at the end of this chapter.

According to this survey the following tendencies are found. Discovery of problems and opportunities are frequently done in the process of long-range planning. Determining the basic policy of projects is also carried out in the process of planning. However, the formulation of new ideas are made outside of the planning process and the development of the details of a plan are made outside the planning process. Ranking and resource allocation are performed within the process of long-range planning in many cases.

The other survey in 1989 on long-range planning practices of 249 companies observed that about 25 percent of new strategic ideas are presented in the process of long-range planning, but that 75 percent of new strategic ideas are suggested outside of the process of long-range planning.

There are two kind of projects, active or ongoing projects and tentative or new projects. Ongoing projects are usually integrated into the long-range plan, but new projects are not necessarily integrated into the long-range plan.

Reasons for conducting project planning outside the process of long-range planning are as follows.

(a) Strategies are studied all the time, not only in the process of comprehensive planning. As a result, the project plan is decided outside of the long-range planning process.

(b) Timing is important. For example, opportunities for acquisition and joint-ventures appear suddenly. Unless timely decisions are made, opportunities will disappear. Uncertainty is another reason. Where forecasting is difficult, or the analysis is not yet finished, the project is not yet formally authorized.

(c) Delegation of authority is necessary. The detailed projects of foreign subsidiaries are not integrated. Although the outline of the production of parts and finished products and the outline of capital investments are integrated, there is an inter-relationship between the long-range plans of other subsidiaries and the parent company.

For the same reason, small projects are not integrated. On the other hand, the advantages of decision making on strategic projects in the process of comprehensive planning is the following.

(a) Strategic information can be assembled systematically and the most profitable opportunities can be discovered. In other words, it becomes easier to find the strategic issues.

(b) From among many strategic alternatives, a company can select the most profitable alternatives. When each decisions on a strategic issue is done independently, then the decisions tend to be taken on a piecemeal approach. Further, many intuitive ideas and chance discoveries, as well as opportunities brought in from the outside are not profitable. They can be precluded by comprehensive planning.

(c) Better integration is attained. Comprehensive planning makes it possible to allocate resources in order of importance. If there is no comprehensive plan, then the projects proposed earlier in time receive resource allocations and for projects proposed later in time no resources remain, even if they are more advantageous projects.

In order to attain these advantages, it is necessary to pinpoint issues and make policy decisions first, and then rank the projects and allocate resources as part of the process of long-range planning.

As we stated earlier, there are "emergent strategies" in addition to intended strategies, and these make the planning system more flexible. The more uncertain the environment is, and the more innovative the company is, the more emergent strategies will appear. However, these emergent strategies can be evaluated quickly and properly by having long term strategic policies.

1.5 The concept of corporate strategy and long-range planning

The subject of long-range planning is corporate strategy. Some of the strategies are decided outside the formal long-range planning process, but still it can give the basic guide-line to the individual strategic decisions, and also it can coordinate individual strategic decisions. We therefore need to know the concept and scope of strategy and the models of strategic decisions. The formal planning system tries to improve strategic decisions.

1.5.1 The scope of corporate strategy

There are three views on the nature of corporate strategy

(a) It is a broad policy. It is a kind of patterns of decision. It states the objective of the corporation, range of business, policy on organization and policy on resource allocation. It is used for long years, thus specifies the patterns of decisions. (Andrews, 1971; Chandler, 1962; Steiner, 1977)

  According to this view, only a part of the long-range plan, the long-range corporate strategy, is the actual strategy. Most of the medium-range plan is not called the strategy.

(b) It is a plot. The competitor or the enemy, will respond to the move of their part and will change their own move. The company has to take into consideration this response of the opponent. The strategy aims to select the best action that will bring the maximin or maximum-of-minimum pay-off. This view is typically taken by the game theory (J. Neuman & O. Morgenstern, 1944; Luce & Raiffa, 1957). This view can go further to the action to manipulate the opponent.

  According to this view, competition strategy in the long-range plan should be emphasized, and the long-range plan should be flexible, depending on the tactics of the competitor, if the long-range plan is to be a strategic plan. If the move of the competitor is hard to predict, the long-range plan should have contingency plans or should prepare strong competitive edges (looking for "dominant" strategy) or should diversify (having "mixed" strategies). The maxi-min evaluation criteria is too conservative, it is not usually used, but rather a satisficing principle is used by considering the amount of risk the company can bear.

(c) It is to change the goals, product-market strategy and the structure of the organization.

  The core of a strategy is to change the style of adaptation of an organization towards the environment. This view can be classified into two. One view does not include consideration of goal, an other view does not include considerations of the resource structure. These views put an emphasis on the product-market strategy as the core of the strategy. Ansoff states that strategy has four areas; product mix, growth vector, competitive strength and synergy.

He also deals with the goals of the corporation. Hofer and Schende define the concept and components of strategy as follows: (a) Scope or domain, (b) resource deployment, (c) competitive strength, (d) synergy. They do not analyze the goals. There are some differences in definition but, most of the research on corporate strategy deal with the three areas – goals, product-market strategy and structure, with somewhat more emphasis on the product-market strategy (Ansoff, 19645; Hofer & Schendell, 1978; Kono, 1984; Kono, 1985; Rowe & others, 1985; Glueck, 1984; Yavitz, 1988; Johnson & others, 1989).

This view is the most common definition of strategy and indicates the typical contents of long-range planning.

Among the approaches which deal with goals, product-market strategies and structures, we can classify three schools.

(c.1) Analysis of principles on the patterns of product-market strategy

This view puts an emphasis on the analysis of the cause-effect relationship on diversification, vertical integration competition, multinational management, acquisition and merger. It also deals with organizational structure. This approach tries to find out the principles underlying these specific areas of strategy (Rumelt, 1974; Williamson, 1975; Harrigan, 1983; Porter, 1985; Kono, 1985)

Long-range planning uses the principles thus developed, but it puts an emphasis on the decision making process.

(c.2) Contingency approach

This approach puts emphasis on the fit between strategy and structure; Miles and Snow state there are four types of strategic decisions: (1) the 'defender' has a narrow and stable domain, strong in cost-efficient technology and centralized control, (2) the 'prospector' has a broad domain, has multiple technology, problem oriented planning and decentralized control (3) the 'analyzer' has a core business and new products, has dual core technology and a matrix organizational structure. (4) The 'reactor' is not able to respond to changes in the environment. The authors state that if there is a good fit between domain, core technology and organizational structure each of the three, excepting the fourth, can attain good financial performance (Miles and Snow, 1978). The classification of mechanic and organic organization is famous (Burns & Stalker, 1961; as other research, Lawrence & Lorsch, 1967).

Long-range planning usually deals with both the product-market strategy and organizational structure, and this places an emphasis on the fit between the product-market strategy and the structure.

(c.3) Dynamic process

Strategy and structure evolve; Company starts with specialization, then proceeds to diversification and then into a multinational company. The structure changes with the transition of these product-market strategies (Greiner, 1972; Abernathy, 1980; Galbraith and Nathanson, 1978).

According to this view, Long-range planning should plan the transition of strategy and structure in the corporation.

1.5.2 Decision-making process

The strategy formulation process is an unstructured decision-making process. Different views on this process can be classified into three.

(a) Analytical decision process.
This view put an emphasis on the rational and analytical process of strategy formulation. This approach studies the rational process of strategy formulation, starting with goal setting, information collection, idea generation, evaluation, resource allocation and implementation. Most of the books on the corporate strategy and on the long-range planning follow this approach (Steiner & Miner, 1977; Rowe and others, 1985; Hofer & Schendel,1978; Glueck and others, 1984; Yavitz and Newman, 1988; Johnson, & Scholes & Sexly,1989; Wheelen & Hunger, 1983; Comerford & Callagham, 1985).

(b) Types of strategic decision-making and the non-analytical approach
This view places an emphasis on non-analytical strategy formulation. Quinn describes the incremental approach for strategy formulation, in which he maintains that strategy formulation is not conducted just like the solving of simultaneous equations. It is conducted on a piece-meal basis. There are two reasons for this. There is uncertainty in the environment, and it is hard to make concrete decisions beforehand, it is better to proceed after some experimentation. Another reason is that the minds of people do not change easily, it is better to spend appropriate time in letting them understand the needs of new strategy (Quinn, 1980).

Minzberg illustrates three modes of decision-making – entrepreneurial mode, adaptive mode and planning mode (Mintzberg, 1973b). Miles and Snow state four types of strategy formulation defenders, prospectors, analyzer, and reactor. He states that if there is consistency with the internal subsystems, each of these (excluding the fourth) can have high performance (Miles and Snow, 1978). Lindblom and Allison show similar typologies (Lindblom, 1959; Allison, 1971).

This approach seems to defy the value of comprehensive long-range planning. But this approach is not completely irrational, it is one method of analytical approach under uncertainty or under conflict situation. Even in the formal long-range planning this approach is used for some projects when prediction is hard. For example, for foreign investment, a small plant (on even large land) will be built first, and after learning through experience the plant will be expanded.

(c) Self-change model
How to change the strategic decision-making style is a problem. In order to change

strategy, the decision-making style has to be aggressive. If the corporate culture is conservative and stagnant, it has to be changed. Sometime the discrepancy between decision-making style and strategy becomes necessary in order to change either of them. Contingency theory, which stresses the fit between strategy, structure and decision-making style, holds that this will tend to result in a static equilibrium. This approach tries to analyze the process of changing the decision-making process, or to create discontinuities in decision-making style. The study of this approach is a recent development.

The research on corporate culture belongs to this approach. Also the study of creative organization deals with this area. (Weick, 1969; Shein, 1985; Burgelman and Maidique, 1988; Kono, 1988).

It should be emphasized that the long-range planning system can have the effect of changing the corporate culture. Here, we will try to focus on this side of long-range planning. The new view is illustrated in table 1.3.

This new view considers the role of long-range planning as one of the tools to change corporate culture. Different approaches on corporate strategy and on strategic decision give us several suggestions about the approaches to long-range planning. The study of long-range planning systems focus on the decision-making process, so we will not dig into the details of this type and principles of strategy. We will concentrate our analysis on the strategy formulation process.

We will follow the rational, analytical process of decisions mostly, but we will pay great attention to the role of long-range planning as a tool of changing corporate culture or of changing decision-making pattern. Japanese corporations place an emphasis on this role of planning.

Table 1.3   Two approaches to long-range planning systems

	Rational view	Culture-change view
Role of top management	Decision maker	Culture changer (When not, plan to change the attitude of top management)
Subject of planning	Straight analysis of corporate stategy	How to change corporate culture
Information	How to collect information	How to enhance sensitivity towards changes in environment
Idea generation	Analytical	Planning is a process of learning. Spontaneous. Many new ideas
Evaluation	Clear criteria, ex., ROI	Evaluation by long-term strategy Sometimes no evaluation
Integration	By planning	By sharing the common goals
Revision	Annually	Planning system frequently changes, depending upon needs
Planning department	Many planning departments, uniform planning style	Many strategic planning departments, using different style of planning
Key role of long-range planning system	Rational dicision-making	Identifiying issues, clarifiying visions to change corporate culture

Summary

1. Long-range plan builds a formal, written and comprehensive plans. The subjects of the long-range plan are goals and philosophies, product-market strategies and key resource structures. Innovation in these three areas is necessary for the corporation to adapt to changes in the environment.

     It describes the courses and schedules of action in the future, based on long-term forecasts.

     Formal long-range planning are the plan is not a plan in the brain of top management which is not made public, an individual long-range project plan, a plan for short-range operations, the rules and standards for operations.

2. The effects of long-range planning are, firstly, to find out the strategic issues of the com-

pany. Organizations tend to have inertia, because people do not like change, they tend to work under "Gresham's law of decisions". By identifying threats and opportunities the company will be "unfreezed". This is attained through regular scanning of problems by the long-range planning system.

The company will become future oriented and outside oriented and will improve their sensitivity towards environmental changes.

By having a long time horizon, the company can increase strategic options, because the lead-times for decisions have become longer. Instead of responding to past stimulus, the company 'responds' to future stimulus.

By having comprehensive planning, better coordination of projects becomes easier. Sharing the common goals is important means to integrate the activities of various departments.

3. There are limitations to long-range planning. (a) There is a difficulty in forecasting. (b) People are more concerned with daily operations, particularly when their merit rating is based on short-range performance. The cooperation of line departments in building good long-range strategies is hard to get. (c) When goals and long-term strategy are not clear, the ranking of projects is not easy. (d) When the follow-up is not carried out well, the long-range plan is not implemented. These problems have to be solved in order for the long-range planning to be successful.

4. Project planning is not necessarily carried out in the process of comprehensive long-range planning. The reasons are (a) strategic projects are studied all the time, not only during the planning process, (b) new projects emerge suddenly from new opportunities, (c) delegation of authority is necessary. However, even in this case when the issues are identified and strategic policies are formulated beforehand, the evaluation is relatively precise and the decision can be reached without delay.

5. The subject of long-range plan is corporate strategy. There are several concepts to this: (a) it is a broad policy, (b) it is a plot, (c) it deals with goals, product-market strategies and resource structures. The subject of long-range planning is the last one – goals, product-market strategy and resource structures.

Strategic decision-making has three models: analytical, non-analytical and self-change models. The long-range planning uses the analytical approach, but progressively the self-change model, or the change of corporate culture, is becoming important.

Table 1.1.b   Effects of long-range planning
What are the effects of long range planning?
(please describe three important effects)

	number of companies	249 co.
Effects		% of total
1. Strategy orientation and innovation		
1–1 Issues finding		
(1) Could identify strategic issues		17
1–2 Future orientation and strategy orientation		
(1) To orient to the environment, to the future		10
(2) Strategy orientation recognition of the importance of strategy		20
(3) To tackle strategic problems		14
1–3 Increasing strategic options		
(1) Long-range goals are clarified furure directions are made clear		23
2. Integration		
2–1 Sharing common corporate goals		29
Formation of consensus among top management team, better coordination of goals of divisions and better communications among them		
2–2 Better resource allocation		8
3. Motivation		
3–1 Providing the members with dreams for the future Communicating long-range goals		14
3–2 Providing opportunities for participation in strategic decisions		4
4. Strategy and performance		
4–1 Change of strategy		6
4–2 Improved performance		7

(   ) * Because of unstructured responses, the number of responses is low
       * Survey in 1989
       * Number indicates the percentage of responding companies

Table 1.2b   Strategic projects and the long-range plan are strategic projects integrated into formal long-range plan?

Number of corporations	110 co.
(1) Finding problems and opportunities	44 (%)
(2) Determining basic policy of projects	50
(3) Formulation of new ideas	37
(4) Developing detailed plans	39
(5) Ranking and resource allocation	46

Note (1)   Frequency was computed as, 'never' = 0, 'in very little cases' = 0.2, 'in many cases' = 0.6, 'in very many cases' = 0.8, multiplied by number of responses

    (2)   Survey in 1982

Chapter 2 Systems and types of long-range planning

"We have changed the planning system from a set of numbers to an emphasis on projects". "We have changed the planning process from a bottom-up approach to an interactive approach, with more emphasis on strategic thinking rather than the contents of the plan". These are the typical changes to the planning system.

2.1 The position of the long-range plan within the overall planning process

A plan is a predetermined course of future action. The relation of long-range plan to other plans is shown in Table 1.1. The long-range plan puts an emphasis on goals, product-market strategy and structured change. The short-range plan places an emphasis on operations.

Using either means-end analysis or the premise-follower relationship, plans are constructed as shown in Table 2.1.

Table 2.1 The plan system

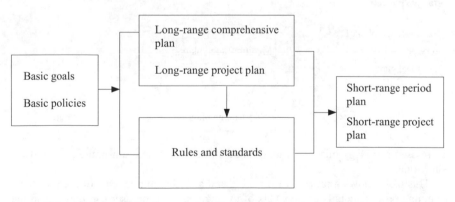

(note) This table is essentially the same as table 1.1.

The 'basic' goals are the premises for long-range strategies and short-range plans follow this. Rules and policies also follow strategy. This implies that appropriate long-range plans are the preceding condition of good short-range plans.

On the other hand, many corporations start planning from the corporate philosophy and from the budgeting, then rules and policies are stipulated, and finally the long-range plan is introduced. This means that, in the beginning, implicit strategies or informal strategies are used, so because of this the strategy tends to be simple and because the size is small, the products are specialized.

2.2. Components of long-range plan

The basic components of the long-range plan is comprised of four parts: basic goals, product-market strategy, structure and outline of operations. These four components are developed into groups of decisions and Table 2.2 is a simplified model of a long-range plan. It is comprised of premises, long-range strategy and medium-range plans. Then, the short-range plan follows.

Table 2.3 is the system of the long-range plan used by C company. Their plan is also

Table 2.2   A simplified system of a long-range plan

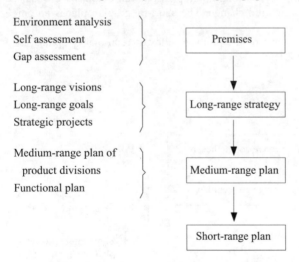

composed of (1) premises, (2) long-range strategy, (3) medium-range plan and (4) short-range plan.

This table shows a process of planning and also the components of the plan. The planning process details components of the plan, so that the user can understand the reasons for the plan.

Table 2.3   The plan system of company C

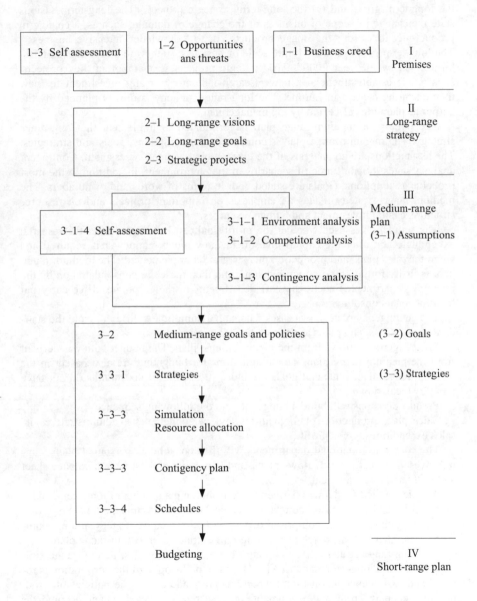

The long-range strategy covers six years, and it states (a) the long-term visions (b) the long-term goals and (c) the long-term strategic projects. The long-term visions state the change of scope of business or the change of domain, such as, a change in product-mix to words "the image products" or to "knowledge intensive business". The long-term goals state the future scale of business, such as to attain "sales of 100 billion yen by the year 2000". The strategic projects state important key projects, such as the establishment of a new research laboratory or any investment for new manufacturing centers in Europe. The long-range strategy is mostly planned by the corporate planning office and by top management.

The three year medium-range plan is formulated to implement the long-range strategy. The medium range plan is composed of assumptions, goals and strategies. The assumptions are an analysis of the environment and self-assessment. Contingent analysis states the multitude of scenarios in the environment, in addition to the most probable assumptions. Goals are stated both in terms of words and of numbers. The medium range strategy places an emphasis on important projects and on resource structure, capital investment and human resources.

The simulation is used whether the profit goal can be attained after the research expenditure and after the capital investment, how much manpower is required and when the sales plans and production plans are to be implemented. The medium range plan is firstly formed by product divisions, and then these are consolidated on by the planning department. Functional staff departments in the corporate office carry out the functional consolidation.

The contingency plan shows cases where an assumption is different from the standard assumptions, and plans to cope with these contingencies.

The budgeting follows from the medium-range plan. The budget policy is derived from the medium range plan. The assumptions for budgeting are also based on the medium-range plan. Financial goals are more stressed. Last six months do not have monthly break down.

Product divisions will build a budget around the following sequence:

Sales plan, production plan, facilities and personnel plans, administrative and sales expenditures, gross profit.

The corporate functional departments will then consolidate personnel plans, capital investment plans, funds flows plans, and then build and estimate a balance sheet and profit and loss statement.

A more detailed model was derived by consolidating a number of long-range planning cases used by successful companies. Table 2.4 illustrates this model.

The long-range plan is comprised of two parts: long-range strategy and medium-range plan. That is, long-range plan = long-range strategy – medium-range plan.

The long-range strategy has two major components. The first is long-range strategic policy and long-range goals (A1). The basic philosophy of the corporation is revised and basic concepts on future directions are made clear. The policies on product-mix, on new product development, on research and development become the policy on product-market strategy. The latter also contains policies on organizational

Table 2.4   The system of a long-range plan

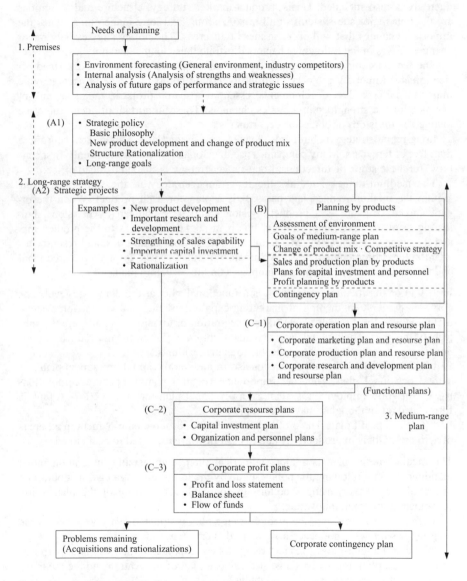

Note: A1 ... Coporate goals and policies   ) Long-range plan
        A2 ... Corporate long-range stretegy
        B ... Division plan or line department plan   ) Medium-range plan
        C ... Comprehensive plan, functional plan and some important projects

structure, on personnel and on capital investment. A long-range policy on productivity is also included. Goals, product-market strategy, structure and operations are the four major sub-systems of all organizations, and long-range policy states the important changes that will occur in these four areas. The policy stresses only major changes. Cases in the following chapters illustrate these long-range policies.

The second component is strategic projects at the corporate level (A2). Head office initiates important projects, even in diversified companies. The projects may be important new product developments, essential research projects, major capital investment or the strengthening of sales channels. These important projects cannot be planned by divisions or other line departments.

Long-range strategy is built from longer-time predictions, usually covering more than five or ten years. Many companies use the slogan "Towards the twenty-first century" for these strategic directions. Long-range strategy is shaped by head office.

The medium-range plan links the long-range strategy to the short-range plan. Within the medium-range plan, part (B) is a plan for each product. When the organizational structure is a product-division style, it is planned by divisions. Following from the long-range strategy, this plan contains changes to the product mix and the competition strategy. Marketing and production capabilities, and resource allocation for equipment and personnel are also planned. These form a structured plan, and the medium range plan puts an emphasis on this structure plan.

Part (C1) of the medium range plan is a functional plan at the corporate level. The corporate-wide strengthening of marketing capabilities, the total production system, including new locations of plants and concentration or division of plants, are the subjects of this part. They include sales channels commonly used by all products and innovative cost-reduction plans applicable to many products.

Part (C2) of the medium-range plan consists of an overall capital investment plan and a total personnel plan. They are important structural plans. Japanese corporations have a life-time employment system, so a personnel plan for even the lowest rank is formulated, even though it may be a simple one.

Part (C3) is a profit plan. The profit plan clarify the resource employment in all areas of activities. Goals in productivity and in cash flow are expected to be attained.

The medium-range plan is a more numerical plan, emphasizing integration rather than innovation. Following the policy set up by the long-range strategy, it is built in a decentralized manner, using a bottom-up approach. The nature of the plan is improvement rather than innovation.

With respect to revision, the medium-range plan is updated every year, whilst the long-range strategy is not necessarily revised every year.

Dividing the long-range plan into two parts corresponds to the two major purposes of long-range planning. Long-range strategy is a plan of innovation and the medium-range plan stresses improvement and integration.

What kind of effects can be expected by dividing long-range planning into a long-range strategy and a medium-range plan?

Firstly, emphasis on strategic issues is made possible by using strategic plans. An innovative product-market strategy usually has a long lead-time. It is necessary to forecast five years ahead, perhaps or more, to make preparations today. At the same time, by utilizing a longer time horizon, freedom of choice increases as does the number of alternatives, and the company can make far-reaching and innovative plans.

Next, by having a medium-range plan, the company can strengthen its competitive power and also strengthen its resource capability. The subjects of these areas fit a two or three-year time horizon. At the same time, competitive strategies and resource planning requires quantitative analysis, so the medium-range term is appropriate.

The medium-range plan also makes it possible to integrate a variety of plans and to allocate resources properly. In order to give priority to strategies and to implement them, resources have to be allocated to each strategy. What amount of capital investment and human resources have to be allocated to carry out a strategy? What should the ranking of these projects be and what should the amount of resource allocations be? For such kind of resource plans, a three-year time span is appropriate.

According to our survey, approximately 30% of Japanese corporations have a two-plan system, as is indicated in Table 2.1.b.

Types of long-range planning are described in the next paragraph. But first we wish to comment on the relationship between a two-plan system and other types of long-range planning. The forecastive-type long-range plan and the quantitative-type long-range plan contain only a medium-range plan. These are shown as part (B) and part (C) on Table 2.4. These types lack a strategic plan. The goal-type long-range plan contains only the elements listed in part (A1) of Table 2.4. It lacks a detailed implementation plan. A type which has an emphasis on projects but also has qualitative consolidation would include every part of Table 2.4, that is Parts A + B + C.

A survey of the detailed components of a long-range plan is shown later in Table 2.5.b.

2.3 Types of Long-range plans

2.3.1 Difference in focuses on the process

Decision-making has the following processes: problems finding – information collection – goal setting – idea generation evaluation – final decision. Depending on where the emphasis of long-range planning is, long-range plans can be classified into four types; (A) forecastive, (B) goal-type, (C) individual project planning (not comprehensive), (D) comprehensive and problem-solving.

The forecastive-type long-range plan predicts the future of the company assuming that present strategy is not changed, and it tries to detail out what kind of problems may arise. It is an issue-finding long-range plan. The issue finding is the starting point and solutions have to be worked out by project planning that is outside the long-range plan.

The goal-type long-range plan states what the goals and domains of a company should be in the future. It describes the position of the company in a predicted future world but it does not have detailed planning of means by which to attain the goals in the plan. The author's investigation on this type of planning discloses that projects and planned steps taken to arrive at the goals within the plan documents or outside the long-range plan. Goal type plans also detail plans for each year. What is different about this plan from other types of plans is that this type emphasizes the goals or visions of the company. Japanese long-range planning emphasizes that a long-range plan be used to clarify goals.

The comprehensive and problem solving type of plan is the most authentic type; it includes forecasting, goal setting and tries to find solutions able to reach these goals. Successful companies in planning (subjective judgment) use this latter type more frequently than less successful companies.

When companies use two plan systems, then the long-range strategy focuses on clarifying goals, the medium-range plan places an emphasis on comprehensive problem solving. In this case, the division of function is clear.

2.3.2 Types of plans, according to the contents and amount of detail

The long-range plan can be classified as to whether it is quantitative or has a project emphasis. There are four types: (A) Quantitative long- range planning, (B) All inclusive and too-many-programs-type planning, (C) Project-emphasis planning, and (D) planning with an emphasis on projects and quantitative consolidation. According to survey material, as shown in Table 2.5, of companies with one long-range plan, thirty-eight percent have quantitative long-range plans and thirty-eight percent have an "emphasis on projects and also quantitative consolidation" plans. In the case of corporations with two time-horizon plans, the long-range strategy is usually a "project emphasis" type and the medium-range plan is about project emphasis and quantitative consolidation.

It is a problem that there are too many companies which emphasize quantitative plans, particularly in the case of companies with one long-range plan. In industries where there is little chance of product innovation, such as construction and oil refining the long-range plans tend to be quantitative. More successful companies in planning (subjective judgment) have (d) project emphasis with quantitative consolidation type.

When a company is diversified, it uses different kinds of planning systems. A corporate planner of one pharmaceutical company state that he had different kinds of plans. For existing products, plans were detailed, with numbers and schedules. For new products, only the goals and policies were stated. For profit planning, capital investment and personnel planning, numbers are important.

Generally speaking, when the environment is analyzable, the plan can be detailed, but when the company wants to explore new opportunities, the plan cannot be detailed. Thus, the more innovative the plan is, the less detailed and the more stress there is on goal-clarification. In other words, for innovation purposes, the long-range plan tends to be goal clarifying and tends to focus on selected key projects; for integration purpose the plan tends to be quantitative or tends to have many programs.

2.3.3 Time horizon and two-plan systems

The time horizon of a plan depends on three factors. One is a lead time from idea to implementation.

preparation ——▶ construction ——▶ completion ——▶ operation

The 'lead time' is that time required from the conception of an idea to designing (preparation), to construction and completion of construction and to the introduction of a product into the market.

The second factor is the length of impact a decision has on an organization, or how long a decision binds an organization. When a company builds a plant, for example, it will have to use the equipment involved for more than ten years, depending on the terms of depreciation. If the use is changed, then the company will have to bear a sunk cost.

The above two factors regulate the time horizon. But a third factor may shorten the time horizon. It is question about the predictability of the future: too long in the future is meaningless for planning.

The time horizon of planning for Japanese corporations is three or five years in the case of a one-plan system (Table 2.1.b). Where a company uses a two-plan system, the time span of strategic long-range planning is more than seven years and the medium-range plan covers three years (Table 2.2.b). Approximately thirty percent of companies surveyed have a two-plan system.

The long-range strategy decides on innovation and is more goal-clarification oriented and centrally formulated, whilst the medium-range plan focuses on integration, is qualitative and is built by divisions and staff departments.

The time span for budgeting is usually one year, but six-month systems have some frequency. (See Table 2.3.b)

2.3.4 Revision of the long-range plan

Surveys show that fifty (36% + 14% = 50%) percent of companies with one long-range plan do a plan revision every year. Although this yearly revision system has the highest frequency of use, some companies have fixed terminal dates and revise the plan as occasion demands,. Companies with two-plan systems revise the medium-range plan every year, but revise their long-range strategy less frequently. This difference comes from differences in the nature of the two plans.

Compared with planning practices in the U.S. and U.K., Japanese corporations conduct revisions less frequently, and a significant percentage of Japanese companies have a fixed revision date and do not revise their plans every year. There are two reasons for this difference. Firstly, it takes time to revise a plan and when a plan is revised every year the contents tend to be less innovative. For the same reason, some American companies (as is the case with GE) and European companies revise their plans less frequently. However, generally speaking, in the U.S. a long-range plan is a commitment of a division manager on the to the division's strategy, so a plan tends to be detailed and revised every year.

Another reason is that when a plan is revised every year its goals can become unclear. When the long-range planning is of a goal-oriented type, it is not practical to revise the plan every year. However, when the environment changes, it is necessary to change strategy. Thus, a majority of Japanese corporations revise their long-range plans every year.

The above analysis does not explain the principles of revision of long-range plans and of action programs. What are the principles of revising a plan in general?

A revision of a plan changes decisions. A revision becomes necessary in the following cases. (a) The environment changes; new, better alternatives emerge and the old plan becomes obsolete. This includes the situation where the actual condition of the environment has greatly deviated from the predicted status. If the company has a contingency plan, it can revise its actions quickly. (b) There is no error in forecasting, but a new, better strategy is found, say, by a break-through in technical research or by new marketing research. The priorities in resource allocation would change in that event. This case also includes a situation where new information is added over time, and planning in more detail becomes possible. This is sequential decision-making. When new, better alternatives are found, these should replace old plans. (c) Predicted values of goals deviate from the expected value of those goals, or are expected to deviate in the near future. For example, if the sales of a certain product are 20 units in the first year but the goal was 100, then the product has to be improved or some new marketing plan has to be devised. In the goal-means chain, if goals cannot be attained, the means have to be revised. On the other hand, if the result is much higher than the goal, then resource allocation has to be changed. Precisely what amount in percentage of deviation leads to a revision is a problem. In Japan many companies revise a plan when the deviation is larger than 10 or 20 percent. If the deviation is in future value, the percentage can be larger.

The revision of a plan tends to decrease the authority or credibility of that plan. Revision also takes time.

A plan is not revised if the following three instances occur. (a) The result of the plan is not yet clear. Many research projects are examples of this. (b) Large capital expenditures or some other resource investments have already been committed, so that the revision of the plan would not be profitable. In this case, future costs should be the basis of any decision. (c) The plan can be achieved by further efforts, and the premises have not changed. Efforts should be increased, and the plan not be revised. (For a further discussion of plan revisions see Kono, 1975)

2.4 Contents of a plan at the corporate level

Long-range planning is formulated both by head office and by line departments and product divisions. Head office builds the plan which contains goals and strategic policies (A1), corporate level projects (A2) and a company-wide functional plan (c) (see Table 2.4). Table 2.4.b shows that this is the actual practice.

To what extent the head office should conduct the above function is a problem. How to divide the responsibility of strategic planning between the head office (staff departments and line departments in the head office) and divisions, plants and sales branches needs to be analyzed.

Generally speaking, the head office performs the following function. (a) planning, deciding and promoting corporate level strategy, which contains (1) head office specific strategy (2) orientation or guide line for divisions. (b) Staff functions, which contain (1) specialist service (2) planning and controlling service (for example, budgeting and auditing) (3) services as the "service staff" (for example, computing, centralized purchasing) (4) staff functions in recruitment, training and distribution of key resources, such as financial resources and personnel. Planning of 'synergy' among divisions is included in this function. (c) Controlling function, which include indoctrination of corporate values and polices formulating a reporting system, establishing the performance evaluation system of personnel. Depending on the selective centralization of authorities conducting these functions, the head offices can be classified into four types.

(a) the strategic type which focuses on corporate strategy, (b) the staff type which places an emphasis on staff functions, (c) the centralized type which follows the above three to the maximum. Many Japanese corporations belong to this type. (d) Small head office, which does the above functions to the minimum. Many American corporations belong to this type.

Among the strategic duties of the head office, many authors lists the following duties as important; (a) Goal setting, (b) management of product portfolio, (c) company acquisition, (d) resource procurement, and management of synergy. (Yavitz & Newman, 1988; Hofer and Schendell, 1978; Porter, 1985)

According to our survey, the head office carry out the following functions with respect to strategic decisions, as is shown in Table 2.4.b.

(a-1) Statement of long-range visions, (a-2) corporate goal and policy (overall guide-line to divisions). (a-3) In many cases (66%), guide-lines are detailed and head office gives specific guide-lines to each division. (b) Corporate level projects. These are important projects or strategies which do not belong to any divisions. (b-2) Sometimes the corporate level plan may be the only plan. (c) Resources procurement, fostering and resources allocation. This is usually called the "functional plan". (d) Consolidation of long-range plan and coordination of the planning activities of each divisions.

The survey shows that head offices have higher levels of concentration in strategic planning. What factors, then, affect the level of concentration of strategic decisions?

(a) Needs for integration. The head office formulate long-range goals and policies to integrate the planning of many divisions. (b) To fill in inevitable gaps in information, head offices collects more information. When the environment changes rapidly, head office will have more information on new developments and can generate more new ideas. It can also form new strategies beyond the product line of existing product divisions. (c) Advantage of concentration. The head office may maintain the advantage of having decision-making concentrated on it. For this reason, resource allocation is performed by head office. Resources are fostered by, and distributed by, head office. The functional plan is built by head office.

When the speed of changes in the environment is fast, the need for planning by head office, the need for a top-down approach and the need for concentration increases for the above three reasons. Japanese corporations do not subscribe to the policy of "the doer is the planner". Instead, new departments are created for the implementation of strategy, for example, a new business department.

The faster the change in the environment, the more delegation of decisions is better – this principle can be applied to repetitive operations, but it cannot be applied to strategic decisions. Instead, such strategic-planning departments as a research laboratory, development department, planning office or new business department are reinforced. It is these departments which build the strategic plan. This is a new trend in Japan: the concentration of decisions rather than their decentralization.

It is usually stated that the diversification affects levels of concentration. In a specialized-product company the head office is large and it does most of the planning, whilst in a diversified company, product divisions play a more important role. However, our survey shows that there are differences, but that the difference is not so large. When the environment is changing, head office has to be responsible for planning changes to strategy.

2.5 Consolidation of the plans of subsidiaries within the plan of the parent company

The method of consolidation of plans of subsidiaries within the plan of a parent company is shown in Table 2.8. American corporations make little distinction between divisions and subsidiaries, so the plans of related subsidiaries are integrated within the plan of the parent company. The long-range plan is used to control the subsidiaries. In Japan, there is a sense that subsidiaries are different from product divisions, so integration of the plans of the related companies are conducted only to a lesser extent. As Table 2.8 shows, approximately forty-one percent of the companies integrate the long-range policies of two companies. Overall integration is seen in only ten percent of companies. And forty-four percent of companies do not integrate the plans of two companies at all.

2.6 Historical development of the long-range planning system

The long-range planning system has evolved as the environment changed. Surveys conducted by the author during the past thirty years are shown in Table 2.5 and Table 2.6.

(1) Individual Project Planning 1950–60
After the Second World War the economy had to be reconstructed. Reconstruction of factories and plants destroyed during the war was the first priority, and companies drew up long-range plans for the reconstruction of equipment. But there were no comprehensive plans at this stage.

(2) Quantitative Plan 1960–70
After the economy entered a high-growth period, the government announced an ambitious national economic plan, which gave a great stimulus to the behavior of management in general, and to business planning systems. Comprehensive long-range planning became widely adopted among large corporations.

The planning was mostly quantitative, however, because expansion by capital investment was the most important strategy, and in order to attain the balanced achievement of goals, it was necessary to integrate capital investment through a long-range profit plan. Many specialized companies had forecasting-type plans, which made clear the gaps between the needs and the availability of capacity and the financial results of capital investment. On the other hand, many diversified companies had goal-clarifying-type plans. Top management assigned goals to each department, and each department drew up quantitative plans to implement the goals using a bottom-to-top approach.

(3) Project Emphasis, but Too Many Projects 1970–1974
The economy continued to grow at a high rate, but the demand structure was changing. Quantitative planning changed to a type that put an emphasis on project-market

Table 2.5   Transition of the long-range planning system

Years	1950~	1960~	1970~	1974~	1978~	1985~
Environment	Economic reconstruction	High growth period	From high growth to stable growth	Oil crisis	Stable growth	'soft economy' Internationalization
Types	(1) Long-range plan of projects →	(2·1) Forecastive and quantitative → (2·2) Assignment of goals and quantitative →	(3) Strategic and all inclusive →	(4) Rationalization oriented →	(5) Strategy oriented →	(6) Long-term visions
Components	• Long-range plan for projects	• Comprehensive • Emphasis on capital investment • Quantitative • Assignment • Emphasis on capital investment	• Too many items • Important strategies are separately considered • Two long-range plans	• Emphasis on cost reduction • PPM and contingency plans studied	• Aggressive long-range strategy + Medium-range plan	• Visions for 21st century • Enhancing R & D capability • Multinational management • Change of corporate culture
Planning Process	• Centralized planning	• Build up approach	• Interactive or build up approach • Use of simulation	• Interactive	• Corporate level strategies are important • Strategic planning departments are strengthened	• Top-down approach

strategy. In Table 2.5, we notice that the comprehensive problem-solving type plan (A(4)) increased in 1970, and the emphasis on projects and quantitative consolidation (B(3)) also increased in 1970.

However, many companies took up too many issues, so that their priorities were not clear and resources were not allocated appropriately. The important strategies tended to be built outside the long-range planning process. To overcome the above defects, some companies started to have a two-plan system, the long-range strategic plan and the medium-range plan, and for the latter, computer simulation was frequently applied.

(4) Suspension of Long-range Plans, and Rationalization Plans, 1974–1977

The oil crisis resulted in increased uncertainty, and many companies suspended their long-range planning as a result. The low response ratio in Table 2.10 in 1976 indicates this. The companies that resumed long-range planning laid stress on cost-reduction plans. The growth-share matrix model attracted a large amount of attention as a tool of rationalization. The time horizon of the plan became shorter because of uncertainty.

(5) Emphasis on Selected Key Strategies, 1977–1984

When the economy entered a low-growth period, companies began to notice that rationalization planning (cost-reduction planning) on its aim was too defensive, and that they needed to take positive action to take advantage of the new emerging opportunities. In Table 2.6, the increase of goal clarifying-type plans (A(2)), and the increase of emphasis on projects and quantitative-consolidation-type plans (B(3)) in 1979 indicate this awareness. Many successful companies selected five to ten key strategic issues around which they formed their long-range strategy. At the same time they built up medium range plans to integrate the strategies and to integrate the allocation of resources. Long-range strategies were built using a top-down or interactive approach at head office.

(6) Long-term visions, 1985 to date

The Japanese economy has experienced two important challenges. One was further advancement of technology in the areas of electronics. In this field Japanese companies could gain more competitive power around the world. One effect of this was the application of information technology to every area, to new products, to communication systems and to production systems. Thus the economy became a "soft economy", an information intensive economy or software intensive economy.

Another trend was internationalization. Because of the increased competitive power of Japanese products, exports increased and to avoid friction, investment in multinational management and foreign production has also increased tremendously, and multinational management has become an important subject for planning.

With these changes, the planning system has experienced and continues to experience the following shifts. The first shift was in the importance of 'future visions'. In order to cope with the uncertainty caused by the advancement of information tech-

Table 2.6 Transition of long-range planning system in the past thirty years

Period		2·1	2·2	3	4	5	6
Year		1963	1967	1970	1976	1979	1989 (2)
Number of corporations		254	268	160	57	327	170
Response ratio (%)		17.9	25.8	25.0	13.8	28.4	20.8
Focus	A (1) Forecastive	22 (%)	23 %	14 %	14 %	19 %	14 %
	(2) Clarifying goals	41	43	23	16	46	61
	(3) Individual problem-solving	8	2	1	0	3	2
	(4) Comprehensive, including all of the above	34	32	61	68	30	23
Components	B (1) Mostly quantitative		53	46	46	41	38
	(2) Emphasis on projects		3	3	7	10	4
	(3) Emphasis on projects and also quantitative consolidation		37	46	51	46	38
	(4) All inclusive, too many projects		–	–	–	–	19
Time horizon	(1) Over 10 years	1	1	1	2	2	4
	(2) 10 to 7 years	6	5	13	4	4	2
	(3) 5 or 6 years	50	59	60	56	34	32
	(4) 4 years	3	5	2	2	5	4
	(5) 3 years	30	35	29	32	47	54
	(6) 2 years	6	6	1	5	5	4

(note) (1) Comparison of seven mail questionnaire surveys conducted by the author in the past twenty-three years.
(2) In 1989, only the companies with one long-range plan are exhibited for simplification.

nology and the unexpected high growth in the economy, companies needed only future visions, instead of detailed plans. Goal nature planning increased. Secondly, increased resource allocation for research and development became necessary. Management of creativity has also come to attention. Thirdly, planning for multinational management began to appear on the stage. Fourthly, the management of corporate culture also begin to receive some attention. Changes of strategy resulted in the changes in the needs of culture, research activity in laboratories needs creative culture and multinational management needs transplanting of the new culture to foreign plants. The long-range planning process is useful in unfreezing the old culture by disclosing future gaps, is useful to stimulate new direction by symbolizing the future visions of the corporation. (On the new trends in other countries see, Glueck, Kaufman & Walleck, 1980; Carpenter, 1986; Taylor, 1986)

The above is a simplified account of the transitions in the planning systems of Japanese corporations over the past thirty years: changes of planning systems tied in with changing environments and the resulting change of strategies in corporations. On the other hand, the accumulation of experience and improvement of technical knowledge for planning was another of the forces of change for the planning systems.

Summary

1. The long-range plan lays the foundation of the short-range plan and rules and standards. If it is not stated formally, the informal plan will play this role.
2. The long-range plan is composed of assumptions, long-range strategies, medium-range plans from which the short-range plan follows. The two plan system makes possible the planning of long-term visions and long-term innovative strategies, the medium-range plan makes possible the strengthening of the resource structure and its integration with resource allocation. The structure of the plan is composed of goals-means sequence, but for implementation, the means-goals sequence is followed. Thus, the medium-range plan is a schedule for implementation.
3.1. The decision-making process follows the sequence of information collection, goal setting and problem solving. When the long-range planning places an emphasis on information collection, it becomes the forecast type. When goal setting is emphasized, it is becomes the goal-setting type. When problem solving is emphasized, it is the problem-solving type.

    The goal-setting type has a high frequency of diffusion in Japan, and when innovative goals and visions are set, new ideas and discontinuous strategies will be stimulated.
3.2. A set of numbers cannot be a strategic plan because they are the results of implementing strategies. The long-range planning is effective when key strategies are selected and resources are dominantly allocated to them.
3.3. The time horizon of planning is affected by lead time, duration of effects and possibilities in forecasting. Two time horizon type plans are becoming popular in Japan.

    The plan is updated when assumptions change, but annual updating, or rolling plans, have merits and demerits. When the plan is revised every year, the plan tends to fall into a set of mere mannerism.
4. Corporate level strategic plans includes guidelines, strategic projects and functional plans. When the environment is changing, the centralization of strategic planning becomes necessary.

5. Consolidation of plans of subsidiaries is selective, depending on the extent of mutual inter-
    dependence. The consolidation of future plans of foreign subsidiaries is difficult because
    estimations about exchange rates is involved.
6. The planning system has evolved historically. During the high growth period in Japanese
    history, the plan was quantitative and a bottom-up process. Then it became to more project
    emphasis going from too many projects to a focus on key projects. Now the visions of 21st
    century are important issues and the change of corporate culture has become one of the im-
    portant subjects.

Appendix. Detailed components of the plan

We have already seen the outline of a long-range planning system in Table 2.3, and
with that outline in mind, the detailed contents of a long-range plan were surveyed.
Table 2.5.b shows the results.

The companies with one long-range plan frequently have the following items. As
for product market-strategy: new product development (8.1), a change of product mix
(8.2), new market development (9), multinational management (10), a strengthening
of marketing competitive power (11) all have a high frequency of diffusion. Cost reduction (12) and information systems (13) have recently become important. A research and development plan to support this product market strategy (15) also have a
high frequency of diffusion. A company acquisition plan (14.1) has a very low frequency of diffusion. This shows that this strategy is not important for Japanese corporations.

With regard to a structure plan: a capital investment plan (18), a strengthening of
marketing capability (19.1), a manpower plan (21.1), a change of corporate culture
(21.2), and a training and management development plan (22) all have a high frequency of diffusion.

For implementation: assignment of the plan to responsible departments and scheduling (28) have high frequency.

The companies with a two-plan system have the following contents in their plans.
For long-range strategy: new product development (8.1), a change of product mix
(8.2), new market development (9) and multinational management (10) have high frequency. In the medium-range plan: a strengthening of competitive power (11), a cost
reduction plan (12), a capital investment plan (18), a strengthening of the marketing
capability (19) and a manpower plan (21.1) are frequently included.

The difference between components of the long-range strategy and the medium-
range plan has been explained in Table 2.3, and this is further evidenced by the survey.

If we look at the historical transition of the components of a plan, the present
long-range plan puts more emphasis on product-market strategy (from item 7 to item
15 in Table 2.11). This means that long-range planning has become more strategic.

Table 2.1.b   Characteristics of a long-range plan

Corporations with long-range plans	1979	1989 (A) Corporations with one long-range plan	1989 (B) Corporations with two long-range plans	
			Long-range strategy	Medium-range plan
	327 co.	170 co.	79 co.	79 co.
(A) a. Forecast only	18 (%)	14 (%)	0 (%)	11 (%)
b. Clarifiying goals	45	61	91	17
c. Comprehensive, and problem solving	29	23 *	7	54
d. Individual problem-solving, not comprehensive	3	2	1	16
(B) a. Mostly quantitative	41	38	13	35
b. All inclusive, but too many programmes	–	19	25	10
c. Emphasis on projects	10	4	32	4
d. Emphasis on projects ans also quantitative consolidation	46	38 *	30	51

(note) (1) Asterisks (*) indicate that the successful companies in planning (subjective judgement) have higher frequencies of these approaches.
(2) There are high corretations (< 5 %) between (Aa) forecast only and (Ba) mostly quantitative; between (Ac) comprehensive ans problem solving and (Bd) emphasis on projects and quantitative consolidation; between (Ad) individual problem solving and (Bb) too many programmes.

Table 2.2.b Time span of the long-range plan

	1979	1989 (A) Corporations with one long-range plan	1989 (B) Corporations with two long-range plans — Long-range strategy	1989 (B) Corporations with two long-range plans — Medium-range plan
Corporations with a long-range plan	327 co.	170 co.	79 co.	
	2 (%)	4 (%)	37 (%)	1 (%)
a. Length of periods				
Over 10 years	2	4	37	1
7 ~ 10 years	3	2	37	0
5 ~ 6 years	34	31	20	26
4 years	4	4	0	4
3 years	47	54	7	64
2 years	4	4	0	4
b. Plans for each year				
Only final year	15	20	83	7
Plans for each year	71	40	17	93
c. Inclusion of 'business cycle'				
Included	45	56	36	69
Not included	42	44	63	31

	1979	1989
Cooporations with long-range plan	327 co.	249 co.
	0 (%)	0 (%)
Related question — Length of periods for budgeting — a. 1.5 year	0	0
b. 1 year	48	66
c. 6 months	55	25

Table 2.3.b Revision of the long-range plan

Corporations with long-range plans	1979	1989 (A) Corporations with one long-range plan	1989 (B) Corporations with two long-range plans — Long-range strategy	1989 (B) Corporations with two long-range plans — Medium-range plan
	327 co.	170 co.	79 co.	79 co.
a. Revised annually adding another year	41 (%)	36 (%)	7 (%)	46 (%)
b. Terminal date is fixed and the plan is revised annually until that date	6	14	1	10
c. Terminal date is fixed and the plan is revised as occasion demands	20	23	23	25
d. Terminal date and plan are revised as occasion demands	22	17	34	10
e. Terminal date and plan are fixed	9	10	35	9

Table 2.4.b The structure of the long-range plan, particularly the contents of corporate level strategy

Corporations with long-range plan		1985 384 co.	1989 249 co.
(1) Length of period	A. Two plans systems, long-range strategy and medium-range plan	18 (%)	32 (%)
	B. Single long-range plan (or single medium-range plan)	82	67
(2) Contents of corporate level strategy and corporate level plan	(a–1) Statement of long-range vision (Corporate long-range strategy)	60	68
	(a–2) Corporate goal and policy (Overall guide line)	89	91
	(a–3) Division goals an strategies to be achieved (Specific guide line)	47	66
	(b–1) Corporate level projects	30	32
	(b–2) Corporate level plan is the only plan		12
	(c) Summary of overall functional plan (Overall marketing plan, overall profit plan)	65	62
	(d) Summary of division plan or plan by products or plan by areas	50	57
(3) Consolidation of plan of subsidiaries	A. Plans of parent company and plans of subsidiaries are not integrated	47	44
	B. Plans of parent company and plan of subsidiaries are worked out separately but plans of some closely interrelated subsidiaries are integrated	35	41
	C. Plans of parent company and plan of closely inter-related subsidiaries are integrated, and consolidated financial plans are made	5	5
	D. In addition to C, plans of closely related foreign subsidiaries are integrated	2	6

(Note) 1. Survey in 1985 and in 1989
        2. Numbers indicate percentage of responding companies

Table 2.5.b Contents of a long-range plan

Corporations with long-range plans		1979	1985 (A) Corporations with one long-range plan	1989
		327 co.	315 co.	170 co.
Premises	1. Missions and objectives of the company as a whole	30 (%)	38 (%)	52 (%)
	2.1 General environmental forecasting	59	77	78
	2.2 Industry forecasting and competitive analysis	–	59	76
	3. Analysis of corporate strengths and weaknesses	57	78	91
	4. Forecasting future of own company under present policy	36	50	55
	5. Clarifies problems and opportunities of the company	42	76	93
Goals	6. Goals and policies of company as a whole	91	90	100
Product-market strategy	7. Vertical integration	1	12	17
	8.1 New product development	49	74	85
	8.2 Change of product mix	–	52	46
	9. New market development	31	65	61
	10. Multi-national management	27	41	43
	11. Strengthening the marketing competitive power	42	47	60
	12. Cost reduction plans	56	56	87
	13. Information systems	16	51	69
	14.1 Company acquisitions	0	6	10
	14.2 Strengthening the subsidiaries as a group	–	37	60
	15. Research and development	33	70	75

* continued

Table 2.5.b Contents of a long-range plan (cont.)

Corporations with long-range plans		1979	1985 (A) Corporations with one long-range plan	1989
		827 co.	315 co.	170 co.
Operations	16. Marketing plan	59 (%)	76 (%)	69 (%)
	17. Production plan	49	63	54
	18. Capital investment	72	81	81
	19.1 Strengthening the marketing capability	37	54	60
	19.2 Rationalization of logistics	–	32	33
	20. Material plan	18	30	31
Structure	21.1 Manpower plan	77	91	95
	21.2 Change of corporate culture	–	27	52
	22. Training and management development	31	47	55
	23. Employee welfare	11	22	31
	24. Planning of organization	24	45	54
Profit	25. Estimated profit and loss statement	63	78	66
	26. Estimated flow of funds	66	67	66
	27. Estimated balance sheet	40	45	40
Others	28. Responsible departments and schedule	13	39	40
	29. Problems remaining and how to solve them	21	32	34
	30. Contingency plans for adverse situations	8	11	10

Chapter 3 The process of planning

3.1 Features of strategic decision-making

In order to understand the decision-making process of long-range planning, we should recognize the features of strategic decision-making as compared with those of repetitive operating decisions. A decision on the development of a new pharmaceutical product, for example, is very different from the operational planning for existing drugs. In the former case, there are many opposing opinions, there are many ambiguities.

Overall features

The strategic decision is ill-structured. Causal relations and qualitative relations are not clear. For example, the ultimate user and the amount of demand of a new product may be hard to predict. Repetitive operating decisions are well-structured, causal relations and quantitative relations are clear. In strategic, ill-structured decisions, people need to understand ambiguity, and need to challenge complicated problems. There are many opposing opinions, so many opinions need to be collected and many alternatives need to be generated (McCaskey, 1982).

The 'birth' of issues is not automatic. The company needs to find out future gaps and issues when the operation of present products is profitable. On the other hand, the 'birth' of issues concerning operating activities is regular and repetitive.

(1) Effects on goals. Strategic planning deals with goal setting itself. The effects of goals lie in future time, they may decrease the profit in the short range. Research and development for example decreases present profit, but bears the fruit in the future. The operating decision deals with present profit, which can support new strategy.

The strategic decision is related to many values, affects the interests of many people and can be a cause of conflict.

(2) The character of initial informations. Strategic planning needs an outside information, information about future, because opportunities and threats lie outside the corporation. Top management and all staffs need to be outside-oriented. Internal information and information about past are not useful for strategic decisions.

Information for strategic decisions involves much uncertainty, this could be reduced by collecting more information, but at the same time some intuitive decisions and determinations based on faith are needed.

(3) Idea generation. Ideas for strategic decisions are new combinations of elements.

Table 3.1   Features of strategic planning as compared with operational planning

Kinds of planning	Strategic planning	Repetitive operating planning
Subjects of planning / Features	Goal setting, innovative change of product-market strategy and resource structure	Production and sales of products from continuous production process
(overall) 0.1 Complexity 0.2 Birth of issues	ll-structured Not automatic	Well-structured Cyclical, automatic
(Goal) 1. Effects on goals	Future effects, discontinuous	Short-term effects, incremental
(Information) 2. Character of initial information	Outside, future information	Inside, past information
(Idea) 3. Repetitiveness	• No precedence and single use • New combination of elements	• Repetitive • Best method in the past
(Time horizon) 4. Lead time and duration of effects	Long	Short
(Evaluation) 5. Ease of evaluation and risks	• Evaluation is difficult and risk is large • Affects the interests of many people	• Evaluation is easy, operation can be done over again • Less conflicts

There is almost no past model for these, there are many alternatives, so creative idea generation is needed.

(4) Time horizon. Lead times are long and the effect of a decision lasts long, thus a present decision binds future decisions. The development of a new drug takes about ten years, a construction of a large factory takes several years, and thus strategic problems need to be planned in the long-range plan.

(5) Evaluation. The evaluation of strategy is difficult, because decisions are related with many values and estimations of future results is hard to achieve. It is necessary

to forecast the worst case to analyze risks, and, also, a sort of resolution is necessary. This resolution is based on a faith on success. If we can anticipate opposition, if we can conduct a force field analysis (Hensey & Blanchard, 1977), if we can identify who may support the new project and who may oppose the project, we can take a 'political' approach to the project.

The above features are summarized in Table 3.1.

3.2 Types of strategic decisions

The characteristics of strategic decisions have been studied above, but they are normative and ideal in many ways. In actual practices, there are many types which fit into certain situations. Mintzberg states there are three types of decisions; planning mode, entrepreneurial mode and bargaining mode, and all three, he argues, are successful in certain situations (Mintzberg, 1973). Ansoff classifies the organization into four, initiative, anticipatory, reactive and stable (Ansoff et al, 1976). Miles and Snow classify the organization into four types, defenders, prospectors, analyzers and reactors (Miles and Snow, 1978). Allison classifies the decisions into three: rational, organizational and bureaucratic polities (G. T. Allison, 1969). Okochi classifies decision styles into analytical, intuitive and experimental (Okochi, 1978). With these classifications in mind, we classified strategic decisions into four, as is shown in Table 3.2. The four types are combinations of innovative versus conservative, and analytical versus intuitive. The reasons for these classifications are that these four combinations are frequently seen in practical cases, and they affect the performance of the organizations. (They are a classification of the upper corporate culture, and essentially the same as the classification of the corporate culture in the next chapter.)

Organizational level. The features of type (1) innovative and analytical, are that the decision style is rather top-down, top management makes use of planning staff, by interactive communication with the planning staff, they collect enough informations and listen to many ideas. The planning staff (including the research laboratory) are strong and they work effectively to formulate the strategy.

In case of (2), the innovative and intuitive type, the top management presents the idea first. The president, after talking with the presidents of other companies, may make sudden decisions on a joint venture project. This pattern may result in failures, but may bring great success if the president is competent.

(1) Goal setting. In the case of (1), the innovative and analytical case, the goal is clearly decided on and is made public. The goal is high. Even for exploratory projects in the research laboratory, the basic directions are set first, and then they try to attain the goals. In the case of (2), intuitive decisions, the goals are not clear, they are determined in the course of detailed planning or implementation. In these cases it happens sometimes that people cannot understand the aim of a project after it is implemented.

Table 3.2 Types of strategic decisions

Decision process \ Types	(1) Innovative and analytical (planning mode)	(2) Innovative and intuitive (enterpreneurial mode)	(3) Conservative and bureaucratic (bureaucratic mode)	(4) Conservative and intuitive (reactive mode)
Organizational level of planning	Polanning staff and top Management	Top down	Relatively bottom-up	(Miscellaneous)
1. Goal and policy	Clear goals High goals	Unclear goals Value in innovation	Idealistic and perfectionist 'Safety first'	Unclear goals Value in safety
2. Information collection and idea generation	From information to ideas, sensitive to new information	Intuitive ideas, sensitive to new opportunity	Reluctant to make decisions until sure of enough information, avoid uncertainty	Ideas by hunch and experience
3. Search	Aggressive search Many alternatives	Aggressive search and adventurous Few alternatives	Conservative search Few alternatives	When problems happen
4. Time horizon	Long (for ahead of competitors)	Long	Short	Short (a follower)
5.1 Evaluation	Deliberate evaluation Considers the worst case	adventurous, quick decisions, without considering resources	Do not cross the stone bridge, suboptimization.	Avoid risk
5.2 Integration	Integration by comprehensive planning	Build-up approach First-in first-out	Integraton is done within the limit of present resources	Build-up approach
5.3 Size of move	Innovative and large	Innovative and large	Incremental	Incremental or imitative
Fitting decisions	Large projects	Small projects		
Fitting departments	Top management, planning department	Marketing department	Personnel department Finance department	

(2) Information collection. In the case of (1) innovative and analytical, the organization is sensitive to the changes of the outside environment, they collect enough information on the future environment. There are many uncertainties, and the information is not very dependable, but the organization tries to collect much information.

In the case of (2) intuitive type, ideas are presented first based on existing information, then related information is collected afterwards, or it goes straight to implementation. 'Thinking while running' is the feature of this type. This type of decision is fit for a small projects.

(3) Searching process. The analytical type, (1), looks for new opportunities positively. The scope of searching is worldwide, the organization generates many alternative. Strategic decisions have few established models, so the organization tries to combine new elements creatively.

In the case of (2), innovative and intuitive type, the search is also positive, but the alternatives are few. In the case of conservative and intuitive plans, the search for new ideas is negatively done and action is taken after some problems happen.

(4) Time horizon. The (1) innovative and analytical type has long-term visions, forecasts long-term environments and looks for new opportunities, and estimates the long-term future results of their own company. The longer the time horizon, the more alternatives the company can find out, the better they are prepared for long lead time projects. The company can take steps ahead of the competitor.

The time horizon of (2) innovative and intuitive type is also long. But the time horizon of conservative types is short, they have a focus on short-term results, conduct only short-term forecasting and cannot take large moves.

(5.1) Evaluation. In the case of analytical type plans, the results of a decision is analyzed, particularly the worst case is forecast, and risks are taken into consideration. Strategic decision affects many values and affects the interest of a variety of people, opposing opinions can easily arise, so the decision maker analyzes the risk on human relations and carries out informal communication or "nemawashi" with the supporters and opposers. But the final decision is taken with faith.

In the case of the intuitive type, evaluations are optimistic and adventurous.

(5.2) Integrations. The innovative-analytical type does the coordination of projects by comparing their effects, ranking them and allocating their resources by the cost-performance ratio.

In the case of intuitive type plans, the project is decided in the order of occurrence of ideas, and is decided by satisfying principle, is decided immediately if it satisfies a certain level of criteria. The decision is taken by a first-in first-out approach. If, however, a profitable project is found out later, there may be no resources left to allocate.

For better integration, a broad policy is decided on first, and then detailed decisions are taken. In the case of analytical decisions, a broad policy is decided on first and then detailed decisions follow.

In the case of intuitive types, detailed decisions are taken first and, by the accumulation of many detailed decision, an overall direction is recognized.

We did not explain the case of (3) conservative-bureaucratic type: it puts an emphasis on the safety, on perfect play. And does not cross the stone bridge even after enough 'test tapping'.

Cases the three types fit with.

Among these four types, the (1) innovative-analytical type seems to be the best. However, the analytical type has several problems: it is expensive to collect information, it needs to have many staffs for analysis and the final decision tends to be too late. There are many uncertainties in strategic decisions, so the decision may not be successful even if the company collects enough information, because of the risks involved. Thus, different decision types fit into some situations.

For small projects, using small amount of resources, intuitive decisions which have cheaper information costs, are appropriate. For example, a new food product which can be produced by using existing facilities will be sold first, and if it is successful then the sales can be increased gradually. On the other hand, for large projects, the analytical type of decision is appropriate. For example, the development of a new car requires billions of yen invested in development and production, the success or failure of the new car determines the financial performance of the company greatly and even its survival may be affected. Enough analysis has to be done. Even in the process of such a new product development, the intuitive approach may be used in the early stage, but in the later stage, the analytical approach may be applied.

Peters and Waterman states in their book "In Search for Excellence", that excellent companies use experimentation or commitment or venture team approach frequently (Peters and Waterman, 1982). The small product development at 3M may fit with the experimental approach, but even at 3M, two approaches are used; to formulate the long-range planning, a large amount of information is collected.

Secondly, different decision types fit with different departments or different kinds of jobs. Top management and the planning department will use an analytical approach when they deal with large projects. The marketing department may use an intuitive approach to make decision on pricing strategies, but may be analytical on establishing sales channels. The personnel department and the finance department may use a bureaucratic mode, because failures in their jobs may be serious.

Four types of decisions and long-range planning

Formal long-range planning tries to use the innovative-analytical approach, because it deals with changes to corporate strategy, because the innovative-analytical approach tends to result in better performance. In the following chapters we will focus on the analysis of this approach.

The actual practices of long-range planning are classified into several types, but this classification is based on different categories, and all types intends to be innovative-analytical approaches. Sometimes the intention will not be successful, particularly when it is a bottom-up or a forecastive or a number-emphasis type, but all types intend to be innovative and analytical.

There are many decisions included in the long-range planning process, and some may be taken using an analytical approach but some may be carried out by an intuitive approach-depending upon the issues. This appropriate mixture is evidenced by our survey.

When the overall decision style of the corporation is not an innovative-analytical type, what can be achieved by a formal long-range planning system is another problem. That is, how can the company change the decision-making style from the type II to I, and from type III or type IV to type II or type I? What is the role of long-range planning in this shift? The effects of formal long-range planning have been already studied in Chapter 1, particularly in Table 1.1.b. We will here focus on the change of decision-making style in the formal planning process and outside the formal planning process, and will explain the reasons for it.

The long-range plan discloses future gaps in performance, makes clear strategic issues, unfreezes present inertia, and can encourage strategic thinking.

It can enhance sensitivity towards the changing environment by a regular scanning of the outside-world.

It plans new strategic projects and assigns the resources to implement them. Thus, the company can realize the importance of innovation. The long-range planning system needs to construct a data base for strategic information, and by constructing a data base, an analytical approach is stimulated. The company can learn the value of information.

However, too much analysis will disturb creative thinking and will lose a flexibility in behavior. Thus, the plan will concentrate on strategic issues. The plan may be a goal-type. There will be rooms for emergent strategies and 'bootlegs'. This problem has already been shown in Table 1.5. (On the role of long-range planning in this respect, see Lenz and Lyles, 1985; M. A. Carpenter, 1986)

The strategic decision style as seen in Table 3.2 is one of the aspects of corporate culture. It is a pattern of behavior. It is an upper corporate culture. The change of strategic decision-making style is a sort of change in corporate culture. The formal long-range planning gives one of the means to change corporate culture. There are some other means, such as change to top management, establishment of a new corporate philosophy, or the trial of a new strategy.

Such means have to be tried in addition to formal long-range planning, or as part of the contents of long-range planning. If the corporate culture is not 'vitalized', or the top management is not in the analytical mode, the company cannot have an effective long-range plan.

3.3   The process of planning

The basic model of the analytical planning process follows the sequence of several steps. They are, basic goals – information collection – detailed goals and issues – idea generation – evaluation and decisions.

Another basic process is from broad policy to detailed planning, from outline to details. This process brings about better decisions.

The actual planning process does not proceed in only one direction. It is composed of a multiplicity of processes, and has feed back processes. A group of decisions are followed by another group of decisions and earlier decisions become the premise of the following decisions.

1. A model of the planning process

This model was arrived at by observing many cases of the planning process in successful companies in Japan. (For other models of process, see Ansoff, 1965; Steiner, 1969; Andrews, 1971; Hofer and Schendel, 1978.) There are four phases (Table 3.3).

Phase 1. Establishing premises
A plan of the plan is worked out at the starting point. The system for the plan, the process of planning and the assignment of responsibility for planning are all decided on.

An atmosphere or organizational attitude that favors the long-range planning needs be exist. If it does not, the organizational culture or beliefs of people have to be changed. In many cases, line men say that they are too busy to be engaged in long-range planning. Many people say that the future is ambiguous. These thoughts have to be changed.

Innovations about the change of the corporate culture has been briefly stated in the last paragraph. We will here explain the actual practices of formal planning process changing attitude. It is a problem whether culture change should precede these changes or whether first or the formal long-range planning can have a changing effect on corporate culture, but here we will discuss a formal planning process that can change the attitude of people. There are three processes to change corporate culture.
(a) Unfreezing process. Future gaps in the performance of company is disclosed by the planning department. "If we do not change direction now, we will go bankrupt".
(b) Change process. The involvement of top management and frequent speeches and gestures on the importance of formal long-range planning and implementation are the most effective.

There are some other approaches. One company distributes questionnaires to managers asking what the important issues are for the company, and what should be done. These ideas are classified into strategic issues, administrative problems and operating problems. While many of them are helpful in generating ideas for corporate strategy, it is much more important that these question and answer exercises foster strategic thinking and orient the managers' attention to long-range planning.

Another company formed a project team to look for strategic issues. Members of the team were assistant directors of departments or managers of sections. They analyze opportunities and threats, strengths and weaknesses, and then generate strategic ideas.

Developing planning guides is another approach. This has the effect of ensuring that long-range planning becomes a formal system within the company.

Starting from an imperfect planning system is another approach. Instead of establishing sophisticated plans, the company starts from simple plans, and in the

Table 3.3   A model of the long-range planning process

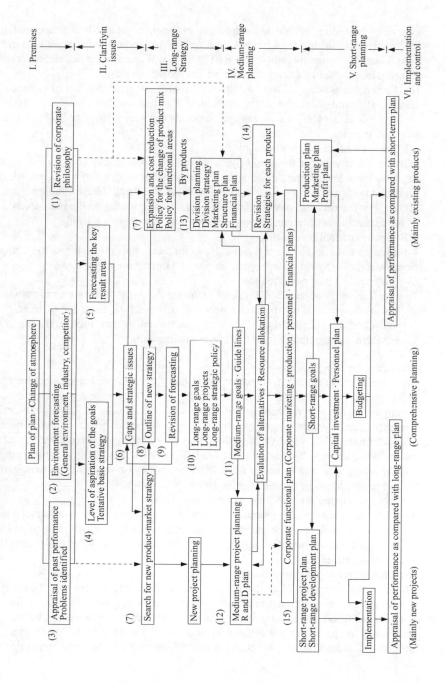

course of planning, people learn through experience. Matsushita suspended their long-range plan during the oil crisis, and restarted planning with "a set of number" type. Later, the company built "Action 61" which was quite strategic, aiming at transforming the product mix towards more information equipment.

(c) Refreezing process. If the contents of the plan are innovate, it can refreeze any change. The implementation of the long-range plan can stabilize change.

In the course of efforts to change corporate culture, trying the following three steps are in order.

(1) Revision of corporate philosophy

What is the mission of the company, what are the roles of the company in society, what business should the company be in, what is the priority of goals-growth over profitability, what is the social responsibility of the firm? These problems are analyzed. For the revision of corporate philosophy, stakeholder analysis or an analysis of the expectations of interest groups related to the company are useful.

(2) Environmental forecasting

Information is collected on the general environment, the industry and the competition. By forecasting the future, opportunities and threats are made clear.

(3) Appraisal of past performance

Past performance is compared with past plans for the purpose of improving planning. It is also compared with the performance of competitors, in order to identify the strengths and weaknesses of one's own company and it is measured over time to discover whether performance is improving or deteriorating.

Phase 2. Clarifying issues

(4) Levels of aspiration of corporate goals and the tentative basic direction of the company.

Following the above three steps, the levels of aspiration of multiple goals are determined. The desirable rate of growth and desirable rate of return on investment are also determined. The tentative basic directions of the company establish the points on which the company wishes to exert leadership, what the image of the company should be, compared to its competitors, what the policy on international management should be etc. Many of these decisions are value judgments.

(5) Forecasting the future performance of key areas.

What the performance of key areas will be when the present strategy is pursued is examined. This discloses what the fate of the company will be when innovations such as new products or new businesses are not developed, and when only capital investment is carried out.

(6) Identification of strategic issues

The levels of aspiration of goals and the tentative desirable direction of the company are compared with estimated future situation, and gaps of goals and gaps of direction are then identified. Here, not only are problems or weaknesses found out, but new opportunities in the future are discovered and issues are identified. For example, the progress of biotechnology, the development of electronics, the development of new materials, or a conflict on foreign trade will present the company not only with threats but also opportunities. For example, if South America has not been considered as a market so far, it could become the subject of investigation. These are some examples of strategic issues.

Phase 3. Long-range strategy
Following information collection and issue identification, a new strategy to close strategic gaps is sought.
(7.1) Search for a new product market strategy
In order to close a strategic gap, such strategies as entry into a new business, new product development, vertical integration, multinational management, an acquisition of another company or a joint venture agreement are searched for and important strategies are listed in the order of priority. This is the most important process.

These searches for new strategies are carried out not only during the period of building the long-range plan, but all the time, all the year around. To do this, the corporate planning department of each division, the development department, the research and development laboratory, project teams which invent new strategies, and, what is more important, a management committee play an active role.
(7.2) Improvement of present business and cost reduction
Present products are evaluated by the attractiveness of the industry and the competitive position of one's own company. Then products which should be supported, products which should be maintained and products which should be discontinued are selected, and different rates of resources are invested depending upon the status of the products. This means that a change of product mix and the strengthening of production and marketing capability may be changed. Cost reductions in every area are also searched for.
(8) Tentative new strategy and policy for improvement.
Ideas for new strategies and the plans for improvement of existing businesses are put together and integrated, and the best policy mix is arranged accordingly. This process means that projects and improvement plans are classified and integrated; sometimes they are divided or sometimes the two plans are put together. Projects are investigated and ranked by priority. In so doing, two or three alternative policy mixes are made. Ranking is done by evaluating the effectiveness of the resources employed and by the ease of implementation.
(9) Revision of the future estimation of performance.
Assuming that the above strategies are carried out, future performance may be forecast. Future performance is compared with the levels of aspirations of goals, and if the gaps are not closed, then the process in (7) is repeated again. This repetition is called the "piston system" by one company.

If the revision of the future estimation of performance is carried out by the use of a computer simulation model, many alternative strategies can be searched for and computation can be done quite rapidly.
(10) Deciding long-range goals, long-range projects and strategic policies

If the gaps in the aspired level of goals and gaps in the desired direction of strategy are closed, this aspired to level becomes the practical goal level and the desired direction of strategy then becomes the policy which is be followed. The strategic projects to fill the gaps are also decided on. These projects are the central part of long-range strategy.

The long-range strategy is comprised of three parts. First is the strategic policy in important areas of management, for example, how to change the product mix, what the direction of new business should be, and what the basic personnel policy is. The second part is strategic projects used to implement the above policy. This part is the most important part of long-range strategy. The third is the goals for key areas, such as the approximate size of sales, the product mix, the percentage of new business, rate of return on total assets and the equity ratio. These goals can be attained after implementing the above strategic projects.

Phase 4. Medium-range planning
The medium-range plan is a plan covering two or three years ahead. Following the long-range strategy, the plans for each product, project plans and functional plans are formed. They are planned by each line department and staff department. The medium-range plan is built by the bottom-up approach. It puts more emphasis on numbers and aims at the integration of resource allocation.
(11) Medium-range goals and guidelines for each department
Goals for the next two or three years of the whole company, of each product line and of each department are described. The long-range goals of step (10) could be used, but this is a guideline for the departments and goals vary from department to department. For example, when a company uses the growth-share matrix model, some products are supported, others are discontinued.
(12) Medium-range project planning
Strategic projects in the long-range strategy have resources allocated to them, and have responsible organizations assigned or new organizations created. Then stages for development are set. A medium-range project plan includes a medium-range plan of the research and development department, project planning at the corporate level and the development plan for already decided projects.
(13) Medium-range plan of each product
Products are grouped and plans for each product line are developed. When the company is organized by product division, the division develops this plan.

The product line is divided into a certain number of products, a growth-share matrix analysis is applied and resources are allocated depending upon whether the product is a 'problem child', a 'star', a 'cash cow' or a 'dog'. A guideline is given for each product line from head office, but among one product line each product has a different location on the growth-share matrix, so the product line itself may be growing but some segments of it may be 'losers'.

The improvement of the location of the products on the growth-share matrix is made possible by competition strategy – it is an important part of the medium-range plan.

A plan setting the sales amount of each product supported by a strengthening of marketing capabilities, a production plan including strengthening of production capabilities and a simplified plan of facilities and personnel are then created. These are the plans which reinforce the structure. The profit plans for each product make clear whether the goals of the product line are attained or not.

(14) Evaluation of alternatives and resource allocation

The medium-range project plan and the plan of product lines are reviewed to see whether they are directed toward the long-term goals and policies, whether there is any overlapping or shortages and whether there are other alternatives. An appropriate amount of resources are then allocated.

(15) Corporate functional plan

The marketing capabilities plan of each product line are consolidated. The sales channels, sales personnel and service facilities are also consolidated. Besides consolidation, sales channels common to all products and common sales promotions are planned.

The plan for strengthening the production capabilities is treated in a similar manner. A policy for production technology, a policy for vertical integration, consolidated facilities and a personnel plan are developed.

The total manpower plan, the capital investment plan and the organizational structure plan are company-wide resource structure plans which cover the research laboratory and the head office. These structure plans are the most important ingredients of the medium-range plan.

The profit plan of the whole company includes an estimated profit and loss statement, an estimated balance sheet and an estimated flow of funds. The profit plan makes possible a review of whether financial goals can be attained. The medium-range profit plan is useful not only to predict and set goals for profitability, but also to see whether the balance of goals is appropriate.

The characteristics of this process of planning are as follows. (a) It makes gaps clear. The process does not aim at maximizing performance, but attaining a satisfactory performance. The satisfying principle of decision rather than maximizing principle is applied (Simon, 1957). (b) It builds up a long-range strategy first. It analyzes key strategies and sets the guidelines for medium-range plans. It proceeds from general decisions to detailed decisions. (c) It emphasizes projects, rather than a set of numbers and is not a mere collection of all-inclusive programs. (d) The long-range strategy emphasizes innovation and is developed by a top-down approach. The medium-range plan emphasizes integration and is formed by a rather bottom-up approach. Thus the model uses different processes of planning for two different kinds of planning.

3.4 Cases of planning process

1. Canon
Canon's planning process is indicated in Table 2.3. Features of planning process of this model are as follows.

a It has two plans, the long-range strategy and the medium range plan. The long-range strategy states the size of the company, the change of corporate domain towards image products and knowledge intensive products, change,in other words, towards a multinational company. The medium-range plan puts an emphasis on the resource structure.
b. Enough information is collected before the strategic ideas are generated.
c. Simulations are used to forecast the results of and to attain the balance of, performance after resources are allocated to a number of projects. The simulation is computed twice, firstly, to estimate the future performances of the company when the present strategy is not changed, and after consolidation of new strategies to forecast the future results of these new strategy mixes.

2. Case of Nihon Sanso Co. (Nihon Oxygen Co.)
The process is indicated in Table 3.4. Characteristics of this case are as follows:

(a) The strategic issues are found out and eight issues are selected by the planning department and by top management. These eight issues are then studied by eight committees headed by eight vice presidents, helped by the planning department. These issues are the most important contents of ten year long-range corporate strategy, which describes new businesses, restructuring of present products, new multinational management strategies, establishment of new information system and so on.
(b) The medium-range plan covering three years is comprised of two parts. One group is corporate level project planning, planning for research, planning of administrative departments of head office and the resource allocation plan. Another group is planning by divisions. Division plans starts from guidelines and then informations are collected. Strategies are of two kinds: one is strategies assigned by head office, another one are the division specific strategies. Finally, all plans are integrated and summarized into a corporate medium-range plan.
(c) To summarize, the process of this corporation places an emphasis on strategic project planning.

3. Case of Taisei Corporation (Construction)
The process is indicated in Table 3.5. The features of this process are as follows:

(a) Twentieth century visions are formulated first. The planning department collects a large amount of information and formulates 30 pages of visions.
(b) Then, the five year strategy is formulated by the corporate planning department. This contains strategies on (1) existing business, (2) related businesses, (3) new

Table 3.4   The Long-range planning process used by Nippon Sanso

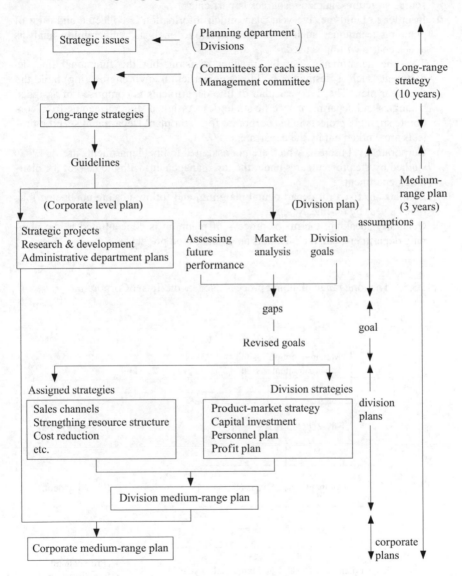

businesses, (4) projects on multinational management, (5) strengthening of resource structures, human resources in particular.

(c)   In order to build the five year plan, much information is collected and a lot of
      planning techniques such as product portfolio analysis, vulnerability analysis
      and scenario writing is used.

(d)   The line departments (not the product division, but the functional line de-
      partments such as designing, buildings construction, civil engineering) build the
      five year plan. The five year plan of line departments is comprised of assigned
      strategies and department specific strategies. Assigned strategies come from cor-
      porate strategic projects in the corporate five year plan. Department specific pro-
      jects are worked out by the department.

(e)   Corporate level projects which are not assigned to line departments are
      studied by the project teams under the top management with the help of the plan-
      ning department.

(f)   Formats are fixed for departmental planning, and follow-ups are conducted four
      times a year by on-line systems.

(g)   Generally speaking, the major process of planning is concentrated in the plan-
      ning department, and the plan puts an emphasis on projects.

Table 3.5.   The long range planning process used by the Taisei Corporation

(a)   System

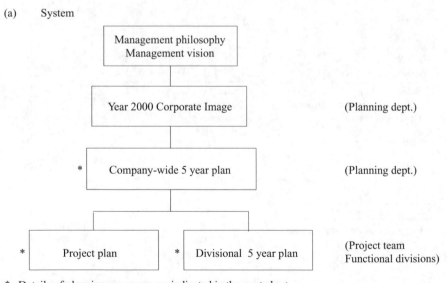

*   Details of planning processes are indicated in the next chart.

(b) Process

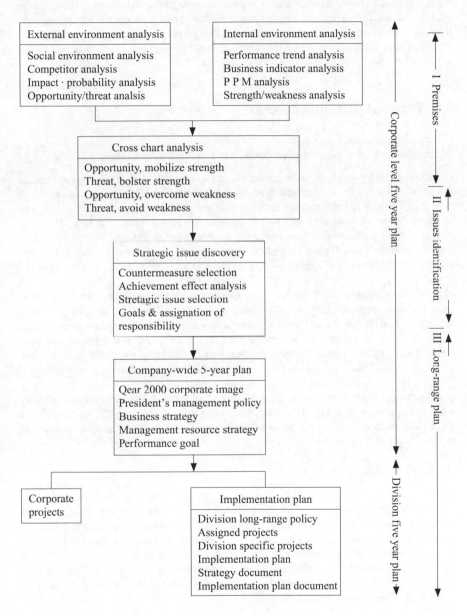

These three cases are slightly different but they are very similar to the model of Table 3.3 in that, (a) they have two plan system, planning proceeds from the long-range strategy to medium-range planning, from broader policy to detailed planning, (b) they are project-emphasis types, (c) there are two kinds of projects, that is, corporate level projects which are planned by corporate level project teams, or assigned to operating units, and operating units specific projects.

3.5 Types of planning process

(a) By idea generation processes
At initial stages, idea generation processes can be classified into three.

(1) The build-up approach. Ideas are collected first, and then checked to see whether the gaps are closed by the implementing of these strategies. This process is similar to type 2 in Table 3.2. Informations are collected after the ideas are presented. But, unlike type 2, the projects are ranked and resources are allocated accordingly. This process is used in a company where incremental opportunities are abundant, where their domain is in the growth stage and where few innovative projects are needed. This approach tends be the "too many projects type", and also tends to be a bottom-up approach.
(2) Goal assignment and build-up type. Goals set by the president are assigned to each division, who then look for informations and ideas. There are no corporate level strategies, and strategies are searched for at divisional level. This process is used where ideas are abundant in line departments, and there is less needs for searches for 'innovation'. In this sense, this type of approach is similar to the build-up approach. If the goals are too aggressive, there is a risk of losing the balance of goals, particularly between the growth rate and return on investment.
(3) Analytical type. This type belongs to type 1 of table 3.2. It follows the ordinary analytical process, starting with goals and information collection. Our model and three cases belong to this type, most of the long-range planning processes are of this type.

(b) By the evaluation method,

(1) maximizing approach and (2) satisfying approach. This classification was made clear by Simon (Simon, 1957) In the former approach, best efforts are attempted, and sometimes the needs for innovative strategies 'are not made clear. In the latter approach, levels of desired goals are made clear, gaps and issues are looked for. Since gaps of performances are made clear, the immediate targets are visible, the motivation to strategic thinking is stronger. Most of the planning processes follow this process. Our model and three cases belong to this type also, because goals are set first and gaps and issues are studied secondly.

3.6 Three types of organizational process

The planning process in the organization may be classified into bottom-up, top-down and interactive types, and each type fits into a certain situation. The three types are explained here as simplified models.

All three types are concerned with where the basic idea or basic policy should be presented, where the plan is reviewed and where the plan is decided. In all models the final decision is taken by top management, the differences lying in the process of initiating and reviewing.

A bottom-up approach implies that the corporate planning department is small, the planning format is given to it, but that information collection is mostly carried out by operating units. Goals, strategies, a plan of each product, functional plans of divisions – all are initiated by operating units. This is a decentralized process of planning. The corporate planning department initiates only the format, and coordinates the planning activities of operating units. It should be noted, however, that even in the bottom-up process, some key strategies are prepared at the corporate level. They are acquisitions and new product developments which do not belong to any existing divisions.

In the case of the top-down approach, basic information, the goals of each department and key strategies are decided at the corporate level. They are given to operating units as guidelines, and the operating units build a "tactical plan". In this approach the planning department is stronger, and plays a more important role. Operating units have less authority to decide on strategy.

The interactive process forms a path between the two. The ideas are formulated by interaction between top management, the planning department and operating units. The planning department will collect environmental information and will submit strategic issues to the top. Top management will then decide on the goals and the broad directions. By vertical interaction, strategies are formulated. In addition, there is a hierarchical division of labour. Some strategies such as acquisitions, joint ventures and new projects which are not assignable to departments are studied by the corporate planning department or by a corporate development department, and are implemented at the corporate level. Operating units will follow guidelines given from the top, build on strategies specific to the division and build operational plans from these.

If there is a two-plan system, long-range strategic plans are worked out mostly at the corporate level and medium-range plans are worked out by operating units.

These three organizational processes are a version of the type 1 model of Table 3.2. All intend to be innovative and analytical, but bottom-up approaches might result in somewhat conservative planning.

Two cases are shown in the following pages. One company is a specialized company producing rubber tires, the other is a diversified electrical products manufacturing company.

Case of a specialized company – a Tire and Rubber Company – Top-down approach.

Table 3.6 Three types of planning or organisational processes

	Bottom up	Top down	Interactive
Planning department	Small	Large	Medium
Contents of guide line	Only format (Occasionally goals of divisions)	Format, goals of whole corporation (Goals of divisions are not indicated)	Format, goals of whole corporation and goals of divisions
Assessment of environment	Mainly by divisions	Planning department	Planning department and divisions
Goals of divisions	Divisions (or planning department)	Planning department	Planning department and divisions
Planning of new strategy	Divisions	Planning department	New business is assessed by planning department. Improvement of present business is assessed by divisions
Planning by products	Divisions	Divisions	Divisions
Functional plan	Divisions	Divisions and staff departments	Divisions and corporate staff
Budgeting	Divisions	Financial department and divisions	Financial department and divisions
Reviewing and final decision	Top management	Top management	Top management
Follow up	Divisions	Top management	Top management and divisions

Note: (1) Planning department refers to the corporate planning department of head office
(2) In functional organizations, divisions mean line departments.

The founder and president of the company was very plan-oriented, and he himself wrote a detailed future blueprint of the company. It was then discussed in a management committee, and was used for actual decisions. As the company grew, more formal planning was adopted and the president's office was established. The first formal plan covered 1967–8 and the second plan 1969–71, but these were quantitative plans, mostly expressed in numbers. They were useful in an expansion period, but top management could hardly set their own plans in the project because the number were too complicated and mutually interdependent. The third plan, covering 1972–5, was changed from a quantitative plan to a more strategic or issues-oriented plan, composed of long-range policy and medium-range financial estimates. There were too many issues, however, and the plan was too all-inclusive. A computer simulation was used for the medium-range plan which was tried as a means to integrate the strategy. In this case, there were too many all-inclusive issues without any ranking, and the issues lacked detailed analysis. During their planning period, the oil crisis occurred and the plan was modified to stress efforts in cost reduction.

The recent plan, started in 1976, has two salient characteristics. First, it stresses five key strategic issues, and second, the issues are initiated and discussed by top management. The planning process is exhibited in Table 3.7.

The first phase is to collect environmental information. This is mostly carried out by the planning department on a continual basis. The second phase is the identification of issues. The functional department works for three months to identify opportunities and threats. Their findings are presented to the management committee, five key issues are found and five committees are set up, chaired by five of the top management including the president (CEO). The five issues are rather broad issues, as shown in Table 3.7. In the third phase, five strategies and over-all strategies are decided by the management committee and checked by simulation. Then, the five-year goals, basic strategies and long-range policies are decided. In the fourth phase the medium-range plans are formulated. They are based on the long-range strategy, and drawn up by each of the product departments and by the functional departments.

The characteristics of this process are that the long-range strategy focuses on five key issues, that simulation is used to guide the medium-range plan, and that the planning process is relatively centralized.

The older systems were somewhat defective, but still could contribute to the strategy formulation. The strategy of the company has been to expand the production facilities aggressively, to undertake construction during the depression period, to emphasize research, and new-product development. These strategies were successful largely because of long-range planning.

Case of a diversified company – an Electrical Products Manufacturing Company – Interactive approach.

Unlike the former company, this company is a diversified company, and the planning process is more decentralized. This company started formal long-range planning in 1959, and used it continuously for strategic decisions, the only break being during the three years after the oil crisis in 1973. Plans in the earlier stages were of the fore-

Table 3.7 Planning process of a tire and rubber corporation

Phase	Planning			Department in charge
I Premises	1.	Purposes of planning		Planning department ↓ Each department Management committee
	2. Environment forecasting	Economic forecasting Demand analysis Competitor analysis		
II Issue identification	3. Strategic issues	Appraisal of past performance Issue finding 1. New products 2. Cost reduction 3. Organization and personnel 4. Multinational management 5. R & D		Functional department (Three months) ↓ Management committee
III Long-range strategy	4. Key strategies	Five key strategies Strategy of each function		Five committees (Two months) ↓ Management committees
	5. Financial estimation	(Simulation) 3 years sales, production, inventory capital investment and personnel		Finance department
	6. Long-range strategy	Long-range goals Long-range strategies Functional strategies		Management committees and president
IV Medium-range plan	7. Medium-range plan	Products	Marketing plan Production plan Personnel plan Facilities plan Profit plan	Each department
		Plan of each function		

First-year goals
Annual plan

casting type, stressed numbers, and were built up using a bottom-up approach, by divisions. Since 1976 top management leadership has been emphasized, and a new style of planning introduced. The new planning system has two characteristics. It emphasizes strategy and policy rather than financial estimates. It emphasizes strategies such as a change of product mix, new business areas, new directions for the company, and how to strengthen the capability structure. It introduced two new approaches, the contingency plan and growth-share matrix model. The most important changes are that top management now initiates the basic strategy and guidelines and that the interactive process is stressed.

The planning process is shown in Table 3.8. Phase one is to collect environmental information and to analyze one's own company. This is done by the planning department, which is also engaged in gathering strategic information all year round.

In the second phase, strategic issues are looked for. Some issues are presented by top management, some are discovered by the planning department through the collection of strategic information, and some are identified through a follow-up of the previous plan. The growth-share matrix model is used here to some extent.

In the third phase, corporate goals and business policies are drawn up by the planning department. They include the size of the company, new business, the future product mix and other basic policies. Next, these goals and policies are discussed by the policy committee which is another name for the management committee, used when it discusses strategic issues. In the guidelines, a contingency plan to be incorporated in the division plan is called for.

In the fourth phase the division plans are worked out. The contents of the division plan are shown in the bottom of Table 3.8. We find that the financial estimate is simple, and strategies are emphasized.

The planning department consolidates the division plans and identifies the issues. This is the second round of issue finding, following phase two. Then the plans and issues are presented to the policy committee, and discussed, and a revision of the plan is requested. This revision is coordinated by the planning department.

In phase five, the corporate plan is drawn up. This includes items similar to those in the division plans; however, it is not just a consolidation of the division plan, but also stresses the future strategy that was discussed in phase three. In this case, the sequence of the phases is a little different from the model on Table 3.3. We find that the flow is not straight, but oscillates back and forth. The issues and corporate strategies are found and discussed in the earlier stages and also in the later ones.

Table 3.8   The corporate planning process of an electrical products manufacturing company

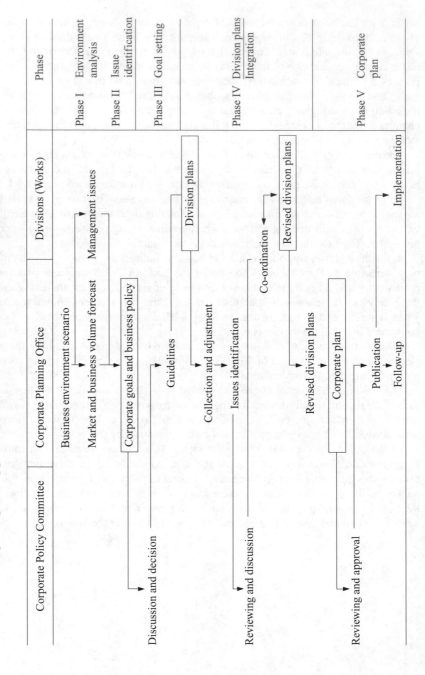

(Legend of table 3.8)

Contents of the Long-range plan – the Division Plan

(1)   Fundamental plan (five years)

(1–1) Volume of business (five years)
       New order, sales, net income, number of employees
       Investment in equipment and figures connected with these items.
(1–2) Long-range strategies on business activities (five years)

       1. Outline of business environment and important strategies.
       2. Review of product mix.
          a. Important existing markets and new markets.
          b. Important existing products and new products.
          c. Products to be discontinued.
       3. Methods to strengthen sales ability.
       4. Strategies and tactics for international business.
       5. Other issues to be solved.

(2)   Contingency plan (three years)

(3)   Summary and implementation plan

3.7 Survey on the planning process in the organization

The planning process in the organization is shown in Table 3.9. For companies with one long-range plan, the initial preparation of the plan is developed with the cooperation of the corporate planning department and the divisions or other operating units. Staff departments develop the functional plan. Diversified companies, such as food products, chemicals, machinery and electrical machinery use an interactive or bottom-up approach more frequently. Even in cases of diversified companies, new innovative strategies such as starting a new business, construction of new plants in foreign countries, or increasing the capacity of research and development are planned in head office. Trends are towards more centralization of planning as the innovative planning becomes necessary.

Specialized companies such as construction, oil refineries, finance, electricity and gas supply use a centralized approach, their corporate planning offices playing a more important role.

Reviewing is mostly done by a management committee or by a management committee of a few top executives.

Final decisions are taken by a management committee or by the president (chief executive officer).

In the case of companies with two long-range plans, long-range strategies are prepared by the corporate planning department and medium-range plans are written by

Table 3.9 Planning processes in the organization:
Which department prepares, reviews and finally decides on the long-range plan

Corporations with long-range plans	(A) Corporations with one long-range plan (170 co.)			(B) Corporations with two long-range plans (79 co.)					
				Long-range plan			Medium-range plan		
	Preparing	Reviewing	Final Decision	Preparing	Reviewing	Final Decision	Preparing	Reviewing	Final Decision
a. Planning department	80 (%)	17 (%)	0 (%)	56 (%)	1 (%)	1 (%)	70 (%)	8 (%)	0 (%)
b. Division or line department	46	7	0	15	4	0	70	10	0
c. Corporate staff department (Personel facilities and financial departments)	26	6	0	8	4	0	29	9	0
d. Special committee (for particular problems or for functional areas)	10	7	0	5	4	0	9	11	0
e. Project team	9	4	0	23	3	0	10	0	0
f. Comittee for long-range plan	8	13	2	8	5	0	2	5	1
g. Meeting of managing director and department (divisions) executive	1	14	1	0	10	0	2	15	0
h. Management committee	2	39	35	1	29	29	1	42	39
i. Management committee of a few top executives	3	37	20	1	34	18	2	43	29
j. President and CEO	1	6	36	4	5	23	1	6	32
k. Board of directors	0	5	22	0	2	18	0	9	22
l. Chairman	0	0	2	0	1	1	0	1	1

1. Survey in 1989   2. Numbers indicate the percentage of companies

divisions or by operating units. Recently, many companies have formulated a 21st century project team to study the visions of the company in the next century. This is the reason why the use of project teams is seen to be so frequent in the survey. In many cases the team is composed of young managers who are expected to be key persons in the next century.

For both plans, reviewing is done by a management committee or by a smaller management committee of a few top executives. And for both plans, the final decisions are made by a management committee or by a management committee of a few top executives, or perhaps by the managing director (CEO).

Generally speaking, companies with a single long-range plan use the interactive process and companies with two plans use the top-down approach for long-range strategy and the bottom-up process for the medium range plan.

The survey shows that the management committee plays an important role in reviewing and in final decisions based on consensus. The management committees of Japanese corporations, usually comprised of about ten top executives, make decisions as a group.

This planning process can be compared with the process in the U.S. and in the U.K.

In the United States, there is more of a tendency to have planning as a bottom-up process. Based on author's personal visits to companies, many have bottom-up processes, some use interactive processes, and the top down process is rarely used in any large company.

Decentralization comes partly from diversification and multinational activity, but there are some other reasons.

In the philosophy underlying American management, corporations are more division oriented (Steiner, 1975), and more decentralized. Long-range planning is used for integrating the strategy of divisions, and also for control purposes of division managers. The long-range plan is a promise of the managers of the divisions.

Japanese corporations are more centralized. There are many papers describing that the Japanese style of decisions is bottom-up and group-decision oriented (for example, Johnson and Ouchi, 1974). According to the author's survey, this cannot be generalized. The strategic decision-making process is not always bottom-up, but it may be top down or interactive. The reason for this is due to a faster change in the environment. Japanese corporations have had to make top-down innovations. Top management is a group body and innovation-oriented.

In addition to these facts, Japanese corporations are less diversified and have less of a spread of divisionalization. They use acquisitions to a lesser extent as entry strategies. This is another reason for centralized organization.

For operational decisions, the situation is different. Operational policy is decided on by the staff department, and ideas are submitted from the middle, and group decisions are used.

In the United States, operational policy may be decided by the participation of many departments, but working decisions are taken by responsible individuals. This system may come from the social setting which is more individualistic than group oriented.

3.8 Planning schedules

The schedule of planning varies depending on the kind of plan. Strategic issues may be investigated by project teams all the year around. The long-range strategic plan may be formulated once in two years. However, the comprehensive medium range plan and long-range plan have regular schedules in many companies. By having regular schedules, the company can review the strategy regularly. Strategic issues tend to be forgotten when daily operations occupy most of the time of the top management.

Our research on the schedule of long-range planning, and the results of survey on 249 companies were the following. – Long-range planning starts between June and September and it is completed between December and March in many companies.

The average time spent for planning is six months.

The fiscal year starts in April, this means that budgeting is completed before March. In order that the contents of the long-range be included in the budget as implementation plans, it is necessary that long-range planning is concluded before the budgeting starts. For this reason, many companies complete the long-range planning between December and March.

Summary

1. The process of decision-making has the sequence of goals setting – information collection – detailed goals – idea generation – evaluation – final decision. The planning process is composed of many groups of this process. Usually the planning proceeds from a broad policy to detailed planning.
2. The above process varies depending upon the types of strategic decision making. There are four types. (a) planning mode, (b) entrepreneurial mode, (c) conservative bureaucratic mode, (d) reactive mode. The long-range planning tries to change the other decision-making styles to (a)the planning mode. However, other styles work well in particular cases. In large projects with high risks, the planning mode is appropriate. The incremental approach which is considered as one of the analytical mode (planning mode) fit with decisions with high uncertainty, such as research and development. In this case the basic direction or broad policy is formulated in the formal plan. Small projects fit well with the entrepreneurial mode.
3. The long-range planning system has the effect of changing the decision-making style, but on the other hand, to attain the above effect, the corporate culture needs to be strategy-oriented, otherwise the innovative long-range planning cannot be formulated.

   In order that the people in the organization are motivated to be strategy oriented, the following unfreezing process is recommended. (a) A sense of crisis is emphasized. (b) Many experimental innovations, a new product development, for example, should continue beside the formal planning process. (c) Top management is committed to innovation. These are the measures taken in Asahi Brewery and Nissan Motor, explained in the next chapter.
4. The long-range planning process has four steps: establishing premises, finding issues and fixing goals, formulating long-range strategy and then medium-range planning. By collecting information, strategic options can be increased, and by finding strategic issues, the

plan can be innovative. The issues should be of limited number, so that resources can be allocated predominantly to projects of high priority.

5. The more intensive the study on strategic projects, the less the need to update them every year.

6. Corporate strategic projects can be studied in two ways, one is by the corporate project teams, another is by the operating divisions. The large projects requiring different skills from present products are carried out by the corporate project teams.

7. The long-range planning process can be classified on three axis: (a)types of organizational process, (b)where the decision-making starts, (c)where the emphasis is placed in the decision-making process. The levels of these three axis are correlated, and we can simplify the combination into three as is seen in Table 3.10. We see that organizational process is the key dimension, and the interactive process is fit for innovative strategic decisions. The appropriateness of this grouping is evidenced by the correlation matrix in Table 7.3.b.

Table 3.10.   Grouping the different types of planning

	Types	I	II	III
(1)	Organizational process	Interactive	Top down	Bottom-up
(2)	From where planning starts	from information	dividing and allocating of goals	from ideas
(3)	Focus on decision process	problem solving	goal type	forecastive
(4)	Contents of plans	key projects	key projects	too many projects
Fitting with 1.	product-market strategies	diversification	specialization	diversification
2.	environment	unstable	unstable	stable
3.	future strategies	innovative	innovative	conservative

Chapter 4 Organization for strategic planning

Many departments participate in the planning process, as is indicated in Table 3.10. Top management, the corporate planning department, product divisions or other operating units, staff departments, project teams and planning committees all have a planning role.

This chapter deals with the departments which are mainly engaged in constructing corporate strategies, and in turn, studies how the long-range plan should try to construct these departments. The structure should precede strategy, the structure should not follow strategy.

There are three new directions on the change of organizations for strategic planning: (a) the strengthening of strategic planning departments, (b) more flexibility in organizational structure and, (c) the change of corporate culture towards a vital one.

The first direction includes the strengthening of top management, the planning department, the research and development laboratories and incubator departments for infant products. Thousands of people in the laboratories, and a few people in the manufacturing factories this is a new trend. The second direction includes the frequent use of project teams, frequent changes in organizational structures and flexibility of job assignments. The third one is the vitalization of corporate culture. Corporate culture is the pattern of decision-making and of the behavior of members. If the corporate culture is vital, the company can develop excellent strategies and it can expect the implementation of strategies.

4.1 Top management

The roles of top management in general management are four. They are a value builder. They sets goals and visions, taking into consideration the demands of stockholders. They detail the goals of the company, and the new direction of the company. They are a strategists. They define the relationship between the organization and the environment, and make decision on product market strategy. They are a great organizer. They take decisions on key personnel and on organizational structure. They motivate people to implement the strategy, by symbolic actions and by visit to the company laboratories and marketing fronts. They are constructors of culture. Through the above three roles, they try to cultivate a vital culture in the corporation. (On the role of top management, see Holden et al., 1941; Drucker, 1974; Katz & Kahn, 1966; Minzberg, 1973).

4.1.1 Top management team and the management committee

Top management is the most important organ for making strategic decisions, for the success of long-range planning. The hierarchy of top management of Japanese corporation is as follows: board of directors – president (CEO) – management committee – senior managers of departments (staff, line departments and product divisions). Among these top bodies the management committee is the most important decision-making body (See Table 3.9). The board of directors is not the real top management, because the majority (19 out of 21 directors on the average) are recruited internally. The management committee is comprised of about such ten 'inside' senior directors. They meet three or four times a months and make decisions on strategic issues as well as operational problems. Holden, Fish and Smith classified the types of general management levels into four: one chief executive, management committee (council of general executives), assembly of department heads (chief executive and council of divisional executives), and the board of directors working as general management. (Holden, Fish and Smith, 1941). In Japan, the management committee has a very high rate of diffusion. (According to a survey by the Kansai Branch of Japan Productivity Center in 1985, 70% of 293 surveyed companies have such management committee)

The number of members is about ten on the average, much larger than the average of American corporations, whose number is about 3 to 5.

The members meet once a week or two or three times a month. They make decision as a group (MITI, 1987).

4.1.2 Effects of group decision-making at the top

The effects of group decision at the top seem to be as follows.

(a) Decisions taken by groups usually exhibit greater degrees of risk. It has been said that group decision tended to be conservative and to be mediocre. Under certain conditions the opposite applies, however. R. D. Clark indicates three reasons for the group to shift in this way, towards, risk taking (R. D. Clark III, 1971). Through group discussions, much more information becomes available and uncertainty is reduced, and with more information the committee members become willing to take risks. Secondly, group decision frees each individual from full responsibility, since he perceives that the decision has been shaped by the group. And lastly, in group discussion risk taking opinions tend to have higher value than conservative opinion, and relatively cautious member will eventually follow moderately risky opinions. This shift of value towards risk is observed when the consequences of failure are not severe. In Japanese corporations, the group decision is used at every level of organization, and this is one of the reasons why Japanese corporations have been innovative.

(b) In order to persuade many members towards a group decision, information has to be collected and provided and this results in rational decisions. This situation is different where one responsible person as an individual makes a decision based on less information, or based on intuition. Also in a group decision, diverse information is available when the group members all represent various fields of knowledge.

(c) The member of the group can be a linking pin with groups on a lower level, and thus decisions can be conveyed to lower levels effectively (The concept of linking pin comes from R. Likert, 1967). The senior executive is usually responsible for several departments, and decisions at the top can make use of information and ideas from lower levels and can be easily implemented. The group decision can thus be used as a means of fostering participation.

4.1.3 Problems of the management committee

As the management committee has become more popular, some defects have become apparent. One is that their members tend to show more interest towards operational issues than strategic issues, because the former are clearer and less risky. Another one is that members are supposed to be concerned with general management, but the committee can come to represent the interests of the departments concerned, because the members (usually the senior director) is responsible to some area of functions or products, though the responsibility is very broad. To solve these problems, several measures are taken.

(a) Two management committees. In addition to the ordinary management committee, many companies have created another body the senior management committee. This is composed of the chairman, president and a few senior executive directors, in all between 5 and 6 members. The "senior management committee" discusses only the strategic problems and refers issues to the management committee for final decisions. The senior committee is a free discussion or brainstorming body for strategic issues. In other cases the issues are divided into two; the strategic issues are discussed and decided by the senior management committee and operational issues are discussed and decided by the ordinary management committee.

(b) The members of the management committee are not charged with the responsibility of departmental heads, but are responsible for broad areas. They are not responsible for the decisions of the departments concerned.

(c) The subject of decisions of the committee are rotated weekly. The subject of decision in one week will be a strategic one, but in the next week, the subject will be an operational one.

(d) The planning department will submit strategic issues to the management committee on continuous basis. The planning department is, in effect, the clerical office of the management committee, selecting the subjects to be placed on the agenda, so it is possible for the planning department to merely establish out the strategic issues and places them on the agenda for discussion.

4.1.4 Role of top management in the long-range planning process

As top management plays key roles in every aspect of strategic decision making, so it is with long-range planning processes. Among the many key success factors to long-range planning, top management involvement ranks first. Then what are the roles of top management? We have already briefly mentioned four roles, and we will repeat them here again.

(a) Creating a climate for strategic orientation, as a value builder and a culture constructor. Top management will present their own ideas and spend much time discussing the issues with planners. They will discuss strategic issues on many occasions, as indicated in table 4.1.b at the end of this chapter.

(b) Top management as a planner, as a strategist.
The top management team will make decisions on future visions or promote the formulation of the future visions by organizing study teams staffed by selected middle managers, or by corporate planning staff.

(c) Top management as promoters of formally described plans, as great organizers.
Top management will make force field analysis and will try to persuade opposing departments and personnel of their view. They will perform symbolic actions so that the implementation of the plan can be understood as important for the success of the company. Symbolic actions may be, for example, the president's comment on the plan in the new year's speech, or talks with employees on the front.

They will conduct follow-ups of plans in the management committee frequently, in particular reviews of the progress of important strategic projects.

4.1.5 The changing of attitudes

What can be done when the top management is not committed to strategic planning? This is an often asked question by corporate planners. General principle of attitude change can be applied.

If top management is a team (as is case in Japanese corporations), then the change of attitude should be the change of all members of the management committee. However, the president and CEO are the most important, because they are leaders of the team and have actual power to select and to appoint directors, although the legal power for selection rests with stock holders. Here we will discuss only the change of attitude of the president or CEO.

(a) Change of the president
This is the most effective, but this is out of control of the corporate planner. Past cases show that only the change of a president is not enough. There are many companies where presidents have changed but where the corporate culture did not change. The problem is the presence of CEO who is aggressive and strategy oriented.

Most of the corporate planners do not have the power to fire the president, so a possible way is to try to change the attitude of the present president. How this can be done is the real problem.

(b) Unfreezing. To change the perspective of the CEO, the crisis the company will face in the future can be analyzed and presented to the president or members of management committee. Future crisis may invade a continuing decline of market share, a weakness in competitive power of the company, a position of the product on the product life cycle or an estimated decline of sales and profit.

(c) Change. An opportunity will be created by the planning department where information on the need for change may be delivered from the top of other companies to whom or which the president pays respect. If there is a director who recognizes the importance of a strategic planning, who is trusted by the president and is influential, he can help the planning department change the attitude of the president.

Series of reports on cases of leading companies which are successful in restructuring in the world market place will be provided all the time.

Experiences. Top management will try a small experience in innovation, such as a new product development or a change of wage system. They will make plant visits to observe successful changes in production systems. The president may also be encouraged to make plant visits or visits to sales offices to see the reality of the situation.

Sanction. Reports on poor performance in newspapers, concerns from stockholders, criticism by outside board members are also useful. A decline of share price is another area in which the president can easily know.

(d) Refreezing. A change of strategy is confirmed by a formal plan. New corporate creeds and goals will be formulated to bind top management.

These are the practices of many companies which actually changed the attitude of top management and changed the planning system successfully by the initiative of the planning department.

4.1.6 Demographic and other characteristics of top management

According to a MITI survey of 598 companies in 1986 (MITI, 1987) and the author's survey of 102 companies in 1984 (Kono, 1984), the demographic and other characteristics of top management members are shown in Table 4.2. Here, top management members means the directors. The majority of directors of Japanese corporations are inside full-time members, they are not only the members of the board of directors, but the members of management committee. Many are also department heads who may be called vice-presidents in American terms, although not all department heads are necessarily directors. The analysis of directors therefore can be the analysis of top managers in a corporation.

Table 4.1   Demographic and other characteristics of top management

	Directors	President, CEO
1.1 Age	5 8. 1 years	6 2. 3 years
1.2 Years as directors	7. 7 years	6. 6 years
2 Functional background		
Technology and production	3 8. 5 %	
Marketing	2 9. 3 %	
Finance and accounting	1 6. 7 %	
Personnel and planning	1 5. 4 %	
3 Percentage of shares held by total directors		
Average	3. 9 %	
Large corporations	1. 4 %	
Medium-sized corporation	7. 8 %	
4 Educational background		
Natural science	4 4. 2 %	
Social science	4 9. 6 %	
Other	6. 2 %	
5 Salary in a year	20~30 million yen	40~60 million yen
	Relative to income of average worker	
	7 times	14 times

(Note)   (1) no 1 ~ no. 3 – MITI survey of 598 manufacturing companies in 1986.
         (2) no. 4   – Kono survey of 102 manufacturing companies in 1984.
         (3) no. 5   – Varied sources.

(1) Age of directors. Average age of directors is 58.1 years and that of the president (CEO) is 62.3 years. These ages are almost the same as those of American corporations.

(2) Functional background

The functional background of directors shows what capabilities are the key resources for the company, although top management is in charge of general management. Technology and production and marketing have the highest frequency of. This is different from the background of the top of American corporations, many of whom are from financial backgrounds. Technology intensive industries such as the iron and steel industry, electronics appliances and precision mechanics industries have more than fifty percent of technology and production backgrounds. Managers from technology and production backgrounds tend to be more sensitive to technological development.

(3) Stock ownership

Stocks held by the directors are only 1.4% in the case of large corporations. This shows one aspect of the separation of management from ownership. The distribution of stock ownership of major large corporations is also dispersed, without a single person or a group having majority ownership. The details of this problem are beyond the scope of this book. We state here only that the divorce of management from ownership is seen in the majority of Japanese large corporations, and it is one of the causes of the long-term view and of growth orientation seen in Japanese corporations.

(4) Educational background

About 44 percent are graduates from the natural science departments of the university. This is related to the functional background in corporations.

(5) Remuneration

Remuneration for the Japanese directors is much lower than that of American top management. They are motivated by the job itself, by a devotion to the company. (On top management, see Kono, 1984; Kudo, 1988 and Merwe, 1985).

4.2 Planning department

In this section, we will study the corporate planning department's role in the head office. In operating departments below the head office there are many planning sections. The number of planners in these operating units may exceed the number of personnel in the corporate-level planning department in the head office. Nevertheless, here we shall concentrate on the central planning department.

1. The role of the corporate planning department

The corporate planning department,which may be called by other names, such as the president's office, or sometimes the general administration department, engages in the study and promotion of corporate strategy. There are five important roles that the corporate planning department takes. (See Table 4.2.b)

Firstly, it promotes strategic thinking. It appeals to the top and middle management on the importance of corporate strategy. People tend to be more interested in daily operations than in strategic problems, because people do not like dealing with uncertainty, with things which bear fruit only in the long-term future or with things which involve many risks.

Secondly, the corporate planning department collects strategic information. It assesses the general environment, it looks for new businesses and conducts macro-predictions of the industry. It also conducts internal analyses of the firm. These ana–

lyses do not overlap with the information collection of the divisions because they are macro-analyses. The departments do, however, carry out some overlapping analysis of the industry which is the key area for their company, and the analysis of their most important competitor.

Thirdly, the department performs a planning function: it determines basic goals and policies, and presents innovative ideas on strategy. These basic goals and policies cover not only the total organization but sometimes include the goals and policies of divisions. When the company employs the growth-share matrix model, the corporate planning department tends to have centralized authority. Also, new business which does not belong to any existing operating units has to be sought out by the corporate planning department.

The fourth role is the coordination and integration of the strategic plans of operating units. One means of coordination is resource allocation, initiated through a long-term profit plan and a personnel plan.

The fifth role is that of follow-up on the implementation of the plan. The planning department compares the actual results with the milestones set for the projects. It also assesses the quantitative performance of the plan. Actual follow-up and performance appraisal are part of top management's task, but the planning department prepares information on performance. It also draws up the standards to be used in performance appraisal.

Unexpectedly, many planning departments carry out budgetary control, and use appraisals of performance in comparison with the budget. If the planning department is responsible for budget preparation and control it will have the power of resource allocation. With that power it becomes easier for the planning department to collect information from inside and to give planning instructions to operating units, and it also becomes easy to collect information on implementation. This is one advantage in having the planning department responsible for budgeting. However, if this is to occur, the planning department has to spend a lot of time in planning and coordinating the short-range plan. If it also has to perform budgetary control, it will have to give approval to many planning documents, and will have little time to spend in developing innovative strategic plans. The source of the power of the planning department should, therefore, be found elsewhere.

If the planning department's duties have a heavy emphasis on the collection of strategic information, the department may be classified as a research-type office.

If the duties mainly involve the preparation of corporate strategy, the office may be classified as a strategic-planning-type, or may be termed a "general staff office" in the military sense of the description. Many Japanese planning departments belong to this type.

If there is more emphasis on coordination, the planning department can be called a coordination-type office. The planning departments of diversified American corporations mostly belong to this type.

Survey results on the responsibilities of planning departments in Japanese corporations are shown in Table 4.3. The survey illustrates that the above-mentioned five functions are important and that the planning departments of Japanese corporations seem to belong to a strategic-planning-type.

In the case of planning departments of diversified companies, the staff members are assigned to each product. The department considers the strategy for each product line viewed from head office, and tries to give a direction to the divisions. In the case of H Company, for example, the planning department members are divided into an environment-assessing group, a product-line group, a planning group and an industry-analysis group which analyze the competition in the home country and abroad.

Also, in the case of B company, staff in the planning department are divided into a macro-economic analysis group, an industry-analysis group, a competition-analysis group, and a planning group. Each member is also responsible for a certain product line. Thus one person performs two or three duties.

2. Number of personnel in the corporate-planning department

According to the survey of 249 large companies in 1989 the median number of personnel in the planning department is approximately 7.5. If assistant members such as female secretaries are excluded, the average number of planning staff is 5.5 and among them 2 are natural science graduates, and 3.5 are social science graduates. In the electricity and gas supply industry, the number of personnel in the planning department is very high: the median number is 55.

3. Power of the planning department

One of the conditions needed for a planning department to be successful is the power to make top management and departments become involved with strategic planning.

In order to analyze this power relationship, it is useful to refer to the theory of power. The influence or power to make another person take a certain action, originates in an unequal exchange. If one gives more than he receives, he has influential power. (There are many studies on power, for example, Homans, 1974.) As a subject of exchange, resources are the most important. The budget department has power, because it controls the resource of money. What is the resource that the planning department has? It is information. If the planning department has unique knowledge and information, it can provide top management and other departments with this knowledge. The problem is how much knowledge and information it can give. Before giving the information, it first has to collect the data and analyze it. It will collect information from the outside environment, then from the inside environment in order to do this. For this function the planning department can construct a strategic information system. To get information from within, it is important that the planner should be able to distribute strategic information, and be able to walk around like an journalist, gathering information from a network of acquaintances. Trust from line department is one of the key success factors.

Trust from top management is also important. Before obtaining this trust, the planning department should have abundant information and knowledge to give them. Once the planning department obtains the trust of top management, easy access to top management can be a source of influence towards other staff and line departments.

A planning department which proves to be a failure usually has some of the following characteristics. It is staffed with incompetent and "problem workers". Perhaps it includes a concentration of overly narrow specialists. It may contain staff who steal information from other departments in order to obtain a higher rating from top management. Or it may simply force other departments at the beginning to construct a full-scale plan for cost reduction (which any department would not like) or a difficult strategic plan, without first starting to persuade on the importance of strategic planning, or without the efforts to change the atmosphere of line department.

4.3 Project team

A project team is formed at the corporate level, at the product division level or at the research and development laboratory. It studies strategic projects, new product developments and other temporary issues. It conducts not only research, but also implements actions sometimes. It is formed by members with different capabilities, works to complete clear goals, with definite schedules and within a certain amount of budget. When the project is completed, the project is delivered to the permanent department, and the team is dissolved. As innovation increases, as new projects increase, so the use of project teams increases.

There are two kinds of project teams with respect to the subject of study. One is a team to study the future vision of the company. For the turn of the century, many Japanese companies have formulated the 21st century vision of the company, by using young managers. Sometimes, the members are selected from among the applicants from many departments. Young members are sure to stay until the 21st century and they are more serious about the long-term future of the company. Usually the planning department helps the teams and provides information to the team.

The other one is a team set up to study a specific subject, such as a new product development, a new information system development or a new capital investment in foreign countries. These sort of teams are very popular.

There are two kinds of teams with respect to members. One is a team with full-time members and the other is a team with part-time members. The full-time team is more powerful, is fit for important project, and for large projects. The responsibility of, and the goals for members, are clear, there is no conflict on the responsibility of the job, no interruption of working and team-work and communication are better. However, some departments many not send competent people to the team, being afraid of the decrease of capability in their own department. According to our survey on new product development in 1985, about half of all teams had full-time member teams, and half part-time member teams.

The author estimates that the extent of use of project teams in Japanese corporations is much higher than in American or British corporations. There are two reasons for this. The Japanese corporation has a relatively centralized authority structure. The profit responsibility of product divisions or line departments are not very strict, so they are willing to send competent personnel to the project team. The other reason comes from the life-time employment system. People are willing to be moved around when employment is assured and promotion to higher status can be expected by being a team member.

The success factors of project teams were also surveyed. Success means that the team members work hard, day and night, almost peripatetetically looking at the problem from a new angle, and complete a successful new product, successful new production system or produce an excellent strategy. The case of the development of crystal quartz watch by Seiko team, the case of the development of Walkman by Sony, the word-processor by Fujitsu are the cases of successful new product development by the project teams.

A survey on the factors of success of project team is shown in Table 4.3.b.

From the observation of many cases and from survey results, the followings are important success factors.

Firstly, the support of top management (1.1) and middle management or the cooperation with related departments (1.2) is important. In order to obtain these supports, the capability of the project leader is important. The reasons for this dual support are three. (a) New projects tend to create conflict, because they affect the promotion prospect of many people. (b) The resource allocation for new projects is essential for success. (c) The temporary organization may not have a stable communication network, yet it still needs to collect much information, so the cooperation of other departments is necessary.

Secondly, the goals and responsibilities are clear, the schedule is clear, but the detail is delegated to leaders and team members. Clear goals are necessary to motivate the team members. (See items 2.1, 2.2 in Table 4.3.b)

Thirdly, outstanding project leaders and the high quality of team members who have different and complementary knowledges are important (See item 3.1 though 3.5 of Table 4.3.b). (On the success factor of project teams, see Kono, 1987; Peters and Waterman, 1982) These problems will be studied further in the section on research organization.

4.3.1 Internal venture team

A venture team is a kind of project team, but it is different in two respects: a venture team is formed by an individual who has conceived a new idea, not by the corporation, and the leader will become the manager of the project and will be able to share in the profit (3M type). This system is not used very much at present by Japanese corporations, because there is a shortage of capable development engineers, in particular electronics engineers, and companies cannot afford to let some staff pursue risky ideas. This system is, however, considered as one of the means to motivate engineers and promote their creativity.

4.4 Incubator departments

Many companies have come to establish an 'incubator' to bring up new products. T Company, which produce tapes for music and for other purposes, has five research laboratories which are engaged in new product development. When a new product development is completed, it is transferred to a "future product department", which is an independent department and conducts profit and loss computation, although the allocation of overhead expenses to this department is slight or none.

Toray, which produces synthetic fibers also has "new business departments", where new pharmaceutical products, thin films and contact lens are developed. The research, production and marketing departments cooperate with other department so that new products will be developed into successful products.

The reason why an 'incubator' is established, and why the new product is not put into related product divisions, is that existing product divisions are more interested in short-range profit and do not like to take care of new products which do not produce immediate profit.

A subsidiary company could be established instead of an inside incubator department. Support from other departments may be better for the inside department than an outside subsidiary company. According to the author's survey on new product development in 1985, about 20 percent of 244 companies have the 'incubator' department.

4.5 Organizational problems of research and development

4.5.1 Types of research policy

There are four types of research policies. (a) Technical leader, (b) Product innovator, (c) Nicher and (d) Follower. (Ansoff and Stewart, 1967). The size and quality of research varies depending on what policy the company is adopting. These policies are, however, not strictly concerned with the research policy itself, but are concerned with new product development policy. One company may take the policy of the follower with respect to basic research, but for new product development, it may take the policy of a pioneer. Many private companies are probably taking this policy to be a pioneer.

We should recognize that the amount required for research is larger than the expenditure for capital investment, when the product is technology intensive. Hitachi, for example, spent about \300 billion on research and development (about 9% of sales) in 1988 and the amount for capital investment in the same year was ¥ 190 billion. Canon also spends about 11 percent of sales revenue for the research and development.

We conducted a survey on research policy, the results of which are shown on Table 4.4.b.

We found that research-intensive laboratories put an emphasis on the mixture of leader and follower (or the product-innovator) and development-intensive laboratories put emphasis on the product-improvement (the product innovator or nicher).

4.5.2 Classification of research

Research is classified into basic research, common elementary technology research, new product development, new production system development and others as is shown in Table 4.5.b.

Common elementary technology is sometimes called applied research, but the latter expression is ambiguous and the former term is commonly used. It is research for common technology which is used for a variety of products and for many production systems. In order to make decision on the subject of common elementary research, the future product mix has to be studied and then common technology will be properly planned. This means that the long-range plan for the future product-market strategy needs to be established.

When the company accumulates outstanding common elementary technology, new product development can be carried out in short period of time and new product can have strong competitive edges, because the new product is the combination of common elementary technology and new development. The successful company has definite plan on the common elementary technology.

The research is classified from the view point of the laboratory, whether it is decided by the laboratory or by the top management or by some other places. Table 4.2 is a case from Hitachi. Independent research is mostly the basic research and common elementary technology research, is decided by the laboratory under the long-range corporate research strategy. Commissioned research is mostly in new product development, and is asked to conduct the works by product divisions and subsidiaries. On the other hand, product improvement is conducted at the works (product divisions). All are based on long-range corporate strategy, although the decision makers on the subject vary depending on the classification of the research.

Table 4.2 Kinds of research at Hitachi Research Laboratories

	Independent Research	Commissioned Research	Product Development
R & D Funding	Head Office	Sponsor (Works, Subsidiary Companies, etc.)	Works
Project Authorization	By General Manager of Laboratory	On Contract Basis (Sponsor-Laboratory)	By Gereral Manager of Works
Target	Beyond 5 years (Risky and Challenging)	Within 5 years (High Percentage of Success)	1–2 years (Product Strategy)
Ratio	9 Corporate Labs.	30 %	70 %	
	Central Research Lab.	50 %	50 %	
	Advanced Research Lab.	100 %	0 %	
	Development Dept. at Works			100 %

(note) (1) The number indicates the percentage of research activities
(2) Kuwahara and others: Planning Research and Development at Hitachi, Long Range Planning, June, 1989.

4.5.3 The long-range planning of research and development.

The 90 percent of the 154 laboratories surveyed responded that they have long-range planning in research and development. The research takes a long time to arrive at the solution. The long-range plan for the research contains the research strategy, the major subjects of research and the resource capacity.

The plan does not intend to decide on the details of research, because the research explores unknown relations, and the subject evolves as discoveries advances.

4.5.4 Centralization versus decenralization of research laboratories

Research organizations are usually divided into central research laboratories, new product development laboratories, and production technology research laboratories. A distribution of resources is shown in Table 2.

Most of the Japanese companies such as Hitachi, Matsushita and Mitsubishi Heavy Industries, have centralized laboratories under the control of head office. American and U.K. corporations, such as Hewlett Packard, Xerox, 3M and ICI have decentralized research laboratories under control of the product divisions, although the central research laboratory is under the control of head office.

This centralization makes possible the concentration of research resources into new strategic projects able to adapt to large changes of the environment. The merit of decentralization is that it makes easier the interface between basic research, new product development, production engineering, production and marketing. Japanese corporations also take other means to improve this interface, so the concentration can have more merits than demerits.

4.5.5 Internal organizational structure

The organizational structure can be classified into division by functions or by products (or goals). The survey shows that research intensive laboratories have more groupings by common elementary technology and development-intensive laboratories have more groupings by products. (See Table 4.6.b)

Project Teams by part time members are not so often used. Projects Teams are suitable for large projects. However, permanent organizations are fit for the situation where the advancement of technology is very fast, because the accumulation of information is easier. On the same grounds, permanent organizations are good for projects which need long time commitment (Allen, 1977). (Our survey does not clearly define project teams, the author assumed that project teams are formed by part time members.)

The room layout of researchers, not experimental facilities, is related to the groupings. There are a number of types: large rooms, large rooms with partitions, medium sized rooms for each group, individual rooms with conference rooms.

The survey shows that large rooms are the most frequently used in Japan, but recently large rooms with partitions are increasing. Large rooms provide good places for mutual communications, though they may be inconvenient for meditation. In the case of Canon's central research laboratory, even the director of the laboratory shares the one single large room with all the other researchers. However, there are many small rooms for individual researcher to read, meditate and write, and many medium sized rooms for conferences and discussions. The facilities for experiment are mostly installed in medium sized rooms and different equipments are combined to conduct definite purpose of research.

Through interviews with many research managers, we can observe the following tendencies.

(1) An individual room for each researcher is appropriate for basic research. However, there are many problems with this. (a) The communication between members, between production and marketing departments tends to be poor. This could be solved by having a common conference room. (b) The facilities tend to be poor: often a small room, without windows. The laboratory cannot afford to accommodate exploding numbers of researchers, who sometimes number over 10 percent of total employees, with deluxe rooms.

(2) Shared rooms or large rooms are suitable for new product development, and development for production engineering. They are also used for basic search in Japan because they have the following merits. (a) Shared rooms can facilitate communication between members in the group and other departments. (b) Large rooms with partitions are becoming popular. (c) For mediation and for reading, many small rooms and a library can be used. For meetings within the group and with other members, conference rooms can be provided.

4.5.6 Combination of divergent capabilities

In order to achieve creative inventions, the laboratory needs to have creative personnel and divergent capabilities.

There are many researches on the traits of creative personalities. (Van Fange, 1959; Steiner, 1965; Nystrom, 1979; Akiyama, 1975) This is not the place to dwell on these past researches, but we will describe our own research results here. Free description of the unstructured questions on creative personalities are as follows: (1) likes to challenge complex problems, (2) has T shape or V shaped knowledge, deep specialized knowledge and wide knowledge, (3) looks at things from new angeles, has strong intuitive ability, (4) has strong faith and strong individuality and maintains his own opinion, (5) can work on one subject for long years and patient in the pursuit of one problem. Our survey shows that patience is the most emphasized trait.

Creative invention can be achieved by a group or people of divergent knowledges and divergent approaches. A combination of complementary knowledge is essential but it is a matter of course. A combination of research men, production engineers and marketing men is frequently used for the development of new products. This is one of the patterns interfacing different functions.

The divergence of personalities is related to the creativity of the group. Combinations of different approaches, such as a long-term approach vs. short-term approach; inductive vs. deductive; concrete vs. abstract; grand imagination vs. incremental approach; simple question vs. logical construction; image vs. concrete investigation; integration vs. analysis; and flexible and wide vs. specialized are used.

The combinations of these divergent approaches are fruitful for creativity, as is shown in Table 4.7.b.

The difference of values is a problem. The difference of value means that whether the researcher places a value on promotion within the company or places value in writing a creative paper and in obtaining prestige from academic circles, or whether the researcher is devoted to research or is enjoying life. There are two opinions on the workability of the divergence of values. One opinion is that it is not desirable because the cooperation of researchers is difficult. Another opinion is that when the value is different, there is less competitive conflict among members so cooperation will be better.

The divergence of capability level is another problem. There are different opinions on this. According to interviews with many research managers, for basic research, a group of first class researchers works well because they stimulate creative ideas in each other. But for development, when goals are clear, a mix of first class and second class researchers is desirable, because control is more important.

One of the means to ensure diversity is to recruit experienced researcher form outside and to mix them with the existing researchers. According to our survey, the percentage of recruitment of experienced researchers, not the recruitment from university graduated, among total recruits is 8.5 percent for basic research and 6.6 percent for developmental research. This is relatively high rate for Japanese corporations.

The percentage of doctors and assistants is as follows.

Average number of researchers in a laboratory surveyed

	192	(68%)
(Doctors of research	20	(10% of researchers))
Assisting engineers	61	(21%)
Clerical workers	32	(11%)
Total	285	(100%)

The survey shows that the number of doctors is less than that of the US and the number of assisting engineers is also less than in US laboratories. Generally speaking, high technology research laboratories use sophisticated equipment, and the researcher himself handles machines for experiments, the number of assistants is very few. At Canon central research laboratory and at Hewlett Packard central research laboratory at Silicon Valley, there are no assisting engineers.

4.5.7 Interface between research, development, production engineering, production and marketing

The interface between research, development, production engineering, production and marketing affects the research results, the speed of development, quality and cost of new products. For example the length of time for a new car development of Japanese car manufacturers is three years, while that of the US companies is about four to five years. These difference of lead time are explained by (1) the interface, (2) enthusiastic activities of researchers and their long working hours, (3) the shorter cycle of the new product introduction, (some home electric appliances are every six months), (4) vertical integration (or quasi-vertical integration) of components suppliers and sales channels, who ensure good cooperation for new product development.

Here we will analyze the interface only. A good interface means that there is good cooperation between the departments engaged in research and development. Where the interface is good, communication between basic research, common element technology research, new product development, production engineering research on production equipment and production process, plant production and marketing and consumer research is good. The means to improve communications are the following:

(1) Relatively strong production engineering laboratory. The number of researchers in these are many and the prestige of production engineers is relatively high. Honda has a production engineering department to produce equipment and to study production processes, the number of researchers and workers is about 2400. (The research and engineering department has 7700 persons, the main company of Honda in Japan had 30,000 employees excluding the above two departments in 1989). The high status of production engineers makes possible the cooperation between the research and new product development and production engineering.

(2) Participation on deciding the subject of research. The strategy of research and key areas of research are decided by long-range planning, because research is one of the key factors of its success. Under these strategies, ideas for research are presented from production departments and marketing departments with budgets (See Table 3). These commissioned researches account for a high percentage of research activities of laboratories. This participation improves the interface.

(3) Interchange of personnel. Researchers will be transferred to development laboratories and to production engineering laboratories and will come back after any technology transfer, so that the opposite transfer is also carried out.

(4) Parallel development. At the idea stage, several concepts will be studied and compete with each other, but after a certain stage one concept will be selected (The case of Honda). Other types of parallel development occurs between the stage of development. Between the research, development and production engineering, there is overlapping of the end of schedules of the preceding stage and the head of schedules of the next stage.

(5) Project teams are formed with staff in development, production engineer, production control and marketing departments. At Honda, the team is called DPS team meaning that D = development, P = production engineering, S = production and sales. Nissan uses this sort of team at early stages of car development, and could develop many successful new cars such as Cyma, which is a driver oriented car, because of this.

(6) Frequent meetings. Researcher will visit the plant, the offices and the customers frequently.

What are the reasons and conditions for this good interface? The location of research laboratories in the plant site is sometime used (Sumitomo Electric) but it is not a usual solution. Research laboratories are rather centralized, as was already mentioned. The following will be important reasons. (a) Group spirit or group orientedness is the fundamental attitude, thus mutual cooperation is the usual pattern of behavior. (b) Relatively equal status between researchers, development engineers and production engineers exists. (c) The pressure from competition in the market is strong. (d) Top management's involvement in research is high. About half of top management are from the science backgrounds, thus they are able to understand the technological issues involved. (Kono, 1984)

4.5.8 Planning and freedom in research management

Research and development is planned as part of formal long-range planning because it is one of the most important strategies for the corporations. The survey shows that 90 percent of 154 laboratories have long-range planning for research. The subject of long-range research planning is the basic policy of research, basic areas of research, and the capacity of research, that is, the facilities and the number of researchers. For the pharmaceutical industry, the development of one drug costs the company about 10 billion yen and the time required to complete it is about ten years, so long-range planning is an essential matter. On the other hand, in electronics industries, there are many research themes, and many research subjects are initiated by the researchers in the research strategy.

In the case of basic research (including common element technology), subjects are proposed by the researcher, and they are coordinated and decided by the top of the laboratory or by head office. For development (the new product development and production technology development), the strategy is set first and then the concrete subjects are decided by the researcher. (See Table 4.8.b). In either case, the complete

Table 4.3 A continuum on control and freedom of research

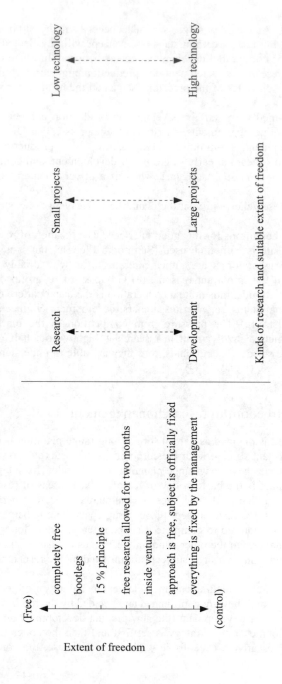

freedom of the researcher on the decision of the subject does not always lead to the success, because the research needs to be a good fit with the interests of cooperating colleagues and with corporate facilities, and research has to bear fruits of some sort to recycle the resources invested.

Freedom in research is, on the other hand, a source of motivation for researchers. The creative researcher likes to challenge new and complex problems. He wants to make full use of his strength to explore these problems. He wants the subjects of research to be along his strength and along his interests. He wants to select the subject of research according to his own interest. However, complete freedom does not result in the success as was already explained. Thus, the harmony between strategic planning and freedom of researchers becomes necessary. Table 4.3 shows this continuum in the freedom of research.

Basic research, the small project and low technology research are fit for the frees approach. Development, the large project and high technology research are fit for the planned approach. Our research result shows these principles.

Summary

This chapter studies the organizational structure used to formulate and implement long-range planning. An appropriate structure has to be constructed before strategy is worked out.

Three principles are important. (1) Strategic planning departments are strengthened to carry out new strategies. (2) Flexibility of organization, such as the use of project teams, become more important. (3) The corporate culture needs to be a vital one. The last problem will be studied in Chapter 6.

There are three departments in the organization. (a) Operating departments, which are engaged in today's operation, producing profit now. (b) Strategic planning departments which sow seeds to harvest the profit in the future, but consume profit now. (c) Staff departments which support the above two. Recently, the second listed departments are becoming larger and larger and more complicated. Technology intensive companies, in particular, are spending about ten percent of sales on research and development. "Few people in the plant site, and thousands of people in the laboratory" is the reality of the situation.

1. Top management is an important strategic planning department. Most Japanese corporations have management committees comprised of about ten members, and they make decision as a group. Group decision-making tends to be innovative. The commitment of top management to long-range planning is important, and among many behaviors, symbolic behaviors such as going to the field where an important strategy is being carried out is considered as important. An analytical approach is needed for group decision-making in order to arrive at a consensus, and long-range planning can be used for this purpose.

   The functional background of about forty percent of top management is technology and production and about thirty percent is marketing. With respect to their educational background, about forty-four percent of them come from natural sciences. These fact results in a sensitivity to technological changes in the environment.

2. The planning department conducts the analysis, the initiative of strategic ideas and the coordination of long-range planning. Depending on the difference of emphasis placed on the above functions, there are three kinds of planning offices, the strategic planning type is the typical type of Japanese corporations.

3. Project teams are frequently used by Japanese corporations. The centralized organization structure makes it easier to form project teams.

4. The incubator departments are necessary to nurture infant products, so that projects will not be crushed by existing departments which are more concerned with the short term profit. It is an independent department, but has imperfect profit responsibility. It is different from research departments, because it has marketing staff, and it tries to complete new products. It is different from a spun out subsidiary company, because it is an inside department. It can have easy access to the assistance of other departments. It is different from internal venture teams, because it is an officially formulated department. Kirin Breweries has established six incubator departments such as pharmaceutical products departments, real estate departments and others in the two years since 1988.

5. The expenditure for research and development is expanding in the technology intensive products company. The ratio of R&D expenditure accounts for more than ten percent of sales, which is larger than the capital investment (there is an overlapping between the two, about 16 percent of R&D expenditure is capital investment)

(1) There are four types of basic policy in research. The company needs to have a mixed policy of leader and follower in order that the recycling of resources is possible.

(2) Research and development can be classified into basic research, common elementary technology research, and several development researches. The concept of common elementary technology research is important, because the accumulation of it makes the development time shorter and enhances the quality of the product. This research can be planned after setting the long-range strategy on future product mix.

(3) When research and development laboratories are centralized, large scale research is made possible, the research on completely new products is made possible, and thus it can support the innovative change of strategy.

(4) The organizational structure of the laboratory can be classified into functional, grouping by product and project team of part time members. For the basic and common element research, the functional (particularly grouping by common element technology) is used, and for development, grouping by product is frequently used. The permanent organizational structure is suitable for the accumulation of knowledge, thus for long-term research and research in uncertain environment. For room layout, large rooms with partitions are becoming popular.

(5) Combinations or diversity of researchers tends to bring about a creative research performance. The mixture of divergent approaches, of divergent values, can affect the creativity of groups. For basic research, a mix of first class researchers functions well. For the development of products, a mix of first class and second class researchers works better.

(6) The interface between research, development, production engineering, production and marketing affects the speed and quality of research. It affects the decision on the subject of research and the process of research. As the means for improving interface, the following is used. (1) Relatively strong production engineering laboratories. (2) The production units and marketing department participate in deciding upon the subject of research. (3) Interchange of personnel. (4) Parallel development. (5) Formation of project teams by members from production and marketing, as well as research and development. (6) Frequent meetings and mutual visits of R&D, production and marketing staffs.

(7) The balance between the control and freedom results in creative development. At the level of basic research, more freedom is suitable, at the development more planning and control is appropriate. In both cases, too much freedom does not produce creative results.

Table 4.1.b The role of the top management in long-range planning

Number of Corporations	249 co.
1.1 Top management presents ideas from the beginning, spends much time in discussion with planning and other departments.	25 %
1.2 Takes many actions to push corporate culture towards strategic orientations.	44
1.3 Committed to long-range planning, discusses it continuously.	57
2.1 Presents to vision of the long-term future of the corporation, or encourages the staffs to formulate one.	68 *
2.2 Listens to opinions of many departments on the future of the corporation.	42
2.3 Initiates ideas on strategic projects, or promotes the implementation of projects.	31 *
3.1 Tries to arrive at a consensus on the contents of the long-range plan, and tries to persuade the opposing members of the value of this	6
3.2 Takes symbolic actions on its importance, such as explaining the contents of the plan in important speeches or talking with the staff of many departments, or going to factories to see the implementation.	73 *
4.1 Planning and implementation are reflected on the merit rating of heads of departments.	14
4.2 Orders the formulation of the implementation plan and its integration with the budget.	37
4.3 The president and the management committee conduct regular follow-ups of the long-range plan.	36 *

(note)

Asterisks (*) indicate the successful companies in planning (subjective judgement, 146 co.) have higher frequency (< 5%)

Table 4.2.b Responsibilities and organization of corporate planning departments in the head office

Items		1985 384 co.	1989 249 co.	Related departments
(1) Planning system	1) Overall system of planning	62 (%)	59 (%)	
	2) Promote strategic thinking	84	56	
(2) Assumptions	3) Environmental forecasting	63	64 *	Marketing department
	4) Analysis of competitors	43	39	Divisions
	5) Appraisal of past performance and strength and weakness	70	64	
	6) Others	74	73	
(3) New projects	7) Preparation of policy for existing products	48	52 *	Divisions
	8) Preperation of policy for new business area	55	56 *	Development department Personnel department
	9) Planning of rationalization	36	21	Facilities department
	10) Planning of important facilities	40	35 *	Development department
	11) Clerical assistance to project teams	37	41	Divisions
(4) Goals	12) Preparing long-term corporate goals and policy	78	90	Divisions
	13) Prearing division goals and policy	26	19	
(5) Co-ordination	14) Co-ordination of division plans and projects	50	41 *	
	15) Preparation of long-range (and medium-range) plan documents	68	68	
(6) Budget	16) Preparation of budget	43	45	Financial department

* continued

Table 4.2.b Responsibilities and organization of corporate planning departments in the head office (cont.)

	Years / Companies	1985 384 co.	1989 249 co.	Related departments
(7) Performance appraisal	17) Appraisal of performance as compared with long-range plan	62	62 *	Financial department
	18) Budgetary control and appraisal of performance as compared with budget	39	38	
	19) Preparation of standard for appraisal of departments and managers	27	27	
(8) Others	20) Information processing by computer	29	14	Financial department · Computer department
	21) Auditing	12	7	Financial department
	22) Analysis of organization structure and recommendation for improvement	46	51	Personnel department

(Note) (1) Survey in 1985 and in 1989
(2) Numbers indicate the percentage of companies
(3) Asteriks (*) indicate successful corporations in planning (subjective judgement, 146 co.) have a higher frequency (< 5 %) of these items

Table 4.3.b   Success Factors for Project Teams of New Product Development
(Free Description)

	Success factors	Number of corporations (total 173 co.)
1–1	Top management commitment	48 co.
1–2	Co-operation with related departments	25
2–1–1	Clear goals and responsibilities	38
2–1–2	Delegation to the leader, like a minature business	10
2–2	Clear schedule	9
3–1	Outstanding project leader (positive, confident, appropriate problem analysis, access to resources)	63
3–2	Quality of team members (outstanding specialists)	38
3–3	Co-operation and enthusiasm among team members	28
3–4	Full-time team	18
3–5–1	Capability of team members and related departments	17
3–5–2	Understanding and support of the head of despatching dept.	4
4–1	Information on needs, on movements of other companies	13
4–2	Good planning, right selection of subject	7
5–2	Adequate resource allocation	10
7	Evaluation with long-term view	3

(Note)   1. Survey in 1985 on new product development.
2. Percentages are not computed because of the free descriptions given.

Table 4.4.b Policy on research and development

	(1) Total laboratories	(2–1) Laboratories with an emphasis on research (The total of basic research expenditure and elementary component research expenditure is more than 54 %.)	(2–3) Laboratories with an emphasis on development (The total of basic research expenditure and elementary component research expenditure is less than 22 %.)
Number of responses	154	37	41
Policy on research and development. That kind of policy does your company take? (Computed as very frequent = 3, frequent = 2. rare = 1)			
① The company conducts unique research and development which other corporations are not conducting.	1.71	1.80	1.80
② In many cases the corporation follows the research and development which other corporations have already started. The corporation believes that it can 'catch up' even if it starts late.	1.72	** 1.48	1.80
③ Mixture of above two.	2.01	2.03	1.86
④ The corporation emphasizes improvement research and development.	2.07	** 1,85	2.29
⑤ The company puts an emphasis on improvement of production process rather than new product development.	1.27	1.17	1.31

(note) (1) The number indicates, very frequent = 3, frequent = 2, rare = 1
         (2)** indicates the difference is significant at 5 % risk, * at 10 % risk, the difference is compared between (2–1) and (2–2)

Table 4.5.b Kinds of research and development

Number of responses	(1) Total laboratories	(2–1) Laboratories with an emphasis on research (The total of basic research expenditure and elementary component research expenditure is more than 54 %.)	(2–3) Laboratories with an emphasis on development (The total of basic research expenditure and elementary component research expenditure is less than 22 %.)
	154	37	41
That is the percentage of distribution of resources among the following kinds of research. (Computed by the distribution of research personnel or research expenditure)			
① Basic research	10.7 %	** 15.2 %	4.4 %
② Common elementary technology research (applied research)	28.0 %	** 56.1 %	8.9 %
③ New product development	31.9 %	** 18.5 %	46.2 %
④ Development of new production technology (excluding ②)	8.6 %	** 2.7 %	13.6 %
⑤ Improvement and testing	8.1 %	** 3.7 %	10.6 %
⑥ Research on reliability and safety	5.2 %	** 2.1 %	7.7 %
⑦ It can be called a research on elements. It is a research on common technology applied to various products. Examples are microprocessing technology or the mixing of unpure materials. It could be called applied research. The classification 'basic research, applied research and development' is based on the basicness of research. Here, research is classified by the process to the corporations goals.	3.3 %	* 1.3 %	5.8 %

(note) (1) The number indicates the percentage of resource allocation
       (2) The asterisks indicate the level of significance (** at 5%, * at 10%)

Table 4.6.b Groupings of researchers

Number of responses	(1) Total laboratories	(2–1) Laboratories with an emphasis on research (The total of basic research expenditure and elementary component research expenditure is more than 54 %.)	(2–3) Laboratories with an emphasis on development (The total of basic research expenditure and elementary component research expenditure is less than 22 %.)
	154	37	41
What is the room layout or grouping of researchers (excluding experiment room, administrative office or computer room)?			
① Rooms or groupings by the field of science (physics, chemistry, electronics and so on) … % of researchers	18.7 %	* 21.9 %	10.7 %
② Rooms by common elementary research (microprocessing technology, control technology and so on) … % of researchers	31.2 %	** 47.4 %	20.2 %
③ Rooms or groupings by products … % of researchers	33.0 %	** 16.5 %	45.3 %
④ Rooms or groupings production process … % of researchers	7.0 %	** 3.1 %	12.3 %
⑤ Project teams (temporary team) … % of researchers	10.4 %	11.3 %	7.6 %
⑥ Others … % of researchers	3.3 %	0.2 %	5.8 %

(note)   (1) The number indicates the percentage of researchers
(2) ** < 5%, * < 10%

Table 4.7.b Diversity of researchers

	(1) Total laboratories	(2–1) Laboratories with an emphasis on research (The total of basic research expenditure and elementary component research expenditure is more than 54 %.)	(2–3) Laboratories with an emphasis on development (The total of basic research expenditure and elementary component research expenditure is less than 22 %.)
Number of responses	154	37	41
What kind of diversity of capability in a research team is the key of the success of research? (Please check) Computed as, very important = 3, important = 2, not important = 1)			
① Combination of complementary knowledge	2.57	2.44	2.53
② Difference of approach (Example, longterm approach vs. short-term approach; inductive vs. deductive; concrete vs. abstract)	2.22	2.27	2.12
③ Difference of value (Example, promotion vs. good paper)	1.39	1.39	1.44
④ Others	2.11	2.33	2.00

(note)   The number indicates, very important = 3, important = 2, not important = 1

Table 4.8.b   Decision of research subjects

	Total laboratories
Number of responses	1 5 4
(a) Basic and elementary component research:	
① The subject is fixed by the researcher freely.	4 9. 6 %
② The subject is decided by co-ordinating the ideas presented by the researcher.	8 1. 0 %
③ The strategy is set up first and then concrete subjects are decided by the researcher.	6 2. 7 %
④ The concrete subject is decided by the manager and they are presented to the researcher.	2 6. 7 %
(b) Development:	
① The subject is fixed by the researcher freely.	14. 2 %
② The subject is decided by co-ordinating the ideas presented by the researcher.	5 7. 8 %
③ The strategy is set up first and then concrete subject is decided by the researcher.	8 2. 7 %
④ The concrete subject is decided by the manager and it is presented to the researcher.	6 7. 4 %

(Note)   The number indicates the percentage of responding companies.

Appendix

Method of Survey on Management of Research and Development of Japanese Research Laboratories

1. Design of research

Toyohiro Kono
Professor of Business Administration
Takashi Uchino
Associate Professor of Business Administration
Both of Gakushuin University
Mejiro, Toshima, Tokyo

with the Cooperation of
Japan Productivity Center, Tokyo

2. Date of Survey
   Mail questionnaires were sent in January, 1988.

3. Respondents of the Survey
   Mail questionnaires were sent to 487 laboratories and 154 laboratories responded (31.6% response ratio).

4. Distribution of response by industry

Industries	Number of Laboratories
1. Mining & Construction	9
2. Food & Fisheries	13
3. Fiber, Pulp & Paper	9
4. Chemicals & Drugs	20
5. Petroleum, Rubber, Glass & Stone	9
6. Iron, Steel & Nonferrous Metals	13
7. Machinery	11
8. Electrical Appliances & Precision Machine	31
9. Transportation Equipment & Machinery	11
10. Transportation & Communication	2
11. Electricity & Gas	2
12. Research Company & Others	24
Total	154

Chapter 5   Analysis of the environment

5.1 Characteristics of strategic information

The collection of strategic information aims at finding the opportunities and threats in the environment and the strength and weakness of the company. The strategic information system (SIS) is different from the operational management information system (MIS). The followings are major characteristics;

(1) The needs for strategic information are not clear, while the needs for operational information are clear and regularly cycled. Some companies do not collect any strategic information regularly and can continue its business operations without doing so, but the company cannot dispense with operational information. For example, a monthly production plan requires information on inventory and the next month's demand forecasts.

The sensitivity towards environment and towards opportunities is one of the important keys for the success of corporate strategy and differences of sensitivity results in the difference of collection of strategic information. Recognition is also selective, one company may not see an opportunity in the environment that another does. The long-range planning system has the effect of orienting the needs of strategic information, to collect orderly information and to disseminate strategic information to the decision-making points.

(2) The source of strategic information is external to the organization. A planning department of one company collects clippings from daily newspapers, and files them by the classification codes of the strategic information of the company, and at the same time the company has long-term contracts with several newspaper companies for on-line retrieval systems. This sort of information is quite different from the internal operational information system.

(3) The time horizon of strategic information is for long-term future, three to ten years hence, whilst the information for operations deal with past information. The forecasting of the future is difficult and may be erroneous, but because of the ambiguity, there lie opportunities which other companies may not see.

(4) The communication network for strategic information is different from that for the operational information channel. It needs to establish different networks. For example, the planning department will collect information on the general environment and the industry environment, and will publish weekly and special reports on important trends in the environment. One company lists key persons involved with each

issue and inputs them onto a computer disc. (On the characteristics of strategic information, see Hayes and Radosevich, 1974.)

The computerized operational information system is sometimes called SIS (strategic information system), because it strengthen competitive power, often by introducing the POS system, CAD, CAM system and CIM (computer integrated manufacturing system). This sort of information system is not useful for innovative strategic decisions, such as decisions on new product development, or on foreign direct investment. Even for capital investment for the expansion of present products, future information has to be collected and operational information has no use.

There are several problems in the collection of strategic information. (a) The forecasting of the future environment is difficult and the company has to cope with uncertainty. The forecasting may result in an error. (b) Competing companies collect information from similar sources, they conduct similar forecasting, and they bring forth similar strategic ideas. Thus, they enter into the same growth areas, they invent similar new products. The more information, the more similar strategies to their competitors they will have.

The two problems are different, but are related to some extent. The two problems are explained by the economy of information. The effect of information collection is the improvement of decisions. The improvement of decisions – cost of information = efficiency of information.

Even if the forecasting contains errors, the decision is better than one with no information. This is the effect of information. In addition, there are many ways to cope with uncertainty, this will be studied in Chapter 13. Further, there are more opportunities in uncertain futures than in known situations.

Too much information costs more than the improvement of decisions. The company can identify needs, and can select the information. Thus, the company can avoid "paralysis by analysis".

The same information source may also bring the similar ideas for strategies. However, if the company does not collect information, it will lose the competition. Many bankrupt companies did not collect enough information, and depended too much on intuition, by doing nothing or taking overly aggressive decisions. The problem is, after collecting similar information, how to explore a niche, how to invent a unique product, how to find out a strategy with differentiation, and how to add intuitive creativity.

5.2 Kinds of information

Information is classified by its contents into, (1) information on the situation (usually called the data), (2) knowledge and (3) information on the ideas. If we use the term "base", these are the data base, the knowledge and model base and the idea base. This classification can be explained by the structure of decisions. The structure of decision can be expressed by the following model:

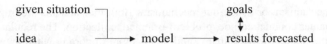

Under a given situation, a decision maker looks for ideas and through the use of the model, the results are estimated and they are compared with the goals. Thus the content of information is composed of three kinds.

The sources of information, can be classified into two; the external source and the internal source.

Examples classified by these two axes are shown in Table 5.1. For strategic decisions, information on external situations, new knowledges and new ideas from external sources are important. In the following section, we will study only the information on the external situation and technological knowledge.

Table 5.1   Kinds of information (examples inside)

contents \ sources		External	Internal
Situation or data	External situation	Political, economical, societal. Trends of consumer and of competitor	
	Internal situation		Value system. Production and sales operation. Facilities and personnel (resource structure)
Knowledge	Theory	Theoretical books Technological knowledge	Research findings Knowledge from development
	Models	AI models	Simulation models
Ideas	Ideas	External ideas	Policies Ideas from inside members

5.3 Identifying needs in strategic information

The needs of strategic information are not self-evident. Identification of needs is necessary for effective strategic information system.

On the regularity of collection, there are two kinds, one is the regular and continuous scanning mechanism, or outside-in mechanism, the other is the irregular, problem oriented mechanism, or inside-out mechanism. Both mechanisms are important, but most companies conduct ad-hoc, problem-oriented, collection. The regular mechanisms vary from company to company, and this is more important when it comes to arriving at distinctive strategies.

Regular and continuous scanning systems are useful to find out the issues, opportunities and threats lying in the environment, and also to find out the strength and weakness of the company. However, there may be too much information and some sort of concentration on the information is necessary.

The formulation of the structure of data base, or the classification structure of the data base is the first steps in this concentration. Chart 5.2 illustrates the conceptual

Table 5.2   Structure of information of external environment

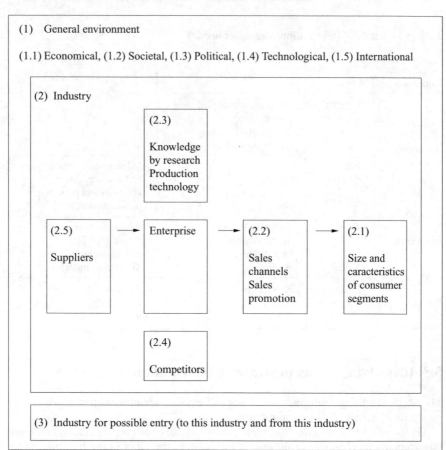

(1)   General environment

(1.1) Economical, (1.2) Societal, (1.3) Political, (1.4) Technological, (1.5) International

(2) Industry

(2.3)

Knowledge by research Production technology

(2.5)

Suppliers

Enterprise

(2.2)

Sales channels Sales promotion

(2.1)

Size and caracteristics of consumer segments

(2.4)

Competitors

(3) Industry for possible entry (to this industry and from this industry)

framework on the structure of the environmental data base. The details of this data base are explained in the next paragraph.

In order to specify the detailed items of the environmental and other strategic data base, the following processes are made available.

(1) From the preliminary basic strategy.
(2) Time series analysis of key factors.
(3) Impact and probability analysis (vulnerability analysis).
(4) By issue finding project teams.

The basic strategy orients the direction of information and ideas, but the strategy has to be generated from information. There are interactions between them.

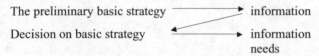

The preliminary basic strategy ──────────▶ information

Decision on basic strategy ◀──────▶ information
                                                  needs

The first preliminary strategy is formed by the accumulated information from the past. Then, the preliminary strategy is reviewed and made into a more detailed strategy and this specifies the important information. For example, if a steel company wants to enter into the computer related products, then the information on computer industry becomes one of the items of this regular information base. If a car manufacturing company wants to do a strategic alliance with a foreign car manufacturing company, world wide car manufacturers become the data base.

Time series analysis of the past key factors on the company performance can suggest the future key factors for performance. This is an analysis on the past cause-effect relationships, but it is useful for finding out future keys issues.

Table 5.3 illustrate the concept behind the time series analysis. Past performances are analyzed over ten years and the key causes of the changes of performance are made clear. As for performance, the growth rate of sales, share of the market or the rate of return on assets may also be used. The environmental causes are, for example, changes of demand, import restriction and new products from competitors. The examples of internal causes are, new products of own company, strengthened sales channels, cost reductions and new production systems.

The impact-probability matrix is illustrated in Table 5.4. This analysis is sometimes called the vulnerability analysis, but this name tends to suggest the analysis of only threat. The opportunity is the event enhancing the performance, with a high probability of occurrence. The development of the sea front, for example, and deep earth is an opportunity for the construction company. The threat is an event with negative effects and a high probability of occurrence. The entry of foreign competitor is one of these cases.

These analysis are usually carried out in brain storming meetings of several informed staffs for half a day. They can establish hundreds of issues, then issues may be arranged by the size of impact and probability of occurrence.

Table 5.3   Time-series analysis of key factors affecting performance

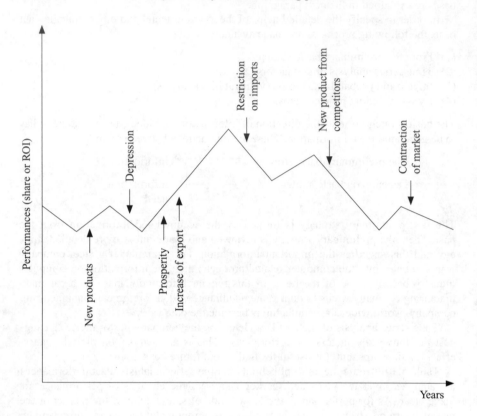

The listed opportunity and threats are combined with the strength and weakness of the company, and strategic ideas are generated, as is seen in Chart B of Table 5.4. The strength is used not only for utilizing opportunities, but also for coping with threat. The weakness is to be strengthened to make use of opportunities and to avoid threats. Thus, the possible strategies and strategic issues are found out and they are evaluated (Chart C of Table 5.4).

The team will meet five or more times to discuss what sort of strategic information should be collected, and what sort of on-line information net-work should be utilized. The planning department will consolidate the plans of each team, estimate the cost of information, evaluate whether the overlapping collection is desirable or not, the department responsible for collection, and the required regular reports on this collected information to be sent to the decision centers.

Table 5.4   Impact and probability analysis

A. Analysis

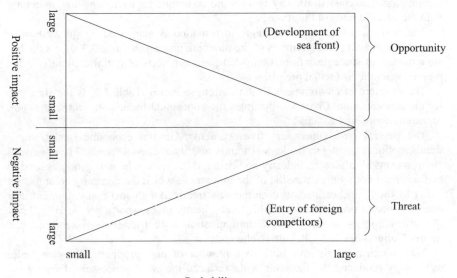

B. Generation of strategic idea

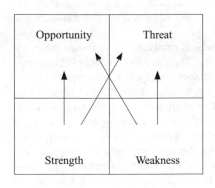

C. Strategic issues

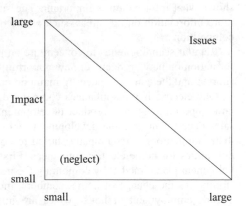

5.4 Data base structure and data collection

The classification system of strategic information makes clear the needs for information, it motivates the information collection, and makes possible the retrieval of information. The classification system should be unique for each company, matching with the specific traits of the strategy.

The basic structure of the strategic information is suggested by the system of long-range planning. The premises of the planning process in Table 3.3 shows the basic structure of strategic information. There are two sorts of premises, one is value premises, another is factual premises.

The structure of environmental information, shown in Table 5.2, is the first step for the concentration. Chart 5.2 illustrates the conceptual framework on the structure of the environmental data base.

The general environment has five segments; General economic trends, social trends, political trends, technological trends and international trends. These general environments all affect the industry and demand structure. The new products tend to be forecasted not by the extension of the industry to which the company belongs, but rather by the logical estimation from the new trends in the general environment. For example, health orientation → health foods, health clubs, sports goods. High level life orientation → sporting car. Communication with friends → restaurants, tea rooms. Cultural life → VCR, culture classes.

Technological trends give birth to a number of new products. The electronics technology produced the facsimile and produced the word processors. Driving the old typewriter manufacturers out of the market.

The information on industry is the most important. Table 5.1.b shows the items and their relative importance, as measured by the frequency of responses. The system is arranged by the flow from materials to finished goods and markets. The survey shows what information is important. The successful companies in planning collect more information on key areas, such as the direction of research, sales amounts and competition.

Regular scanning tends to concentrate on present products, but it should cover information on new products, or new opportunities. The product life cycle is becoming shorter, and the company needs to maintain continuous analysis on new opportunity.

One electric home appliances company did not conduct the regular scanning on new opportunities; new product development used to start upon the request of the sales department, and the development tended to imitate hurriedly new products of their competitors. The company started to conduct regular scanning on the new opportunities for home electric appliances. Firstly, the company built a long-range development plan aimed at by combining the needs of home life and technological possibility. As the change of home members, increases in aged people and increases of outside employment of house wives are important in this respect, they cause the change of needs in home life. As the general needs change, needs for labour savings, for health (home care of the aged), for enjoyable home life (air conditioning), for safety (crime protection equipment) are expected to increase. As for technology seeds, control technology, information technology, energy and services (robots) are important. Through this matrix of 'needs and seeds', ideas for the new products are generated. Their ideas are evaluated, schedules of development are formed, they are discussed with the development department and the production department.

The second stage is a survey on the market segment. The reasons why the customer recently bought the products of the company are asked. By such regular scanning of the customer, the time series changes in the demand, for example, of electric stove appliances is found out.

Third stage is a regular survey on attitudes towards new products recently introduced by the company and by competitors. The survey is conducted at large sized retailers. The company tries to grasp the trends of new successful products.

The new business or the new product are produced by the changes of needs and by new technology. The regular scanning on technological development is important to conduct scientific research and to create new products. The author conducted a survey on scientific research methods, and asked the research laboratories what sort of scientific information they were collecting. Table 5.2.b shows the result. The survey shows that not only formal sources but also the informal sources are important. For formal sources, on-line information is becoming important. For informal sources, attendance at academic meetings and interaction with other researchers in various research organizations are important.

We can know that this sort of information is quite different from operational information system, such as POS or CAM systems. But there is a similarity, both are regular scanning systems.

5.5 Data sources

The 'data source' refers to both the medium and the originator. The medium includes newspapers, magazines, books, tapes, discs and other materials, and various on-line sources. The originator means the writer, and the publisher and other senders. In order to identify the data source both items have to be known.

The data source is classified into formal and informal. The formal source is printed matter which is published. The informal source is a person who knows the information. The information is only held in his brain. Informal information is obtained through a human network. One trading company, for example, lists key persons who know key information and they are classified and inputted onto computer, and utilized when necessary.

Informal information can disclose facts behind formal information and can tell the meaning of formal information. Informal information can be obtained faster than formal information. However, informal information is not necessarily systematic. It is not accurate, depending the quality of the source.

Information on the competitor is critical for competitive strategy, but access to that information is considered as difficult. The survey on the practices used is shown in Table 5.3.b.

The analysis shows that much formal information is collected, particularly the annual report and periodicals of competitions. Inside reports from employees are very useful, if available. In this survey, the newspaper is not listed, but this is also an important source, although it is more useful for general environmental scanning.

In this survey, the on-line sources are not listed. Newspaper companies, patent offices and other organizations provide on-line data, and these sources are becoming more popular as sources of competitor information and of general environment information as well.

Informal information is used extensively; friends, reporters, bankers and distributors are important sources. The analysis of competitors products, or reverse engineering is also used. In this survey, the customer or user is not listed, but the user knows information on the competitors, and it can be grasped through salesmen or through sales channels.

As was already stated, one trading company lists the key persons as sources of important strategic information, not only the information about competitor but also other environmental information, and the names and knowledge areas are inputted to the data base, and can be retrieved by key words.

The successful companies in planning (subjective judgment) tend to collect more information through such sources as internal report, public relations report, industrial periodicals, through friends and bankers and to conduct more surveys.

5.6 Collectors

The planning department is one of the important collectors and processors of strategic information. At C company, planners read the newspapers for thirty minutes in the morning, and clip and classify them, then, the title, key words, date and source are stored on a computer data base.

The planners also are specialized by different areas of concentration. They are specialized by products, by geological areas and by languages, having multiple responsibilities. They collect information from a number of sources.

The research laboratories and the research management department in the head office also collect information on technological trends. The information is summarized in reports and disseminated to the top and the departments concerned. Sources of information are shown in Table 5.6. The salesman collect the information on consumers and competitors. One company has a format of the report of the salesman, which includes items on the behavior of the consumer and the competitor. The format was decided with the participation of the corporate planning department, and the weekly report is delivered to the corporate planning department.

The library collects books and periodicals for general information. Books include the knowledge rather than the data. Periodicals are stored not only at the library, but also at relevant departments. Depending on the value of information and the cost, duplicate collection is more economical.

Ad hoc information, or problem oriented information is collected by project teams or it is ordered from outside consultants.

For regular scanning, it is important to assign the responsibility for collection to the appropriate departments. Unlike operational management information, the needs of information and communication channel are not self-evident, so the assignment of responsibility for collecting information is important.

5.7 Processing

The processing of information involves selection and evaluation, classification, in order to find the key words, to understand meaning, to draw the line through the dotted points and to conduct the forecasting of the future. Drawing a line through the known points means the discovery of unknown points and to draw a picture or detail scenarios. It means the forecasting of the future. The processing aims at the utilization of information for generation of ideas and for strategy evaluation.

Demand forecasting is an area of information processing which is used for the above purposes. Table 5.5 illustrates types of demand forecasting.

According to the survey, the time-series analysis is most frequently used for existing products. Time-series analysis is simple, easy to process and easily understood by top management. Among regression analysis, single regression analysis is more often used than multiple regression.

Demand forecasting of new products is different from that of existing products, because there is little previous data. It is not practical to make use of a statistical method like time-series analysis or regression analysis. Rather, a direct survey of the plan of the purchaser, or logical assumptions are more frequently used. (For a discussion on demand analysis, see Kono 1975.)

What is important in demand forecasting is that, while the company is conducting a quantitative analysis, it should forecast changes of key factors in the environment and estimate what the impact of each change will be. For example, the rising price of oil created a discontinuous change in the demand for small cars. Production costs of the petrochemical industry rose sharply.

One company alone cannot conduct an overall forecast of the general environment to use as a premise of demand forecasting, but it can make use of already published predictions by the government and other organizations.

The survey shows that many different methods are used by companies. Applying multiple forecasting methods to the same product and comparing them with each other is useful to obtain a more accurate expected value of a prediction and its variance.

Table 5.5 Method of demand forecasting (226 manufacturing corporations)

Method of forecasting		Products	Existing products	New products
(1) Time-series extension		Linear extension	38 (%)	14 (%)
		Curved extension	34	19
(2) Regression analysis	Single regression	Linear	24	12
		Nonlinear	12	6
	Multiple regression (with more than two independent variables)	Linear	16	6
		Nonlinear	8	4
(3) Analogy		Trends of similar product	36	46
		Trends of demand in foreign countries	21	27
(4) Direct survey of the plan of purchaser		From their purchase plan	29	19
		Marketing test	4	12
		Market research through questions	8	18
(5) Logical assumption		From the required unit of material	20	11
		From the relation with competitive products	17	28
		From the relation with complementary products	8	8
		Market research	40	41

(note) 1. Survey in 1979
2. Number indicates the percentage of responding companies

5.8 Communication, storage and retrieval of information

The planning department writes regular reports and special reports on strategic issues with actions recommended. They are presented to the top management or to the management committee and to the departments concerned. In the case of B Tire Company, this report was an important trigger for the development of the radial tire, which resulted in a substantial increase of the share in the market of the company.

The research management department in the head office and the research laboratories write the report on the technological development inside the company and outside the company.

The salesman will write reports on the format which details the behavior of the consumers and of the competitors.

Project teams will write reports on the research results of new projects.

These reports are important data bases for long-range planning. The formal long-range planning specifies the needs of information, gives a stimulus for collecting the information of the external environment, and once collected, it is an important media for disseminating strategic information. The assumptions are agreed assumptions, they are used for many kinds of strategic decisions. The decided strategy becomes the assumptions of the project planning and short-range planning.

For retrieval, the proper classification of strategic information and indexing are essential. Most of the strategic informations are filed as documents, but some are stored on tapes or on disc. In the latter case, access to this information is easy, but usually the retrieval is limited to certain personnel who can open them with the use of identification numbers.

Human problems affect the communication of information. At Ataka Trading Company, the huge accumulation of uncollectable accounts receivable was not reported to the top management, because one executive did not want to disclose his failure. The company went bankrupt. Generally speaking, when a planner of a project wants to promote his project, he will communicate an optimistic estimation. The hockey stick estimation is another case. Easy plans and greater resource allocations are made possible by the hockey stick estimation.

Summary

1. Strategic information is different from operational information. The needs for strategic information are not self-evident, the sources are external to the organization and future results are relevant. The designing of strategic information systems needs a different approach to the operational management information system.

    Sometimes, the computerized operational information system is called a SIS (strategic information system) in the sense that it reinforces competitive strength, by introducing the POS system, AI (artificial intelligence) and CIM (computer integrated manufacturing system). This sort of arrangement of computerized management information systems will be studied in Chapter 9, as the 'resource structure'.

The effects of information is to improve decision making. If the forecasting results in some errors, the company can still improve on decisions by collecting information.

The information does not produce ideas automatically, a creativity or a sort of intuition is needed for formulating excellent strategies which have competitive edges.

2. Information is classified into three types, information on the situation (or data base), knowledge (or model base) and information on ideas (idea base). In this chapter we studied the collection of information on the situation.

3. Perception is selective. Some companies do not collect strategic information at all. The strategy follows the old pattern or strategy is decided by intuition. Other companies collect the environmental information extensively with research oriented planning department, but the information is not utilized well.

   The needs of the strategic information can be identified by having a proper structure of information. Specific needs in the structure are found out by time series analysis of performances, opportunity and probability analysis and the brain storming of teams.

4. There are two sorts of scanning: regular systematic scanning and problem oriented scanning. The regular, comprehensive scanning tries to find out issues. This scanning varies from company to company. After finding issues, an issue oriented search is conducted.

5. The sources of information mean mediums and holders. There are two kinds of sources: formal and informal. The informal information is verbal, is held by persons and communicated through a human network. The informal information details the facts behind formal information and can be obtained quickly. As a formal source, the on-line data source is increasingly important.

7. The collection of strategic information is carried out by many departments depending on their speciality. Unlike operating information, the needs of strategic information are not self-evident, the responsibility of collecting departments should be made clear, so that there is no shortage of information. A proper format and reporting system is useful.

7. The processing of information is to evaluate, to understand the meaning and to forecast the future. For the method of forecasting, time series estimation is most frequently used.

8. The formal long-range planning specifies the need for strategic information, motivates the external oriented attitude, and can be used to disseminate strategic information.

   (References for strategic information: Kono, 1985; Kono and Watanabe, 1975; Takagi & Kosaka, 1990; Morita ed., 1989; Hofer and Schendel, 1978; Glueck, 1980; Rowe et al. ed.: 1985; Johnson et al.; 1989; Yavitz and Newman, 1988; Hayes and Radosevich, 1974; Rodriguez and King, 1977; King, 1983; Porter, 1985.)

Table 5.1.b Collection of information on industry

What kind of information on industry is actually collected by the head office, by the corporate planning department?
(Please check the most important ten items)

Years			1985	1989
Corporations with long-range plans			384 co.	249 co.
Subjects of information on industry	(1) Supply of raw materials and components	A. Change of raw materials	27 %)	12 (%)
		B. Demand and supply	45	38 Δ
		C. Concentration of supplier	9	3
		D. Trend of costs	44	41
		E. Barriers on export and import	9	5
		F. Trend of suppliers		18
	(2) Research and development and production	A. Direction of research of industry	56	58 *
		B. Level of research and development	31	10
		C. Trends of production technology	45	32
		D. Trends of cost structure	23	18
	(3) Competition	A. Sales of each competitor	75	51
		B. Diversification of competitors	38	21
		C. Strength and weakness of competitors	53	48
		D. Change of emphasis of competition (Quality of products, raw materials, production technology, cost and so on)	47	45
		E. Product differentiation	33	35
		F. Entry barrier	15	6
		G. Cost competetiveness		41

(continued)

Table 5.1.b Collection of information on industry (cont.)

Years			1985	1989
Corporations with long-range plans			384 co.	249 co.
Subjects of infor- mation on indus- try	(4) Sales channels	A. Sales channel network	41	——— 34
		B. Exclusiveness of sales channel	11	⊢— 15
		C. After service	17	⊢ 10
		D. Media advertisements	13	⊦ 3
		E. Quantity of advertisements	9	⊢ 4
	(5) Size of the market and characteristics of each segment	A. Sales by each segment (Sales by each customer and so on)	55	——— 43 *
		B. Size of total segments (Sales amount, quantity and so on)	60	⊢— 41
		C. Growth rate	78	—— 71
		D. Competition	59	—— 52 *
		E. Business cycle and season cycle	23	⊢ 8
		F. Elasticity of demand (on price and on service	22	⊢ 10
		G. Trends of new products	62	——— 49
		H. Loyal customer	10	⊢ 8
		I. Profitability	57	⊢—— 52

(Note) 1. Number indicates the responding corporations
2. In 1989, responses were restricted to the most importand 10 items. This is the reason why the response ratios are less.
3. Asterisks (*) indicate the successful companies in planning (146 co.) (subjective judgement) have higher frequencies (< 5 %).
Triangle (Δ) indicates, they have less frequency.

Table 5.2.b Sources of technological information

1. What are the important formal, documented technological information sources which your corporation collects?
   (Computed as, very important = 3, ralatively important = 2, less important = 1)

Number of laboratories	154
(1) Academic periodicals	2.68
(2) Report on patents filed	2.68
(3) New books	1.78
(4) Reports on the documents on technological information	2.35
(5) Resume on scientific documents	2.03
(6) On-line information	2.34

2. What are imported informal, external, technological sources of information? (Please rank from 1st to fifth)
   (First = 5, second = 2.5, third = 1.5, fourth = 1.25, fifth = 1)

(1) Friends of the researcher	1.55
(2) Attendance at academic meetings	2.35
(3) University researchers	1.95
(4) Communication with the researchers at public research laboratories	1.35
(5) Researchers in the laboratories of other corporations in the home country	1.30
(6) Researchers in the laboratories of foreign corporations	0.80
(7) Suppliers	0.75
(8) Purchasers	0.05

(note) 1. Survey in 1988.
        2. Questionnaires were sent to 487 laboratories and 154 responded.
            (response ratio = 32 %)

Table 5.3.b   Collection of information on competitors. Which kind of following information on competitors are actually collected?

Years					1985	1989
Corporations with long-range plans					384 co.	249 co.
Sources of information on competitors	Formal information	Competitors		A. Annual reports	67 (%)	88 (%)
				B. Financial reports	67	71
				C. Reports for employees	25	25 *
				D. Publications for public relations	24	26 *
				E. Catalogues	49	50
		Universities		F. Published papers	39	41
		Associations		G. Periodicals by associations	61	72
		Banks		H. Statistics by associations	62	78
		Periodicals		I. Reports by banks	50	57
				J. Articles of industry periodicals	72	85
				K. Articles in management periodicals	62	72
		Government		L. Statistics by government	60	75
				M. Report on patent	52	56
	Informal information	N. Personnel in similar jobs of other corporations			39	40
		O. Alumni of universities			34	23 *
		P. Personnel in associations			43	43
		Q. Personnel in banks			49	38
		R. Reporters of industrial periodicals			48	46
		S. Reporters of business periodicals			38	27
		T. Government officials			29	30
		Distributers and suppliers		U. Wholesalers and retailers	27	34
				V. Advertisment agent	15	22
				W. Suppliers	30	34
				X. Carriers	16	17
		Survey organizations		Y. Survey	29	36 *
				Z. Panel of wholesalers and retailers	12	12
				A. User panel	13	15
		B. Analysis of the products of competitors			41	46

(Note)   1. Numbers are computed as "always collected" = 1, "occasionally collected" = 0.5
2. Number indicates the percentage of responding corporations
3. Many companies increased the collection of competitive information
4. Asterisks (*) indicate that successful corporations in planning (subjective judgement, 146 co.) have higher frequency (< 5 %) of these items

Chapter 6 Internal analysis and the changing of corporate culture

Fittest will survive. The internal analysis aims at finding the strength and weaknesses of the firm, and at constructing a strategy to make use of strength and overcomes the weaknesses.

There are two problems with internal analysis. One is that financial analysis is used too often. Financial analysis does not disclose the causes of the results, does not make clear the strengths and weaknesses in strategy and resource structures, thus it leads to easy measures to improve them, such as cost reduction or acquisitions of other companies. The second problem is that weakness are not fully analyzed. The analysis of weaknesses tends to mean criticisms against the present top management, because the weaknesses could be the result of mismanagement. In this case, external sources could be used, or the external analyzer could be used to uncover the weaknesses and defects in present practices.

6.1 Types of internal analysis

There are two types of analysis, one is static, cross-sectional analysis, the other is dynamic analysis.

1. Static analysis

(1) Comparison of actual results with the long-range plan or the short-range plan. This analysis shows how the plan was implemented and what are the causes of deviations. This analysis is fed back to the next planning cycle to improve it.
(2) Comparison of strategy, structure and performance with those of competitors and with the practices of excellent companies or of industry standards. By this analysis, relative strengths and weaknesses can be found out. The defects of this approach are that analysis is mostly done based on the present strategy of another company, which does not necessarily consider the opportunities and threats in the environment. However, this analysis, being easier than the following approach, is popularly used. This analysis also appeals to top management, because competitors are existing and differences are visible and are easily proved.

2. Dynamic approach

This approach does analysis over several years and estimates future strength and weaknesses.
(1) Time series analysis
    Historical analysis of past performances and their causes, future estimation of gaps of performances and resource structures are carried out. Historical analysis discloses change in the environment and the strategy against it as the cause of changes in performances of in the past several years. This was already explained in Chapter 5.
    In addition to historical analysis, future estimation is conducted. The future age distribution of employees and equipments and future sales and profit when no change of strategy is considered are estimated. Thus, strengths and weaknesses are analyzed. If the company uses a simulation model, future results are estimated by the use of a model, assuming that there will be no change of major strategies, or assuming that some minimal actions (such as replacement of equipment, regular introduction of improved products) are taken.
(2) Comparison of the company status with future opportunity and threat. This approach was explained in Chart 5. This is usually called WOTS analysis or SWOT analysis (strength, weakness opportunity and threat analysis) (Steiner 1977; Rowe, 1985; Johnson, 1989)

An example of the Matsushita Electric Company (conducted by study groups at the Business Research Institute in Tokyo) is shown in Chart 6.1. The future opportunities and threats are forecasted, strengths and weaknesses at present and in the future are disclosed by comparing the situations of the company with future opportunities and threats. Then future strategies are proposed.
    This approach is different from other approaches in the sense that the strengths and weaknesses are found by comparing the company with the environment.
    The simplified structure of this approach is indicated in the following:

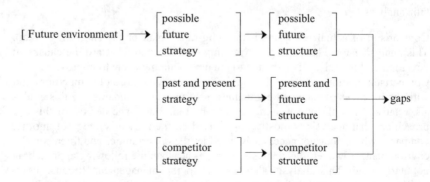

Table 6.1   Strength and weakness analysis of a home appliances corporation

(Opportunities)	(Threats)
Information society (increase of OA, FA)	Increase of trade restriction
Old-aged society (increase of HA)	Stronger NIES
Increase of female employees (increase of HA)	Maturing of home appliances market
Divergent values (from family use to individual use)	More competition in OA market

(Strength)	(Weakness)
1. High profitability Financial resources	1. Overly homogeneous corporate culture 1. Short-term profit orientation of divisions
1. Clear corporate philosophy	2. Delay in entrance into computer related products
2. Largest electrical home appliances manufacturer, strong brands	2. Excessive 'weight' on home appliances
3. Strong elementary technology, strong mass production technology	3. 'Sectionalism' of product divisions
3. Good cooperation between development, production and marketing	3. Many overlapping activities between product divisions
3. 25,000 exclusive and selective retail stores	

(New proposed strategies)

1. Renewal of corporate philosophy
1b Emphasis on individual creativity
2. 50 % of sales from non-home appliance products, entering into computer related products
2b To systems products, to information products
2b 50 % of production in foreign countries
3. Better cooperation between product divisions, interchange of personnel between divisions
3b Centralization of research laboratories under the head office
3c Better co-ordination between the foreign production plants
3d Enhancing the capabilities of the sales channel, from home appliances to OA instruments

Note   (1) OA = office automation, FA = factory automation, HA = home automation, NIES = newly industrialized east Asian regions.
(2) 1 ... goals, 2 ... product-market strategy, 3 ... resource structure

Estimation of the future environment makes clear the opportunities and threats and this leads to a conception of possible strategy and desirable structure. They are compared with the present and future status of the company and of the competitors, thus gaps or strengths and weaknesses are identified and then strategic issues are identified.

In this sense, the comparison with competitors and time-series analysis are also used, so this approach is a comprehensive one, integrating the other methods.

6.2 Systems of internal analysis

There is too much emphasis placed on the financial aspects of internal analysis, but financial performance is only the result of strategy, structure and competitive power. Internal analysis can be systematized by following the sequence of factors affecting the performance of one's own company.

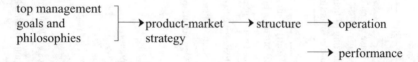

This model is the same as the model illustrating the subjects of corporate planning, shown in Table 1.1. They show the four sub-systems of a corporation. Following this sequence, the system of internal analysis is described in Table 6.2.

An internal analysis examines, firstly, whether financial goals have been attained. Financial performance is the result of strategy and structure but it can also provide resources for strategy and structure. If the profit is large, the company can have sophisticated facilities, can spend large amounts of money for research and development and can produce high quality products.

If the past financial performance is below the desired level, thus leaving a gap in the financial performance, it might be an indication that there were some mistakes in the past strategy and structure. A past gap is useful to forecast a future gap. To close gaps in the future, the company has to find a new strategy.

At the same time, the goals and philosophy of the business themselves may be outdated and have to be critically reviewed. For example, a company may put too much emphasis on stability and short-range profit, and thus have a growth rate that is too low, because growth products were not developed. This will cause dissatisfaction among employees, and the survival of the company may be in danger.

Generally speaking, the goals of organizations are formulated by the expectations of key resource holders. Surveys on the aspirations of key resource holders, usually shareholders, managers and key staff are conducted by the company to update its goals.

The corporate philosophy, or the business creed, expresses key elements of the goals, strategy and code of behavior, in words which emotionally appeal to em-

Table 6.2   System of internal analysis

(The strength and weakness of the host corporation are evaluated into five levels: highest, high, medium, lower, and lowest.)

1. Overall performance

	Three years before	This year (estimated)	Future estimation	Evaluation
Sales				
Return on total investment				
Equity ratio				
Share of market				

(2) Top management
Top management .... ( )
Planning department ...... ( )

(3) The strength and weakness in product-market strategy (diversifiction, multi national management, vertical integration and so on.) in relation to the opportunities and threats

11. Analysis by divisions and departments
(4) Capability of each functional area

Items	Function	New product development	Marketing	Production
Criteria of capability (quantitative measurement)				
Resource	Knowledge and system			
	Organaizational structure			
	Human resource and organaizational climate			
	Facilities			
	Allocation of financial resources			

(5) Competitive power of each product

Items	product	New product development	Marketing	Production
		X1	X2	X3
Quality				
Price and cost				
Sales channel				
Sales promotion				
Linkage with the customer				

(Notes)   1. Level of strength and weakness are evaluated as follows: highest among corporations in the same industry = highest; avove average = higher; average of the all companies = medium; below average = lower; lowest among the companies = lowest

ployees and to the public. They affect corporate culture. But they could become obsolete. For example, the business creed of Matsushita Electric Industrial Company, "To provide the society with home electric appliances at the cheapest price like water" had to be reconsidered, when its strategy shifted to include selling of office equipment. When the Keihin Railway company tried to diversify into housing, the creed "the spirit of railway" was too old, so it changed its creed to "business that supports the pleasant urban life of people". By this change, the company stated its intention to change corporate culture and strategy. In general, it is necessary to re-examine the corporate creed once every five years.

Next, an internal analysis assesses whether the top management team is excellent and whether the planning staff, which assist them, are competent. It is not easy to assess the strengths of top management teams, but it is very important. If the president (CEO) is capable, and if the top management team is excellent, this results in high performance.

A good product-market strategy is produced by an excellent top management team, and if the product-market strategy fits with structure, the performance is high. To evaluate the strengths of the product-market strategy, the features of diversification, multinational management, vertical integration and competitive power are reviewed.

The fourth part of the analysis is on structure. A company's structure is simply a cluster of its corporate capabilities. These capabilities are comprised of a product development capability, a production capability, and a marketing capability. As is shown in Table 6.2, these functional capabilities are composed of several elements: knowledge of the system of management, organizational structure, personnel capability and quality of equipment. These are the resources. These functional capabilities may be strong or weak, depending upon the products, so they are assessed in relation to products.

An important but difficult area of internal analysis is the analysis of the corporate culture. If the company can assess corporate culture – whether it is viable or stagnant – it can make a plan to improve corporate culture, so that there will not be a gap between strategy and corporate culture.

Fifthly, an analysis of the competitive power of each product or each product line reviews the strengths of each product displayed in the market battlefield. These strengths consist of the quality of products, their price and cost, the strengths of the sales channel, the quantity and quality of sales promotional activity and the linkage of the accumulation of the above four factors with the customer. These direct competitive edges originally come from functional capabilities, and they also originate in the quality of the product-market strategy, the quality of top management and the level of financial performance.

Survey on the items of internal analysis

What the items of internal analysis are and to what extent they are used are shown in Table 6.1.b. The results show that the system of internal analysis stated in the previous section is actually used. Among five areas, (1) financial performance, (3) strength in product mix, (4) strength in functional capabilities and (5) the competitive power of each product have a higher frequency of use.

There are some differences among industries. The industries which are in severe competition such as food and electrical machinery collect more information on internal analysis than industries which are less competitive, such as the textile, pulp and paper, and oil industries. Competitive industries collect more information on the strength of functional capabilities in particular.

The successful companies in planning put more emphasis on top management and middle management capabilities, and high performance companies put more emphasis on the analysis of the product-market strategy.

6.3 The use of growth share matrix (product portfolio matrix)

Growth share matrix analysis or PPM analysis is useful for internal analysis. This approach locates each product on the matrix of the attractiveness of the industry (or growth rate of the industry) and the competitiveness of one's own product (or market share of the product). The matrix is divided into four or nine segments.

The analysis of product-mix by the use of the portfolio matrix is firstly done by time-series analysis. Any changes of the position of each product is reviewed, if there are any abnormal shifts, such as, from the star to the problem child or from the cash cow to the problem child, then in these cases there are some errors in strategy.

The second analysis is to see the balance of products, whether there is a good balance between tomorrow's products, today's products and yesterday's products. If the product mix is composed of only the problem child and the star product, the company will have a shortage of internal supply of financial resources. If the product mix is composed of only the cash cow and the dog, if future products are not cultivated, the company will have troubles in the future.

How the growth share matrix or PPM is used is surveyed in Table 6.2.b. In that table, 35 percent of the companies are using the growth share matrix, and among them 27 percent of companies are using it informally. Such industries as food products, textiles, chemicals, machinery and electrical machinery are frequent users; from 50 percent to 60 percent of these companies are using it, because they have diversified products.

Many companies are using a simple four-segments method. In one third of these cases, positioning is done by head office, in one third it is done by operating units and in the remaining one third both parties consult about the positioning. In most cases positioning is done according to the present situation rather than after efforts in improvement. The former approach may be easier to do and there are less problems. The most important purpose of using the PPM method is the discovery of problems with the product mix. Matsushita Electrical Machinery Manufacturing Co. uses it informally by four cells; positioning is initially done by the head office and then is used to discover problem with the product mix.

The problems of PPM analysis are that, (1) it is an analysis of present products, does not look at the new products, new opportunities in the environment, (2) it does not analyze the resource structure, (3) it does not see the synergy between the products. (On PPM analysis, Rothchild 1976; Hofer and Schendel, 1978 and others.)

6.4 Sources of data

The data source of internal analysis is usually the documents of the company, or the opinions of the staff. However, the external sources are useful, if the external sources know the facts, and if they can express their opinion frankly, like a jury. At Asahi Brewery, long before the change of corporate culture started in 1980, the diagnosis of a consultant company was conducted. The analysis said that (1) the image of Asahi Brewery is low, (2) new product development tended to be technology oriented, not consumer oriented, (3) there was little effort by the company to deliver the mind of products to the customer, (4) little efforts were tried to distribute fresh beer to the consumer. This report described the weaknesses exactly, but it was disregarded, because top management had no desire to listen. Five years later, the report was taken up and used for restructuring the company.

In 1983, a CI (corporate identity) study team of the same company conducted an interview survey with exclusive wholesalers, retailers, university professors and reporters in mass communications, and obtained similar opinions from them.

There outside sources could related frank and honest evaluations of the company. These two outside assessments proved to be very useful in restructuring the company, to change corporate culture and to formulate the formal long-range plan.

6.5 Corporate culture and long-range planning

Corporate culture is composed of three elements – shared values, decision-making patterns and overt behavior patterns. It is called an organizational climate, corporate style, corporate ethos, and, sometimes, beliefs, assumptions, schemes, corporate eye glasses and common maps. (Shein, 1985; Davies, 1984; Kilmann, 1986; Harris, 1989; Kono, 1988; Umezawa, 1986)

There are two reasons why corporate culture has begun to draw the attention of researchers. One is that as the environment changes strategy has to change, but culture tends to stay the same and there arises the discrepancy between strategy and corporate culture. The second reason is that initiatives of members have become more important for activities in every area. Researchers need to be creative, and marketing personnel need to be alert to changes in consumer behavior. These active behaviors cannot be expected from situations controlled by rules.

Motivation is a little different from corporate culture, because motivation is a behavior to cooperate with duties already set by the organization. Corporate culture is the pattern of looking for new opportunities.

1. Long-range planning and corporate culture change

Long-range planning has the effect of changing culture in the following aspects
(a) Unfreeze. The analysis of the environment and the self-assessment of the company discloses problems, issues and future gaps of financial performance. These analysis could evoke a sense of crisis.
(b) Change. Regularly every year, it forces the reconsideration of the product-market strategy and the personnel management system, thus changes to corporate culture.
(c) Refreeze. Ideas generated from many departments do not flow away, but they are written down, formally authorized, implemented and followed up. This system is different from informal decisions, and it provides the conditions for re-freezing changes. Thus, formal planning provides the conditions for culture change.

The initial conditions of corporate culture affect the nature of long-range planning in the following way.
(a) When the culture is lively. In this case, long-range planning can be easily built. The detailness could be one of two extremes. The plan could be detailed (for example, the case of Canon), because people are willing to formulate strategic plans. The other extreme is that the plan could be relatively simple (The case of Asahi Chemicals, for example), because a vital culture could complement a simple plan, people do innovative actions an their own initiative.
      The cause-effect will be as follows

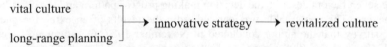

vital culture ⎤
              ⎬ ⟶ innovative strategy ⟶ revitalized culture
long-range planning ⎦

(b) When the culture is stagnant. In this case, the culture change and strategic planning have to be carried out simultaneously. There are two approaches.

(1) Long-range planning first. This approach aims to formulate long-range planning by a top down approach and try to change culture and strategy.

                                              ⎡⟶ change of culture
Issue finding ⟶ long-range planning ⟶ ⎨
                                              ⎣⟶ change of strategy

This process is made possible by the strong leadership of top management. The process can be incremental, that is, the plan need not be comprehensive but partial and strategy change could be incremental. Symbolic change of strategy could affect culture change. (for example, in the case of an advertising company.)

(2) Culture change first. This approach takes the following process:
Activities to change culture – partial change of strategy – comprehensive long-range planning – comprehensive strategy change (The cases of Asahi Brewery and of Nissan Motor)

This process tries to change culture first and implement partial change of strategy. After the company culture becomes more strategy oriented, then comprehensive planning is installed to promote and refreeze strategic innovations.

2. Types of corporate culture

Before we plan changes to corporate culture, we have to identify what types of corporate culture will breed an aggressive corporate strategy.

A. Measurements of corporate culture

Corporate culture is composed of three groups of elements, that is, the values held by the members of an organization, their method of decision-making or way of thought and their overt behavior patterns. In this study, the author does not define corporate culture as the beliefs or assumptions of its members but rather defines it as the actual decision making patterns, because these patterns are easier to observe and measure, and they affect the performance of the organization and the satisfaction of its members.

Detailed factors of three groups of measurements of corporate culture is shown in Table 6.3.

There are seven factors: (1) values that the members believe, (2) information collection, (3) idea generation, (4) evaluation of ideas and risk taking, (5) cooperation, (6) loyalty to the organization, and (7) value of the task to the employee, or morale of the member.

These seven factors describe the decision making process pattern and the overt behavior pattern. The above table was derived from the results of an extensive questionnaire survey that the author conducted in November 1987. Questionnaires were sent to 126 companies (908 pieces), and 88 companies and 265 persons responded. One set of questionnaires contained 126 questions, of which 67 questions were related to the expression of corporate culture. Each answer had five levels from definitely yes to absolutely no. Answers were analyzed by computer factor analysis, and we found that the above seven factors were the key ones. The contents of Table 1 illustrate important elements selected from the responses and classified according to the seven factors.

B. Types and performances

The classification of corporate cultures is useful to identify the position of culture of a corporation, and to discover the relationships between culture and the strategy of the organization, its performance and the satisfaction of its members, because there is a specific cause and effect relationship for each type.

We used three axis to classify culture, innovative vs. conservative, analytical vs.

Table 6.3   Elements and types of corporate culture

Elements \ Types	1. Vitalized	2. Follow the leader and vitalized	3. Bureau-cratic	4–1 Stagnant	4–2 Stagnant and follow the leader
General characteristics	Value in innovation Many ideas presented	Follow the leader	Procedures and rules are respected.	Tradition oriented	Follow the leader
① Value	Innovation oriented	Following the leader is a value.	Procedure-oriented Safety first	Safety first	Safety of self Safety first
② Information	Information collection is oriented to outside environment.	Information comes from the higher ranks	Oriented to technical knowledge	Internally oriented	Top down
③ Idea Presentation	Many spon-taneous ideas presented Many oppos-ing ideas	Do only what are told to do No opposing ideas	Perfect and completed plan is necessary. High level of spezialization	Habital few new ideas No opposing ideas	Few new ideas presented Do what are told to do
④ Risk taking	Are not afraid of failure	Failure is the responsibil-ity of the leader	Arc afraid of failure	Are afraid of failure	Are afraid of failure
⑤ Co-operation	Little social distance between the leader and the follower Good team-work	Follow the leader Mutually competitive	Hierarchy is necessary. Responsibil-ity and author-ity are clear.	Do not trust the higher ranks Mutually separated	Large vertical social distance Mutually separated
⑥ Loyalty to the organization	Two extremes	Work for lifetime	Work for lifetime	Quit the company if better opportunities are available	Quit the company if better opportunities are available
⑦ Motivation	High sense of responsibility	Little sense of responsibility	Follow the rule	Low sense of responsibility	Low sense of responsibility
Examples	**Canon Hitachi Sony**	**Kyocera Nippon Gakki** in early times	Public office Large manu-factures of materials	Old National Railways Old ship building companies	**Van Jacket** (in later years)

intuitive and the social distance between the levels of hierarchy. We assume that these axis are related with the performance and the satisfaction of employees to a great extent. We also found that a lot of common expressions describing the corporate culture of many companies, such as Matsushita is a 'merchant', Mitsubishi is a 'lord', Sony is an 'innovator' and other similar expressions can be classified on these three axes. The combination of three pairs with two levels makes 8 kinds of culture, but since there are some correlations between the levels, the kinds of culture are reduced into five, as is shown in Table 6.13.

(1) Vitalized type
The vitalized culture type has the following characteristics. The members put emphasis on innovation, have a sense of one family or one community and share common values. The goal of the organization is clearly understood, and the members understand the meaning of their jobs clearly. Information is actively collected from the outside, and is customer- oriented. The organization has good communication both vertically and horizontally.

Ideas for improvement are presented voluntarily, and members perform duties in anticipation of the expectation of others. Opposing ideas towards seniors and colleagues are presented. Members take risks. Members also feel that there is little social distance between them and their seniors, thus they do not hesitate to call their seniors by name, instead of by the name of the senior's position.

The vitalized culture tends to give birth to good new strategies, to implement them well and have a high productivity.

(2) Follow-the-leader and vitalized type
The feature of this type of culture is that its members follow a strong leader, usually the founder of the company. The members trust the ability of the leader, and important information and ideas come from top management. As long as the top makes good decisions, this type works well, but once the top gets older and begins to take wrong decisions, this type shifts to the (4-2) type described below.

(3) Bureaucratic type
In companies with this culture, rules and standards increase, the behavior of members is bound by these rules, and members do not try to take risks. This type is found in old companies and in mass-production material manufacturing companies.

(4-1) Stagnant type
The members of this type of culture only repeat old patterns of behavior, and their information collection is inner-oriented and not sensitive to changes to the environment. Members also do not present new ideas. This type appears in companies with monopolistic market shares and in public organizations.

(4-2) Stagnant with strong leader type
Here, the top management is autocratic, but their decisions are wrong and the members, who have to obey orders, lose the initiative to do anything. A company with a type 2 culture might develop into this type, when the top management stays in position for many years.

Table 6.4 Measurement and performance of each type of corporate culture

Types / Elements	1. Vitalized corporate culture	2. Follow-the-leader and vitalized	3. Bureaucratic	4-1 Stagnant	4-2 Follow-the-leader and stagnant
Responding corporations	34 corporations	7 corporations	32 corporations	8 corporations	7 corporations
Persons	157 persons	20 persons	161 persons	25 persons	28 persons
1. Shared values					
(1-1) Take risks, not afraid of failure	55 *	58 *	47 *	38 *	40 *
(1-2) Take initiative, rather than follow the leader	52 *	43 *	47 *	52	52
(1-3) Know business philosophy and business creed	53 *	54	47 *	43 *	46
2. Communications					
(2-1) Much horizontal communication	53 *	62 *	47 *	36 *	46
(2-2) Make a decision after collecting enough information	53 *	56 *	47 *	44 *	45 *
(2-3) Put emphasis on intuition and experiments	51	59 *	45 *	49	51
3. Idea presentation					
(3-1) Present opposing opinions to the senior leader	53 *	59 *	48 *	39 *	42 *
(3-2) Present opposing ideas to colleagues	55 *	54	46 *	43 *	40 *
4. Evaluation					
(4-1) Are not afraid of failure	51	52	50	43 *	45 *
(4-2) Do not think merit rating is made by deducting systems	53 *	50	48 *	47	42 *
5. Social distance and co-operation					
(5-1) Small social distance between higher level and lower level	55 *	42 *	49	40 *	49
(5-2) Good cooperation between departments	55 *	53	47 *	31 *	45 *

continued

Table 6.4 Measurement and performance of each type of corporate culture (cont.)

Types / Elements	Responding corporations / Persons	1. Vitalized corporate culture	2. Follow-the-leader and vitalized	3. Bureaucratic	4-1. Stagnant	4-2. Follow-the-leader and stagnant
		34 corporations	7 corporations	32 corporations	8 corporations	7 corporations
		157 persons	20 persons	161 persons	25 persons	28 persons
6. Loyalty to the organization						
(6-1) Like to work for lifetime		52 *	51	49	43 *	48
7. Motivation						
(7-1) Report the mistakes to the senior		54 *	58 *	46 *	43 *	41 *
(7-2) Our section is eager to work hard		53 *	58 *	49	38 *	43 *
8. Performances						
(8-1) Yearly growth rate of sales	(%)	10.4	19.7	7.1	3.2	5.6
(8-2) Rate of return on total asset	(%)	7.4	9.4	5.8	3.0	5.2
(8-3) Equity ratio	(%)	40.0	44.8	28.0	19.2	26.4
(8-4) Total performance = (1) + (2) + 1/4	(3)	28.3	40.5	20.0	12.5	17.5

(Note)
(1) From 1 to 7 the figures indicate the standardized value.
    The value $Y = 50 + 10$ t (t = (values measured − average value) ÷ standard deviation)
(2) Annual growth rate was computed between 1977 and 1986. Return on total assets were computed by averaging the 1980 and 1986 results. Equity ratios were the averages of the 1980 and 1986 figures.
(3) Classification of companies into types of corporate culture are judged by responses to several key questions.
(4) The good performance of type 2 comes from the fact that many young companies are included.
(5) The difference between the averages are almost significant at the 5% level.

Many companies tend to start from type 2 and then shift by the following sequence: (2) – (1) – (3) – (4). To avoid this shift, the rejuvenation of the organization's culture is necessary.

The relative performance of these various classifications were examined, and the results are shown in Table 6.4.

The classification of companies was determined by the distance between the values of answers relating to key elements from the standard values of each type. The survey results show that a type 2 culture has the highest value of vitality followed by type 1. The best financial performance is also seen in type 2, and again type 1 follows. The reason why the financial performance of type 2 is the best is that many of the companies in this type are newly established and fast growing companies and have vital cultures. In contrast, the performances of the stagnant culture companies are the worst.

An analysis of Table 2 shows that the method of classification is meaningful, and that companies should try to possess a vitalized corporate culture, should try to shift to type 1 if they are some other type, and should try to remain at the type 1 culture.

3. Factors that formulate a corporate culture

We assume that a corporate culture is formed by four factors (a) the corporate philosophy (b) the product-market strategy, (c) the organizational structure and personnel management system, and (d) the attitude of top management affects the above three.

The relationship between these factors are outlined in Table 6.5.

There are three factors that affect personal attitudes: one is information or education, one is learning by experience and the last one is rewards and punishment. These three factors roughly correspond respectively to the above three factors. The corporate philosophy describes the desired values of the corporation and the desired way of thinking, and thus affects the pattern of behavior. The product-market strategy determines the job positions which affect the behavior pattern through experience. We found that corporate culture varies from industry to industry, this means that the product-market strategy affects the types of corporate culture. Finally, the organizational structure defines the communication pattern and the responsibilities of each member, the personnel management system stipulates the reward and punishment system. Thus they influence the corporate culture.

As a specific example of how these factors influence a formation of corporate culture, the case of Honda Motor Corporation is described in Table 6.6.

Honda has a vibrant and energetic culture, which has been cultivated by the leadership of the top management, who retire at the age of 55. Its corporate philosophy puts an emphasis on "dreams and youthfulness". It aggressively introduces new products quite frequently, thus it stimulates an innovative atmosphere. The personnel management system is deliberately designed. It tries to recruit diverse capabilities from diverse sources, for example, recruiting university graduates from as many universities as possible. Honda utilizes job rotation of employees on planned schedules

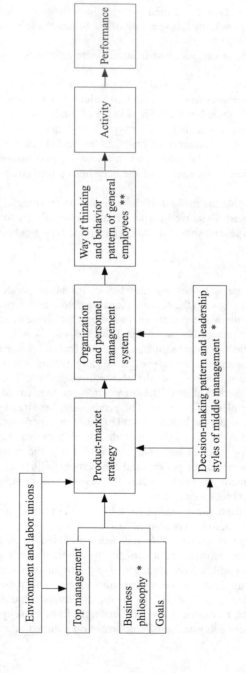

Table 6.5 Factors affecting corporate culture

(Note)
* ...... Upper corporate culture
** ...... Lower corporate culture

Table 6.6 Factors affecting the corporate culture of Honda Motor Corporation

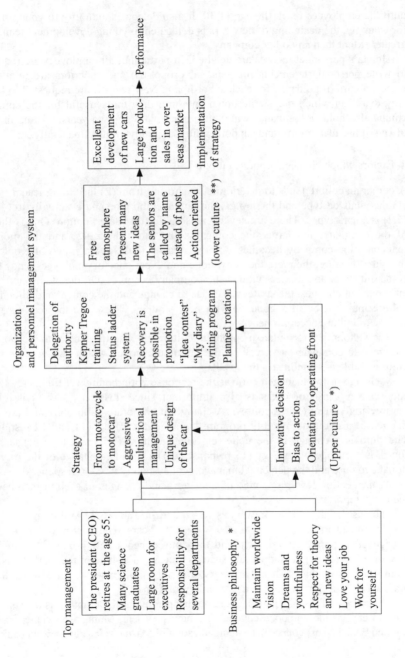

Top management

The president (CEO) retires at the age 55.
Many science graduates
Large room for executives
Responsibility for several departments

Business philosophy *

Maintain worldwide vision
Dreams and youthfulness
Respect for theory and new ideas
Love your job
Work for yourself

Strategy

From motorcycle to motorcar
Aggressive multinational management
Unique design of the car

Innovative decision
Bias to action
Orientation to operating front

(Upper culture *)

Organization and personnel management system

Delegation of authority
Kepner Tregoe training
Status ladder system
Recovery is possible in promotion
"Idea contest"
"My diary" writing program
Planned rotation

Free atmosphere
Present many new ideas
The seniors are called by name instead of post.
Action oriented

(lower cutlure **)

Excellent development of new cars
Large production and sales in overseas market
Implementation of strategy

Performance

until the employees reach the age of 30. It also delegates authority to young people, for example, the designing of new cars is delegated to young development teams to a greater extent than any other company.

Honda's personnel records are detailed. In particular, all employees are requested to write personal statements (or personal proposals) and superiors are required to write a record of guidance for each subordinate. New recruits are requested to keep a "my diary" in which they write down anything they think useful for the company. Honda also holds a company- wide "idea contest" every two years, costing millions of yen. It has idea rooms, and supports voluntary study groups financially.

4. Factors which change corporate culture

A corporate culture tends to deteriorate by shifting from (2) the strong leader type to (1) the vitalized type and then to (3) the bureaucratic type and eventually to (4.1) or (4.2) stagnant types. There are several reasons for this deterioration. One is the size of the company: the larger the company, the more the rules, and the more bureaucratic the company becomes. Another reason is the average age of employees: the older they are, the more the knowledge and experience of employees tends to become outdated, and the less vibrant the company becomes. On the other hand, if the environment changes, the strategy also has to change and the content and direction of culture may not be in a good fit with new strategy. These are the reasons why a change of culture becomes necessary.

The factors that formulate a corporate culture are also the factors that change the culture. We conducted a survey on the important factors which change a corporate culture. Table 6.3.b indicates the results.

A change of top management was the response with the highest frequency (56 responses). A sense of crisis is also important since this may make possible the "unfreezing" effect (30 responses). A change of corporate philosophy and the introduction of a corporate identity program have similar effects (11 and 12 responses). The third is a change in the upper corporate culture (9,12 and 8 responses). The fourth is a change of strategy (15 responses). The fifth is a change of the organizational structure and the personnel management system (25, 8 & 6 responses)

At the section level, a change of managers and changes of section members are the most important.

The case of the Asahi Brewery is illustrated in Table 6.7. Asahi's market share had continued to fall from 36% to 9% over 35 years. The new president started a change of corporate culture first, and then introduced a new product "Asahi Super Dry Beer". It resulted in a dramatic success and Asahi's share of the market has risen from 9% to more than 20% in two years. The old culture was "we are always the losers", but the culture changed to a live and vibrant one.

The success of Asahi's new beer did not happen by itself, but rather as a result of efforts to change the corporate culture. The new president, Murai, who came from Sumitomo Bank had experience in the reorganization of Mazda which almost went bankrupt.

Table 6.7 Changing the corporate culture of Asahi Breweries

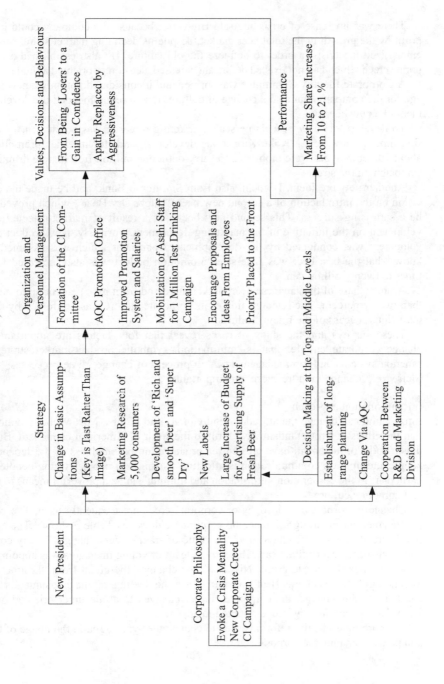

Corporate Philosophy

New President

Evoke a Crisis Mentality
New Corporate Creed
CI Campaign

Strategy

Change in Basic Assumptions
(Key is Tast Rahter Than Image)

Marketing Research of 5,000 consumers

Development of 'Rich and smooth beer' and 'Super Dry'

New Labels

Large Increase of Budget for Advertising Supply of Fresh Beer

Decision Making at the Top and Middle Levels

Establishment of long-range planning

Change Via AQC

Cooperation Between R&D and Marketing Division

Organization and Personnel Management

Formation of the CI Committee

AQC Promotion Office

Improved Promotion System and Salaries

Mobilization of Asahi Staff for 1 Million Test Drinking Campaign

Encourage Proposals and Ideas From Employees

Priority Placed to the Front

Values, Decisions and Behaviours

From Being 'Losers' to a Gain in Confidence

Apathy Replaced by Aggressiveness

Performance

Marketing Share Increase From 10 to 21 %

There was no sense of crisis at Asahi Brewery , because the company could gain profit by the growth in the total beer market, despite its declining market share. Murai emphasized the crisis in order to defreeze the old culture. He also established a corporate creed which had not existed before and stressed a customer oriented attitude.

A Corporate Identity Committee was formed and it considered not only a new image for the company, but also a change of culture. It also recommended the development of a new beer.

To develop this new beer, large scale marketing research was conducted for the first time. A new beer, "Koku Kire", was developed, and, for its sales promotion, about 700 employees were mobilized to carry out a one million free sample drinking campaign on the streets.

Another new president, Higuchi, also from Sumitomo Bank, and he made the decision on the introduction of a second new beer, "Super Dry Beer", which proved to be a surprising success. This second new beer was a result of market-oriented development on the initiative of the marketing department. Formerly, new product development was conducted by the development department which was assumed to know what the best beer was. The sales promotion budget was also increased four times to twenty billion yen.

Asahi's share of the Japanese beer market increased from nine percent up to more than twenty percent. The revitalization of its corporate culture was reinforced by this marvelous success of their new products.

These surveys and the study of cases reveal that four factors are important to change corporate culture, that is, information, symbolic product-market strategy, sanction systems and top management. As a process of change, three processes – to 'defreeze', 'change' and 'refreeze' are important.

(a) Information approach

Information can change the attitude of individuals and groups. Max Weber mentions that the ethics of Protestantism gave birth to the spirit of American capitalism. Buddhism and Confucianism have created the organization-orientedness of the Japanese people and in mass communication is affecting the spirit of people, young people in particular. In the corporation, information and training can be a powerful means to affect corporate culture.

Change in corporate philosophy or corporate creed are frequently used. The corporate creed has a strong influence on corporate culture, as Table 5 shows. The corporate creed needs to be changed as the value of stakeholders changes. Many companies change it every five years. Recently, a team of young managers was appointed to study a new corporate creed. Nissan Motor changed the creed from "Distinctive Technology" to "Feel the Beat" meaning that the feeling of the consumer is respected. By this change, the corporate culture changed to a consumer oriented one. After that, successful new models started to appear.

The corporate identity reform is used to change the symbol mark, the image of the company, to change the corporate culture.

The behavior of Top management, its speeches and writings have a symbolic effect in changing the employees.

A member of channels of communication are used to appeal to the employees on the importance of change, on the direction of change. The company newspaper, morning meetings, a variety of movements and the employee training are used to deliver the new philosophy, the new creed, a success story of some departments.

(b) Learning through experience of new product-market strategy and the diffusion of the spirit of experimentation

A new experience can change attitudes. The value system and behavior patterns are formed through experiences since childhood. Likes and dislikes towards some foods, patterns of eating foods, attitudes towards readings and towards other people, all are formed through experiences.

When a person experiences a new thing which is not consonant with old conceptions, he will change his attitude when the new experience is a convincing one. This is explained by the theory of cognitive dissonance. For this reason, a success in new product-market strategy will change the confidence of the corporation. For example, the success in the new products "Pulser" and "Be 1" of Nissan Motor gave a great impact to the culture of the company, the employees realized the importance of consumer orientedness. The impact of success of the new beer at Asahi Brewery has been already explained.

There are many cases, however, where new products do not result in the change of corporate culture. Neither the oil well development nor the operation of a branch of Teijin Synthetic Fiber, nor the soft contact lens of Toray served to change corporate culture.

What then, are the conditions in which a partial change of strategy can influence corporate culture?

Firstly, new strategy needs to succeed, and needs to become a symbol of new culture. It should indicate the new direction of behavior patterns, and it should be supported and authorized by the top management through simple praise, through prizes, by the ceremonies or be made into a myth.

Secondly, the experience should be imitated and similar experiences should be practiced by other departments. At Nissan, after the success of new car developments, new activities to improve the culture were encouraged and new components supply systems at production plants were tried, new groups of old aged workers were formed and new ways of working for the elderly were explored, and many other new experiments were tried.

Thirdly, the transfer of personnel. At Asahi Brewery, 600 people from all departments were mobilized to a sales promotion campaign to let one million consumers on the street try the new beer. This had an effect to make employees understand the feelings of consumers. At Mitsubishi Electric, the managers at one plant who produced a successful new home appliances were transferred to other plants in the same line, the new approach was transplanted, and many new, successful products were produced thereafter. Innovators in one department become opinion leaders, they are scattered to many departments and transmit the new spirit to other departments, or they may transmit the new spirit to the opinion leaders already existing in other departments. Opinion leaders play important roles in transmitting the new way of thinking evidenced by new experiences such as new product developments.

(c) Sanction system

The change of organizational structure and personnel management systems are the third factors used to change corporate culture. Organizational structure affects responsibility of members, and delegation of authority tends to activate members.

The personnel management system includes recruitment, training and rewards systems. Practices by many corporations to activate corporate culture are collected and listed in Table 6.8.

Table 6.8   Personnel management system

		Activating system	Stagnating system
1.	Recruiting	• Recruit those who like to take risks • Recruit experienced personnel from outside and mix them with insiders	• Recruit high score students • Promotion from within, only
2.	Promotion	• Merit appraisal system (Addition only) • Promotion by capability • Loser recovery system	• Demerit appraisal system (Deduction only) • Too rigid length of service system • Fast track system
3.	Job assignment	• Planned rotation • Assign the capable to key projects	• Early specialization
4.	Training	• Training decision-making process	
5.	Wage and salary	• By merit	• Strict length of service system
6.	Personnel information system	• Self statement, self evaluation	• Evaluation by the senior

Among these practices, the merit assessment system, not demerit rating, is drawing attention. The manager tends to see the demerits or failure of subordinates, because it is easier to identify. Those who do new trials tend to be failures. If these failures are punished, nobody will dare to run the risk, and behavior will become conservative. In order to encourage new trials, real "merit" ratings have to be introduced. Merit rating tries to see the process, not the results. One company gives a prize to those who committed a failure, because he tried a new thing. The company evaluated the effort and the process.

In order to install the "merit" rating, the company needs to have self-statement system, a kind of management-by-objective system. The employees are encouraged to make a plan to improve his job or to do some new trials or a plan to develop himself. The plan will be reviewed by himself and by his boss.

In order to activate the employee, there should be many opportunities for rewards. Most Japanese corporations have a system of status ladder promotion system in addition to promotion on the job classification ladder, and annual wage increase by merit on wide rate ranges. These many extrinsic rewards system can support the operation of real merit rating.

"The loser recovery system" is another way. If one person is slow in promotion, he can have many challenges set to recover his slowness, and eventually he could go ahead of his colleagues. In order to reevaluate those who are slow in promotion, the personnel manager will review those who are behind their colleagues, and try to reevaluate them, and provide them with faster tracks to recover their positions. One company selects 20% of slow movers and reevaluates them. Another large bank has about ten interviewers in the personnel department, and do interviewing with about 20 percent of all employees in a year, and hear what are the problems for them. Data is used to provide opportunities to recover this slowness.

5. Process to change corporate culture

Change in the corporate culture takes the form of the process of 'unfreeze', 'change', and 'refreeze'. This process is similar to the process of 'brainwashing' applied to war prisoners held by the communist bloc during the Second World War.

First, 'prisoners' preconceptions were destroyed by pointing out the 'contradictions and errors' of capitalism (unfreeze). Next, they were taught the 'correctness' of communism. For those who did not change their minds, food rations were reduced, and for those who accepted this change in thinking, rations were increased (change). The change was then fixed and reinforced by peer pressure exerted by fellow prisoners, etc., (refreeze).

(A) Unfreeze

To unfreeze is to destroy conventional values. To achieve this, people are taught that their conventional values or ways of thinking are erroneous. In the case of an individual, each person is taught to reflect inwardly and confess the error of his ways.

In the case of Asahi, the process of 'evoking a crisis mentality' corresponds to 'unfreezing'. In Asahi, despite the steady loss in market share, there had always been profits due to the overall expansion of the beer market; therefore, the employees did not feel that the situation was critical. A feeling of crisis was evoked by educating them about the declining market share and the deterioration of the company image in the minds of consumers. Also, a consulting company was employed in order to diagnose and criticize the company management.

(B) Change

There are three ways to affect a cultural change:

(a) The information approach teaches a new way of thinking. In the case of Asahi, a new management philosophy was established, and the top management, including the president, promoted new philosophy among employees at a new CI Campaign, which emphasized consumer and market orientation.

(b) The experience approach consists of having employees solve problems themselves, go through new experiences and force them to take new measures. This is most effective for creating changes in the corporate culture. This is to change strategy, particularly the development of new products and their subsequent success. For Asahi, it was the development and success of a new draught beer (Koku-Kire Beer) in 1986. This deepened the understanding of the importance of a customer orientation, and the company emerged from having an 'underdog' corporate culture and acquired a new culture filled with confidence. The mobilization of the employees in the 1-million subject trial sampling provides an example of the approach through action. The phenomenal success of Super Dry in 1987 put new energy into the corporate culture.

c) The approach through reward and punishment involves rewarding preferable actions and punishing undesirable ones and is mainly achieved by changes in personnel management. The execution of various campaigns and corresponding performance commendations awarded to participating employees fall under this category.

(d) Finally there is the 'comprehensive approach', This includes all three approaches, and requires a replacement of top management. Asahi used this method i.e. information, experience, reward and punishment.

(C) Refreeze

In order to 'refreeze' a change, it is necessary continuously to reward and punish, to teach new ways of thinking, and to provide new experiences which reinforce the correctness of the change in culture. In the case of Asahi, the success of the first beer was followed with the development of second new product, 'Super Dry', thus refreezing the new way of thinking. To refreeze a change and maintain the impetus, a continuous revolution such as the continuous development of new products is required. Maintaining the momentum of the revolution by the continuous development of new products and business is essential to maintain a revitalized corporate culture.

Long-range planning has the effect of refreezing by formally writing down the new strategy and structure. In order that the long-range planning is used effectively to change corporate culture, the above processes and means need to be planned in the document, and at the same time, above actions need to be taken inside or outside the long-range plan.

Summary

1. The fittest will survive. The company can find out strengths and weaknesses, and it can make use of future opportunities by applying its strengths, it can avoid future threats by using its strength. Weaknesses can be identified, it can be reinforced so that the strength can work effectively to utilize opportunities.

   Strengths and weaknesses are a relative concept, they can be identified by comparing the company with opportunities and threats in the future. The opportunity and threat assume the strength and weakness, so they are interactive relationships. The strength and weakness can be a dynamic concept, the future result is important, the future gaps should be analyzed. The analysis of weakness tends to disclose the mismanagement of the top, so it is not necessarily easy to conduct.

2. The system of internal analysis has a sort of hierarchy, and it contains four elements; goals and top management, the product-market strategy, the resource structure and the operations, or the competitive power.

3. The product portfolio analysis is one of the useful instruments for internal analysis. It is useful to follow the movement of the location of the products on the matrix, and to uncover the reasons for this. It is also useful to check whether there is a good balance of future products, today's products and yesterday's products.

   The analysis, however, does not consider the needs of allocation of resources to the birth of new products or to research and development. The focus is on present products; in this sense the principle is conservative. The strategy on the cash cow is very negative, the core product could lose the competitive power.

4. Internal analysis could be distorted by the politics of the company, so outside data sources can be used. The opinions of the customer, of the retailer and wholesaler, of the supplier, of the reporter could provide objective judgments. The consultant company is sometimes used, although the use of consultants in Japan is definitely less than in other countries.

   (References. Most of the books on corporate strategy deal with internal analysis. Kono, 1985; Hofer & Schendel, 1978; Rowe et al., 1985; Glueck et al., 1976; Johnson et al., 1989; Yavitz and Newman, 1988; Rothchild, 1976)

5. Corporate culture is composed of shared values, decision-making patterns and behavior patterns. There are five types of corporate culture, and it is important to recognize to what types of corporate culture the company belongs.

   Corporate culture affects strategic decision-making and the contents of strategy, as is seen in case of the Nissan Motor Company.

   If the corporate culture is vitalized, the long-range plan can incorporate innovative strategies, and strategies are implemented well (The case of Canon and Bridgestone)

   If the corporate culture is stagnant, the change of corporate culture has to be planned. Long-range planning has an effect on changing culture. It makes clear what threats lie in the future. It enforces the company to generate new ideas every year.

However, these functions are hard to expected when the culture is stagnant, the other measures to change culture have to be looked for.

There are four factors used to change culture. Information, successful implementation of small and symbolic new strategies, sanctions and change of top management. The symbolic new strategy has the highest impact.

There are three processes to change the corporate culture, that is, defreeze, change and re-freeze.

Table 6.1.b Items of internal analysis
Waht kind of the following items are used for the internal analysis of the corporation?

Years		1985	1989
Corporations with long-range plans		384 co.	249 co.
(1) Financial performance	a. Sales (or growth rate)	98 (%)	92 (%)
	b. Return on total assets	70	63
	c. Equity ratio	81	68
	d. Share of market (corporation as a whole)	63	72
(2) Top & middle management	a. Capabilities and ages of top management	8	20
	b. Capabilities and ages of middle management	27	32 *
	c. Organization of tcp management	23	34 *
(3) Strength and weakness in product market strategy	a. Strength and weakness in product mix	72	70
	b. Strength and weakness in multinational management	2	13 ○
	c. Strength and weakness in vertical integration	9	17 ○
	d. Strength and weakness in grouping of companies	12	23 ○
(4) Strength in each functional area	a. Capability to adapt to the company to change of environment	24	44
	b. Capability in product development, capability in basic technology for development	47	55
	c. Capability in marketing	43	53
	d. Production capacity, capability production control, capability in production technology	56	55
	e. Financial capability	57	60

continued

Table 6.1.b Items of internal analysis
Waht kind of the following items are used for the internal analysis of the corporation? (cont.)

Years		1985	1989
Corporations with long-range plans		384 co.	249 co.
(5) Competive power of each product	a. Quality of each product	60	62
	b. Price and competitiveness of cost	66	64
	c. Strength in sales channel	39	49
	d. Sales promotion	36	50
	e. Linkage with the customer	40	53
	f. Share of market	64	66
	g. Product differentiation	36	55
	h. Market segmentation (favoarable niche)	17	34
	i. Service	27	47

(Note) 1. The number indicates the percentage of responding corporations
2. Asterisks (∗) indicates more successful companies in planning (146 co., subjective judgement) have higher frequency (< 5 %)
Circel (○) indicates higher performance corporations have a higher frequency (< 10 %)

Table 6.2.b USe of PPM (Product Portfolio Management (or Matrix); growth share matrix; BCG model)

Corporations' with long-range plans			384 co. 6 (%)
(1) It is used formally			6 (%)
(2) It is used informally			29
(3) Not used			61
(4) When you are using	(a)	a. By four cells	22
		b. By nine cells	7
	(b)	c. Positioning of each product is done by head office	11
		d. Positioning of each product is done by each division	10
		e. By both levels	8
	(c)	f. Positioning of the product is done according to the present situation	25
		g. Positioning of the product is estimated after the efforts to improve it are finished	5
	(d)	h. Positioning of the industry is done according to the present situation	23
		i. Positioning of the industry is located after some efforts at improvement, (for example to extend the life cycle)	5
(5) For what purpose are you using PPM?		a. To find out problems of product mix	21
		b. To bring up or to decease the product	10
		c. To allocate the financial resources	6
		d. To allocate personnel resources	5
		e. To use standard strategy	10

(Notes) 1. Survey in 1985   2. The number indicaes the percentage of responding company

Table 6.3.b Reasons for the change of corporate culture, in the whole corporation
and your section
(Free response. 260 persons out of 391 persons responded. Number is
the number of persons)

Company as a whole		In my section	
1.	Change of top management members and lowered average age	56 (persons)	1.	Change of managers	38 (persons)
2.1	Increase of sense of crisis by the change of environment and by deteriorating financial performance	30	2.1	(Same as the left column)	15
2.2	Due to improved financial performance, the vitality and enthusiasm of the corporativon increased	13	2.2	(Same as the left column)	7
2.3	Diffusion of corporate philosophy and goals, and enthusiasm of top management	11			
2.4	Introduction of corporate identity movement	12			
3.1	Change of attitude of top management towards aggressive and innovative behavior	9	3.1	Clear goals for the sections and individuals, management by objectives	11
3.2	Improvement of daily operations and making efforts to improve the attitude of the members	12			
3.3	Improvement of administration system	8	3.3	(Same as left column)	7
			3.4	Introduction of quality control movement	5
4.	Introduction of new business and change of product-market strategy	15			
5.1	Change of organizational structure and delegation of authority	29	5.1	(Same as the left column)	7
5.2	Introduction of merit system and improvement of personal management system	8			

Continuation Table 6.3.b

Company as a whole		In my section	
5.3 Recruiting of new employees	6	5.3 Change of members and lowered average age	41
		5.4 Change of jobs and improvement of working place	11
		6. Others	11

(Note)   The meaning of the head numbers
1   Top management
2   Business philosophy and goals
3   Decision making of upper echelon
4   Product-market strategy
5   Organizational structure and personnel management

Appendix to chapter 6

Method of survey on corporate culture

Designing of survey   Toyohiro Kono, Professor of Business Administration
                      Takashi Uchino, Professor of Business Administration
                      Both of Gakushuin University, Mejiro, Toshima-ku, Tokyo

Date of survey   Mail questionnaires were sent in November 1987.

Number of responses   Mail questionnaires were sent to 126 corp. (908 pieces)
                      88 companies and 391 persons (4.4 persons per
                      one company) responded
                      Response ratio was 70.0% by corporations
                      and 43.1% for persons

Distribution of response by industry

1.	Mining and construction	7 corporations	(36 persons)
2.	Food and fisheries	4 corporations	(30 persons)
3.	Fiber, pulp and paper	4 corporations	(10 persons)
4.	Chemicals and drugs	13 corporations	(67 persons)
5.	Petroleum, rubber, glass and stone	8 corporations	(34 persons)
5.	Iron, steel and nonferrous metals	4 corporations	(14 persons)
7.	Machinery	6 corporations	(27 persons)
8.	Electrical appliances and precision machinery	23 corporations	(88 persons)
9.	Transportation equipment	4 corporations	(19 persons)
10	Finance and insurance	5 corporations	(31 persons)
11.	Commerce and services	7 corporations	(23 persons)
12.	Miscellaneous	3 corporations	(12 persons)

Total 88 corporations   (391 persons)

References on Corporate Culture

In Japanese

Ishikawa, J. (1987): Asahi Beer no Chosen (Challenge of Asahi Breweries, Ltd.), Japan Management Association, Tokyo

Kagono, T. (1988): Kigyo Paradigm no Henkaku (Change of Corporate Paradigm), Kodan-sha, Tokyo

Kono, T. (1985): Gendai no Keiei Senryaku (Corporate Strategy), Diamond-sha, Tokyo

Kono, T. (1987): Keieigaku Genri (Principles of Management), Hakuto-shobo, Tokyo

Kono, T. (1988): Henkaku no Kigyo Bunka (Change of Corporate Culture), Kodan-sha, Tokyo

Matsuura, K. (1984): Shafu no Kenkyu (Study of Corporate Culture), PHP, Tokyo

Organizational Science, Special Edition on Corporate Culture, 1983, Vol. 17, No.3

Umezawa, T. (1983): Soshiki Bunka no Shiten kara (View-points on Corporate Culture), Gyosei, Tokyo

Umezawa, T. (1986): Kigyo Bunka no Sozo (Creation of Corporate Culture), Yuhikaku, Tokyo

In English

Davis, S. M. (1984): Managing Corporate Culture, Ballinger Pub., MA

Deal & Kennedy (1982): Corporate Culture, Addison-Wesley, MA

Diesing, P. (1955): Non-economic Decision Making, Rowe & Mason, ed. Strategic Management & Business Policy, 1982, Addison-Wesley, MA

Frost, P. J. & others ed. (1985): Organizational Culture, Sage Pub., NY

Harris, S. G. (1989): A Shema-Based Perspective on Organizational Culture, a paper presented at Annual Meeting of Academy of Management, August, Washington, D.C.

Kilmann, R. H. (1984): Five Steps for Closing Culture-gaps; in Beyond The Quick Fix, Jossey Bass, CA

Kilmann, R. H. & others ed. (1986): Gaining Control of the Corporate Culture, Jossey Bass, CA Kilmann, R. H. & others ed. (1988): Corporate transformation, Jossey Bass, CA

Likert, R. (1967): The Human Organization, MacGraw-Hill, NY

Litwin, G. H. & Stringer, R.A. Jr. (1968): Motivation and Organizational Climate, Harvard Univ.

Morris, G. C. (1982): Psychology, an Introduction, Prentice-Hall, NJ

Nakajo, T. & Kono, T. (1989): Success Through Culture Change in a Japanese Brewery, , Long Range Plannig, December

Peters & Waterman (1982): In Search of Excellence, Harper & Row, NY

Roethlisberger & Dickson (1939): Management and the Worker, Harvard Univ.

Hofsteade, G. (1980): Culture's Consequences, Sage Pub., NY

Shein, E. (1961): Management Development as a Process of Influence, Sloan Management Review, May 1961

Shein, E. (1985): How Culture Forms, Develops, and Changes, in Kilmann & others ed.

Shein, E. (1985): Organization Culture & Leadership, Jossey-Base Publishers

Wilkins, A. L. & Ouchi, W. G. (1983): Efficient Cultures, Administrative Science Quarterly, Sept. 1983

Chapter 7 Strategic issues and long-range goals

The corporation has an inertia, and unless strategic issues are explored intentionally, the company will not be able to formulate an innovative strategy. An aggressive search for new strategic ideas will bring forth outstanding strategies which bear fruit in the future. The search for strategic issues is one of the most important processes in long-range planning.

7.1 The meaning of strategic issues

The strategic issue means three things: (a) opportunity and threat in the environment, (b) strength and weakness of the corporation, (c) new tentative ideas for new strategies. In this chapter, we will focus on the last one.

Strategic issues have a hierarchy, there are the following areas: Goals and philosophies – Product-market strategies – the resource structure – the operations.

A case of a Nihon Sanso (Oxygen) illustrates this issue finding process. The company firstly decided on the overall goals on the product-mix: the proportion of industrial goods to consumer goods would be 6 to 4 in the future.

The next part was a new corporate creed. The formulation of the new creed was necessary, because in the past the company was production-oriented, was not customer oriented, and it was too conservative, did not even cross the stone bridge. The new corporate creed placed emphasis on the customer orientedness, the merchant mind, and it stressed the challenge mind.

Thirdly, eight strategic issues were raised. They were (1) the improvement of profitability of present products, (2) new product development in the present industry, (3) new product development in the consumer industry, (4) internationalization, (5) strengthening of research and development capability, (6) change of organizational structure, (7) hange of corporate culture.

These philosophies and strategic issues were developed after the analysis of the environment and an internal analysis, by the top management committee, with information provided by the corporate planning department and the product divisions.

Then eight committees were formed to study these issues. Each committee was composed of one senior vice-president and several directors of the departments and a member from the corporate planning department. They studied the issues for one month and wrote reports to the senior management committee. Then all inside directors of the board stayed at a resort hotel for several days to again study the issues.

The issues were finally decided by the senior management committee, they became the core long-range strategy for the 21st century and was called the "NS-21 Plan".

Then, a three year plan was formed as an implementation plan. There are two kinds of medium-range plan has. The corporate level projects are either studied by head office project teams or by product divisions as assigned projects. The division specific plans are studied by the product divisions.

The finding process of strategic issues in this case is aggressive and analytical, and also uses a rather top down approach.

7.2 The process to find strategic issues

In some case, a strategic idea is suddenly brought in, and is decided by top management through intuitive judgment. At K company, everytime the president meets with the top management of other companies in foreign countries, he makes sudden agreements on licensing to introduce new products. Many new products turned out to be failure products. In an other company, a chance to buy a company was brought in, and the top management made a sudden decision on acquisition without enough information.

In another case, strategic ideas were generated after collecting enough information and after selecting from among many options, as was described in the Case of Nihon Sanso.

Thus, strategic ideas can be generated by either an intuitive approach or an analytical approach. An analytical approach starts from the collection of information, while the intuitive approach starts from idea presentation. How ideas are actually generated has been surveyed.

In Table 7.1, analytical idea generation means idea generation done by interactive communication between top management and lower management (A-c), from the collection of information (B-a), from broad policy (E-a), and by aggressive searches (F-a).

Intuitive idea generation is that done by a top down approach (A-a) or by a bottom up approach (A-b), the collection of ideas rather than from information (B-b), a random approach rather than by policy (E-b), or by ideas submitted from other sources (F-b). According to the survey in Table 7.1, the analytical approach is more frequently used than the intuitive approach. That is, information is collected and ideas are generated by an interactive process. It should be noted, however, that the random or piecemeal approach is also frequently used. Successful companies in planning (146 companies, subjective judgment) use analytical approaches more frequently. They collect more informations, present ideas in comprehensive planning, from policy and aggressive searches.

The mutual correlations coefficient is computed and it is shown in the Appendix, Table 7.3.b at the end of this chapter. This computation shows that the elements of analytical decisions have a high correlation coefficient, thus it can be one type of de-

Table 7.1   The manner of strategic decisions

Corporations with long-range plans	1979 327 co.	1985 384 co.	1989 249 co.
A a. Mostly by top management	14 (%)	25 (%)	18 (%) * ○
b. Mostly by bottom-up (by middle up)	32	25	33
c. Interactive ←	48	65	46
B a. Mostly from collection of information ←	78	67	79 * ○
b. Mostly from collection of ideas	13	21	17
C a. By the use of systems, such as life cycle analysis or PPM	8	7	8
b. Without the use of systems	82	82	97
D a. Mostly from comprehensive planning processes	20	22	25 * ○
b. Mostly from piecemeal searches	71	68	71 Δ
E a. Mostly from broad policy decisions ←	36	44	45 * ○
b. Mostly from random approaches	53	47	51 Δ
F a. Mostly from aggressive searches ←	53	51	56 * ○
b. Mostly by ideas submitted from outside sources, without agressive searches	36	38	40 Δ

(Notes)   1. Number indicates the percentage of responding corporations.
2. The arrow (←) indicates the use of an analytical approach.
3. Asterisks (∗) indicate that successful corporations in planning (146 co.) have higher frequencies of this method (< 5 %). Triangles (Δ) show less frequency.
4. Circles (○) indicate that hig performance corporations (30 companies) have higher frequency.

cision. Also, the elements of intuitive decisions have moderate correlations, thus it is another type of decision.

The relationship between decision-making style and company performance is analyzed. The high performance companies (30 companies) use the analytical decisions more frequently, as is indicated in Table 7.1.

As for the causes of strategic decision, the types of long-range planning are also investigated. The correlation between comprehensive and problem solving type long-range planning and the aggressive type of search has a high correlation. Thus, we can establish the following cause-effect relationship.

The style of long-range planning → the style of strategic decision making → high financial performance

However, we should notice that intuitive decisions are also used frequently. The intuitive decisions may have some areas of fitness. The intuitive decision has the following structure of decision.

(1)

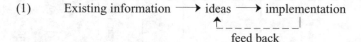

feed back

(2)

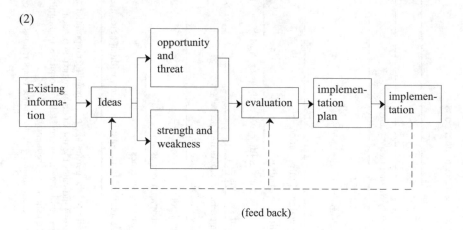

(feed back)

The first type is highly intuitive, but the second type is less intuitive, because the evaluation is done after the idea is presented.

The intuitive type of decision is actually used in two cases. (a) When the project is small. The cost of information processing is less for intuitive decisions, so it is appropriate for small projects. (b) When there is uncertainty. In this case, information is hard to collect and intuition is required. If possible, information is collected after the ideas are presented, or the results of implementation are fed back to the next decision. If the decision can be divisible, this is a sequential decision, or an incremental approach. (c) When creative ideas are required. In the intuitive approach one is freed from past information, knowledge and experience and one can obtain a fresh idea or a discontinuous concept. These may be the reason why many articles criticizing the analytical approach have recently appeared. (Eg. see Peters & Waterman 1982, which stresses the experimental approach and field data; Weick 1979, which emphasizes the intuitive approach. Also, Lindblom, 1959; Quinn, 1980.)

The analytical approach takes the following process (See Table 7.2):

(3)

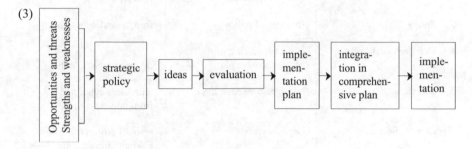

Notice that the process is somewhat the reverse of the second process in the above. This sort of decision is appropriate for (1) the large projects, such as the development of a large new product like new cars, new computers; or foreign direct investment, large replacement or expansion of manufacturing plants. (2) It is appropriate for projects in which the conflicting interests of people arise and on which persuasion is required. Information is useful for persuasion.

In the analytical process it is more expensive to process the information. The analytical process tends to arrive at similar ideas when similar information is collected by competitors. On the other hand, the analytical approach has two advantages. (a) One can obtain the best idea, or at least, one can find an alternative with less risks by performing enough analysis. (b) One can persuade others on the reliability of the plan by having sufficient information.

Table 7.2   Two types of decision-making processes for strategic issues

Processes \ Types	Analytical	Intuitive
1. Organizational process	interactive	top down or bottom-up
2. Information collection	from information	idea first
3. Policy	from broad policy	from a random approach
4. Comprehensive plan	in the processing of comprehensive plans	by piece-meal searches
5. Search	by aggressive searches	with ideas submitted from outside sources
Appropriate decisions	large projects	• small projects • when information is uncertain

(note)   This table is essentially a part of Table 3.2.

7.3 The organizational process

For the turn of the century, many companies started to form a project team to build a dream of the company in the 21st Century. One company publicly solicited their members throughout the company, many applied and the company selected about ten young members from among hundreds of applicants. They met on Saturday afternoon or on Sunday, sometimes stayed together at a hotel for days. They were supported by the planning department, to obtain information. They presented a report on strategic issues and visions of the company in the 21st Century. This sort of team has the potential to present new and fresh ideas. However, since it lacks power, the report has to be supported by the planning department and by top management.

The organizational process is surveyed and is shown in Table 7.1.b at the end of this chapter. The cases where issues are raised by the top management and through the discussion of the management committee have a high frequency of diffusion. The Nihon Sanso case belongs to this type. If the top management has enough information provided by the planning department, and if the top management has an innovative mind, then this approach might be able to find the basic issues of the firm. Implementation may be easier, because top management has power.

The presentation from the planning department, and the interaction between the planning department and the planning section of various departments has the merit of having enough information. The issues may be based on detailed experiences and information. In case of Taisei Construction Co., a large size report on issues and visions was prepared by the planning department. The use of project teams has the merit of mixing a variety of information and ideas. The team members may be high level directors (Bridgestone Co.), or middle class managers (Eisai Co.), or young staff (Lion Co., Shiseido).

The operating units and staff departments may present issues. In this process, some basic issues which do not belong to any existing departments will be lacking. The use of consultants is not very popular in Japan, but the members of cases are increasing, as is seen in Table 7.1.b.

7.4 Long-range goals

The goals of a long-range plan have a hierarchy. This hierarchy is comprised of four levels. The first is basic goals (A). They are stated in detail according to items, measurement, and desired levels for each year. Components of basic goals are growth, profitability, stability, and goals for the participants. The next are levels and policy on product market strategy (B), levels and policy on structure (C) and desired levels and policies on operation and productivity (D). These four have a means-end relationship. (B) and (C) are means to attain the (A) goals, so a plan is built by a sequence of (A) – (B) – (C) – (D), although sometimes a plan starts from (B).

Among these four areas, three areas (except basic goals (A)) are outlines of a long-range plan. Therefore, a survey on the goals also indicates the components of a long-range plan. Table 7.2.b shows what items are used for the goals of the long-range plan.

As basic goals, the growth rate (1, 1.2, 2, 10), goals on profitability (3, 12), goals for stability (4, 5, 11), and goals for the participant (6, 7, 8, 9), are important. Japanese corporations put emphasis on the growth of the company.

For the goals of profitability, the amount of profit, the rate of return on total capital and the rate of return on sales are frequently used. Earning per share is used to a lesser extent by Japanese corporations, but the frequency is increasing compared with the last survey. This may be due to the increased use of issuing new stock at market price (in many cases stocks are sold by par value to the present stock owners) and to the increased issue of convertible bonds in foreign countries. These trends increase the demand by shareholders that more attention be paid to earnings per share.

As a measurement of the rate of return on total capital (A3b), the ratio of profit before interest and tax divided by total assets has the highest frequency of diffusion.

Corporations in the U.S.A. are currently using this measurement. This measurement makes it possible to compare the rate of return with the general interest rate, and to compare the rate of return between companies with different debt ratios. And it also makes possible the comparison of the rates of return among different product divisions, in order to fix a cut-off rate for project planning. However the rate of return after interest and before tax (3-c), the rate of return after interest and tax (3-d) are used to an unexpected extent. The rates of return after interest and after tax may be used instead for the measurement of stability.

As goals of the product market strategy, the product mix, the ratio of new products and the policy for multinational management are considered as important. The policies for company acquisitions and business combinations have low frequency of diffusion.

For structural goals, the amount of capital expenditure, the policy on capital investment, the number of personnel, the amount of expenditures and the policy for research and development are considered as important. For operational goals, goals for productivity and the policy on rationalization (cost reduction) are emphasized.

7.5 Process of deciding the goal levels

According to our observation of many cases, deciding goal levels is done as follows:

Level of aspiration of goals

$\left. \right\}$ → Gaps of goals → Search for → Revised estimation → Filling → Attainable

Future estimated value of goals
when present strategies are followed   new strategy   of goals   of gaps   level of
                                                                                                                                   goals

How are levels of aspiration of goals formulated? In theory, one's level of aspiration is determined by the actual condition of reference groups. This theory can be applied to the goal level of corporations. For example, L Company looks for the actual level of comparable companies in the same industry, and selects the level of the best one-quarter. Usually this level is chosen by considering (a) the average value of all companies, (b) the value of excellent companies in the same industry and (c) the value of similar companies in the world.

The aspired level becomes a realizable level by filling the gap between aspirations and the expected value through implementation of new strategies.

7.6 The international comparison of goals

Comparative analysis of goals in the long-range planning process makes us understand what the similarities and differences of goals are in corporations (See Table 7.3).

There is a hierarchy of goals of the long range plan, i.e. basic goals, goals for product-market strategies, goals for structure or resources and goals for productivity. Here, only the basic goals and productivity goals are analyzed. It is generally said

Table 7.3   Comparison of goals of a long-range plan

	U.K. (%)	Japan (%)	U.S. (%)
Year of survey	1980	1985	1975
Number of company	74 co.	384 co.	23 co.
A. Basic Goals			
(1) Sales	51	94	63
(2) Rate of growth (sales or profit)	59	71	65
(3) Profit			
(a) Amount of profit	53	84 *	57
(b) Profit ratio to total capital (before interest and tax)	⎫	27	⎫
(c) Profit ratio to total capital (after interest, before tax)	⎬ 59	20	⎬ 52
(d) Profit ratio to total capital (after interest and tax)	⎭	20	⎭
(e) Profit ratio to equity capital	18	17	57
(f) Profit ratio to sales	37	64 *	44
(g) Standard deviation of profit (or limit of profit in the worst case)	0	11 *	9
(h) Earning per share	37	23 *	52
(4) Market share	50	40	48
(5) Capital structure	41	27	71
(6) Dividend	30	40	39
(7) Share price	8	4	26
(8) Employee compensation	8	35 *	17
(9) Quality level of products	32	22	17
(10) Basic policy of growth	49	57	70
(11) Basic policy of stability	14	31 *	30
(12) Basic policy on profit	47	57	61
(13) Basic policy on social responsibility	16	20	13
B. Operational issues (productivity goals)			
(1) Target value added	15	31 *	4
(2) Investment per employee	10	11	9
(3) Target productivity of labour	37	46	13
(4) Ratio of assets turnover	30	30	39
(5) Policy for cost reduction	54	35 *	44

(Note) (1) The star (*) indicates the level of significance is 10 percent, comparison is between the U.K. and Japan only.

(2) All mail surveys were conducted by the author with the cooperation of London Business School and Graduate School of management, UCLA, respectively.

that U.S. and U.K. companies are short-term profit-oriented and that Japanese companies are long-term growth-oriented. According to the survey, there are more similarities than differences, probably because the responding companies in the U.S. and U.K. are more long-term growth-oriented than the non-responding companies.

In both countries, sales, profit and market share are important.

There are some differences, however. In the U.S. and U.K., return on total capital (or total assets) and earnings per share are important. Simply speaking, financial goals are more strongly emphasized.

In Japan, the amount of sales and profit (both used as indicators of growth), employee compensation, value added and labour productivity have higher priority. Simply speaking, growth and employee welfare are considered as more important.

What are the reasons for these differences? The U.S. and U.K. are more shareholder-oriented, because of stronger pressures from shareholders and institutional investors; and because there is a threat of being taken over by some other company if the price of the shares are low. The Japanese company is less shareholder-oriented. Most of the funds come from banks, and banks regard the corporation with a long-term view. The need for growth is also stronger in order to provide jobs for employees who are employed for their whole working lives.

7.7 Long-term visions and corporate philosophies

A. Long-term visions

Many companies started to formulate long-term visions of their company. The reasons are that the 21st century is approaching, and that the companies wanted to make public the directions of restructuring itself in the changing environment.

The vision is a sort of long-range strategy, but it is a little different from a formal long-range strategy. (1) The time horizon is usually very long, more than ten years. (2) It describes the future size of the company, the future domain and the product mix. The case of Kirin Brewery and of NKK in Table 7.6 shows these features. It also describes the image of the company. (3) Unlike formal strategy, it is not confidential, is made public and thus it intends to motivate people and to form a image of the company. Unlike formal strategy, it is not detailed. It is supported by the long-range plan, but the vision itself does not have any schedule.

The formation of future visions is usually done by head office, not by divisions. Project teams are frequently used. The project team is sometimes organized by public solicitation and selection of young people. In other cases members are appointed. In many cases, it is built by the planning office.

It is revised in three or in five years, when necessary. NKK, for example, revised the Future Vision to the New Future Vision in three years.

The effects of long-term visions are three fold. (1) They orient the company to a new direction. The vision usually shows a large change of product mix or the change of domain of the company. Thus, the innovative company will build visions, but the conservative company does not formulate visions. (2) It shows to the outside public an image of an excellent company. It enhances the image of the company. (3) It motivates people, by showing the future dream of the company, by showing that the company will be a worldwide excellent company. The member will be able to imagine that their status and remuneration will be improved.

Table 7.4   Long-term visions and corporate philosophies

A. Visions
  1. **Kirin Brewery**
      1. Sales ... 1,700 billion yen. It will be ioncreased from 1,250 billion yen in 1990 to 1,700 billion yen in 2000.
      2. Sales of non-beer products will be 60% of sales.
         Diversify into biotechnology, construction engineering, information systems and service industries.
      3. The corporation will become of global importance.

  2. **NKK** Future vision in 1983 (growth oriented)
      1. Sales will increas from 1,500 billion yen in 1983 to 2,000 billion yen in 2000.
      2. Sales of steel will be less than 50%. Company will enter into high growth areas, such as new materials, machineries, services.

  New future vision in 1988 (emphasis on profitability)
      1. Basic policy
         • Strengthen steel and related core business
         • Enter into high growth and high value added area
      2. Corporate image
         • High technology
         • Devotion enhancement of home life and industry infrastructure
      3. Size and product mix
         • Sales 1,600 billion yen in 2000
           (1) Core business
               • Steel ... 50%
               • Construction engineering ... 25%
           (2) New business
               • City development ... 12.5%
               • New materials, electronics, biotechnology ... 12.5%

B. Corporate philosophy
  1. **Hitachi's** Odaira Spirit
      1. Devotion to society in quality products for the society
      2. Frontier spirit, self-help and aggressiveness
      3. Harmony and friendliness

(continued)

2. **Sony** spirit
   Sony is a trail blazer, always a seeker of the unknown.
   Sony will never follow old trails, yet to be trod.
   Through this progress **Sony** wants to serve mankind.

3. **Honda's** management policy
   1. Proceed always with ambitions and youthful spirits
   2. Respect sound theory, develop fresh ideas, and make the most effective use of time

4. Management philosophy of **NEC**
   Throug C & C (computers and communication)
   NEC tries to improve the understanding of people in the world
   Tries to help realize the afluent world
   Where people can express fully their own personalities

5. **Canon's** change of "corporate objectives"
   1. We will create the best products, we will devote ourselves to the enhancement of world culture
   2. We will create an ideal company, and will prosper forever

   ↓ changed in 1987

   To achieve the success as a global corporation, we believe that mutually rewarding coexistence must be the guiding principle of all our actions

6. **Nissan Motor's** change
   Strength in Technology

   ↓

   Feel the beat (Feel the sentiment of the consumer)

7. **Keihin Railway's** change
   Enhance the welfare of the society through railway transportation

   ↓

   Devote to the society through the activities to improve the urban life.

8. New Image of **Kenwood**
   1. High quality company
   2. Pioneering company, top runner in technology
   3. Sensitive to the changes in society
   4. Company as a polyhedron, a congregation of divergent individualities
   5. Employees are not afraid of failure.

(continued)

Corporate creed of **NKK**
1. Corporate philosophy
   - To take advantage of future needs, to supply the best quality goods from material to service
   - To devote ourselves to the construction of an affluent human environment through the supply of industrial and domestic goods
   - To have a global view, to look into the future, to renew ourselves continuosly, to build a strong company
2. Basic policy
   - To construct a profitable company
   - To develop new business and diversify
   - To promote would wide business
   - To try to change corporate culture

3. Code of bahavior
   - Look to the outside world
   - Challenge all the time, take aggressive action
   - Express your individuality
   - Be profit conscious

B. Corporate philosophy

Most Japanese corporations have a clearly stated corporate philosophy. The book on the excellent companies in the U.S., written by Peters and Waterman (1982), also found that excellent companies have a publicly stated corporate philosophy.

Corporate philosophy means a statement on the selected essence of mission, social responsibility, goals, product-market strategies, and guides for behavior. It is stated in a few words, in the words and symbols which appeals to the emotional feelings of people. It states the basic common value and the basic direction of the company. It is expressed in the company creed. It is called ideology, the entrepreneurial spirit, style of management, ethos.

The corporate philosophy is different from the corporate vision in many ways. It stresses the core values of the corporation. The corporate philosophy covers wider areas of decisions, and it contains the cord of the behavior of employees. It gives the direction and the policy rather than quantitative goals.

The corporate philosophy does not specify the time of achievement, it should be used for longer than the long-term visions.

We understand that the corporate philosophy is stated in the corporate creed, that the both are the same. The corporate creed has three parts. The first one states the basic goals of the company, their mission in society and their social responsibility. Devotion to society, quality products, consumer orientedness, enhancement of employee welfare are frequently used words. The second part describes basic policy on management, that is, basic policy on decision making, on new product development, on research and development, on marketing and on creativity.

The third part states the desired cord of behavior. Attitudes towards the organization, towards the job, towards seniors, colleagues, subordinates, and towards self are stated. (Kono, 1988)

The case of NKK in Table 7.3 illustrates these three parts. The corporate creed is an explicit expression of the corporate philosophy. We consider that corporate creed is the same as corporate philosophy. Some companies may not have stated a corporate creed, but may have an implicit corporate philosophy, In this case, the philosophy does not become the shared value of all members. We study here a stated corporate philosophy, that is the stated corporate creed.

Hitachi's corporate philosophy is comprised of three statements, it affects the corporate culture and the strategy to a great extent. It was established by the founder Odaira, through his long-term experiences. The devotion to society means that quality products should be supplied to society, resulted in a strategy which placed emphasis on quality, at the sacrifice of marketing. The frontier spirit means aggressive attitudes, to respect creative and original technology. This resulted in the profit center system of the factory. Harmony and philosophy means mutual respect, to respect the opinions of each employee, to make full discussion on problems.

Although this philosophy had some dysfunctions, such as too much emphasis on technological strength at the sacrifice of marketing, the profit center system resulted in an emphasis on short term profit, but it was the important source of the strong competitive power and the vitalized corporate culture of Hitachi.

The Hitachi spirit is indoctrinated to employees through the speeches of managers, through panels on the wall of the plant, and various movements and through the training of new recruits.

The Sony spirit also provides for a basic direction on the way of thinking, particularly on creative new product development.

The company which has a clear philosophy is called a company with a thick corporate culture, and the company which does not have it is called an organization with a thin culture.

The effects of having corporate philosophy, having a thick culture are as follows:

Firstly, the philosophy makes clear the common value of the company, enhances the emotional upheaval of employees. The employees do not necessarily behave by rational judgment, but rather emotionally respond to corporate philosophy, to the symbol of the company, to the company song. Japanese people are trained as such since elementary school, because every school has a school creed, school song, school flag and school symbol. Sharing in common values enhances the sense of identification with the organization and makes detailed rules unnecessary.

Secondly, business creed makes clear the mission, the social responsibility, the goals of the organization, and helps employees to understand the meaning of daily work, and promotes the voluntary initiatives of the members, by satisfying their self-realization needs.

Thirdly, it clarifies the important directions of the company, it relates what information is important, what ideas are respected, thus it simplifies decision-making. At Sony, the creation of real new products have a high priority.

Fourthly, it communicates the image of the company to the outside world. It is one of the activities used to clarify corporate identity. (Some opinion on this see, Peters and Waterman, 1982)

There are some limitations to corporate philosophy. Every principle has its dysfunctions. For example, an emphasis on creative technology at Hitachi resulted in the neglect of the marketing viewpoint. The other problem is that it will homogenize the organization, as happened at Matsushita, when their philosophy is over-emphasized. The harmony between a uniform culture and a differentiated culture is important. Lastly, philosophies deteriorate and become obsolescent as the environment changes. Thus the revision of the philosophy becomes necessary.

There are several principles for success regarding the contents of corporate philosophy. Successful philosophies have the following characteristics: (1) They are customer oriented. "Customers first" is the popular word. (2) They emphasize innovation. "Frontier spirit" is one of the typical words. (3) They respect people. The wording "work for your self" is used at Honda. (Same findings, Peters and Waterman, 1982) These characteristics are seen in Table 7.6.

The mistaken philosophy goes against these principles. The corporate creed of bankrupt Eidai Industries (home construction), for example, had the following creed. "Use your brain to produce ideas; those who cannot have ideas work hard with sweat; those who cannot have ideas nor sweat should leave the company quietly" This creed does not respect people. Van Jacket (suits for young people) also went bankrupt. The president also emphasized "Enjoy your job, enjoy your life". It lacked customer orientation and lacked rational thinking.

The change of corporate philosophy is needed because of the change in the values of society, the value of employees and the change of the product-market strategy.

Canon changed the corporate creed, as seen in Table 7.6. Canon recognized that one way communication and supply of goods does not result in the prosperity of the corporation, that mutual prosperity and double loop communication is necessary for success.

Nissan Motor changed their technology oriented philosophy to a 'feeling sensitive' philosophy. This change resulted in a remarkable success in new car development.

Keihin Railway also changed their philosophy to change corporate culture to a more aggressive one.

To change the corporate philosophy in many corporations, teams are formed to study new philosophy. In old times, the creed was determined by the founder. Recently the participation of various levels of employees were used in many cases, and they collected a large amount of information to arrive at the draft of a new philosophy. Participation and the analytical approach is a recent trend in the changing of philosophy.

Corporate philosophy should have both continuity and the ability to change to adapt to the transition of external and internal environments. Generally speaking, the revision of it in every five years is effective in freeing it from obsolescence.

Some companies think that their old, traditional philosophies are not outdated. Hitachi and Sony think as such, because they put emphasis on change and innovation.

7.8 The implementations of the long-term strategy

Long-term visions and long-term strategies tend to be considered as the products of elites or only the dream of top management. They are considered as something different from daily operations, different from the thinking of laymen in the lower echelons. The future vision may meet with the resistance of the departments which may lose their dominant status in the company. These problems may disturb the formation of implementation plans, or the inclusion of them in the medium-range plan.

At NKK, the president visited the operating front a number of times to explain the new future vision. These sort of efforts from top management are needed to implement the future strategy.

In order to indoctrinate new corporate philosophy, many companies deliver to every employee a small card which describes the new philosophy, and sometimes it is read in the morning meeting. In every speech of the president, the new philosophy is emphasized. It is referred to in many kinds of planning documents.

Summary

1. Organizations tend to have inertia. The aggressive search for strategic issues enables the organization to take advantage of future opportunities, not to simply follow the changes of the environment.
2. To find the strategic issues and to form the original ideas of the strategy, there are four approaches, – seen in Table 3.2. In this chapter, the two approaches, the analytical and intuitive approaches are studied. The survey shows that both approaches are used. Large projects are fit for analytical approaches and small projects are fit for intuitive approaches. The information processing cost of the analytical approach is more expensive. Successful companies in planning and high performance companies use the analytical approach more frequently. One problem is that, if jumping and creative thinking is not added to the process, the new ideas of analytical process tend to be similar to competitors.
3. As an organizational process, top management does the study of strategic issues most frequently. Recently, project teams of young managers are used to formulate the long-term visions of many companies.
4. Long-range goals have a hierarchy: basic goals, product-market strategy, resource structure and operations are the levels of goals.
5. The items of goals and the levels of goals are determined by the holders of key resources.
6. Japanese corporations place more emphasis on long-term growth, and the welfare of employees.
7. The long-term visions make public the future size and the future product mix or the domain of the company. The corporate philosophy is the declared basic value of the company. It

states the selected essence of the missions, goals, product-market strategy and code of behavior. The wording tries to appeal to the emotion of employees. Clear visions and clear philosophies are useful to motivate people and to vitalize the corporate culture.

As the external and internal environment evolves, the corporate philosophy needs to be changed, and this is one of the important processes of long-range planing.

8. In order to overcome the resistance against new visions, top management has to make efforts to diffuse the thoughts. The new vision tends to be seen as something like a "floating dream without roots" over the real world. The indoctrination of new philosophy also needs large efforts. Many companies distribute to every employee a small card which describes the new philosophy.

(References: Kono, 1985; Kono, 1988; Cyert & March, 1963; Richards, 1978; Steiner and Miner, 1977; Sutton, 1956; Yavitz, 1988; Johnson, 1989; Peters and Waterman, 1982)

Table 7.1.b Organizaitional processers used to discover strategic issues

Years	1985	1989
Corporations with long-range plans	384 co.	249 co.
A. By Top management	30 %	31 (%)
B. Through discussions in the management committee	54	50
C. Presentation from corporate planning departments	38	42
D. Through an interaction beween corporate planning departments and the planning sections of each department	40	52 *
E. Through a meeting of top management staying at a hotel	3	6
F. By a project team get up to discover key	17	20 *
G. With questionnaire surveys distributed to various departments	2	3
H. From specific investigations and presentations of various departments	65	66
I. External consultants	–	16

(note)   1. Asterisks (*) indicate that successful companies in planning (146 co., subjective judgement), have higher frequencies.
2. The number indicates the percentage of responding corporations.

Table 7.2.b   Goals of a long-range plan
In what specific terms are the goals and policies of your long-range plan stated?
(Please tick as many as neccessary.)

Corporations' with long-range plan	1979 327 co.	1985 384 co.
1. Sales	88 (%)	94 (%)
1.2 Value added	36	35
2. Rate of growth (Sales or profit)	64	71
3. Profit a. Amount of profit	88	84
b. Profit ratio to total assets (before interest and tax)	–	27
c. Profit ratio to total assets (after interest, before tax)	42	20
d. Profit ratio to total assets (after interest and tax)	–	20
e. Profit ratio to equity capital	27	17
f. Profit ratio to sales	61	64
g. Standard deviation of profit	16	11
h. Earning per share	18	23
4. Market share	41	40
5. Capital structure	32	27
6. Dividend	43	40
7. Share price	2	4
8. Employee compensation	39	35
9. Quality level of products	14	22
10. Basic policy of growth	50	57
11. Basic policy of stability	34	31
12. Basic policy on profit	51	57
13. Basic policy on social responsibility	19	20

Basic goals

Table 7.2.b   Goals of a long-range plan

In what specific terms are the goals and policies of your long-range plan stated? (Please tick as many as necessary.) (cont.)

Corporations' with long-range plan	1979 327 co.	1985 384 co.
B. Product-market strategy		
1. Product mix (Ratio of new products)	54 (%)	58 (%)
2. Ratio of exports	32	36
3. Policy for diversification	56	69
4. Policy for new product development	46	55
5. Policy for company acquisition and business combination	3	9
6. Policy for multi-national management	28	34
7. Policy for sales channel	28	30
8. Policy for strengthening the competitive ability	54	65
C. Structure		
1. Amount of capital investment	63	71
2. Number of personnel	78	78
3. Expenditure for research and development	25	44
4. Amount of policy cost such as cost for advertising or employee education	13	21
5. Policy for capital investment	61	70
6. Policy for recruitment	52	64
7. Policy for research and development	40	58
8. Policy for purchasing the materials	12	12
9. Policy for organizational structure	28	35
10. Policy for improvement of communication	8	18
D. Operational issues (Productivity goals)		
1. Target value added	31	29
2. Investment per employee	11	14
3. Target productivity of labour	46	39
4. Ratio of assets turnover	30	27
5. Other operating ratios		23
6. Policy for cost reduction	25	40

(Notes)   The number indicates the percentage of responding corporations

Table 7.3.b Correlation coefficient matrix of decision styles

		A			B		C		D		E		F	
		a	b	c	a	b	a	b	a	b	a	b	a	b
	Corporations with long-range plan													
A	a. Mostly by top management								0.18				0.19	
	b. Mostly by bottom-up (or middle up)													
	c. Interactive ←									0.21			0.18	
B	a. Mostly from collection of information ←							0.19						
	b. Mostly from collection of ideas													0.15
C	a. By the use of systems, such as life cycle analysis or PPM													
	b. Without the use of systems				0.19					0.22				
D	a. Mostly in comprehensive planning process	0.18												
	b. Mostly by piecemeal search			0.21				0.22			0.50	0.51	0.40	0.42
E	a. Mostly from broad policy ←								0.50				0.51	
	b. Mostly by random approach									0.51			0.51	0.52
F	a. Mostly by aggressive search ←	0.19			0.18				0.40	0.42	0.52			
	b. Mostly by ideas submitted from outside source					0.15						0.52		

(note) 1. Only the positive correlations are listed
2. Level of significance < 10 %
(3) The arrows (←) indicate the analytical decisions

Chapter 8 Development of the product-market strategy

The product-market strategy affects directly the performances of the corporation, and it is one of the core elements of long-range planning. High performance companies have products in high growth areas, have high market shares, and change the product mix flexibly as the market and technology change.

The product-market strategy is a selection of the environment, to find out the fittest domain. The subjects of the product-market strategy are, the product-mix, vertical integration, competition strategy, foreign direct investment, and external or internal growth strategy.

8.1 Approaches of the product-market strategy

The product-market strategy can be analyzed by various approaches.

A. Growth or retrenchment (growth – share matrix model)

The attitude towards growth may be positive or negative, depending on the policy of top management, or on the status of the product. The product portfolio model classifies strategy into several policies which fit with the status of products. The typical models are as follows:

(1) Share increasing strategy. Increase of position in the market is the most important, profit is not important, resources are allocated to specific products fully with high priority. This strategy is fit for "question mark" products, if the product is a hopeful product. The product should be supported by a cash cow product.
(2) Growth strategy by maintaining share. The total market of products is in the high growth stage of the life cycle, and if the share is maintained, sales can increase. Share maintaining is most important, the profit could be moderate. The resources are allocated with high volume. This strategy is appropriate for the "star" product.
(3) Profit strategy. Present profit is the most important, and it is used for supporting question mark and star products. The investment should be moderate. This is appropriate for the cash cow product.
(4) Market concentration and asset reduction.

(5) Liquidation or divesture strategy.
   These two are negative strategies which try to reduce the market share. They are used for "dog" products and "question marks" which are evaluated as hopeless.
(6) Turnaround strategy. If lost share can be recovered, every effort is taken to improve the position and resources are moderately allocated. This could be applied to products which traditionally had a high market share, but lost the share lately. (These explanations were mostly taken from Hofer and Shendel, 1978. See also Henderson, 1979; Rothchild, 1976; Hax, 1984)

This model is well known among Japanese corporate planners and is applied to a certain extent. However, there are two problems with this model. Firstly, the core product, or cash cow product, will become weak, will lose market share and eventually lose profit by the "profit strategy", by the negative strategy, by neglecting aggressive investment to improve the product, to maintain market share. Honda (in motorcycles, once a cash cow product) and Kirin (beer) followed this strategy, lost market share and now follow aggressive strategies. Secondly, the liquidation or divestment of the dog are difficult in Japanese corporations, because of life time employment. The divestment is usually the closing of a plant, not the sale of it to other company. It is carried out slowly, so that the employee can be transferred to growth products, instead of discharging them.

There are some other models on growth or retrenchment, of the company as a whole. Rowe states the following model (Rowe et al., 1985, chap. 4)

(0) status quo, (1) concentration, (2) horizontal integration, (3) vertical integration, (4) diversification, (5) joint venture, (6) retrenchment, (7) divesture, (8) liquidation, (9) innovation.

Among the above, 0, 1, 6, 7, 8 and 9 are negative strategies and 2, 3, 4 and 5 are positive growth strategies. Many Japanese corporations take the growth strategies.

B. Growth vector model

This model shows the direction, and is typically stated by Ansoff, and is stated by many authors. Ansoff's model states four types, market penetration, product development, market development and diversification. Diversification is classified into six types, horizontal diversification, vertical integration, marketing and technology related, marketing related, technology related and conglomerate diversification (Ansoff, 1965, chapter 6 and 7)

His model is a little simplified by other authors, and Chart 8.1, Model A is Rowe's description (Rowe et al., 1985)

On the horizontal axis, the marketing relations of new products with existing products, or marketing distances are indicated, on the vertical axis technological relations or the technological distance of new products are shown. Thus the distance of new products are indicated by this chart and synergy relations are used to measure the distance.

Table 8.1   Growth vector

(Model A)

Market options / Technology options	Existing market	Expanded market	New market
Present technology (product)	Penetration	Aggressive promotion	Enter into new market
Improved technology (product)	Improvement	Differentiation	Create awareness
New technology (product)	Replacement	Extend product line	Unrelated diversification

(Note)   Adapted, with some modification, from Rowe, 1982, chapter 8.

(Model B) (KONO model)

Use / Technology	Existing	New use	
		Marketing related	Marketing unrelated
Existing	Improved product	Marketing and technology related product	Technology related product
New technology	Replacement product	Marketing related products	Unrelated products

Model B assumes that the difference in life cycle of new products from existing products is important, so the difference of the use of products is measured. The products of the same use cannot change the product life cycle. New products with new uses are classified by the marketing relationship with the existing products and by the technological relationship with existing products. (Kono, 1987)

These models can be used to generate ideas, to find out any new ideas in the segment of the matrix, because the combination is an important approach to generate ideas. This model can be used to locate strategic ideas already presented, and to evaluate ideas. The distance will show the risks involved, and will suggest resource strategies to overcome the weaknesses. Alliances and/or acquisitions could be used for unrelated new products.

This model emphasizes synergy, and is quite different from PPM and the life cycle model. This model does not consider the position on the stage of life cycle, nor the growth rate of the new products.

This model deals with strategy on the product mix, not the strategy of vertical integration nor foreign direct investment.

C. Long-term growth model

The company follows a similar pattern during long-term growth. Greiner states five stages. At phase one, making and selling is the management focus, and organizational structure is informal under an owner manager. At phase two, efficiency of operations is the focus and organizational structure is centralized and a functional one. At phase three, expansion of the market is the focus, the organization becomes decentralized. At phase four, consolidation of the organization is the focus, and product groups are formed. At phase five, problem solving and innovation is the focus, matrix teams are frequently used. He states different organizational structures appropriate for each stage, and problems in each stage. (Greiner, 1972)

Galbraith and Nathanson also state four stages: single product, single product and vertical integration, related diversification and multinational management plus diversification. They state also the organizational structures, research and development, performance evaluations and leadership styles which are fit for each stage. (Galbraith and Nathanson, 1978)

These long-term growth models are almost the same as the growth pattern of Cannon illustrated in Chart 9.2. These models are useful for establishing long-term future visions.

D. Leader or follower by the timing of entry

Some companies take strategy to develop new products as a first entry all the time, while other companies take a policy of entering the market as second entries. Ansoff and Stewart classify these strategies into four. (1) The technical leader is always the first to enter, they put an emphasis on research and have long-term horizons. Sony may belong to this type. (2) The product innovator is second to enter. It emphasizes development, and adaptation is quick. Matsushita and Ajinomoto may belong to this type. (3) The nicher is not the first to run, it specializes in a certain segment. Honda may be an example in the motor car industry. (4) The follower is late to enter, but is strong in cost reduction, cheap prices are their competitive strength. Watch manufacturers in Asian countries may be examples. (Ansoff & Stewart, 1967).

These typologies suggest possible strategic options for late enterers, which are fit for their resource capabilities.

E. Leader or follower by the size of share of market

Some companies hold the largest share of a market for many years, whilst other companies have smaller shares continuously. There are appropriate strategies by the size of the share of market. Kotler states four types. (1) The market leader has the largest share, and a full line policy is the typical strategy. (2) The challenger is the second largest share holder, like Yamaha against Honda in the motorcycle market. It will challenge with cheaper prices or better quality, or develop stronger channels. Many Japanese corporations have been challengers in motor cars (Toyota and Nissan), copier (Ricoh and Canon), construction equipment (Komatsu) in the world market. (For an interesting analysis of Japanese challengers, see Hamel and Prahald, 1990). (3) The follower has the third position in the market, and it imitates the leader in price, quality and service. This type can be found in raw material industries. (4) The nicher has a small share, but it is specialized in producing niche products in which large share holders are not interested, such as high price goods (cameras and cars), order made goods (printings), or used goods (used cars). (Kotler, 1980, chap 11)

This model is useful to develop specific strategies unique to the size of market share. This model is different from Ansoff's model, in that this model does not analyze the timing of entry.

8.2 Options of product-market strategies and basic principles

1. Options of product-market strategy

The product-market strategy aims to select the environment. There are five options, as seen in Table 8.2.

(1) The product-mix or diversification. This strategy is to select the use of the products or the needs of consumers which the products intend to satisfy. To separate the fate of the company from the product life cycle is the major goal.
(2) Vertical integration aims to replace the market mechanism with hierarchy, or to internalize the outside trade. It could be either backward integration or forward integration. The major objectives are to reduce uncertainty and to transfer technology.
(3) Multinational management, or foreign direct investment, aims to transfer the core technology and management skill to foreign countries and to produce goods instead of exporting. The objectives are, to replace export (an export replacement type), to produce goods at a foreign production center and export them (a production center type) or to obtain natural resources (a vertical integration type).
(4) The competition strategy aims to increase or to hold the share of the market.

Table 8.2   Relations between five product-market strategies

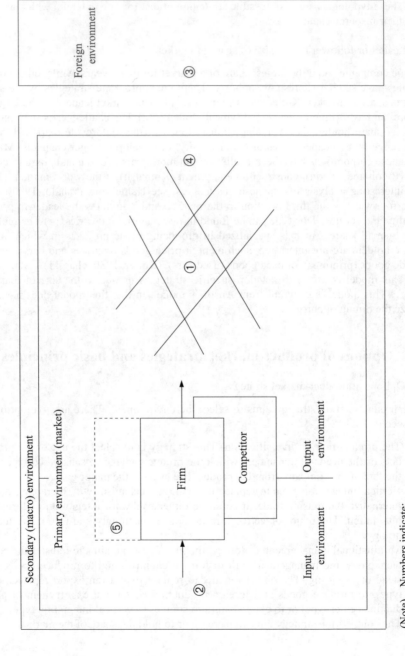

(Note)   Numbers indicate:
① Product-mix, ② Vertical integration, ③ multi-national management, ④ Competition, ⑤ External growth

(5) The external growth strategy. This includes purchase of patents, strategic alliances, joint ventures, purchase of assets, acquisition of other companies. The
characteristics of this strategy is to obtain a completed system of resources, and
also of products.

The relationship between these six strategic options are shown in Table 8.2. The
product-mix strategy aims to select the habitat or domain. The vertical integration is
to expand the border of the system. The foreign direct investment aims to transfer the
superior capability to foreign countries. The competition strategy aims to increase the
share in the existing market. The external growth aims to increase the resource structure. The growth stage model is one of the theories which state the timing or sequential relationship of these strategic options.

In order to succeed in these strategic options, there are key principles which dom-
inate these strategies. What principles are related to what strategic options is shown
in Table 8.3.

We will explain these principles very briefly. Product differentiation aims to avoid
the price competition. It is to differentiate products from the competitor's product, by
changing the design, packaging, naming, services, advertisement and sales channels.
The essential differentiations are quality and cost. By this product differentiation the
company can create a "price indifference zone" (Gutenberg 1964).

Market segmentation aims to recognize that the market is not homogeneous and to
differentiate products and services to fit into segments.

The stages of the product life cycle determine the profit and growth rate of the
product.

Time-based competition is a newly recognized principle on the advancement of
information technology. Computerized information systems can 'compress' time.
The POS system, CIM, CAD and CAM systems shorten the time required for delivery, for purchasing, for production and for the designing of new products. This
principle applies to new product development, for competition. Different methods
and the external growth, also shorten the time required for entry.

The experience curve accelerates the advantage of high market share. This principle means that the average cost is determined by the accumulated volume of production, not by the annual production amount.

The economy of scope is a slightly different concept. This means that a variety of
products with different specification can be produced like a single product by the use
of factory automation. This can be combined with the experience curve principle.

The theory of plant location determines the location of plants in foreign countries.

The strength in common basic technology can be formed by long-range product
strategies. From this strength, the company can develop new products in short periods of time, and can have strengths in every area of the strategy.

'Synergy' is the complementary relations or mutually helping relations between a
number of products by the common use of research, production facilities and marketing channels. This is the basic principle on product mix and vertical integration.

Table 8.3 Options of product-market strategies and key principles

Principles \ Product market strategies	1. Product mix and new product development	2. Vertical integraton	3. Multi-national management	4. Competition	5. External growth
1–1 Product differentiation	O			O	
1–2 Market segmentation	O			O	
1–3 Life cycle model	O				
1–4 Time based competition	O			O	O
2–1 Experience curve and economy of scope				O	
2–2 Theory of plant location			O		
3–1 Strength in common basic technology	O	O	O	O	O
3–2 Synergy	O	O			
3–3 Economy of size of firm		O	O	O	O
3–4 Transplantation of superior technology		O	O		

(Note) (1) Circles (O) indicate the dominating relations
(2) 1–1 ~ 1–4 are marketing related principles, 2–1 ~ 2–2 are production related principles, 3–1 ~ 3–4 are resource structure related principles.

The economy of size of the firm explain the advantage of the large company. The large company can have a competent team of top management, high quality middle managers and powerful research laboratories.

Superior technology can be transplanted to vertically integrated component manufactures and to foreign plants. The knowledge is a "public good" and can be transplanted without cost. The technology in technology intensive industries can be transplanted like a floating boat, to any weather and to any market, if skillful (above certain level) labours are available. Superiority in technology and management skill are the most important competitive edges in foreign direct investment and in quasi-vertical integration. (References. There are many books dealing with the strategic options, but not so many books clearly state the basic principles of this. Kono, 1985, tries to explain their basic principles. On diversification and vertical integration, see Penrose, 1966; Gort, 1962; Rumelt, 1974; Channon, 1973; on vertical integration, Williamson, 1975; Harrigan, 1983; on foreign direct investment, Robock et al., 1977;

Rugman et al., 1985; on competition, Porter, 1985; Teece Ed., 1987; on external growth, Muramatu, 1989; Marren, 1985)

8.3 The process of transformation

The process of transformation or the roadmap of transition is an important subject of long-range planning. Some companies have failed in diversification because it was too fast, without accumulating enough knowledge. Other companies failed because of too large capital investment, too fast expansion. And another company failed because the timing of entry was too late. There are not many studies on the process of transformation. We will study three principles to determine the process of transformation.

1. Decrease of uncertainty

The new project has many unknown aspects and involves many risks. The step-by step approach, from the known area to proceed to the unknown area, will reduce risks. Yamato Transportation, for example, introduced computerized information systems from a partial network to a total system. Matsushita started foreign direct investment from the production of small batteries. Through learning about the small scale production of batteries, the company was able to accumulate knowledge and then expand to the large scale production of many electric home appliances. Canon starts with exports, the construction of a sales network, then constructs a manufacturing plant. These cases are examples of sequential decisions used to reduce risks (On detailed analysis on decision under uncertainty, see Chapter 13, on incremental decisions, Quinn, 1980).

In the case of turnaround from depressed financial performance, the decrease of uncertainty is also an important principle. Usually, turnaround starts from cost reduction in present products and then goes to new product developments, because cost reduction has less risks than new ventures do. (Hofer, 1986). The turnaround of Kenwood (a stereo manufacturer, sales in 1990 were ¥165 million) is am example. The company experienced a loss in 1980. The reasons were, the company placed too much emphasis on high price, high quality, products, whilst the market was rather moving towards increased demand for cheaper and popular products. The company took many actions to reduce costs. Firstly, it sold out ¥1 million of excessive inventory of unsold products, it sold unused land, it stopped new recruitment and it discontinued their recording business. Then it began to take positive action. It entered into car audios in 1980, it was technologically related product with almost no risks. Then it developed the digital compact disc player, increased export to the US and to Europe. The company started to change the CI (corporate identity) and changed their name from Trio to Kenwood in 1986. It constructed a new plant in Singapore in 1987, and entered into the telephone market. This case shows that the strategy for turnaround proceeds from less risky measures to risky, but more profitable, measures.

Uncertainty also arises from internal conflict. New projects may not be implemented because of resistance. A step-by-step approach is again needed to change the minds of people so that people can accept the change of strategy. In the case of NKK, in order to implement the restructuring of the steel business, and to diversify into related areas, the following steps were taken.

NKK wants to change the product mix from a specialized company in steel (about 74% of sales come from steel, the remainder from construction engineering and machines in 1988) to a diversified company (50% of sales from steel, 25% from construction engineering and 25% from city development, new materials, electronics and biotechnology), because steel was in the mature stage, and in 1986 the company experienced a deficit. To change the product-mix and to restructure the company, the change of minds and the prevention of conflict coming from the steel departments were necessary.

In 1983, the CI (corporate identity) committee was formed. A survey on the perception of the company held by employees, the customers and suppliers was conducted, and it found that many felt anxiety over the future of the company. In order to change the corporate culture to a vital and outside oriented one, a new corporate creed was written and was made public. It emphasized (1) market-orientedness, (2) the construction of an affluent human environment, (3) to become a strong company through self change. The president visited the production fronts and sales fronts a number of times and talked with employees on the future of the company. A new company song and slogans were publicly solicited and the name of company was changed from Nippon Kokan (Nippon Steel Pipe) to NKK, to change the image of the company. One of the selected slogans was "we look around 360 degrees".

Then, the "New future vision" was formulated. The change of the existing products, the cost reduction of steel production in particular, was studied by the existing departments. On the three new areas, a project team was formed to study the future environment and the strength of the company, supported by the corporate planning department. They suggested three new areas. Then, three teams were formed to study new areas, they built the detailed plan on the development of new domains.

To implement new future visions, the long-range planning integrated the visions fully. New departments were established to implement new business. Resources for research and development were allocated to new business predominantly. Experienced people were newly recruited to develop new businesses. Existing departments built cost reduction plans for existing business. To those who were against the future vision, the president tried to interview them, and persuaded them on the need for change. This case tells that the change of mind was important, that many measures were taken to change the corporate culture before the change of corporate strategy.

2. Cost-effectiveness of scarce resources

The projects which have higher productivity have higher priority in roadmap planning.

(2.1) High return

From among many independent capital investment projects, higher return projects have a higher priority in the schedule. Text book approaches on financial management states that projects will be arranged by the size of rate of return computed by discounted cash flow, and will be cut off at the amount where the financial resources are limited, or will be cut off by the marginal cost of capital. In this case, the total additional profit amount, and the rate of return on additional capital, will be at their maximum under restricted resources. (If there is no limitation on financial resources, the project could be arranged by the net present value of the project, to maximize the profit amount. (Weston & Brigham, 1975, chap. 7))

This principle can be applied to the scheduling of independent projects. If the company is in need of cash, and earlier payback of investment is desirable, then the payback period can be used for ranking. Many surveys on financial evaluation of projects show that this method is used very frequently.

As NKK's long-range plan, the cost reduction of present steel production and city development had higher preference in the time schedule, because not only were there less risks, but also the rates of return of projects were estimated to be high, and also the payback period was short. They had to support other projects, such as construction engineering, development of new materials, electronics, biotechnologies. The company had a large amount of lands available for city development, so the payback period could be short.

The goals of the company are multiple. Not only profit, but sales amounts, employee welfare and other goals should be considered in the computation of cost-effectiveness.

At a university, for example, there are many projects, such as the expansion of class rooms, of research facilities, of student unions, athletic facilities, dormitories and guest houses. Multiples effects are taken into consideration for cost-effectiveness and for scheduling.

(2.2) Timing in the environment

The value of the project varies depending on the timing of entry. One sewing machine manufacturer entered into the color television production at the mature stage of the product life cycle. It had technology and sales channels, but the project failed. Other companies have failed because a product was introduced to the market too early, without waiting until the breakthrough of technology was completed.

(a) Life cycle. The life cycle determines the timing of entry. The early stage should be selected for entry. Ajinomoto entered into mayonnaise, instant soup, instant coffee, chilled food at the second or third entry, as the challenger, and succeeded in most of the cases, because it entered in the early stage of the life cycle. It had strong marketing capabilities and also used joint venture arrangements with successful foreign companies. If the company is to enter into the market at the later stage, it has to select an appropriate segment.

(b) Turning point of technology.

The company selects the timing when there appears to be new technology or when the company succeeds in a breakthrough in key technology, or when the patent of the leader company expires. Sony started to produce small radios when the transistor was invented. Seiko started to produce the crystal quartz watch when a small semiconductor became available at a cheap price. Canon entered into the copying machine business when the main patents of Xerox expired. The above two companies also completed breakthroughs in key technologies and filed hundreds of patents when they produced new products.

There are countless cases where companies make use of the turning point of technology to enter into new business. The new life cycle starts, so this principle could be included into the life cycle principle.

(c) Establishment of entry barrier.

Early entry tends to establish an entry barrier. It is established by strong brands and also by the cost competitiveness which the experience curve effects.

3. Cause-effect relationship

Causes have to arise before effects can be obtained. In order to develop a new product, research has to be started, and the longer the lead time, the earlier the starting time.

(3.1) PERT principle

The PERT chart is seldom used for long-range planning, but the concept of PERT is a basic principle of scheduling. The planner can daw a fish-bone chart, or a bar chart or a PERT chart and the critical path should be found.

The lead time is a simpler concept, and when the lead time is long, starting times needs to be earlier. At the pharmaceutical company, the development of a new drug takes about ten years. In order to attain the goals ten years on, the company needs to start research this year. The motor car company has a cycle of new car development and the starting time of development is determined by the lead time of development.

(3.2) Dynamic synergy

Dynamic synergy determines the sequence of new product development and diversification. Dynamic synergy means that when two or more products have time-series relationships in technology or marketing, new products can have stronger competitive power in quality and cost, and also that existing product can get benefits from the new products by a mutual help relationship.

A case of the Citizen Watch Company (Sales in 1990, ¥ 225 billion, watch and watch related products) is illustrated in Table 8.4.

The company produced machines which produced watches, and this technology was applied to produce the machine tool, the numerically controlled lathe.

Table 8.4   Transition of product-mix and dynamic synergy at Citizen
Corporation

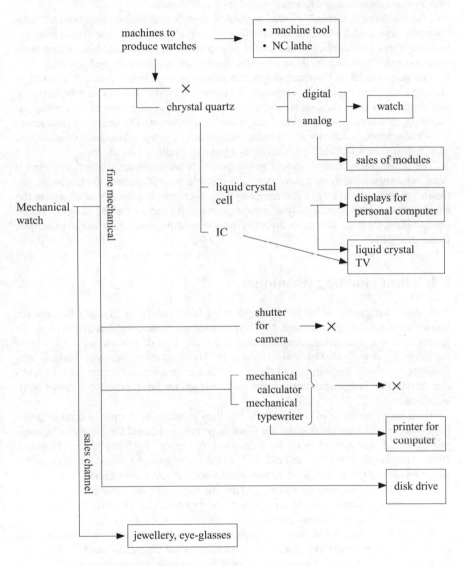

(Note)   (1) ☐ indicates successful products
(2) ✕ indicates discontinued products

The development of a crystal quartz watch not only brought success in maintaining their share of the watch market, but the technology was applied to the display of personal computers and to small liquid crystal television.

Fine mechanical technology was applied to printer and disc drive products. Sales channels were used for the sales of jewelies and eye glasses. This case shows how dynamic synergy was applied to successful new product development. Notice that there were some products failure; these products were in the last stage of the life cycle.

The stage model of corporate development can be explained by dynamic synergy. Greiner and others explain the corporate development model. It states that the corporation starts from specialization to wider modifications of main products, to vertical integration, to diversification and to foreign direct investment. The organizational structure changes from a functional organizational structure to a product division structure. The case of Canon in Table 9.2, illustrates a good example of this model.

The development model show a grand overview of scheduling the strategy, but it does not explain the reason why it is a profitable growth pattern. This can be explained by dynamic synergy. The company constructs strong resource structures in the specialization stage, an assembly of various capabilities can be applied to other related products and thus the company diversify into related products. (Similar explanation, Penrose, 1959).

8.4 Use of planning techniques

New ideas are generated by combining known laws and facts. In order to combine known concepts, imagination and new original angles of observations are needed. To generate new combinations, models and tools are useful. For example, the brain storming developed by Osborn (Osborn, 1953) to promote creative thinking emphasizes the above principles, and there are other principles and techniques. In addition to intuitive imagination, principles and tools are useful to produce creative combinations.

Tools may limit kinds of combinations, but they increase the number of combinations. If the planner sticks too much to the use of tools, he may be blamed for "paralysis by analysis". (On the limitation of tools, see Peters and Waterman, 1982; Hamel and Prahalad, 1989). The planner, however, can be flexible in the use of tools, he should be aware of the limitations of tools, and should use imagination to find out new combinations.

The techniques to generate strategic ideas are surveyed (see Table 8.1.b).

To analyze information, factor analysis or principle factor analysis, sensitivity analysis and multiple environment scenarios are frequently used.

To generate ideas, PPM analysis (growth share matrix analysis), life- cycle models, a matrix of products and market, and simulation are frequently used. This survey is not exhaustive. Financial analysis methods, for example, are not surveyed.

It is not necessary to explain the tools in Table 8.5, but there are some comments on the use of matrix of product and market model. (no. 10 in Table 8.5) This method

Table 8.5 New product development by combining growth areas with the strengths of the corporation.

Strength of own company \ Growth area		By new technology			By change of needs		
		IC card	Bio technology	Optronics	Adult education	Health industry	Underground room
Basic technology	Electronics						
	Printer						
Market	Dealer and distributers						
	Personal computer						

was already explained in Table 8.1 as the growth vector analysis. This can be used to generate ideas on new products and new businesses and it is also useful to arrange ideas already presented. This method assesses the present market and the new market on a horizontal axis and the present technology and new technology on a vertical axis. These combinations are useful to discover new businesses and new products.

Table 8.5 is another kind of matrix. On the horizontal axis, possible new businesses or new products by technological innovation, or by change in needs of the market are indicated. To find possible new products, large amounts of information are collected and sometimes research laboratories are visited or outside consultants are made use of. The strength of one's own company in technology and the market are evaluated and then the company tries to find new businesses or new products to which it can apply its strengths. If some areas of technology have to be strengthened for new products, then this is planned in the next stage. Companies which make use of this sort of comprehensive and analytical investigation of new opportunities have increased recently.

Summary

1. The product-market strategy aims to select habitat. It affects the corporate performance greatly. There are various approaches.
2. The strategy can be classified by attitudes towards growth. The product portfolio model states that the company can apply growth or retrenchment policies differently to the products depending on their positions on the growth share matrix.
   The growth vector model shows the position of new products by the synergistic relations with the existing product. This model can be used to generate ideas of new products. The strategy varies by the position on the growth vector chart.
3. The long-term growth model states the change of the product mix from specialization to diversification, then to multinational management. The organizational structure, decision style, personnel management and other management systems will change to fit with the change of product-market strategy. This model can be used to construct long-term visions of the company.
4. Leader or follower by the timing of entry. The company can take the policy of pioneering in any product at any time like Sony, or take the policy of second entry like Matsushita. There are several options for late enterers. This model can suggest appropriate strategies fit for the timing of entry.
5. Leader or follower by the size of share of market. The share of market of each company tends to last for a long time after certain stages of the life cycle, and there are different options of strategies which are suitable for each position in the market. This model can be combined with the PPM model.
6. There are five options for the product-market strategy; diversification, vertical integration, multinational management or foreign direct investment, competition strategy and external growth strategy. The mutual relationship is shown in Table 8.2.
7. There are ten or more key principles in the product-market strategy. The success of the strategy depends on appropriate applications of these principles. Product differentiation is one of the principles.

8. The process of transformation in strategic change has not been studied well in management literature. The decrease of uncertainty, the cost-effectiveness of scarce resources and the cause-effect relationship are three important principles. The first one is explained by sequential decisions or by incremental decisions. The second principle contains several principles on timing. The third one is typically explained by the PERT principle.

9. Creative ideas are born from new combinations of known concepts. The tools of decisions can help increase the number of combinations. The survey was conducted to establish what tools for decisions are used and how often, as is shown in Table 8.5.

Table 8.1b Use of planning techniques

Year	1979	1985	1989
Corporations with long-range plans	327 co.	384 co.	249 co.
1. Factor analysis (or principal factor analysis)	21 (%)	21 (%)	25 (%)
2. Sensitivity analysis	12	12	17
3. Risk analysis (or Monte Carlo Simulation)	2	1	6
4. Multiple scenarios on environment	22	18	19
5. Contingency plans	17	13	9
6. Product Portfolio Management analysis	17	22	21
7. Zero base budgeting system	4	6	6
8. Program budgeting	12	12	14
9. Standart strategies for each stage of product life cycle	13	15	15
10. Product analysis by product-market matrix analysis	12	20	20
11. Linear programming	4	4	3
12. P E R T (CPM)	1	2	2
13. Input-output analysis for production planning	3	1	2
14.1 Company-wide comprehensive simulation, with sub-systems for each product	31	20	24 *
14.2 Company-wide comprehensive simulation, without sub-systems for each product		9	13
15. Partial simulation	17	14	17
16. Planning by strategic business units	6	10	19
17. Planning by use of matrix organization	3	7	8
18. Planning & implementation by internal venture system	–	4	5

(Notes) (1) Number indicates the percentage of responding company
        (2) Asterisk (*) indicates that successful companies in planning (subjective judgement, 146 co.) have higher frequency (< 5 %)

Bibliography for product market strategy

In Japanese

Ishida, H., (1981), Kaigai ni okeru Nihon Kigyo no Jinteki Shigen Kanri (Personnel Management of Japanese Corporations in Abroad), March, Journal of Japanese, Personnel Management Association, Tokyo.

Ishida, H., (1985), Nihon Kigyo no Kokusai Jinji Kanri (Personnel Management of Japanese Foreign Subsidiaries), Nihon Rodo Kyokai, Tokyo.

Itami, T., (1980), Keiei Senryaku no Ronri (Logic of Corporate Strategy), Nihonkeizai, Tokyo.

Japan Management Association, (1982), Senryaku-teki Kenkyukaihatsu no Hyoka to Ishikettei (Evaluation and Decision of Strategic Research-and-Development), Japan Management Association, Tokyo.

Japan Management Association ed., (1985), Shinseihin Kaihatsu Handbook (Handbook for New Product Development), Japan Management Association, Tokyo.

Japan Marketing Systems ed., (1985), Shinseihin Kaihatsu Handbook (New Product Development Handbook), Japan Management Association, Tokyo.

Kobayashi, N., (1980), Nihon no Takokuseki Kigyo (Japanese Multinational Companies), Chuokeizai, Tokyo.

Kondo, S., (1980), Gijitsu Matrix ni yoru Shinseihin Shinjigyo Tansaku-ho (New Product and New Business Development by Technology Matrix), Japan Management Association, Tokyo.

Kondo, S., (1981), Gijitsu Matrix ni yoru Shinseihin Shinjigyo Tansaku-ho (New Product and New Business Development by Technology Matrix), Japan Management Association, Tokyo.

Kono, T., (1956), Keiei Keigaku no Riron (Theory of Business Planning), Diamond-sha, Tokyo.

Kono, T., (1974), Keiei Senryaku no Kaimei (Analysis of Corporate Strategy), Diamond-sha, Tokyo.

Kono, T., (1975), Choki Keieikeikaku no Tankyu (Analysis of Long-range Planning), Diamond-sha, Tokyo.

Kono, T., (1985), Gendai no Keiei Senryaku (Modern Corporate Strategy), Diamond-sha, Tokyo.

Kono, T., (1987), Shinseihin Kaihatsu Senryaku (New Product Development Strategy), Diamond-sha, Tokyo.

Kono, T., (1988), Shinseihin Kaihatsu Senryaku (New Product Development), Diamond-sha, Tokyo.

Mori, S., (1981), Kenkyukaihatsu Kanri-Ron (Management of Research and Management), Yushido, Tokyo.

Muramatsu, S., (1989), Kigyo Gappei Baishu (Merger and Acquisition), Toyokeizai, Tokyo.

Nakane, C., 1967, Tateshakai no Ningenkankei (Human Relations in Vertical Society), Kodan-sha, Tokyo.

Nishida, K., (1984), R&D Rema Hakutsu no Management (Management to Create the Subject of R&D), Bunshindo, Tokyo.

Okochi, A., (1978), Keiei Kosoryoku (Conceptual Capability of Strategy), Tokyo University Press, Tokyo.

Uchihashi, K., (1978), Takumi no Jidai (Age of Scientific Craftsman), Sankei, Tokyo.
Ueki, H., (1983), Kokusai Keiei Itenron (International Transfer of Management Styles), Bun-shindo, Tokyo.
Yamanouchi, A., (1986), Kigyo Henkaku no Gijitsu Management (Management of Innovation), Nihonkeizai, Tokyo.
Yasumuro, K., (1982), Kokusai Keiei Kodoron (International Business Behavior), Moriyama, Tokyo.
Yoshihara, H., (1979), Takokuseki Keiei Ron (Multinational Management), Hakuto-shobo, Tokyo.
Yoshihara, Sakuma, Itami and Kagono, (1981), Nihon Kigyo no Takakuka Senyaku (Diversification Strategy of Japanese Enterprises), Nihonkeizai, Tokyo.

In English

Aaker, D. A., (1984), Developing Business Strategies, John Wiley, New York.
Abell, D. F. & Hammond, J.S., (1979), Strategic Market Planning, Prentice-Hall, London.
Abernathy, W.J., (1978), The Productivity Dilemma, Johns Hopkins Univ. Press, Baltimore and London.
Allen, T. J., (1977), Managing the Flow of Technology, MIT Press, Cambridge, Mass.
American Management Association, ed., (1959), Developing a Product Strategy, AMA, N. Y.
American Management Association, ed., (1964), New Products, New Profits, AMA, N. Y.
Andrews, Kenneth, (1971), The Concept of Corporate Strategy, Irwin, Homewood, Ill.
Ansoff, H. I., (1965), Corporate Strategy; An Analytic Approach to Business Policy for Growth and Expansion, McGraw-Hill, New York.
Ansoff, H. I. & Stewart, (1967), Strategies for a Technology-based Business, Harvard Business Review, November–December, Boston, Mass.
Bain, J. S., (1959), Industrial Organization, Wiley, New York.
Berg, T. L. & Shuchman, A., (1963), Product Strategy and Management, Holt, Rinehart and Winston, New York.
Burgleman, R. A. & Maidique, M. A., (1988), Strategic Management of Technology and In-novation, Irwin, Homewood, Ill.
Burns, T. & Stalker, G. M., (1961), The Management of Innovation, Tavistock, London.
Buzzell, R. D., Gale, B. T. & Sultan, R. G. M., (1975), Market Share – A Key to Profitability, Harvard Business Review, Jan.–Feb., Boston, Mass.
Caves, R., (1964), American Industry; Structure, Conduct and Performance, Prentice-Hall, Englewood, Cliffs, N.J.
CB Report 546, (1972), Generating New Product Ideas, Conference Board, N.Y.
Chamberlain, E., (1933), The Theory of Monopolistic Competition, 1933, Oxford Univ. Press, London.
Chandler, A. D., Jr., (1962), Strategy and Structure; Chapters in the History of the American Industrial Enterprise, M.I.T. Press, Cambridge.
Channon, D. F., (1973), The Strategy and Structure of British Enterprise, Macmillan, London.
Conference Board: Evaluating New Product Proposals, (1973), Conference Board, N. Y.
Dore, R., (1973), British Factory-Japanese Factory, University of California Press, Berkeley.
Fayerweather, J., (1982), International Business Strategy and Administration, Ballinger, New York.
Galbraith, J. & Nathanson, D., (1978), Strategy Implementation; The Role of Structure and Pro-cess, West Publishing Company, Minn.

Gilber, X. & Strebel, P., (1988), Developing Competetive Advantage, in Quinn et al, The Strategy Process, Prentice-Hall, N. J.

Giragosian, N. H., (1978), Successful Product and Business Development, Dekker, New York.

Glueck, W. E., (1976), Business Policy, Formulation and Management Action, 1976, McGraw-Hill, New York.

Glueck, Kaufman & Walleck, (1980), Strategic Management for Competitive Advantage, Harvard Business Review, July–August, Boston, Mass.

Glueck & Jauch, (1984), Business Policy and Strategic Management, McGraw-Hill, New York

Gort, M., (1962), Diversification and Integration in American Industry, Princeton Univ. Press, Princeton.

Greiner, L. E., (1972), Evolution and Revolution as Organization Grow, Harvard Business Review, July–August, Boston, Mass.

Grinyer, P. H. & Spender, J. C., (1979), Turnaround – Managerial Recipes for Strategic Success, Associated Business Press, New York.

Gutenberg, E., (1964), Grundlagen der Betriebswirtshaftslehre, Der Absatz, Berlin.

Hamel, G. & Prahalad, C. K., (1990), The Core of Competition, Harvard Business Review, May–June, Boston, Mass.

Hamel, G. & Prahalad, C. K., (1989), Strategic Intent, Harvard Business Review, May–June, Boston, Mass.

Harrigan, K. R., (1983), Strategies for Vertical Integration, D. C. Heath & Co. Mass.

Hayes, R. H. & Abernathy, W. J., (1980), Managing Our Way to Economic Decline, Harvard Business Review, July–August, Boston, Mass.

Hax, A. C. (Editor), (1984), Readings on Strategic Management, Ballinger, Mass.

Hedley, B., (1976), "Fundamental Approach to Strategy Development", Long-Range Planning, Dec., Pergamon Press, Oxford.

Henderson, B. D., (1979), Henderson on Corporate Strategy, Abt Books, Cambridge, Mass.

Henderson & Quandt, (1958), Microeconomic Theory; A Mathematical Approach, McGraw-Hill, New York.

Hersey, P. & Blanchard, K. H., (1977), Management of Organizational Behavior, Prentice-Hall, New York.

Hofer, C. W., (1986), Designing Turnaround Strategies, in Quinn et al, The Strategy Process, (1988), Prentice-Hall, New York.

Hofer & Schendel, (1978), Strategy Formulation: Analytical Concepts, West Publishing, St. Paul, Minnesota.

Hofsteade, G., (1980), Culture's Consequences, Sage Pub., Beverly Hills, CA.

Johnson, G., Scholes, K. & Sexty, R. W., (1989), Exploring Strategic Management, Prentice-Hall, Canada Inc.

Kanter, R. M., (1983), The Change Masters, Simon & Schuster, New York.

Kindleberger, C. P., (1970), "A Symposium, The International Corporation," MIT, Cambridge, Mass.

Kollat, D. T., Blackwell, R. D. & Roberson, J. F., (1972), Strategic Marketing, 1972, Holt, Rinerhart & Winston, New York.

Kono, T., (1984), Strategy and Structure of Japanese Enterprises, 1984, Macmillan Press, London.

Kotler, P., (1980), Marketing Management, Prentice-Hall, Englewood Cliffs, N. J.

Markowitz, H.M., (1959), Portfolio Selection, Wiley, New York.

Marren, J. H., (1985), Mergers and Acquisition, Dow Jones-Irwin, Homewood, Ill.

Miles, R. E. & Snow, C. C., (1978), Organizational Strategy, Structure and Process, McGraw-Hill, New York.
Myrdal, G., (1968), "Asian Drama" An Inquiry into the Poverty of Nations, Pantheon, New York.
Nyström, H., (1978), Creativity and Innovation, John Wiley & Sons, New York.
O'Connor, R., (1983), Managing Corporate Development, Conference Board Report 771, Elsevier Science Publishers.
O'Meara, J. T., (1961), Selecting Profitable Products, Harvard Business Review, January–February.
Osborn, A. F., (1953), Applied Imagination, Scribers, CA.
Ouchi, W., (1981), Theory Z., Addison Wesley, Reading, Mass.
Pascale, R.T. & Athos, A.G., (1981), The Art of Japanese Management, 1981, Simon & Schuster, New York.
Penrose, E., (1966), The Theory of the Growth of the Firm, Basil Blackwell, Oxford.
Perlmutter, H. V., (1969), The Tortuous Evolution on the Multinational Corporation, Columbia Journal of World Business.
Pessemier, E. A., (1966), New Product Decisions, An Analytical Approach, McGraw-Hill, New York.
Pessemier, E. A., (1977), Product Management, Strategy and Organization, John Wiley, New York.
Peters & Waterman, (1982), In Search of Excellence, Harper & Row, New York.
Porter, M. E., (1980), Competetive Strategy, Techniques for Analyzing Industries and Competitors, Free Press, New York.
Porter, M. E., (1985), Competetive Advantage; Creating and Sustaining Superior Performance, Free Press, New York.
Prahalad, C. K. & Hamel, G., (1989), Strategic Intent, Harvard Business Review, May–June, Boston, Mass.
Quinn, J. B., (1980), Strategies for Change; Logical Incrementalism. Homewood, Ill.: Richard D., 1980, Irwin, Homewood, Mass.
Quinn, J. B., (1985), Managing Innovation; Controlled Chaos, Harvard Business Review, May–June, Boston, Mass.
Richman, B. & Copen, M., (1972), "International Management and Economic Development", McGraw-Hill, New York.
Riggs, H. E., (1983), Managing High Technology Companies, Liftime Learning Pub., CA., Wadsworth, California
Robinson, R. D., (1984), Internationalization of Business, Holt, Rinehalt and Winston, New York.
Robock, S. H., Simmonds, K. & Zwick, J., (1977), International Business and Multinational Enterprises, Irwin, Homewood, Ill.
Rogers, E. M., (1962), Diffusion of Innovations, The Free Press, New York.
Rothberg, R. R. (Editor), (1981), Corporate Strategy and Product Innovation, The Free Press, New York.
Rothschild, W. E., (1976), Putting It All Together, AMACOM, New York.
Rothschild, W. E., (1979), Strategic Alternatives; Selection, Development and Implementation, AMACOM, New York.
Rothschild, W. E., (1984), How to Gain the Competitive Advantage in Business, McGraw-Hill, New York.

Rowe, M. & Dickel, (1985), Strategic Management and Business Policy, Addison-Wesley, California.

Rugman, A. M., Lecraw, D. J. & Booth, L. D., (1986), International Business, McGraw-Hill, New York.

Rumelt, R. P., (1974), Strategy, Structure and Economic Performance, Harvard University Press, Cambridge, Mass.

Scott, B. R., (1971), Stages of Corporate Development, Harvard Business School, Boston.

Sharpe, W. F., (1970), Portfolio Theory and Capital Markets, McGraw-Hill, New York.

Simon, H. A., (1957), Administrative Behavior, Macmillan, New York.

Steiner, G., ed., (1965), The Creative Organization, Univ. of Chicago Press, Chicago.

Stopford, J. & Wells, (1972), Managing the Multinational Enterprise, 1972, Basic Books, New York.

Teece, D. J. (Editor), (1987), The Competitive Challenge, Harper & Row, New York.

Weston & Brigham, (1975), Managerial Finance, Holt, Rinehart and Winston, New York.

Williamson, O.E., (1975), Markets and Hierarchies: Analysis and Antitrust Implications, Free Press, New York.

Yavitz, B. & Newman, W. H., (1988), Strategy in Action, The Free Press, New York.

Zaltman, Kotler & Kaufman (Editors), (1972), Creating Social Change, Holt, Rinehart and Winston, New York.

Chapter 9 Resource structure planning

Nintendo was a playing card manufacturer, who once had nothing to do with the modern electronics technology. But it entered into gaming instruments, an electric light gun and an "invader game" which used electronic displays. Through the development of these gaming equipments, it was able to accumulate electronics knowledge and then could successfully develop the "television game". It took more than ten years to accumulate the knowledge on electronics. The sales of this company in 1990 were ¥ 410 billion and the net profit was ¥ 100 billion (profit rate over sales is more then 25 percent).

On the other hand M Sugar Co., an old company, did not try to enter into areas other than sugar manufacturing and sales and profit continued to decline. The company said that they did not have the capability to manufacture any other things, and that they had no resources to attract and formulate future resources. Here, a vicious circle is at work.

The resource structure is a vessel where the research, production and marketing activities are conducted. People are the subject of operations the equipment is the assistant of operations. The resource structure is a storage of distinctive knowledge, which is accumulated over a long time and also deteriorate from time to time.

The resource structure is planed for each project and for each product, but it is also planned and coordinated by functional departments in head office or such as in the development department, the marketing department, the production department or the personnel department. Reasons for such concentration of authority are that the resource structure is the key for success, restrain activities for long years and head office can recruit better resources with a cheaper cost by concentration.

9.1 Areas of the resource structure

Areas of resource structure is shown in Table 9.1. It has two dimensions, one is the functional knowledge area, the other is the element resource area. Element resources mean knowledge, people and equipment which constitute the functional knowledge and also are transferable from one function to another.

The functional areas 1 and 2 are mostly studied in chapter 4, and in this chapter we will deal with areas 3 to 5, and also the mutual relationship between these areas. (For other concept of resource structure, see Ansoff, 1965; Hofer and Schendell,

Table 9.1   Assessment of resource structure

Functional capability / Element resources	Integration of strategy Top management (Planning department)	New product and process development (Research and development)	Production (Production department Manufacturing factory)	Marketing (Marketing department)	Finance (Finance department, accounting department)
Measurement of capabilities	Growth rate R O I New product ratio Share of market Image of company	Number of patents New products sales/ total sales Number of new products 'Leadership' of products	Cost of materials /sales Cost of production/sales Leadership on quality Inventory turnover	Share of market Marketing cost Profit/sales Sales/account receivable Sales/current asset Price competitiveness Brand loyalty Quality of after-sales service	Class of bond Debt ratio PER Cash flow/sales Dividend/profit Price of stock
1. Knowledge and systems	Strategic information system Long-range planning system Budgeting systems	Information system Development system	Information system Production system Quality control Purchasing system	Information system Development system Distribution system Sales-promotion system Service system	Cash management system Asset management system Profit management system (decentralized management system) Use of simulation Accounting system Use of computers
2. Organizational structure	Top management organization Planning department	Number of laboratories Location of laboratories Organizational structure	Organization of production management Organization of manufacturing plant	Number of sales channels Number of exclusive sales channels Share of channels/share of market	Organization for financial management Types of profit centers

continued

Table 9.1   Assessment of resource structure (cont.)

Functional capability / Element resources	Integration of strategy (Top management) (Planning department)	New product and process development (Research and development)	Production (Production department) Manufacturing factory)	Marketing (Marketing department)	Finance (Finance department, accounting department)
3. Personnel and organizational culture	Caliber of top management Value of top management Capability of corporate planners Aggressiveness of top management Decision making pattern	Researchers/total number of personnel Key capabilities Qualities of researcher (doctors) Creative culture	Labour productivity Key capabilities Quality of workers Morale of workers	Number of salesman Share of salesman/share of market Quality of salesman Morale of sales department	Quality of staff in finance and accounting departments
4. Facilities	Location of head office	Floors of laboratories Quality of research facilities Number of books	Plant location Quality of facilities Age of facilities Operation ratio Turnover ratio of facilities	Facilities of sales channel Service facilities Storehouse Sales/current asset	Number of computer Number of banks with close relations Shares of friendly stockowers
5. Resource allocation	Expenditure for strategic information system	Expenditure for research/ sales (for each kind of research)	Capital investment/sales	Expenditure for marketing research /sales Advertisement/sales Sales promotion/sales Capital investment for marketing/sales Training expenditure/ marketing personnel	Expenditure for financial management Training cost for financial management Present Future Issues

(Note)   Three sheets are prepared: present, future estimation and issues

1978; Porter, 1985; Quinn & Mintzberg, 1988; Gilbert & Strebel, 1988 in Quinn & Mintzberg, 1988.)

The resources and functional capabilities have the following principles: (1) Key resources. Key resources are the capabilities to develop new products and to have competitive advantage.

Canon accumulated the ability of light science and fine mechanical technology by recruiting the engineers from closing navy research laboratories at the end of war. Then, they accumulated electronics technology to develop and produce the electronic calculator, and then accumulated software technology and semiconductor technology and communication technology to develop copiers, word processors and other office automation equipment. These capabilities were accumulated through the development of new products and before the successful large scale development of new products.

Canon has a highly automated manufacturing plant. Mini-copiers are produced by an automated manufacturing system with few attending labourers. It has strong sales channels, employing about 7,000 people throughout the world which account for more than 40 percent of total employees. These resources are the sources of successful new product development and competitive edges.

The characteristics of Canon's formation of resources structure are, firstly, as seen in Table 9.2, these resources were formulated before the large scale development of new products and large scale production. For example, sales channels were formed before the production in foreign countries. Secondly, the core technologies are used by many related products and thus synergistic relationships are found. Thirdly, the formation of these resources are planned by long-range planning. The company has had continuous long-range plans since 1957.

(2.1) Substituting relationship

By having distinctive key resources, the company can dispense with some other capabilities. Casio concentrates on development and the designing of new products, development of production technology and marketing, but it does not have production facilities except for experimental production. NEC has the highest share of the personal computer market, and most of its software are produced by outside makers. Qualities of hardware attracted outside software makers, and abundant supply of software in turn appeals to the buyers of hardware. As far as the personal computer is concerned, NEC does not intend to have a software ability. The supply of software could reinforce the sales of hardware. This is a complementary relationship.

Automation can substitute for manual production workers and outstanding product designing can substitute for service activity after sales.

(2.2) Complementary relationship

Highly technological products need high skills for production or highly automated production system and high service skills. Distinctive competences in key resources are usually a combination of several skills. If one ring in the chain is lacking, then the

Table 9.2 Transition of strategy at Canon

Years	1950	1960	1970	1980	1990
1. General (1) Product (2) Market	Camera Home market	Camera related products Exporting	Image products Foreign direct investment	Image and information products Multi-national enterprise	Image, information and communication products Multi-national enterprise
2. Core technology	Optical Fine mechanical	Electronics Physics Chemistry Fine Optical	Software System Material technology Communication	(same as for 1970)	Biotechnology Energy technology
3. Product mix	Still camera Movie camera Lens	EE camera Reflex camera Calculator	Copier Faximile Razor printer Word processor	Office automation Video Word processor Electronic fitting	Audio-visual products OA FA system Information service
4. Production	One plant	Multiple plants	Foreign direct investment	Optimum production location, domestic and overseas	Optimum world-wide production location
5. Sales channel 1. domestic 2. overseas	Outside wholesaler Outside agency	Construction of direct whole sales channel Construction of direct whole sales channel	Strengthening direct sales channel	(same as for 1970)	System integration Cutomer oriented system
6. Personnel	Recruiting	Training	Utilization of human resources	Enhancement of creativity	Enhancement of enter-prenurial spirit
7. Organizational structure	Functional	Preparation product division	Product divisions Functional committees	Group divisions	Global management system
8. Sales (billion yen)	0.4	4.2	44.8	240.7	900.0

Table 9.2   Transition of strategy at Canon (cont.)

Years	1950	1960	1970	1980	1990
9. Long-range planning		1st long range plan (Construction of resource structure for diversification)	2nd long range plan (1968 ~ '72) (Diversification, Expansion of production capacity and sales channel.) 3rd long range plan (1973 ~ '77) (To image industry, to knowledge intensive products. Development of multi-national management)	Excellent company plan (1976 ~ '81) 1000 billion plan (1979 ~ '89 + Medium-range plan) 2nd excellent company plan (1982 ~ '86) (Strengthening Canon group, creative new product development capability, strengthening resource structure)	Global company plan (1988 ~ '92) (To global company and information industry)

(Note)   Original from Nakahara + ISONO, Corporate planning office, Canon Inc.

whole does not work. The production control information system will work with sophisticated mechanical equipments. In planning the resource structure, the complementary resource structure has to be prepared together as one set of combination. Toyota has a group of components suppliers, which provide high quality components to Toyota, delivering several times a day to make possible the just-in-time production system. This quasi-vertical-integration contributes to the low production cost and high quality of Toyota cars. Toyota has complementary resources outside of the company, but it sets up and supports those capabilities. This is one of their strategies for resource structure.

(3) Synergy and economy of scale

Synergy is one aspect of economy of scale. When one resource is used by two products, then the productivity of it increases and thus the cost and quality of two products are improved. Honda produces motorcycles and cars, synergy is one of the reasons why it succeeded in car manufacturing in spite of late entry. When there is a common share of development resource, of production resource or of marketing resource, the company can save the investment to these resources and can enhance the productivity of these resources.

Synergy relationships can be planned as horizontal relationships, on the vertical flow of products and time series relationships. Topcon Company, for example, discontinued the production of cameras, but successfully developed land survey equipment and eye-testing equipment, because there was a time series synergy relationships or dynamic synergy.

(4) Time horizon

It takes a long time to construct distinctive competence, so it has to be planned by the long-range plan.

The long lead time means that costs are incurred now and results come in the future. For this reason the division manager who is charged with short term profit responsibility tends to avoid heavy capital investment or investment in human resources. On the other hand, the division manager desires to build a big castle, he may want to have more allocation of resources, and he may use hockey-stick style planning. Two opposing forces affect the size of request.

The capability lasts long but deteriorates. The durability of superiority varies, depending on the following factors. (a) whether it is protected by patents, (b) whether there is a learning curve effect, (c) whether it has a complementary relationship with other resources, or whether there is a synergy relationship with other products. (d) The durability can be controlled and extended by successive invention, by continuous training of employees and by continuous replacement of facilities.

(5) Resource structure planning and organizational structure planning

The organizational structure shows the resource structure in a visible chart, so the plan can be expressed as future organizational chart. By looking at the organizational chart of the competitor it is possible to compare the resource structure of the competitor with that of one's own company.

If we want to strengthen multinational management, we need to establish an international department in head office; if we wish to improve the cooperation between departments, we need to reinforce head office, or need to set up group headquarters.

The organization chart can show not only the resource structure, but also the lines of authority and reporting hierarchy relationships. The organization chart does not, however, show the quantity and quality of resources.

Product division or functional division

One of the issues of organizational structure is the selection of the product division, or the functional division, structure. As the company diversifies its products, the company assures a product division structure. This trend applies to Japanese manufacturing corporations, as is seen in Table 9.3.

However, the rate of diffusion of the product division structure is about fifty percent, and in addition, many product divisions do not have fully fledged functions. In many cases, research laboratories are lacking, they are centralized under head office. The marketing function is carried out in head office or shared with head office.

Generally speaking, the merits and demerits of the product divisions are considered as follows:

Merits. (a) The decision is delegated, the division can adapt to changes of the environment quickly. (b) The delegation of authority improves morale. (c) The division faces the market directly, thus the appraisal of performance becomes easier, and self-control becomes possible.

Demerits. (a) Cooperation among divisions is difficult and the mobilization of resources, particularly human resources, into large new projects is difficult. The large and discontinuous adaptation of the corporation as a whole is not easy. (b) The division tends to be short-range profit oriented, and declines to invest resources in long-term projects.

The reasons why Japanese corporations prefer functional organizations, or imperfect divisional structure are explained by these demerits of product divisions. The reasons are as follows:

(a) The change of environment is fast, the corporation is aggressive in innovation and large scale innovations need to have concentrated efforts. For example, at Hitachi the development of the computer, the color television and the semiconductor were all carried out by central project teams or at central research laboratories. For a small adaptation, decentralization works well, but for a large and discontinuous adaptation, centralization functions better. This is the reason why at Hitachi the improvements to existing products are conducted at product divisions with the cooperation of the central research laboratories, but why

Table 9.3.A   Organizational Structure (manufacturing co.)

Year Organizational Structure	1967	1976	1980	1985	1989
Samples	102 co.	102 co.	102 co.	235 co.	163 co.
Functional	53 %	45 %	42 %	23 %	13 %
Functional (main products) and product division	7	11	13	20	14
Product division	40	43	44	49	52
Geographic division	0	1	1	8	13
Holding company	0	0	0	0	0

Table 9.3.B   Analysis of product division

Year	1985	1989
Samples	235 co.	163 co.
Product division	49 %	52 %
a Integrate production and marketing	34 %	41 %
b Marketing excluded	9	9
c Matrix of product division and production plant	2	6
d Mostly planning and marketing; production separate from division	3	4
a Research laboratory under head office	15 %	20 %
b Laboratories are both under head office and in the product division	7	11
c Laboratories in product division only	8	13

Source: 1967 ~ 1980, direct observation of company materials; 1985 and 1989, by mail survey on long-range planning.

large scale new product development and research activities are conducted at the centralized research laboratories under head office, with the exception of the home products division.

Under centralization, the research and sales activities are carried out with economies of scale or economies of scope. But at the same time, the coordination between research, production and marketing also becomes difficult. This problem is solved by self-coordination. In many cases, the interface between these departments are done by self-coordination. Self-coordination works well in the group oriented corporate culture of Japanese corporations. (This was studied in Chapter 4).

(b) The quasi-vertical integration of backward processes (or upper streams) of components is a popular strategy also the quasi-integration of forward processes (or down streams) of distribution channels are typical strategies of many corporations. These up and down processes are used by many departments in a company. At Matsushita or Canon, this situation exists. Then it is convenient for the diversified corporation to have centralized marketing departments (actually a wholly-owned independent sales company) to control selective or exclusive sales channels. For the same reason, the centralized production technology department and the production technology research laboratory can transfer technology to the component suppliers which form a group of exclusive suppliers.

(c) Life time employment. Top management does not fire division head because of the poor performance of the division, because of life time employment. The control of head office tends to be strong, the division head tends to consult with the head office frequently on various matters. In this situation, there is less need for delegation of authority, and the merit of concentration works better.

9.2 The decision process

As the construction of distinctive competence takes a long lead-time, the formation of resource structures need to be prepared in advance of its actual use, while the company has enough surplus to pour resources into its construction.

The Taisei Corporation puts an emphasis on the resource plan in long-range planning and it uses similar formula to that of the chart in Table 9.1. The plan in the following process.

(a) What are the problems or weaknesses at present, considering the present strategy?

(b) What are the problems or weaknesses when new strategies are to be prepared?

(c) What are the desirable situations in each segment?

(d) What are the key capabilities, what segments have a high priority to be strengthened?

(e) Selection of key issues. High priority segments are selected as key issues, they become the subjects of long-range planning. From many other cases, a generalized model of decision-making is shown in Table 9.4.

Firstly, in five functional capabilities, their measurements, kinds of element resources and their measurements are articulated. Element resources are arranged following the management process: planning, organizing, staffing and monetary resource allocation. Then the key resources (core resources) necessary for present products are ranked. For example, if research and development are key resources, they are ranked high, they are compared with the competitors and strengths and weakness are evaluated.

Next, the resources necessary for new product-market strategy are identified and ranked. If the company is to enter into the office automation equipment, electronics engineers and software engineer to design the system have a high ranking. Then the future shortage of capabilities are made clear, and this eventually leads to the personnel plan and to the capital investment plans. In the resource plan, the core capabilities are important, if the company has strong core capabilities, it can obtain other resources by collaboration.

The road map to close the gap

The schedule to strengthen the resource structure can be decided by the following principle. This problem has already been studied in Chapter 8, but we will repeat it briefly.

(a) Learning process

Where uncertainty is involved, a learning process or sequential decision process can be used. For example, to introduce a computerized information net work, a CAD system and machining center may be introduced first, the company can then learn about the computerized information system, then gradually the company can expand their information system. This approach was used by Nippon Seiko and Yamato Transportation, whose cases are studied in later sections.

When the experiment starts earlier than that of the competitor the timing of formulating the capacity can be earlier. Since investment in experiments is not so large, the company can and should-start the experiment as early as possible. The more experiments and the earlier the timing, the more innovations can be attained. If the experiment can be extended to the key resources, it should be started earlier. In the case of Nippon Seiko, for example, computerization did not start with office jobs, but from product design and production systems, because these could be extended to CIM, and the company estimated that the CIM (computer integrated manufacturing system) was key capability. Expandability is one of the factors used to decide on the timing of experiments.

(b) High output-input ratio

Projects with high output-input ratios have a high priority. The output can be of two kinds, one is the competitive power of present products, the other is the capability to produce new products. One construction company analyzed that their company had weakness in collecting information on huge national projects such as a road constructions across Tokyo Bay, or the Kansai Air Port construction, so the company decided to establish a new project development department (with ten members) in order to an-

Table 9.4 Decision-making processes in resource structure

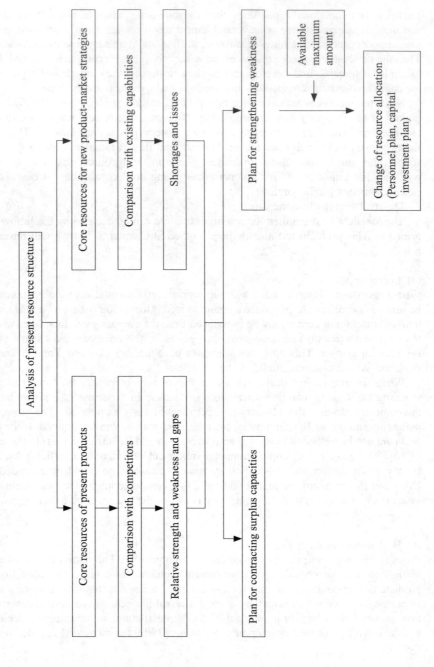

ticipate any development of projects from the beginning. In the past, the company was waiting for orders after detailed plans had been decided. The company estimated that the cost effectiveness of this measure was very high.

Another pharmaceutical company found that their drug division was too strong. The product division structure was appropriate for improving products. However, for exploration of new business and of completely new drugs (for example, a new drug using biotechnology), a cooperation between the departments was needed; so the company decided to reinforce the central research laboratory and to establish a new business development department.

The financial cost of changing the organizational structure, the change of personnel management is low, although the psychological cost may not be low.

On the other hand, capital investment incurs high costs and the output-input ratio needs to be measured carefully.

Complementary relationship (internal consistency). When a change of one resource structure increases the capability of the other resource structure, it can have a high priority. For example when a CAD system not only improves the designing of the product, but also make it possible to present the design of the product to the customer by facsimile, it has a complementary relationship. When an enlargement of the central research laboratory not only enhances the research ability, but also improves the attractiveness of the company for the graduates of natural science departments, it has a synergistic effects.

(c)   Lead time

The lead time determines the schedule. Research and development, the construction of facilities and the training of employees need long years before their effects can be realized. The plans need to be started now based on long-term forecasting.

The stage of the product life cycle suggests the required timing for resource structures. At the introduction stage, the development capability is important, at the growth stage, production technology is important, and at the later stage the marketing capability becomes the key capability.

9.3 From operational plans to resource structure plans

In order to articulate the requirement of resource structures, it is necessary to build a research plan, marketing plan and production plan for each product, and then consolidated these into functional plans. One example of a marketing plan is shown in Table 9.5. From the marketing plans of all product divisions the marketing resource structure plan is consolidated, as exhibited in Table 9.6. This corporate level marketing plan is not only the consolidation of the plans of product divisions, but it includes the corporate level marketing strategy, such as common sales channels for all products and common service centers.

One example of a production plan is exhibited in Table 9.7. From the production plans of all product divisions, corporate level production strategies are formed, as is

Table 9.5 Marketing Plan – Product x

Item	Year	1			2			3		
		Yen	Quantity	Share %	Yen	Quantity	Share %	Yen	Quantity	Share %
1. Sales plan for each product & segment	Total									
2. Marketing trend	i) Market characteristics ii) Demand analysis									
3. Marketing policy	i) Distribution channel ii) Sales organisation iii) Sales promotion iv) New Products v) Price policy vi) Collection policy									
4. Profit plan	i) Gross profit ii) Advertisement iii) Cost of sales iv) Contribution profit		(Per Head)			(Per Head)			(Per Head)	
5. Inventory	i) Inventory									
6. Investment	i) Items ii) Yen									
7. Cost reduction	i) Items ii) Yen									
8. Personnel & organiziation	i) Personnel (by jobs)									
9. Special projects										

Table 9.6 Corporate Marketing Plan

Contents	Schedule	Ranking

1. Strengthening of distribution channel
New establishment of sales office & service center
  A
  B
  Total
New establishment of information system
  A
  B
  Total
 	
Increase of distributors
 	
  Wholesale { increase of exclusive stores
             increase of selective stores
  Retailers { increase of exclusive stores
         increase of selective stores
 	
Increase of sales office in foreign countries		

2. Strengthening of sales promotion activity Advertisement Service Increase of salesman		
3. Total resource allocation (1) Capital investment (2) Investment in sales channels (3) Increase of personnel (4) Increase of expenses		
4. Effects Increase of share of market Increase of sales		

shown in Table 9.8. This corporate level production strategy is not only the consolidation of product division plans, but it plans the policy on production technology for new products or for technology which is common to all existing products, strategies for new plant location which improve the performance of several departments.

This corporate level production strategy becomes the basis of capital investment plans for production facilities.

Use of input-output analysis for production plan.

When there are interchanges of components or unfinished products, the production plan cannot be built straight from the final products. By using the input-output model, we can compute all the inside transactions and required resources structure simultaneously. A model of input-output analysis is shown in Table 9.9.

The notations of each variable are stated in Table 9.9. If the outside sales, B_i and input coefficient a_{ij} are given, then the total production, X_i or X_j, including inside transactions are computed:

$$a_{ij} X_j + B_i = X_i$$
that is, $A\varkappa + b = \varkappa$
then, $\varkappa = [I - A]^{-1} b$ – total production

Thus total production $\varkappa$ or X_i is computed. Table 9.10 shows an example of a computed result.

After computation, we can compare the production capacity, K_i, and required production amount, X_i. Thus we can identify what production capacity is in short and thus the information for capital budgeting becomes available.

If the input coefficient of materials or components are known, then the required amount of these inputs may be computed instantly.

$$\sum_j m_{ij} X_j = M_i$$ – required materials and components

m_{ij} – input coefficient of materials and components

If the input coefficient of one man-hour, l_{ij}, is known, then

$$\sum_j l_{ij} X_j = L_i$$ – required direct man-hour

We can also compute profit; if the prices of all variables are known and if there are limitations of resources, we can use linear programming and thus we can compute the production of X_i which will maximize the profit under the limitation of resources (For these problems, see Kono, 1975).

If the input coefficient in the future can be estimated, and if the outside sales in the long-term future can be forecasted, then the input-output model is very useful, particularly where there are complicated mutual transactions.

Table 9.7 Production Plan – Product

Item		Year	Yen	Quantity	%	Yen	Quantity	%	Yen	Quantity	%
				1			2			3	
1. Production plan	Inside production	Domestic									
		Export									
		Total									
	Outside orders	Domestic									
		Export									
		Total									
	Total	Domestic									
		Export									
		Total									
2. Trends of production cost		Domestic									
		Export									
		Total									
3. Production policy	i) Policy on 'make' or 'buy' ii) Cost reduction iii) Production organization iv) New products v) Research & development										

continued

Table 9.7 Production Plan – Product (continued)

Item	Year	1			2			3		
		Yen	Quantity	%	Yen	Quantity	%	Yen	Quantity	%
4. Profit plan	i) Value added ii) Cost of production (Labour expense) iii) Items iv) Yen									
5. Inventory	i) Amount of inventory									
6. Personnel	i) Head counts by grade (including organization plan)									
7. Capital investment	i) Items and yen									
8. Special projects										

Table 9.8   Corporate Production Strategy

Policy for production

1–1	Policy for production technology
1–2	Policy for information system
1–3	Policy to improve material cost
1–4	Policy for capital investment to increase labour productivity
1–5	Policy on sales of unfinished products
1–6	Policy to level down cyclical changes in production
2–1	Policy to catch up on shortages of capacity and policy for 'overcapacity'
2–2	Policy for shifts, labour hours and operating ratios
2–3	'Make' or 'buy'
3–1	Policy for modernizing the facilities of the plant
3–2	Policy for location, new establishment, discontinuance of plants (including those overseas)
3–3	Policy for manpower
4	Program and priority

Table 9.9 Production plan by output-input analysis

Input \ Output	Process X_1 (ton)	X_2 (ton)	X_3 (ton)	X_4 (ton)	Internal consumption	Outside sales	Total production	Total capacity required	Shortage of capacity
Process X_1 (ton)									
X_2 (ton)		$a_{ij} X_j$			Y_i	B_i	X_i	K_i	H_i
X_3 (ton)									
X_4 (ton)									
Materials E (ton)									
F (ton)		$m_{ij} X_j$			M_i	—	—	—	—
G (ton)									
H (ton)									
Direct labour I (persons)		$l_{ij} X_j$			L_i	—	—	N_i	O_i
J (persons)									

(note) (1) a_{ij} = input coefficient, m_{ij} = material input coefficient, l_{ij} = man-hour input coefficient

(2) X_i, X_j = Total production

(3) B_i = Outside sales

Table 9.10 Computed transactions

Input \ Output	Process				Internal consumption Y_i	Outside sales B_i	Total production X_i
	1	2	3	4			
Process 1	0	995	648	584	2,178	4,000	6,178
2	618	0	1,297	1,068	2,978	2,000	4,978
3	1,853	1,054	0	2,136	5,483	1,000	6,483
4	3,089	0	2,593	0	5,681	5,000	10,681

(note) (1) Outside sales (B_i) is given
(2) Input ratio (a_{ij}) is given as follows

$$a_{ij} = \begin{bmatrix} 0 & 0.2 & 0.1 & 0.05 \\ 0.1 & 0 & 0.2 & 0.1 \\ 0.3 & 0.3 & 0 & 0.2 \\ 0.5 & 0 & 0.4 & 0 \end{bmatrix}$$

9.4 Capital investment

1. Concept and classification of facilities investment

The facilities and equipments not only formulate the physical capacity of output but also determine the quality and cost of products and speed of production because they involve technology. The advancement of technology is embodied in equipment.

Japanese corporations have been aggressive in capital investment, most manufacturing companies have new equipment, more robots and more automated manufacturing facilities than American or European competitors. This is true with the iron and steel industry, automobile industry and machine tool industry. For example, the 1986 production of industrial robots in Japan was worth about 3 billion yen, or about 30,000 sets, 20 percent of which were exported and 80 percent of which were sold domestically. This amount of investment in robots is about five times greater than the amount spent in the U.S. This aggressive modernization of equipment is the results of long- term strategy intended to attain long-term goals and to survive in severe competition. Employees do not oppose this modernization because of the security of jobs by life time employment. At one plant of the Lion Company, which produced laundry detergent, the number of employees was reduced from 250 to 150 by automation in recent years (production amount was about ¥ 25 billion). About 100 employees were not fired, but transferred to three other expanding plants.

In order to make decisions on capital investment, an appropriate classification is necessary. Table 9.11 shows an example of classification. The classification should show a relationship with the product-market strategy, should show the difference of effects, and also the differences in financial sources.

For example, investments for expansion are related with positive product-market strategies, and sources of funds for them can be obtained from outside sources because sales will increase. The modernization of investment reinforces competitive strength, but the sources of funds should be limited within internal funds, because sales will not necessarily increase. Strategic investment does not increase sales in a short period of time and investment should be financed from within.

Another meaningful classification is investment in home country and investment in foreign countries. If the production in foreign countries is planned to be one third of consolidated sales, for example, the capital investment in foreign countries need to be a high percentage of total investment.

One more recent problem is that of resource allocation between research and development and capital investment. About 84% of expenditure for R and D are personnel costs and material cost, but the expenditure for R & D does not bear in fruit short periods of time. It is similar to capital investment, and both are competing for financial resources generated from the inside.

Table 9.11   Corporate Capital Investment Plan – A

	New or continued	Start	Completion	Total	Already invested	Schedule of expenditure				Total of 3 years	Priority
						this year	1 year	2 year	3 year		
(1) Production facilities 1.1. … 1.2. … (Replacement)											
(2) Marketing facilities 2.1. … 2.2. … (Replacement)											
(3) Research and development facilities 3.1. … 3.2. … (Replacement)											
(4) Office facilities Welfare facilities 4.1. … 4.2. … (Replacement)											
(5) Replacement and modernization (duplicated total) 5.1. … 5.2. …											
(6) Overhead cost											
(7) Total											
(8) Depreciation											
(9) Increase of net fixed asset											

Table B.   Other classification of capital investment

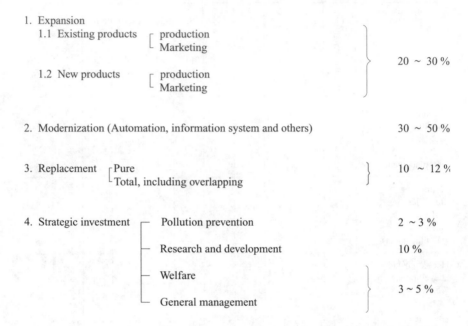

1. Expansion
    1.1 Existing products   ┌ production
                             └ Marketing

    1.2 New products   ┌ production   }   20 ~ 30 %
                             └ Marketing

2. Modernization (Automation, information system and others)   30 ~ 50 %

3. Replacement   ┌Pure   }   10 ~ 12 %
                 └Total, including overlapping

4. Strategic investment   ┬ Pollution prevention   2 ~ 3 %

                          ┼ Research and development   10 %

                          ┼ Welfare
                                                      }   3 ~ 5 %
                          ┴ General management

(Note) The percentage shows the average results of surveys of 407 manufacturing corporation
        by MITI, 1987; of 803 manufacturing companies, by Nihonkeizai, 1985.

2. Decision-making process

The capital investment plan needs to follow corporate strategy, because it is a means of realizing the strategy. A model of decision-making process is indicated in Table 9.12.

The product-market strategy specifies the need for facilities, with respect to both the volume and quality, but on the other hand the needed capital investment is fed back to strategy to evaluate the appropriateness of the strategy. The starting point is the corporate strategy, and the most important criteria for evaluation is the corporate strategy, not the DCF return.

The facilities specific strategy is another premise for capital investment. This includes factory automation policies, the maximum amount of capital investment allowed, the policy on location and others.

The existing facilities are inspected on their age distribution, physical capacity, location and other qualitative characteristics and then gaps and issues are identified. The long-range capital investment plan is formulated to solve these issues. These is-

Table 9.12   Decision-making process for capital investment

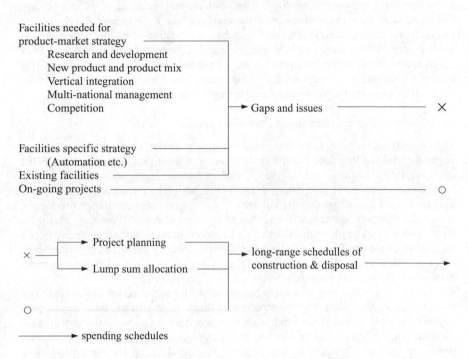

sues are identified for each product-market strategy. The new project plans are worked out for major projects, but for minor projects lump sum amounts are allocated. There are many on-going projects, and together with new projects, long-range schedules of construction and disposals are drawn up. The physical schedule of construction is different from the spending schedule, but the overall capital investment plans are expressed in money terms. The yearly spending plan will not fluctuate too high, if it does coordination has to be worked out to flatten this peak, which is too high.

3. Facility specific strategies

(1) Core technological strength

The facilities embody technology and if the company can identify key technical strengths, these can be the basis of facilities strategies. For example, for Canon it was a precision mechanical technology, mass production technology and then electronics technology and software technology. The core technology changes as the product changes and as the science advances. If the company can have strengths in these core technologies, it can obtain other technologies by collaboration with other companies. In order to identify the core technology, the company needs to determine the future product mix, and to identify common technologies needed for a variety of products. This can be a basic policy for facilities for research and development, production and marketing. (For an interesting analysis on core strength, see Prahalad and Hamel, 1990)

(2) Economy of scope, economy of scale and experience curve

The capacity of facilities is an important strategic problem. Generally speaking, the larger the scale of the plant, the lower the average cost of production, as long as the operating ratio is high.

The experience curve puts emphasis on cost reduction by the accumulation of production not the annual production volume. If the volume of accumulated production is two, then the average cost will be reduced by, for example, 30 percent. This principle results in an emphasis on the share of market, because once a company gets a high share of the market, then it can utilize lower costs by accumulating experience and increase its share of the market. The experience curve is not a different principle from economy of scale, but it is a dynamic side of the principle.

The economy of scope is a different principle from the economy of scale one (Goldher & Jelink, 1983). The principle holds that a variety of products can be produced in one plant, and if the products are in a certain scope, then the cost of production is much lower than production in separate plants. For example, in an automated car assembly plant, a variety of cars are assembled on the same production line. This is made possible by an extensive use of robots and conveyers. At the plant of NSK, a variety of ball bearings are produced by CIM (computer integrated manufacturing system) as will be studied in Section V of this chapter.

The economy of scope principle assumes a flexible production system. The flexible production system is made possible by factory automation and the designing automation use of CAD/CAM systems.

The need for flexible production systems comes from two reasons. The product life cycle is becoming shorter, because of advancements in technology (the semiconductor for example) and by increasing competition The company needs to introduce new products frequently and in shorter development periods by the use of CAD/CAM systems. On the other hand, the needs of consumers are becoming more and more segmented, and small lots of production are needed to meet these individualistic, segmented needs.

(3) Combination of men and machine

The effects of automation are not only the replacement of labour, but improved quality of products and speed of production. But the replacement of labour is one of the factors of automation, and the problem is, how many men the robot (or other machines) should replace at a minimum or; how much investment can we take to replace one man in the maximum. The formula is as follows.

The optimum combination of man and machine is:

(1) $$\frac{\text{marginal productivity of one man}}{\text{wage}} = \frac{\text{marginal productivity of one machine}}{\text{cost of one machine}}$$

In this combination, the cost is minimum (note 1).

When one man is replaced y pieces of machines, then

(2)   marginal productivity of one man = marginal productivity of y machines

From equation (1) and (2), we get

(3) $$\frac{\text{marginal productivity of one man}}{\text{wage of one man}} = \frac{\text{marginal productivity of y machines}}{\text{cost of y machines}}$$

From (2) and (3),

the wage of one man = the cost of y machines

The cost is a ratio of expense on investment, it is called M.
The cost of one man = price (P) of y pieces of machines × M

$$y \times P = \frac{\text{wage of one man}}{M}$$

The left side shows the optimum investment which will save one person. The cost ratio (M) includes depreciation, interest, insurance, tax rate, maintenance cost and operating cost. The operating cost includes the cost of power. For example

$$\text{cost rate M} = \frac{0 \cdot 9}{t} + \frac{1 \cdot 1\,k}{2} + g$$

where t – life of machine, k – interest rate, g – insurance, tax, maintenance and operating cost rate.

The wage rate is the present rate, but the cost of equipment is the future average cost. The timing of replacement is thus determined because when marginal cost equals average cost, the average cost is minimum. This principle is applied on a time series basis. If the total wage and fringe cost of one person per one year is 6 million yen, and if the equipment cost rate is 30 %, 6 million yen ÷ 0.3 = 20 million yen. This is the maximum amount of investment required to save one person.

(4) Total amount of investment

Capital investment projects could be arranged by the height of rate of return and be cut off at the cost of capital. Some projects, however, cannot be evaluated by rate of return. Investment in the research laboratory, for employee welfare facilities and for new products are such examples. Small projects have to be decided on by lump sums.

(1) Maximum amount of capital investment determined by profitability.

The rate of return of on total investment (or total assets) is determined by profit rate over sales and turn-over rate of total assets. Rate of return on total investment = (profit − sales) × (sales − total assets). The profit rate on sales is mostly determined by competition, it is hard to be controlled by one company. Thus the company needs to maintain the turn-over rate a certain level. There are two kinds of capital investment, one is the increase of fixed assets, the other is that of replacement. If the rate of increase of fixed assets is less than the growth rate of sales, then the turn-over rate will not decrease.

> sales ÷ standard turn-over rate of fixed assets = allowable total fixed assets
>
> Allowed fixed assets − present net book value of fixed assets = allowed net increase of fixed assets
>
> Allowed net increase of fixed assets + yearly amount of depreciation = allowed capital investment

The standard rate of turn-over of fixed assets can be obtained from the past actual figures of the company and from the industry average. The average number of manufacturing industries has been relatively stable, it is about four.

(2) Allowed investment determined by liquidity

The fixed asset over long-term capital ratio should be less than 100 percent. If this principle is not observed the capital investment plan needs to be revised.

From the above two considerations, there are a number of partial principles for investment. Arranged by order of conservativeness:
(1) Capital investment ≤ depreciation
(2) Capital investment ≤ depreciation + retained profit
(3) Capital investment ≤ depreciation + retained profit + equity finance
(4) Capital investment ≤ depreciation + retained profit + equity finance + long-term loan
(5) No limitation, invest as much as possible to grow, to make use of the rising price of land, by using long-term debt, short-term debt, lease and accounts payable.

Among the above, (1) and (2) are too conservative. Japanese corporations have been aggressive in pursuing growth and invested in the construction of plants for new products production and for expanding existing products. They did not hesitate to borrow money. To have the balance of growth and stability, principles (3) and (4) need to be applied. Policy (5) is a dangerous one if the estimated rate of return is high. Bankrupt companies have tended to use this policy.

(5) The location of the plant

The location of the plant is determined by many factors – access to markets, to resources, cost of transportation and economic size of the plant. We consider only the
last two factors, and show a simple model. This model can be one of the principles
used in foreign direct investment which constructs a manufacturing plant.

Average cost of production decreases as the size of a plant increases. (See Table 9.13)
The cost of transportation of materials and finished goods increases as the plant becomes
larger and more concentrated. The sum of the cost of production and the cost of transportation amounts to the total cost of delivery. If an import tariff is charged on imported
goods produced outside the country, tariff charged are added to the cost of transportation.

Generally speaking, the higher the cost of transportation, the smaller the size of
the plant. The higher the import tariff from the production plant, the smaller the
plant, because the advantages of economies of size disappear. If the product is produced in a foreign country, the production volume at X, can have a much lower delivery cost and thus the economical size of the plant becomes smaller.

Table 9.13 Size of plant and average cost

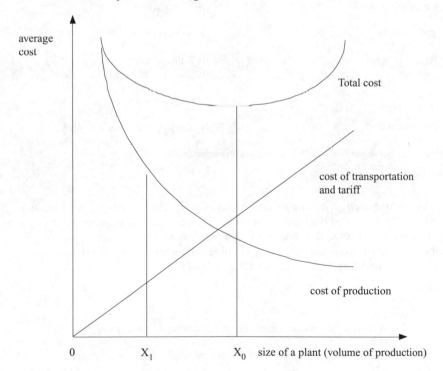

(5) Economic evaluation of investment projects

The evaluation of strategy is studied in Chapter 10, we will here have a quick look at the survey results economic evaluation method. In a survey on the budgetary control practices of 267 companies (of the 267, 175 companies were manufacturing companies) conducted in 1981, the method of economic analysis of capital investment was asked about. The results are shown in Table 9.14 (Japan Productivity Center, 1982).

This survey shows that the accounting pay-back period is the most frequently used evaluation. The payback period does not indicate the profitability of investment because investment which has a long depreciation life may have a high rate of return and a long pay-back period. However, the payback period shows the years in which the company is exposed to risks and relations with liquidity.

Table 9.14   Survey on economic evaluation of capital investment
               (multiple responses possible)

Accounting method		Discounted cash flow method	
1. Cost comparison	... NA	1. Cost comparison	... NA
2. Profit amount	... NA	2. Net present value	... 15%
3. Rate of return	... 32%	3. DCF-rate of return (Internal rate of return)	... 16%
4. –		4. Profitability index	... NA
5. Pay-back period	... 78%	5. Pay-back period	... NA

(Note) (1) Survey in 1981 on 267 companies (manufacturing ... 175 co.).
       (2) Japan Productivity Center

The accounting method of rate of return comes next. This may be easier to understand. The DCF method is not used very often. The estimation of future profit is ambiguous and sophisticated methods of computation will not be very meaningful. Rather, valuation by strategic policy is more important. (On capital investment, Kono, 1975; NAA Report, 1964; NAA Report, 1967)

(note 1)
$$Y = f(K,L)$$
$$Z = mK + wL$$
Y = output, K = capital, m = capital cost, L = labour, w = labour cost,
Z = cost
Y is fixed, and the minimum value of Z is computed. f = the Lagrange coefficient

$$Z\lambda = mK + wL + \lambda \{y^* - f(K, L)\} \dots \text{minimize}$$

$$\frac{\partial Z\lambda}{d\,K} = 0, \quad \frac{\partial Z\lambda}{d\,L} = 0, \quad \frac{\partial Z\lambda}{d\,\lambda} = 0$$

$$\frac{f_k\,(k,L)}{m} = \frac{f_L\,(K, L)}{w} = \lambda$$

Summary

Facilities embody technology, working with human power and determine the quality and cost of products. The faster the technology advances, the more important the modernization of equipment is. Japanese corporations have been aggressive in capital investment, and this is one of the reasons for their strong competitive power in the world. The capital investment plan is one of the important parts of long-range planning because the lead time is long-range planning because the lead time is long, and large amounts of money are fixed in the balance sheet. Many bankruptcies are due to insufficient analysis of capital investment.

To make decisions for investment, product-market strategies and identification of core technologies are the two most important premises for investment. The analysis of investment itself does not necessarily result in the best decision on investment. The economic evaluation of investment is used for appraisal but simple methods are used.

Information technology is integrated into facilities and factory automation has become popular. By using controls by programming, the operation can be integrated with marketing needs and a variety of products can be produced on the same production line. Thus the economy of scope can work. At the same time, the company can respond to market demand quickly, by the use of information systems.

9.5 Information systems

The information system is becoming one of the important elements of resource structure. We cannot imagine any manufacturing company and service company which do not use computerized information systems from the sales front to head office and to manufacturing plant and to suppliers. In this book, two typical cases are studied.

The first case uses a top-down approach, which means that a total system was planned first, and the information system was constructed. This approach is frequently used in the process production industry. The second one uses a bottom-up approach, which is a gradual construction of the information system, from a partial improvement to a total system. This approach is frequently used in the batch production industry, such as the machine production industry and the service industry.

The two cases are the construction of vertical information systems, that is from the customer to production. The other one is not studied here is a horizontal information system, which is a construction of net works with other companies or with outside retailers, by the use of exclusive net work or by the use of a shared net work.

The case of Nippon Seiko Co.

Nippon Seiko is a manufacturer of ball bearings and other precision components for cars, with sales of ¥ 360 billion, 7 plants in Japan and 7 plants in overseas, employing 11,000 people worldwide.

Nippon Seiko started the study of information technology to control the total system of operations in the early 1970s. A project team was formed and a report came out after two years. Unlike other companies, it did not start from computerizing the accounting and payroll jobs, but from the operations of marketing, design, production, sales and physical distribution. The concept of this total system is shown in Table 9.15.

(1) FENICS system works mostly in the design of products and to break down these to production order. When the sales office receives an order for ball bearings, key parameters are relayed to the information system of the R & D department, and then an authorized design blue print is sent by facsimile to the sales office in a few minutes and this is presented to the customer. The contract can be reached quickly.

(2) When an order is received, the specifications of production is delivered to their manufacturing factories (eight factories in Japan). The specifications include the design blue print, materials required, production process, machines to be used, method of operations, cost design and parameters on quality. Any changed of these items can be done easily.

(3) ASPACS links the marketing and production. After an order is confirmed, it is processed by the ASPACS model. If there are stocks of ordered products, the products are delivered to customers, if not, production orders are issued to the appropriate plant. FENICS and ASPACS models are operated in the central information processing department.

(4) CIM in factories. Each plant has its own CIM (computer integrated manufacturing) system. The production specification and the production order are received from the center and they are transmitted by two exclusive telephone lines to the central computer of the plant then sent to mini computers with work stations in each house and to micro computers installed in the machine. On the orders of the operator, the manufacturing starts. After finishing, the products are stored on huge revolving round shelves and are sent to the customer. The huge store houses are operated by only one man.

The quality is assumed by appropriate designing, checking by sensing instruments in the production line, and inspection supports by testing machines.

(5) ASPACS also does inventory control and cost control using actual data.

Nippon Seiko also has information net works with retailers, component manufacturers and overseas plants. The effect of the above information system is as follows. (a) Quick response to the customer, (b) good quality assurance through designing and

Table 9.15   Outline of CIM at Nippon Seiko Co.

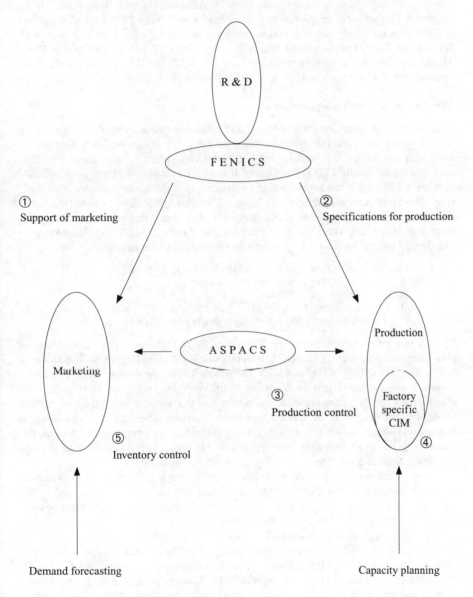

through production control, (c) flexibility of production, by changing the products with short lead times. (d) Cost reduction by reduction of man hours and of inventories. The sales per employee rose from ¥ 14.4 million in 1976 to ¥ 33.8 million in 1989. The inventory turnover (sales – average inventory) rose from 3.0 in 1976 to 9.3 in 1989. The net profit soared from ¥ 1.1 billion in 1976 to ¥ 15.1 billion in 1989. The investment for the computer system was only 0.52% of the 1988 sales. Sales increased from ¥ 111 billion in 1976 to ¥ 301 billion in 1989.

The Case of Yamato Transportation Co.

Yamato Transportation Company is engaged in the transportation of small packages from home to home and some other transportation business. It has sales of 360 billion yen in 1989, employs 32,000, amongst whom 17,000 are car drivers. It hauls about 1 million packages annually, with 17,000 freight cars. It has been in the started transportation business since 1970, but it has specialized in the hauling of small home packages. The company found that there is a niche in the business. The post office and National Railways monopolized parcel transportation, but many company found that there were many defects in their services. The reversal of the policy of the above public organizations provided a new chance for business. The niche and the defects of are as follows:

> Office collection only – we will go to the home to pick up
> Put several address tags on the parcel – no tags
> Package it firmly – put it in a bag
> Bind tightly by strings – no strings
> Complicated price structure – Extremely simple price structure

The transportation system is that the customer will telephone to the sales office, or take their parcel to 'Seven Eleven' Stores or other goods retail stores (230,000 stores nationally) which have a contract with Yamato to handle the goods. The Yamato car drivers will go either to private homes or to the contracted retail stores to collect the goods. They are then transported to the center and the mass transportation of parcels to destination centers is contracted to outside carriers. The parcel is delivered to homes by Yamato drivers the next day. Only both ends are operated by Yamato, because it is the most important service point. The customer can designate the approximate time of collection or delivery, even during the night.

If the parcel is missing or delayed, the company can trace it in the transportation system immediately, and after locating the parcel, the company can respond to the customer in a few minutes. This is made possible by computerized information systems. Thus, the quality of transportation is assured.

The information system is shown in Table 9.16.

Yamato has 17,000 sales drivers who drive, collect parcel and deliver, collect parcels on the orders, of sales offices through wirelesses, the inputting of data to "portable POS" computer (a small computer, POS means point of sales). The data of POS is transmitted to the work station on physical connections, and it is used help to classify and deliver parcels.

Table 9.16 The information network of Yamato

name of center	driver and truck	sales office (center)	intermediate center	computer center
number of centers	17,000 persons 17,000 cars	1,300	32	2
machines	Portable POS	Work station	class CPU	host computer
number of machines	17,700	1,500	35	5
operations	• input, cards are used	• input from PP by batch • program down-load	• classification of parcels	• computing

The input in "portable POS" systems is used for the following outputs. (1) Identification of sales office for arrival, by using telephone numbers, (2) fares are computed by the size and distance of handling, (3) recording of received fare, (4) amount of fees to be paid to the receiving stores, (5) recording of operation of sales drivers, (6) label of destination stores. The bar cord is put on each parcel. The truck has printing instruments, and data is eventually sent to the sales office nearest to the final destination.

The driver delivers the goods, and collects fares if necessary, and if the home is vacant, will leave messages.

The net work of physical distribution is a little different from Table 9.16. The parcels are collected and sent to 1300 sales offices (centers), then to about 50 bases where they are distributed to destination sales offices to be eventually delivered to homes.

The effects of the computerized information system of Yamato are the following:

(a) Complicated transportation from home to home of huge amounts of small pieces of parcels is made possible at low costs.
(b) When trouble in transportation happens, the tracing of the parcel situation is possible, and quick response to the customer are available.
(c) Simple packaging (for example, paper bags) are allowed by the use of dual information systems, the data on the parcel and the data on the computer system. The information arrives at the destination sales office before the parcel reaches there.

It should be noted, however, that this system is supported by human factors, the driver in particular. They are all trained the use of the computer. The one-man driver does both physical transportation and information processing. They are assigned certain narrow districts, and they know everything in that area. Seven or eight sales drivers form a team, they help each other, if necessary, using the wireless phone in their cars. Every morning, a meeting is held in the sales office for mutual communication.

The cost invested for the construction of information systems is hard to estimate because software construction has been a long-term project spanning long years. The running cost in a year is about ¥12 billion, or about 3% of sales.

The construction of information systems as they are today took more than 15 years. Improvement was carried out every five years. In 1969, fare computation and accounting were computerized. In 1974, a country-wide on-line network was completed. In 1980, the ability to retrieve information on troubled packages was completed. In 1986, inputting by sales drivers and by every body was established. Thus the construction of the information system was implemented step by step.

Impact of information technology

Because of the high speed of advancement of information technology, the enhancement of information systems by the use of information technology is becoming one of the key resource structures for the development of new products and for the strengthening of competitive power.

The effects of computerized information systems can be summarized into two. (1) Speed. The time is compressed. By the use of computers, activities can be done in a short period of time. The blue print is presented to the customer in a few minutes, for example. (2) Service. More information is provided by computerized information systems and thus it becomes possible to generate more ideas and more options. The flexible manufacturing system makes possible the production of a variety of goods on one production line, by mass production systems, for example.

The following are the detailed effects of computerization in areas of management.

(a) Research and development

Information retrieval, computation, designing by the use of CAD are made easier by the use of computer. Hundreds of computers are used in the laboratory. The speed of new product development has been accelerated by the use of computer.

(b) Enclosure of the customer. By the use of computerized reservation systems, the terminals placed on air ticket sales office can procure the passenger lists of the air line which distributes the terminal and thus the sales office will sell only the ticket of that airline. Similar effects can be attained by banks and by Security service companies.

(c) Integration of sales and production, faster and more customer oriented services. These effects are seen in the cases of Yamato and Nippon Seiko.

(d) In production. On the production side, there are several levels of factory automation.

$$CAD \rightarrow NC \rightarrow FMC \rightarrow FMS \rightarrow FA \rightarrow CIM$$

This is not the place to describe these concept in details. CAD is computer-aided-designing. NC means numerical control and robotics or numerically controlled tooling machines. FMC is a flexible machining center, which changes tools by programming. It does many kinds of jobs by changes in programmes. FMS is a flexible manufacturing system, which is a larger system than FMC. Automatic transporting systems connect FMCs. FA is factory automation, and has an automatic storage system in addition to FMS. CIM is a computer integrated manufacturing system, which integrates marketing and production. The case of Nippon Seiko is an example of the use of CIM.

A survey on the effects of these factory automations shows that the following are the results actually attained.
(1) Flexibility in manufacturing … 42%. The FA make possible the production of a variety of designs by the change in programmes.
(2) Saving of labour … 24%
(3) Cost reduction … 22%
(4) Shorter delivery time … 18%
(5) Assurance of high quality … 15%
(6) Flexibility towards the change of demands …14%
(7) Reduction of inventory … 11%

The number shows the percentage of responses of 98 companies. 1988 survey by the Japan Association of Industrial Machinery)

(e) At the office

By office-automation, the processes of printing, recording, computing and retrieval are made easier.

(f) General impact of information technology

(1) Risks of factory automation

The factory automation increases the flexibility of production. But this has a limitation. Automation needs a large amount of investment, about fifty percent is on hardware and fifty percent on software development, and these investments cannot be transferred to other lines of products. Flexibility is limited to a line of business, and if the product is losing a competitive edge or at the end of its life cycle, the sunk cost cannot be recovered.

(2) New opportunities. On the other hand, information technology is the key for competition and production, the company can diversify into other areas using technology. Yamato has diversified into other transportation areas, world-wide transportation, for example, using similar systems. Nippon Steel is going to produce computers by using the knowledge on operation control of steel production, Canon diversified from cameras into office automation products, such as copiers and, word processors and printers.

(3) Change of organization. The organization becomes a diamond shape with many middle managers and experts, with very few simple workers.

(4) Change of cost behavior. The cost of production is decided by the design of products, not by rates of labour efficiency. The overhead cost increases and it is allocated by machine hours, not by labour hours.

9.6 Human resource planning

Human resource planning is not the results of strategic planning, but it is the prerequisite of strategic planning and the conditions for success. There are three reasons why strategic human resource planning has become more important.

Firstly, companies are producing more technology intensive goods, are using high-technology facilities and are spending more money in research and development. This tendency is not necessarily seen only in manufacturing businesses but also applies to service industries. This technological orientation can be carried out by having highly educated graduates or by retraining employees.

Secondly, companies are increasing foreign investment, and so need more staff to be sent to foreign subsidiaries, and also need more facilities to train foreign staff and labourers in Japan.

Thirdly, the change of corporate culture becomes important, and the personnel management system has to be considered as one of the important means for changing corporate culture.

The long-range personnel plan in the past tended to be a set of numbers. The numbers are still important even now, to close the gap between the demand and supply. But in addition to a numerical computation, long-range policies and programmes to change the quality of human resources became important.

1. Process of planning

The process of the long-range human resource planning of Japan IBM is shown in Table 9.17.

This process is a comprehensive one and shows a good example of human resource planning.

The business creed on personnel management is the first starting point. Respect for the individual is one of the most important of the three creeds and it contains four principles.

The outside environment is scanned and there is a decrease of high school graduates and a short-term increase of university graduates, but the demand for school graduates from information industries is increasing. Thus, the recruitment of competent high school and university graduates is becoming difficult.

The internal environment is assessed, there is a tendency towards more emphasis on individualism and the value system of employees is becoming more diverse. The average age of employees is not becoming older because of increased new recruits but the number of older employees over fifty years will be doubled within five years.

The product-market strategy puts an emphasis on the development of new hardware and software. Strengthening the sales and service forces is another focus.

In order to realize the product-market strategy, and also to realize the personnel management philosophy, the company constructs selected key personnel programmes within the limitations of external environment and internal environment.

To directly meet the needs of the product-market strategy, increased recruitment of female graduates from universities is planned. This source was not well utilized in the past.

The percentage of female professionals will be increased. To facilitate the continued employment of female employees, a new vacation system for taking care of babies has been established. Home-terminal programmes are another programme for utilizing female human resources.

The training programme has been emphasized so far, and it is to be strengthened. The company plans to spend about 3% of sales for training. This percentage is extremely high compared with other companies.

To meet the need for multinational management, an international personnel management policy was established. Three years, for example, will be the maximum years for dispatching workers to foreign countries.

To meet the needs of the new product-market strategy, and also to respond to the changing values of employees, appraisal and consultation programmes, planned rota-

Table 9.17   Human resource planning process at Japan IBM

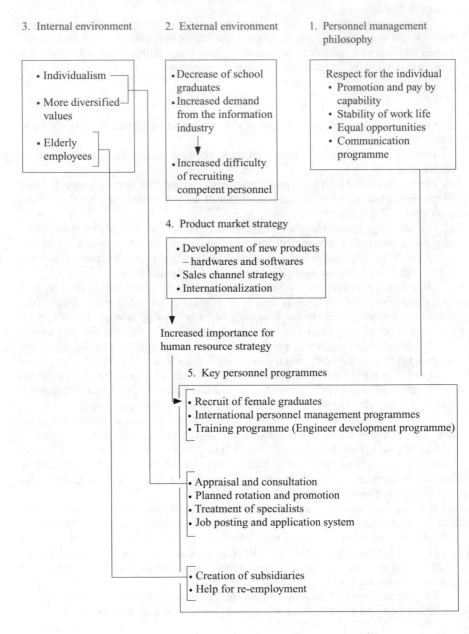

3. Internal environment

- Individualism
- More diversified values
- Elderly employees

2. External environment

- Decrease of school graduates
- Increased demand from the information industry

↓

- Increased difficulty of recruiting competent personnel

1. Personnel management philosophy

Respect for the individual
- Promotion and pay by capability
- Stability of work life
- Equal opportunities
- Communication programme

4. Product market strategy

- Development of new products – hardwares and softwares
- Sales channel strategy
- Internationalization

Increased importance for human resource strategy

5. Key personnel programmes

- Recruit of female graduates
- International personnel management programmes
- Training programme (Engineer development programme)

- Appraisal and consultation
- Planned rotation and promotion
- Treatment of specialists
- Job posting and application system

- Creation of subsidiaries
- Help for re-employment

tion and promotion systems, new treatment of specialists, new jobs posting and application systems are established.

2. The Process of quantitative planning

The process of human resource planning is described in Chart 9.18. From the long-range goals, the product-market strategy is decided. This affects the demand for job content. The capital investment will substitute for labour, and thus it decreases manpower needs. These two produce the demand for manpower.

The supply of manpower from internal markets is estimated by forecasting the levels of retirement age, death, transference and promotion.

The gaps between the demand and supply of human resources are forecasted and means to fill the gaps for job groups are studied. The gaps are filled by new recruits, by rotation and by training. Surplus manpower is also identified, and every means of relocation are studied.

Chart 9.19 shows the future demand and supply of job groups. Gaps for each segment of the matrix are identified and then programmes to fill the gaps are studied.

(2.1) Process of quantitative demand analysis

(A) A Micro approach-demand analysis.

In order to compute the demand for human resources, the assumptions the demand need to be made clear. The future mix of products, organization plan, sales, production, facilities and purchasing plan need to be fixed. There are several approaches to this.

(1) From the organizational structure plan. This is used for projecting the number of personnel for administrative departments, particularly the number of managers.

(2) From new projects. The plan to establish new research laboratories, or to establish manufacturing plants or sales offices are used for the new demand for personnel.

(3) From the number of workers combined with equipment. This is used not only at chemical plants but also at other automated plants. A simple method runs as follows.

> n persons $\times$ 3 shifts $\times$ 1.3 = Y persons
> n   = number of persons stationed per one machine
> 1.3 = Multiple required for holidays and paid vacations.
> Y   = required total number

As the production process is automated, a drastic decrease of stationed personnel can take place.

(4) From standard hours. Where manual works are predominant, standard hours are used for estimating head counts. The final products are composed of the production of components and assembly, and they are composed of a number of operations. A case of such computation from T Company is as follows:

Table 9.18 The process of quantitative planning

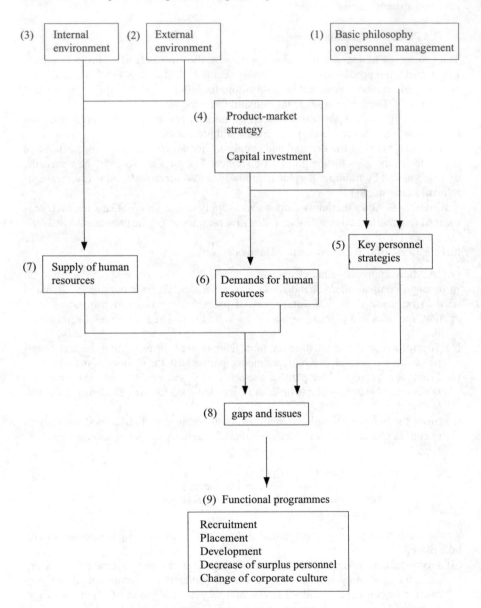

Table 9.19   Personnel plan summary

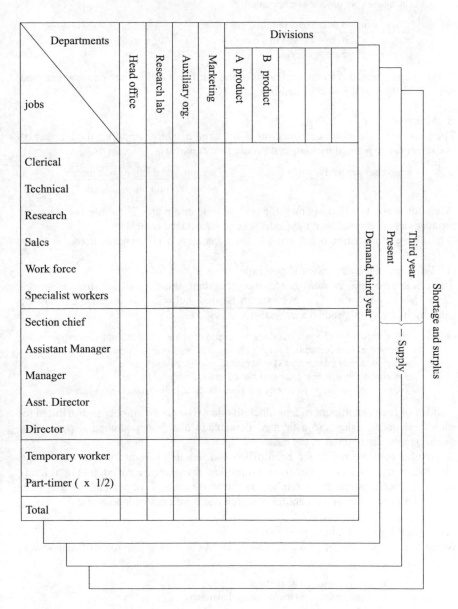

(a)   quantity of one operation in a day × standard hours for one operation =
        man hours per day for one operation

(b) $$\frac{\text{Total standard man-hours required per month}}{\substack{\text{estimated days worked in a month} \times \\ \text{rate of presence} \times \text{working hours in a day}}} = \substack{\text{direct labour force required} \\ \text{for a set of operations}}$$

This is a complicated computation, and for the third year estimation, demand per man hour in the third year has to be estimated.

B. Macro analysis
The basic principle of the combination of men and machines and thus the number of personnel can explained by marginal productivity analysis.

$$\frac{\text{marginal productivity of a labour}}{\text{wage}} = \frac{\text{marginal productivity of a machine}}{\text{cost for one machine}}$$

When the above condition is met, the cost will be minimum. Then, the net marginal productivity is zero and then the profit will be maximized (note 1)
If the above computation is not feasible, the other approach is actually used.

(1) From the expected personnel cost ratio
The labour cost ratio in sales is relatively constant, this means that there is an optimum labour cost ratio. This assumption is used and this rule is considered as the same as the marginal productivity analysis.

(Estimated sales of a product division x ratio of value added × wage cost ratio)
÷ personnel cost per man $(1 + r)^t$ × change of labour composition ×
effect of shorter labour hours) = Required number of work force
r = annual wage increase, t = number of years, change of labour
composition = change of mix of job classification, higher jobs tend to increase.

Number of each department of a product division. The above number is distributed to each department, using the estimated percentage distribution among departments, modifying the distribution in the past.

Number of personnel in the head office and research laboratory. The percentage distribution ratio is used. Numbers of all product divisions are added, and total number of product divisions are multiplied by the above ratio. Five percent, for example, for head office and seven percent for research and development laboratories.

(2) From the goals of labour productivity
Goals of sales per man are used for the basis of computing the goals of manpower. Following examples are used:

        ¥ 300 million / man … sales office
        ¥ 100 million / man … manufacturing department

Sales per person are computed from past data as are the averages of the same industry and estimated future wage increases.

The assumption of this model is the same as the above personnel cost ration method, because;

$$\frac{\text{number}}{\text{of man}}{\text{power}} = \frac{\text{Sales}}{\text{Sales per person}} = \frac{\text{Sales} \times (\text{wage} \div \text{sales per person})}{\text{wage}} = \frac{\text{Sales} \times \text{ratio of wage cost}}{\text{wage}}$$

(3) From regression analysis

(a) Labour equipment ratio
Labour productivity rises as increases in the labour-equipment ratio. The regression analysis is computed by using the labour-equipment ratio as an independent variable. Using Douglas function, total production is calculated thus;

$$Y = aL^b K^{1-b}$$

where Y = production, L = labour and K = equipment

(1) $$\frac{Y}{L} = a\left(\frac{K}{L}\right)^{1-b}$$

next, the total cost is defined as:

$$C = kK + wL$$
where C = total cost, k = cost for equipment, w = wage rate

The condition of minimum cost for certain amounts of production is (see note 2):

(2) $$\frac{K}{L} = \alpha - \beta w$$

Thus, the labour equipment ratio rises as the wage rate rise. We can compute the value of a, b, α, β by regression analysis. From equation (2), we can get the value of K/L if the value of w is known. Then, by using equation (1), we can arrive at the value of L, since Y is already known.

(b) Regression analysis by using the amount of output as an independent variable

> Number of personnel of a product division = $a + bY$
> where Y = amount of sales.

The increase of productivity is expressed in a, since the number of personnel does not increase in proportion to Y.

For other departments, some other intermediate outputs can be used. For example, the production department can use converted physical output for Y, and the sales department can use number of orders for Y.

This method assumes that an optimum number can be obtained by regression analysis.

(4) Input-output analysis
The number of personnel in service departments, in components departments which do not have outside sales and in departments which have mutual transactions can be computed simultaneously by using the input-output model. This model has already been explained earlier in section 9 · 3. The value of input coefficients change and the future values have to be estimated by time series extension or by some other method.

C   Integration of micro approach and macro approach
Macro approaches tend to give normative values, while micro approaches tend to give forecasted values, reflecting the requests of many departments. The numbers which are built up from the micro approach tend to be much larger than the numbers built up from the macro approach.

Generally speaking, the number of the macro approach are preferential, because personnel costs have to be within a certain percentage of sales in order that the company can have competitive power. The gaps between these values by macro and micro approach have to be solved by a personnel reduction plan.

3. Identification of technical skills

Scientific skills are becoming key skills for technology intensive companies. C company and S company are using the matrix of skill to identify their needs. Skills are classified on X, Y and Z axes. X axis shows the educational background or academic skill, Y axis shows the product and the Z axis indicates the basic common technology. By using the matrix that is shown in Table 9.20, the company can identify the supply and demand of scientific skills. The X axis is used for recruiting.

4. Estimation of supply

(1) Use of the transition matrix. The internal supply of human resources can be estimated by the use of the transition matrix. The inventory of personnel placed at a job at the end of a year is computed.

> Beginning inventory − (promotion + transfer + temporary retirement + retirement and death) + (promotion to this job + transfer to this job + returns from temporary retirement) = ending inventory.

> $a_0 \, Qt = a_t$
> a_0 = beginning inventory of each job

Q = transition matrix, a_t = inventory of each job at the end of t years. Q can be estimated from past data, or by a normative model.

Table 9.20   Specification of skills on the XYZ axis

X. Educational background	Y. Products							Z. Technology						
	· · ·	Copier	Printer	Computer	Video	SV	Camera	· · ·	Electric design	Mechanical design	Semiconductor	Material analysis	opto electronics	Opticals
Mathematics physics	○							○						
Applied physics														
Chemical														
Information engineering														
Mechanical engineering														
·														
·														
·														

(b) Age distribution

Forecasting age distribution is considered as important in Japan because of the life-time employment policy, although this policy is not a contract. As the age distribution becomes older, the capability tends to decline, wages will increase under the length-of-service wage system and corporate culture will become stagnant. Forecasting of age distribution is a rough estimation of the supply of capabilities. This forecasting is rather easy, it is frequently used by many companies, although very few measures can be taken to solve the old age problem. The growth of the company is the ultimate measure to cope with this problem, because it makes possible the in-breeding of fresh new blood.

The estimation of age distribution is made possible by a simple simulation.

$$N_{i+1} = N_i(1-r_i)$$

where N_i = number of employees, by sex at the age of i at the end of the year

r_i = retirement rate at the age of i

This is estimated by the retirement rate ri of each age. r_i is estimated by past data. The pattern of r_i is completely different by the sex of employees.

If new recruits are considered, then the model will be

$$N_{i+1} = N_i (1 - r_i) + Y_i$$

where Yi is number of the new recruits of each age.

5. Closing quantitative gaps

Gaps are closed by (1) new recruitment from fresh graduates from universities and high schools, (2) recruit of experienced staff and workers from other companies, which is rather rare in Japan, (3) Transfer of employees, (4) Training. Other means are (5) replacement by machines, (6) enhancement of productivity by improvement of method of operation.

The surplus of personnel are displaced by (1) discontinued new recruitment, (2) increase of retirement by improved retirement allowances, (3) transfer to other departments, (4) transfer to subsidiary companies which in turn discharge old aged employees, (5) temporary transfer to growth companies, motor car manufacturers, for example, (6) temporary lay-offs paying ordinary salary, but where the company can save overhead costs. (7) The final means is discharge, which is rarely used in Japan. There is no temporary lay-off system in Japan.

6. Closing qualitative gaps

The means to close the gap are not the quantitative computation but are mostly in the personnel management system.

The goals can be classified into two: one is to enhance the capabilities for the existing products, the other is to create capabilities for new business. We will study a case of human resource planning of Omron Corporation (a manufacturer of electronic equipment, such as ticket vending machines). A self assessment of human resources disclosed the following defects. (1) Delays of new product development. (2) Delivery of products were late, one or two months after the order. (3) The stock of components and materials was too large, no effort was taken to decrease the inventory. The plan to solve these problems was named as "Action 61". A new policy was established. The policy contained several areas. Firstly, six study teams were formed: technology innovation teams, marketing, purchasing, production, distribution and accounts receivable collection teams, which were expected to plan innovations in these six areas of seven product divisions. Secondly, a new philosophy was established. It stressed (1) learning from the customer, (2) respect for people, (3) a challenging mind towards new trials. Thirdly, the new personnel policy was formulated. For the overall enhancement of the capability of personnel and for the change of attitude, the following was planned. (1) The career system was changed, and two career routes were created, general job career and specialized job career. The latter restricted the working district so that changes of residence were not needed. (2) Interviews were increased. Goal attainment interviews, training interviews, capability development interviews and career development interviews were initiated. Employees received interviews several times a year.

(3) Training programmes were systematized. A new center was created for off off-the-job training. Self development systems were reinforced by financial aids, to correspondence courses, by encouraging to obtain a number of licenses, by providing corporate lecture courses.

For the enhancement of capabilities to develop new products, the following measures were planned. (1) The rotation of personnel was planned and high calibers were allocated to new business development. (2) Internal venture systems were started. (3) Delegation of authority was encouraged in every area. Reporting after decisions was allowed. (4) Seventy percent failure and 30% success probability was allowed for the minimum standard of risk evaluation. Employees were encouraged to try new things, if there was a chance of success of more than 30%. (5) Young men were promoted to important tasks. (6) Two or three years deficit in new ventures was allowed.

These new systems were planned in the long-range plan, and employees were encouraged to implement long-range planning along with these new personnel systems. The visions of the company in towards the 21st century were expected to change corporate culture towards a challenging spirit.

A case of the human resource plans of the Taisei Construction Corporation

This includes the following items: (1) Establishment of two career courses and rules of change of courses. (2) Recruitment of experienced engineers from outside in addition to new recruitment from university graduates. (3) Personnel assessment systems were changed to positive assessment systems, evaluating the efforts to accomplish something and to ignore the failures. (4) The establishment of status ladders in addition to job ladders. (5) To mobilize aged employees new businesses were started.

7. Training programmes

The training programme is an important element of long-range human resource planning, because it takes a long time for the enhancement of capability and to make the capability adapt to new strategic needs. Training also repays its cost in Japanese corporations because of the life time employment system.

Table 9.21 Training courses of Canon Corporation

Types / Trainee	Corporate		Functional		Production	Operating units		Trainer training	Self development
	Training by grade class	Functional	International division	Research and development		Training by grade classes	Functional		
Department directors	Director training	Labour law	Management seminars	CDS director course	I E course K T course U E course S A course			MTP instructor (other 10 courses)	Creative life seminar
Managers	Newly appointed managers MTP		Returnee training Foreign languages	R&D management course CDS manager course	(other 29 courses)	Foreman grid seminar	V E I E		
Middle management and foremen	Middle staff training Middle engineer training		International key personnel training International production staff training Foreign assignee training Foreign assignee spouse training Foreign law English course	R&D leader course Core technology course Comprehensive technology course Soft technology R&D international course		Foreman course Management games Creativity development TWI Conference leader Creativity development	Q C Q A Accounting Computer Cost accounting Cost engineering		Correspondence courses External seminars
General employees	2nd year training new recruit training	Office automation training	Foreigner trainee course Foreigner technical trainee course	Basic technology		Improvement training Basic course New recruit training	Technical skills KYT		Recommended books
Total courses	11	2	13	11	33	15	15	11	–
On the job	On the job training								

Training aims at changes in capability. Capability consists of conceptual skill, human skill and technical skill.

Table 9.21 is a case of the training system of Canon Corporation. The training courses by grade classes and international department training courses stress decision-making skills and human skills, whilst other functional training courses put an emphasis on technical skills.

Training is classified by the place of training, that is, on-the-job training, off-the-job training and self-development. 'OJT' is much more important than the others, but in order to change skill, or to make trainees have different skills than those they are provided by their present jobs, Off-J-Ts have to be used. Table 9.21 shows there are a variety of training courses.

The training is also classified by the sponsor of training. Head office, the international department and the divisional offices mostly do management training, emphasizing conceptual and human skills whilst functional departments carry out technical training.

New employees receive Off-J-T entry training for a week or two before they are trained on the job for more than six months at plant sites and at sales fronts. Through their whole life, the employee has frequent opportunities for training. Under the life time commitment system, training pay are considered as important. Some old companies, such as Hitachi and Tokyo Electric Power Co. have even college courses and high school courses, but these general training courses are decreasing as outside universities and high schools increase.

The long-range planning of training starts from identifying the needs of training, then goes on to plan the training system, facilities and expenditures for training. Tokyo Electric Power Co. has a large central training school, which provides college courses, and a number of other courses and spends about ¥ 2.2 billion ($ 15 million). Total expense in 1988 for off-the-job training are about ¥ 5 billion and the training hours were 12 days per employee. The Canon Corporation provides more than 100 courses for off-the-job training as seen in Table 9.21. On the average, Japanese companies engaged in production of technology intensive products are spending about 0.5 percent of sales for off-the-job training.

8. Ability to recruit competent employees

The gaps of human resources can be filled by an internal market and by an external market. If the company can recruit freely the needed manpower from outside, human resource planning could be easily implemented. However, a vicious circle happens sometimes are this. When a company is losing money, competent people will leave the company while the battle of turnaround is being carried out, and the financial performance will deteriorate still further. On the contrary, excellent companies can attract competent people, thus they can have favorable cycles.

According to a number of surveys, the following three principles for recruitment are important.

(a) The performance and the popularity of the company. The estimated growth rate, profitability, stability and size of the company – these are affected by the quality of the product-market strategy. For example, Toray had number one ranking in 1970s, but since the decline of demand for the synthetic fiber, its ranking has declined.

Attractiveness has the following system, this system is the same as the system of self assessment, studied in Chapter 6.

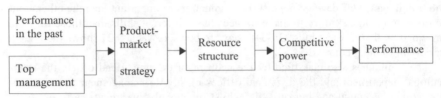

(b) The contents of jobs and how they are consistent with the interest of the applicants. Those who like sales activities will apply for a trading company, and those who are fond of technological research will like to go to technology intensive companies. Employees want to satisfy their self-actualization needs. The above factors, performance and product-market strategy affect the attractiveness of jobs. Diversified companies tend to have higher attractiveness than specialized companies.

(c) Opportunities for promotion and wage increase, as extrinsic rewards. Medium sized companies are more attractive in these respects than large companies, because the number of new recruits is much less, and chances of being promoted are higher.

The level of the above three items need to be higher than the average, or than aspiration levels. If they are higher than the average, they have a substituting relationship. Smaller companies sometimes offer pay that is twice as high as usual for key technological jobs. Consulting companies also offer extremely high pay substituting the size of the company.

(note 1)

$$Y = f(K, L) \quad \text{– production function}$$
$$C = kK + wL \quad \text{– total cost}$$

By fixing Y, minimum can be derived:

$$C_\lambda = kK + wL + \lambda \{Y^* - f(K, L)\} \quad \text{– minimum}$$
$$\lambda = \text{The Lagrange multiplier}$$

$$\frac{\partial C_\lambda}{\partial K} = 0, \quad \frac{\partial C_\lambda}{\partial L} = 0, \quad \frac{\partial C_\lambda}{\partial \lambda} = 0$$

$$\frac{f_k(K, L)}{k} = \frac{f_L(K, L)}{w} = \lambda$$

(note 2) Using the Lagrange multiplier

$$C = kK + wL + \lambda \ (Y^* - aL^b K^{1-b})$$

To arrive at the minimum value of C,

$$\frac{dC_\lambda}{\partial L} = 0, \quad \frac{dC_\lambda}{\partial K} = 0, \quad \frac{dC_\lambda}{\partial \lambda} = 0$$

(1) $$\frac{K}{L} = \frac{1-b}{b} \cdot \frac{w}{k}$$

If b and k are assumend to be constant, then (1) can be expressed as

(2) $$\frac{k}{L} = \alpha + \beta w$$

(References, Kono, 1975; Management Center, 1968; Fombrun, Tichy and Devanna Ed. 1984; Manzini and Gridley, 1987; Niehaus, 1987; Nkomo, 1988.)

9.7 Strategic acquisition of resources

Strategic acquisition means methods other than the internal composition of resources, the recruiting of fresh graduates from schools, capital investment, or than incremental investment. Strategic acquisition has one or three characteristics: (1) it tries to use outside resources, or (2) it is a jumping approach, or (3) it is a round about approach.

(a) External growth
External growth is an attempt to acquire outside resource structures already formulated as a system, to obtain a set of composition of human, capital and information resources.

External growth includes (1) purchase of patents or buying, (2) purchase of assets and business, (3) acquisition of a company, (4) a strategic alliance or a joint venture by contract, the establishment of a joint venture company.

By these methods, a number of product-market strategies are made possible. By these methods also, many functional areas are strengthened or suddenly formulated.

The acquisition of other companies makes possible a prompt formation of resource structures, when one company cannot formulate all capabilities, it can make use of outside resources.

On the other hand, there are some defects.

(1) In Japan, there are few sales of companies, because a company is considered as a 'Gemeinschaft', a community organization of employees. Unfriendly acquisition is considered to be unethical. However, the opportunities for OEM and joint ventures are abundant.

(2) Easy diversification by external growth tends to result in failure.

The use of acquisition by Japanese companies is increasing in foreign countries, by acquiring foreign companies.

Alliances or joint venture, on the contrary imply that more than two companies cooperate to do something on an equal power basis, providing each other with unique capabilities and trying to nurture the effects of synergy. There are the following cases. (1) Quasi-vertical integration. For example, a group of component manufacturers which are exclusive suppliers to Toyota, receive technical assistance from Toyota. (2) Vertical cooperation. A chemical company invents a drug, and another pharmaceutical company sells it. (3) Horizontal cooperation. The joint development of a drug by two companies. OEM production. In automobile industry, there are worldwide cooperations between car manufacturers. (4) Cooperation of sales. Sales channels are mutually utilized between the two companies.

As the required level of technology becomes more complicated one company cannot construct every area of technology on its own effort and cooperation with other companies, even with competitors, becomes necessary. Sony did not sell the patents of the VCR to any other company, but Matsushita (and JVC) sold the patents of VHS to many manufacturers and formed a team of production for VHS-VCR. The result was a drastic overturn of the share of market, supported by increased supply of software.

(b) Construction of a bridgehead

This is not to start a business with sufficient resource structures, but to start a new business without enough capabilities. For example, a steel and iron manufacturing company may start to produce ceramics for semiconductors with a joint venture contract disregarding profitability, and try to learn and accumulate knowledge through experience. A tire manufacturer enters into sports goods, and through producing and selling them with a loss, the company can accumulate knowledge on production and the sales of leisure goods.

(c) Use of foreign resources.

One computer software company employs foreign engineers, British, American, Indian, Malaysian and Singaporian engineers. One company built a research laboratory in the U.S. employing 80 researchers. In the U.S., there are about 250,000 graduates from science and engineering departments, one third of whom are masters or doctors. Japan has almost the same number of graduates from natural sciences, but by employing foreign engineers, the company can employ people with different approaches, different ways of thinking and thus it can form a team of diversified characters to develop creative products, although there are some legal barriers to this.

(d) Recruitment of experienced employees from outside.

There might be some doubt whether the recruitment of experienced researchers is a strategic approach, but in Japan it is not considered a usual method, because the recruitment of fresh graduates from high schools and universities is the usual method.

High growth companies, such as Canon, Sony, Asahi Chemicals and Asahi Glass have been recruiting many experienced engineers. To help this sort of employment, about thirty recruiting companies have started business.

The aims of recruiting experienced researchers are two fold. One is to obtain key capabilities, such as electronics, computer sciences and foreign exchange operations. The other is to vitalize the corporate culture by mixing them with the existing employees. The different way of thinking of new recruits who are coming from other companies with different corporate cultures is expected to stimulate the bureaucratic corporate culture of large corporations.

The ability to attract the new recruits with experience comes from three sources, as was already analyzed. The future of the company, how the new jobs are attractive to their interests and extrinsic rewards.

(e) The cultivation of highly technological knowledge.
The training of employees is nothing new to Japanese corporations, but the change of highly technological knowledge by inside training is a new phenomena. As technology changes rapidly, the company has urgent needs for new technologies, such as electronics and biotechnology, which are hard to obtain from new recruits. Many companies have started to open training courses aimed at changing the knowledge of employees. Konica opened a course in the corner of a plant to train graduates from chemical science and the mechanical engineering to master electronics. Twice a week, half day training continues for two months. NEC has opened five "comprehensive technical training courses" and ten "basic technology training courses". The former educates on communications and information sciences, one day a week for one year. The latter educates a number of new technologies, once a week for one year. These two cases are examples of plans to cultivate new highly technological knowledges in order to close the gaps of strategy and the resource structure, by means of inside training.

Summary

1. The resource structure is a vessel whereby research, production and marketing activities are performed. Distinctive competence in these capacities produces differentiated products and competitive power. These competences are formed by knowledge, information systems, people, facilities and money.

   Some capabilities are key resources for new product development and for competitive edges. These capabilities have to be formed before the strategy is developed.

   Between the capabilities, there are complementary relations and substitution relations. Key resources with complementary relations have high priority for formation.

2. It takes a long time to construct these capabilities, and expenditure comes first, the fruits come in the future, so it has to be planned in the long-range plan with long-term visions. In Japan, internal growth is more popular than external growth.

   The formation of new resource structures start from future strategies which have the utmost importance for successful resource formation. Comparing the needs and supply of re-source capacity, gaps and surplus are identified. Gaps mean both shortages in quality and quantity.

3. Capital investment plans can be planned by the same process as the above. The needs are accumulated from research and development strategies, the new product-market strategy, marketing and production plan. It is checked by using the macro approach whether this amount is healthy from a financial aspect.

4. The information system is one of the key capabilities of the organization. It is advancing everyday by progress in semiconductors and computers. The information technology is ap-plied to research and development, marketing, production and office management.

Information technology has compressed time. The time for designing and for computing has become shorter. The response to customers' needs has become faster. The company can provide a variety of products to the customer using a flexible manufacturing system.

Because of large investment in hardware and software, the information systems have to be used fully. The system becomes a capital intensive facility.

5. Personnel has to be planned, under the life-time employment system, by the long-range planning. However, because of the difficulty of forecasting, detailed head-count planning is difficult, so, rather than the micro alternative, macro planning is generally used. The train-ing programme and personnel system of planning is more important.

6. Strategic approach
Strategic approach means any approach other than that of normal internal growth. It is not an incremental approach, but a discontinuous approach. The chances of their success are not clear in advance, but policy can be planned in the long-range plan.

Bibliography for resource structure

In Japanese

Akiyama, T. (1975), Sozo (Creativity), Baifukan, Tokyo.

Business Research Bureau, (1983), Gijitsu Kaihatsu Senraku to Management (Research and Development Strategy and Management), Kigyo Kenkyukai, Tokyo.

Japan Productivity Center, (1982), Kigyo Yosan no Jisho Kenkyu (Survey on Budgetary Con-trol), Japan Productivity Center, Tokyo.

Kansai Productivity Center, (1976), Keiei Soshiki no Shindoko (New Trends in Business Or-ganizations), Kansai Productivity Center, Tokyo.

Kansai Productivity Center, (1986), Keiei no Shintenkai (New Trends of Management), Kansai Productivity Center, Osaka.

Kono, T., (1956), Keiei Keikaku no Riron (Theory of Business Planning), Diamond-sha, Tokyo.

Kono, T., (1974), Keiei Senryaku no Kaimei (Analysis of Corporate Strategy), Diamond-sha, Tokyo.

Kono, T., (1975), Choki Keieikeikaku no Tankyu (Analysis of Long-range Planning), Dia-mond-sha, Tokyo.

Kono, T., (1980), Senryaku Keieikeikaku no Tatekata (Introduction to Strategic Planning), Diamond-sha, Tokyo.

Kono, T., (1985), Gendai no Keiei Senryaku (Modern Corporate Strategy), Diamond-sha, Tokyo.

Kono, T., (1987), Shinseihin Kaihatsu Senryaku (New Product Development Strategy), Dia-
    mond-sha, Tokyo.
Kono, T., (1988), Henkaku no Kigyo Bunka (Change of Corporate Culture), Kodan-sha,
    Tokyo.
Kono, T., (1988), Keieigaku Genri (Principles of Management), Dobunkan, Tokyo.
Management Center, Editor: Tekisei Jinin (Human Resource Planning), (1968), Management
    Center, Tokyo.
MITI: Keiei Ryoku Hyoka (Measurement of Corporate Capability), (1973–80, 86, 87), Min-
    istry of International Trade and Industry, Tokyo.
Mori, S., (1981), Kenkyukaihatsu kanri-rin (Management of Research and Management),
    Yushindo, Tokyo.
Nishida, K., (1984), R&D Tema Hakutsu no Management (Management to Create the Subject
    of R & D), Bunshido, Tokyo.
Science Bureau, (1985), Kagaku Gijitsu Hakusho (White Paper on Science and Technology),
    Kagaku Gijitsu-Cho, Tokyo.

In English

Allen, T. J., (1977), Managing the Flow of Technology, MIT Press, Mass.
Ansoff & Stewart, (1967), Strategies for a Technology-based Business, Harvard Business
    Review, November-December.
Burgleman, R. A. and Maidique, M. A., (1988), Strategic Management of Technology and In-
    novation, Irwin, Ill.
Burns, T. and Stalker G.M., (1961), The Management of Innovation, Tavistock, London.
Chandler, A. D., (1962), Strategy and Structure; Chapters in the History of the Industrial
    Enterprise, M.I.T. Press, Mass.
Channon, D. F., (1973), The Strategy and Structure of British Enterprise, Macmillan, London.
Clark III R. D., (1971), "Group-induced Shift Toward Risk", Psychological Bulletin, vol. 76.
    No. 4.
The Conference Board: Planning and the Chief Executive, (1972), The Conference Board, New
    York.
The Conference Board: Planning and the Corporate Planning Director, (1974), The Conference
    Board, New York.
The Conference Board: Corporate Guides to Long-Range Planning, (1976), The Conference
    Board, New York.
Davies, S. M., (1986), Managing Corporate Culture, Harper & Row, New York.
Fombrun, C., Tichy, N.M. & Devanna, M. A., (1984), Strategic Human Resource Management,
    John Wiley & Sons, New York.
Galbraith, J. and Nathanson, D., (1978), Strategy Implementation: The Role of Structure and
    Process, West Publishing, Minn.
Galbraith, J. R., (1984), Designing the Innovative Organization, in R.B. Lamb, (1984), Com-
    petetive Strategic Management, Prentice-Hall, N.J.
Goldhar, J. and Jelink, M., (1983), Plan for Economics of Scope, Harvard Business Review,
    November-December.
Haefele, J. H., (1962), Creativity & Innovation, Reinhold, Colorado.
Hershey, P. & Blanchard, K. H., (1977), Management of Organizational Behavior, Prentice-
    Hall, New York.

Kanter, R. M., (1983), The Change Masters, Simon & Schuster, New York.
Katz, D. & Kahn, R. L., (1966), The Social Psychology of Organizations, John Wiley, New York.
Kono, T., (1984), Strategy and Structure of Japanese Enterprises, Macillan Press, London.
Kudo, H. et al, (1988), How US and Japanese CEO's Spend Their Time, Long-Range Planning, December.
Kuwahara, Y. et al, (1989), Planning Research and Development at the Central Research Laboratory of Hitachi, Long-Range Planning, June.
Levitt T., (1963), Creativity is not Enouth, Harvard Business Review, March-June.
Likert, R., (1967), The Human Organization, McGraw-Hill, New York.
Likert, R., (1969), New Patterns of Management, McGraw-Hill, New York.
Manjini, A. O. & Gridley, J. D., (1987), Integrating Human Resources and Strategic Business Planning, AMACOM, New York.
March, J. G. & Simon, H.A., (1958), Organizations, John Wiley & Sons, Inc.
McCaskey M. B., (1982), The Executive Challenge, Pittman Publishing.
Merwe, A. & Merive, S., (1985), Strategic Leadership and Chief Executive, Long Range Planning, February.
Miles, R. E. & Snow, C.C., (1978), Organizational Strategy, Structure, and Process, McGraw-Hill, New York.
Mintzberg, H., (1973a), The Nature of Managerial Work, Harper and Row, New York.
Mintzberg, H., (1973b), "Strategy Making in Three Modes", Winter, 44–53, California Management Review
NAA, (1964), Long-range Profit Planning, New York
NAA, (1967), Financial Analysis to Guide Capital Expenditure Decisions, N.Y.
Niehaus, R. J. (Editor), (1987), Strategic Human Resource Planning, Plenum Press, New York
Nkomos, S. M., (1988), Strategic Planning for Human Resources, Long Range Planning.
Nystrom, H., (1979), Creativity and Innovation, John Wiley, New York.
Osborn, A. F., (1953), Applied Imagination, Charles Scribners, California.
Peters & Waterman, (1982), In Search of Excellence, Harper & Row, New York.
Porter, M. E., (1980), Competitive Strategy; Techniques for Analyzing Industries and Competitors, Free Press, New York.
Porter, M. E., (1985), Competitive Advantage; Creating and Sustaining Superior Performance, Free Press, New York.
Prahalad, C. K. and Hamel, G., (1990), The Core Competence of the Corporation, Harvard Business Review, May-June.
Quinn, J. B., Mintzberg, H. & James, R. M., (1988), The Strategy Process, Prentice-Hall, N.J.
Riggs, H. E., (1943), Managing High-technology Companies, Wadsworth, California.
Rumelt, R. P., (1974), Strategy, Structure and Economic Performance, Harvard University Press, Mass.
Staw, B. M., (1976), Intrinsic and Extrinsic Motivation, General Learning Press, N.J.
Steiner, G. A., (1979), Strategic Planning; What Every Manager Must Know; A Step-by-Step Guide, Free Press, New York.
Thompson, J. D., (1967), Organization in Action, McGraw-Hill, New York.
Von Fange, E., (1959), Professional Creativity, Prentice-Hall, N.J.
Williamson, O. E., (1975), Markets and Hierarchies; Analysis and Antitrust Implications, Free Press, New York.

Chapter 10 Evaluation of strategy
and allocation of resources

A. The evaluation of strategy

Evaluation of a strategy aims to predict the results of strategy, to compare it with the goals and to make a judgment as to whether it will promote or obstruct goal attainment.

Evaluation of strategies is a difficult task, because there are few precedents and the prediction of results is difficult. The strategy changes the course of promotion of people and it relates to a variety of values. There can be many negative evaluations of one project and there can be many other alternatives. Accordingly, the evaluation has to be judged by the top management based on their beliefs. Hitachi entered the computer business in about 1960, much later than other companies and when other companies were divesting their computer businesses. Its top management decided that the company will continue to develop computers. This happened because the Hitachi top management evaluated the importance of computer-related technologies.

Although prediction of the probability of success is difficult, the company will fail only if belief or intuitive decisions are used. Excessive expansion of Yoshinoya (fast food business) or improper diversification by Kojin (pulp, paper, textile and housing) proved to be a failure, because their analyses were not sufficient. A company should conduct an analysis by collecting information on one the hand, and on the other, it should use experiments to generate further information, or should use sequential decisions to avoid large failures.

10.1 Evaluation criteria – rating scale methods

As a tool of evaluation, the goals of the company such as sales or profitability should be used eventually. American corporation use the rate of return based on the discounted cash-flow method, but many planner say that this computation is artificial in many cases. There is no doubt that the goals of the company are bases of evaluation, but intervening variables, such as the size of the total demand, the competitive power of one product or the possibilities of production and marketing are frequently used. Generally speaking, evaluation and measurement are composed of the following items (based on the author's survey; Rumelt, 1980; Tills, 1963).

(1) External consistency
What is the size of the market, the growth rat and the position on the product life cycle curve? Is the environment favorable to projects, is it in harmony with ethical principles and in harmony with social responsibility? In order to evaluate projects from
this angle, it is necessary to forecast future changes in the environmental forces.

(2) Competitive strength – help from existing products and resources
Do the products have competitive strength i quality and cost? How can existing resources or present products support new business? Is there a superiority of resources?
The expertise of technology, location of plant, superiority of equipment, benefit from
the size of the company and strengths of sales channels are also elements. Can existing products provide synergy?

(3) Possibility of production and marketing
Can key resources be obtained? Are patents obtainable? Does the company have
technological or personnel capability or can it procure the funds for capital investments? It is not necessary to overempahsize how these fit with the values of top
management but projects which are not congruent with the values of top management
are hard to have carried out. It is necessary to take into account the opposition of la-
bor unions and employees in general.

(4) Internal consistency – help towards other products
Can the new product support other, existing, products or new projects? For example,
can the technology of this project support the development of technology of an other
product? Can new products provide other products with synergy? Does the new products comply with basic policy or basic strategies? For example, a project to invest in
land to make profit through rise in price may not be in compliance with the basic
strategy that the company should develop new material using high technology. Not
only harmony with the basic strategy but also harmony with the business creed and
business culture is important. The corporate culture can be changed by implementation of small strategic projects, but a large project which is not supported by
corporate culture will not succeed. Generally speaking, internal consistency means
that a new project will vitalize other subsystems of the corporation and that a new
product has synergy with other products.

(5) Direct contribution to goals
How will a new project affect the level of sales? Will it increase profit? Will the rate
of return of the project be high enough? Is the efficiency of use of limited resources,
such as management time, high or not?
    Is the risk large or small? Is the expected loss in the worst case smaller than the
equity capital and can the company stand the risk? The risk is reduced when it is
mixed with other business.
    Timing is important if the value of results will decrease rapidly when projects

Table 10.1 New product evaluation system
"What items of the following are important to evaluate a new product?"

Stage Evaluation items	In earlier stages (from idea to technical development)	In middle stages (from technical development to merchandising)	In final stages (before production & sales)
1. Size & stability of the market (Industry attractiveness)			
(1) Size of the market	74 (%)	39 (%)	29 (%)
(2) Stage of the life cycle	36	31	13
(3) Competition	49	45	37
(4) Stability of demand	33	40	34
(5) Value for social responsibility	22	22	15
2. Possibility of production & selling (Possibility to enter)			
(1) Possibility to obtain technology	72	21	3
(2) Size of expense for research & market development	48	37	7
(3) Size of capital investment	20	62	26
(4) Possibility of obtaining resources	20	40	16
3. Competitive strength (Advantage provided by existing capability)			
(1) Capability of research & development	73	20	2
(2) Support of production technology	23	66	12
(3) Cost of production	15	66	37
(4) Sales capability	19	45	38

continued

Table 10.1 New product evaluation system (cont.)

Stage / Evaluation items	In earlier stages (from idea to technical development)	In middle stages (from technical development to merchandising)	In final stages (before production & sales)
4. Contribution of new product to present product & future product			
(1) Contribution to present market	44 (%)	27 (%)	13 (%)
(2) Strengthening of present sales channel	5	38	44
(3) Expansion of research & development capability	48	27	12
(4) Expansion of production technology	12	54	25
(5) Offsetting the fluctuation of existing product sales by seasonal or business cycles	15	19	23
(6) Diversification of customers	6	18	27
5. Profitability			
(1) Forecast of sales	32	38	31
(2) Increase or decrease of sales of other product	17	37	29
(3) Profit ratio on sales	17	46	45
(4) Return on investment	19	50	31
(5) How many years to reach the break even point	13	45	33
(6) Loss in worst case (After capital investment)	10	34	30

(note) Mail questionaire survey on new product development, conducted in 1980. Analysis of responses from 157 manufacturing corporations

are not implemented on time. It matters when the delay decreases the value or cause loss.

The above five groups of items are usually used for evaluation. These evaluation items are similar to the measurement of PPM (attractiveness of industry and competitive power).

Why are these evaluation items important? (a) The strategy tries to act on the environment, so external consistency and competitive power are necessary. (b) It consumes large quantities of limited resources, and availability of resources are necessary for its success. (c) If one strategy supports another strategy, then it strengthens the corporate resources. This kind of synergy is desirable, that is, internal consistency is desirable. (d) And lastly, contribution to the basic goal of the corporation is essential as the ultimate criteria.

These relations are simply stated in the following model.

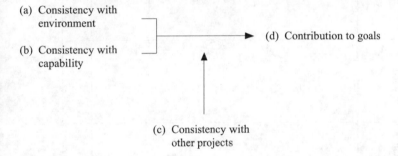

(a) Consistency with environment

(b) Consistency with capability

(d) Contribution to goals

(c) Consistency with other projects

The above theory is supported by the survey results shown in Table 10.1. It shows items used evaluated new products.

The survey is on new product developments and it does not include and evaluation of existing products and is not the evaluation of multinational management nor a vertical integration strategy. But the principles can be applied to the evaluation of all strategies. Looking at the frequency of each item, we find that the above-mentioned five groups of items are important.

The relative importance of each evaluation scale changes as the projects proceed from one stage to another. In the beginning of development, (1) external consistency, (2) competitive strength and (3) possibilities of entering are important to attain goals. In the middle of development, (4) internal consistency and (5) direct contribution to goals become important. In the last stage, capital investment is carried out and direct contribution to basic goals becomes important. Since the quantity of information increases as project is developed, this is one of the reasons for the change of importance of the evaluation items.

An example of evaluation of research projects is shown in Table 10.2.

The items of evaluation seem to be a little different from those items in Table 10.1,

Table 10.2 A Case of Evaluation Scale for Research Projects (Company O)

Criteria \ level	Excellent 5	good 4	fair 3	poor 2	very poor 1	
1. Consistency with basic strategy						

2. Technical strength
   Creativity
   Timing
   Originality
   Patent protection
   Cost						

3. Overall evaluation						

4. Contribution to basic goals
   Size of market
   Share of market
   Size of company sales
   Sales channel
   Labour productivity						

5. Resources required						
Total						

Table 10.3 The Matrix Evaluation Model

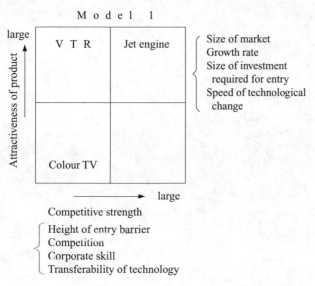

M o d e l   1

large

Attractiveness of product

V T R	Jet engine
Colour TV	

⎧ Size of market
⎪ Growth rate
⎨ Size of investment
⎪   required for entry
⎩ Speed of technological
     change

large

Competitive strength

⎧ Height of entry barrier
⎪ Competition
⎨ Corporate skill
⎩ Transferability of technology

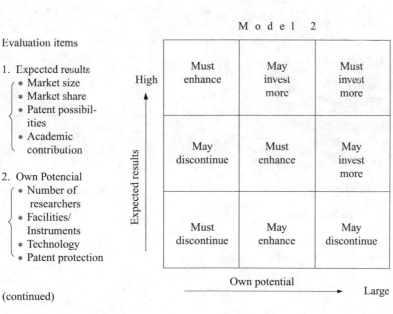

M o d e l   2

Evaluation items

1. Expected results
   ⎧ * Market size
   ⎪ * Market share
   ⎨ * Patent possibil-
   ⎪   ities
   ⎪ * Academic
   ⎩   contribution

2. Own Potential
   ⎧ * Number of
   ⎪   researchers
   ⎨ * Facilities/
   ⎪   Instruments
   ⎪ * Technology
   ⎩ * Patent protection

Expected results

High

Must enhance	May invest more	Must invest more
May discontinue	Must enhance	May invest more
Must discontinue	May enhance	May discontinue

Own potential

Large

(continued)

Table 10.3 The Matrix Evaluation Model (cont.)

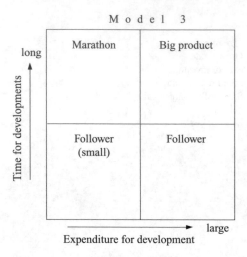

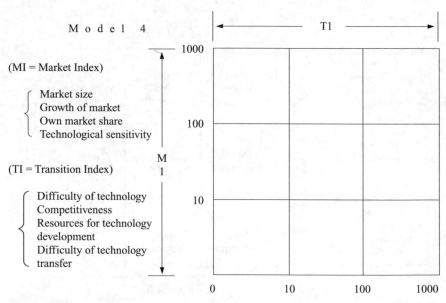

(continued)

Table 10.3 The Matrix Evaluation Model (cont.)

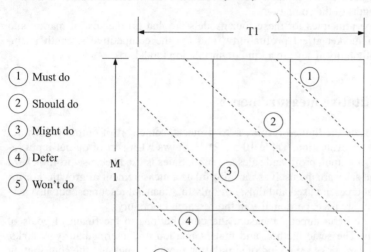

but there are many similarities. That is, (1) consistency with the strategy is a general evaluation and lacking in Table 10.1, (2) technical competence corresponds to (2) possibly and (3) competitiveness of Table 10.1 (4) contribution to goals and (5) amount of resources to be invested may correspond to (5), profitability, of Table 10.1.

10.2 Evaluation criteria – the matrix model

The two axes matrix method is frequently used. Table 10.3 shows many examples. The principles of criteria are the same as for table 10.1, but the matrix model simplifies the criteria, and appeals to visual clarity.

Model 1 is a case of G Company. Two factors, the attractiveness of the industry and competitive strength for the product correspond to items 1 and 3 in Table 10.1. The two factors are the same as the factors of PPM criteria.

Model 2 is used by H Company, and is applied to the evaluation of research projects. The criteria use intermediate items to goals and attractiveness and competitiveness are used for evaluation.

Model 3 is used by C Company. The length of development and size of cost for development is used. This company put an emphasis on "big projects" and "marathon race projects".

Model 4 is used by T Company. It uses the attractiveness of market and technological strengths of the company.

The common principles for these four models are that (a) the size of market and growth rate of market affect profitability, and (b) the competitive strength is important for profitability. They are a kind of simulation model.

10.3 Quantitative measurements

In order to allocate the limited resources to projects, some sort of output-input ratio has to be used for evaluation. Table 10.5 ((2)-1) shows what sort of output-input ratios are used. For output, profit and sales are used. Sales is used because profit is hard to estimate, and sales are themselves meaningful as a measurement of growth. For input, limited resources are used and thus, not only the financial resources, but also personnel resources are used, particularly in the research laboratory.

Quantitative criteria directly measure the contributions to the financial goals of the corporation. The scale method and matrix method use intermediate yardsticks. These midway yardsticks are a kind of simulation model, to measure the contribution to the goals of the corporations.

10.4 Strategic policies

Strategic policies are used for evaluation of strategic projects, as is shown in Table 10.5 ((2)-2). For example,one company estimates that semiconductor are the key elements of the electronics industry with a huge market, and the company can have competitive power in that area, so it decides that it will hold a number one position in the market. With this strategic policy, research in conductors and their production has highest priority. In this case, strategic policy is the evaluation criteria.

However, in order to build strategic policy, strategy should be evaluated, and if it is considered as successful, then detailed projects or programmes are evaluated against strategic policy. This means that strategic policy has to be evaluated in the first place.

10.5 Classification of evaluation

Table 10.4 shows an exhaustive but not mutually exclusive list of evaluation methods.

(1) What are appraised
This chapter is concerned with the evaluation of strategic policies or projects.

Table 10.4   Classification of evaluation method
(Indicates most frequently used method for strategy evaluation)

1–1 Subject of evaluation
- Strategic policy
- Project
- Department
- Individual

1–2 Timing
(1) ex ante … a. Beginning stage
               b. In process
               c. Finishing stages
(2) ex poste … a. Straight
               b. Double loop

1–3 Evaluator
- Planner self
- Planning department
- Committee
- Outside agency
- Top management

1–4 Relationship of alternatives
- Independent
- Compelementary
- Competitive alternatives

1-5 Time horizon
- Long-term
- Short-term

2–1 Criteria
- Financial goals
- Non-financial goals (share of market etc.)
- Intermediate measurement
- Strategic policy
- Interests of individuals
- Accumulation of knowledge

2–2 Maximizing or not
- Maximizing (weighting)
- Satisficing (no weighting)

3. Estimation of results
3–1 Single value
- Discounted cash flow
- Accounting estimation
- Sensitivity analysis

3–2 Multivariate analysis
- Regression analysis
- Estimation of expected value
- Simulation
- Monte Carlo Simulation
- Decision tree
- Canonical analysis
- Path analysis

3–3 Subjective estimation
- Estimation by individuals
- Estimation by pannels

3–4 Linkage effect
- Independent estimation
- Estimation of synergy

3–5 Risk analysis
- Estimation of expected value
- Estimation of worst case
- Estimation of risk reduction
(Capital asset pricing model)

4 Evaluation model (combinations of above classifications)
4–1 Quantitative analytical
a. Discounted cash flow
- DCF – rate of return
- DCF – net present value
- DCF – payback period
b. Accounting method
- rate of return
- net profict
- cost minimum
- payback period
c. Output of limited human resources
d. Linear programming
e. Sensitivity analysis
- Simulation
- Decision tree
f. Heuristic models
(cont.)

4–2 Qualitative
  a. Evaluation scale
    • Rating scale by using five
      discrete steps
    • Scoring method
  b. Matrix model
    • PPM model
  c. Merits and demerits

  d. Semi-analytical
    • Incremental analysis
    • Muddling through
  e. Political model
    • Force field analysis
    • Allison model
  d. Sequential decision analysis

Evaluation of departments or individuals are related with the follow-up of the plan.

Evaluations have to be made before the project is implemented, when a large amount of resources are committed. Evaluations are made many times before projects are implemented. After implementation, evaluation is practiced, and if the next decision can be changed then it is a double loop evaluation or sequential decision. The project has to be divisible.

The final evaluator of large projects is top management, helped by the planning department and the management committee. The attitude of top management affects the evaluation of strategic projects.

If the projects are mutually independent, they are ranked by priority (or accepted or rejected). If two projects are mutually complementary, the two are evaluated as one combination. If they are alternatives, one should be selected.

The time horizon affects whether the short range profit is important or not. Japanese corporations put an emphasis on long-term effects. A popular principle is "projects should break-even in the third year, total loss should be cleared in the fifth year. Losses in the first and second year are unavoidable".

(2) Criteria

Financial goals and non-financial goals (share of market, quality of products, social responsibility etc.) are used, but intermediate measurements such as the size of the market and competitive strength of the company are more important. (See Table 10.1). It is a sort of simulation model. Strategic policies are frequently used, but the policies have to be evaluated first.

Interests of individuals are not formally considered, but they are important for planners. If a project runs against the beliefs of top management, the project will hardly be promoted. Corporate culture matters here.

Accumulation of knowledge is applied to a new experimental project, usually an unrelated product development. The aim is not to get profit, but knowledge. This is called the construction of a "bridgehead".

Rough information on the diffusion of these criteria is seen in Table 10.1 and Table 10.5.

Both the maximizing and the satisficing principles are applied. In the latter method, weighting of criteria is not needed, only go-no go judgments are used. The matrix model is similar to this.

(3) Estimation of results
There are three methods for estimating results. When one value is estimated, we call it the single value analysis, and when many results are estimated, we call it multivariate analysis.

In many cases, subjective estimations are used.

Estimation of the linkage effect is very important for strategy evaluation. The synergy effect is one of them, risk reduction is another effect. In Table 10.1, the synergy effect is considered.

Estimation of risk may be classified into a no consideration, an estimation of deviation of results or the worst case value. The linkage effect of risk also needs to be evaluated, this is the basic thought of the capital asset pricing model (Sharpe, 1970). If the sales or profit of one product vary in the opposite direction of other products, then risk is decreased as an effect of "mixed strategy". (This will be studied further in Chapter 13.)

(4) Evaluation model
Evaluation models are the combination of assumption of values and estimation of results. This is not the place to make detailed explanation of these methods, because there are many books on them.

For quantitative methods, the DCF method is not used very often, but rather accounting estimations are used, and among them the payback period is most frequently used. The planner knows the limitations of the payback period in estimating profitability, but the payback period is one of the measurements of risk. (See the table on capital investment.)

Limited resources are not only money, but researchers and other human resources, so the output of these limited resources is measured. Linear programming can consider the contribution of many limited resources.

For qualitative models, rating scales like Table 10.2 are used frequently, so we spent some pages in their explanation. Matrix models, as seen in Table 10.2, are also used in many cases.

Merits and demerits statement do not use any predetermined format, but state the plus effects or minus effects of goals. Standard evaluation scales are hard to fix because strategies vary. This approach is also popular, although the evaluation might be too subjective.

Incremental analysis by Quinn (Quinn, 1980) and muddling through by Lindblom (Lindblom, 1959) can be classified as semi-analytical, because they are one of the methods used to attain organizational goals, while the Allison model deals with the goal attainment of departments and individuals (Allison, 1971).

Among the many approaches in Table 10.4, marked approaches are frequently used in Japan. This will be explained in the following section.

10.6 The process of appraisal

1. Promoter and reviewer

Strategies are initiated and proposed from a number of levels of hierarchy: top management, middle managers, corporate planning offices, researchers and others. (On who proposes new product ideas, see Kono, 1987.) The promoter tends to present optimistic estimations to get the idea accepted and to have resources allocated.

The reviewer of strategy is ultimately top management. They are expected to make objective judgment, and make resolutions which take into considerations the risks involved. When top management is the promoter, as they are in many cases, they have to listen to the subordinate opinions (or other directors' opinions).

In the case of Japanese corporations, the decisions of top management are usually taken by the management committee, which is comprised of about 8 to 10 directors. They make decisions as a team by consensus. It is a group decision-making process.

There is a misconception that the group decision is conservative, but this is not the case. The group has a tendency to dare to take a risks. The reasons for this were studied in Chapter 3.

The decision is made by consensus, but there might be some opposition. There is an opinion that the more the opposition, the more unique and distinctive the plan will be. If all members agree with an original draft, then the plan will be mediocre. This statement has not been proven, but it has something true about it. There are two processes in arriving at the consensus. The president will persuade other members of the management committee, and the same subject will be discussed a number of times. When Teijin, a synthetic fiber manufacturer, was going to introduce the technology of polyester, from ICI, the alternative was acrylic fiber technology. The researchers and the majority of the management committee members were in favour of the introduction of acrylic fiber technology, because the research of it had already been started. However, the president Oya believed that the market for polyester was much larger than that of acrylic, and with the support of the report of the corporate planning office, tried to persuade other members and opened the management committee a number of times, finally to arrive at a consensus. The production of polyester proved to be a success, and the sales of it became more than 50% of the company total sales.

The group decision-making also tends to results in analytical evaluation, using enough information for appraisal because it is necessary to persuade many members. However, even when enough information is collected, uncertainty remains, so the top management has to take the decision with risks and has to make resolutions. Usually the president takes initiatives to arrive at a resolution. In the case of Sony's Walkman, president Morita took the final step to develop it and sell it. Although the idea of Walkman, a small high quality stereo player without a recording mechanism (a first model), was derived from a market survey which showed the tendency towards increasing demand for better sounds, for personal use, for tapes rather than disc records, there were many negative opinions against the sales of Walkman among the marketing departments. There were many stocks of radio-tape recorders made by a lot of manufacturers in the market. While the prices of were going down, the price of Walkman was about three times as high as an ordinary radio-tape recorders. Nevertheless, the president tried it, and gave a go sign for this final development and production.

2. Other reviewers

When the issues are technical, committees of specialists are formed and evaluated them. According to the author's survey on new product development, about 44% of respondents (173 high performance companies) have committees of specialists who conduct technical reviews of new products, and 33% of 173 respondents have special committees for economic reviewing.

Outside agencies such as consultants are not used very often.

3. Force field analysis and communication

In order to arrive at a consensus in group decision-making, communication on the meaning and implications of the projects to the reviewers before it is presented officially is very important. The proposer will make a force field analysis and identify sympathizers and opponents, evaluate the power they hold, and will deliver enough information to key top management and middle managers. This behavior is called "nemawashi" and it is important in the situation where the group evaluation is used to arrive at a decision.

4. Time horizon

Japanese corporations have longer time horizons. For this reason, the growth of sales and attractiveness of markets are important, and many companies enter into the growth field. The short range profit is not important, even the future profit is not the most important criteria and the DCF method is not used very often. One company uses the measurement that the larger the volume of investment of research and longer the time of development, the more hopeful the new product will be (see Table 10.3).

The reasons for this long time horizon were already analyzed in Chapter 7. The pressure from stockholders is not strong, rather, the welfare of employees is more important.

5. Weighting of criteria and attitude towards risk

The weight of ultimate value items is decided by the value and power of stakeholders. It was already explained that in Japan, the growth of sales and the welfare of employees are more important because top management and employees are considered as more important key resources.

If the weighting of ultimate goals is decided, then the weighting of intermediate criteria have to be decided. Logically, this can be decided by regression analysis or by canonical analysis. In the case of regression analysis,

$$z \ = a_1 \, g_1 + a_2 \, g_2 + ...$$
$$g_1 = x_1 \, m_1 + x_2 \, m_2 + ...$$
$$g_2 = y_1 \, m_1 + y_2 \, m_2 + ...$$
$$\cdot$$
$$\cdot$$
$$z = \ w_1 \, m_1 + w_2 \, m_2 + ...$$

z – weighted value of goals of the company
a_i – weightings, which are assumed to be known
g_i – sales, ROI and other goal items
m_j – intermediate criteria
x_j, y_j – weighting of intermediate criteria

Computations of this sort are rarely seen, but this is a logical explanation.

The frequency of responses to each item in Table 10.1 may be used for weighting. This approach aims to use the average value of other companies for weightings. This not a logical method, but is one method.

Weighting is necessary when ranking is needed, when a maximizing principle is used. If the satisficing principle is used, then weighting is not needed. In this case, cut-off levels have to be decided. The matrix model is similar to the use of the satisficing principle, although weighting is used for the items of each axis. It is a mixture of maximizing and satisficing principles.

Some companies use rating scales but do not put weight on each items, the judgment is made subjectively considering the status of a project on each item. This is also similar to satisficing principles.

Evaluation of risk is important for large projects which involves the investment of a large amount of money. The method of evaluation of risk is studied in Chapter 13, but here we are concerned with the attitude towards risks. Most companies look at results in the worst case, which have to be considered to persuade groups to make decisions. Some companies went bankrupt with the overly aggressive capital investments, or by overly conservative attitudes towards new product development to lose the share of a market of a product line. Generally speaking, aggressive attitudes are successful in Japan, because of the high speed of change in the environment. Many companies do not put emphasis on the reverse of situations. The steel industry and car manufacturing industry were very active in the expansion of capacities and the modernization of their facilities. This is the reason why the Japanese steel industry and car manufacturers have increased their share in the American market. The electrical equipment manufacturers were aggressive in increasing the expenditure for research and development, which are the cause of competitive strength in the world market.

The reasons why growth is more important than safety, are the same as the reasons why corporations are long-term oriented and competition oriented.

6. Timing of evaluation

Evaluation is performed many times in the course of developing a project. In the case of new product development, evaluation is carried out three or four times, in the idea stage, in the evaluation research stage, in the middle of development and at the end of development and before capital investment and then again after mass marketing. The evaluation criteria (or weighting) change as the development progresses, as is shown in Table 10.1. In the case of technology intensive products, technical experiments are conducted; in the case of marketing-intensive products such as foods and textiles, market experiments are conducted. This sort of interactive information collection and evaluation is called a double loop evaluation (Rumelt, 1980) and it is an important success factor for new product development.

Once, mass production facilities are constructed and mass production and mass sales starts, then change in the plan are difficult.

Sometimes, evaluations are not taken, or purposely delayed. The bootleg researches are seen in creative research organizations, where some researches start by the personal interest of researchers, and they are allowed to use company's resources up to a certain stage. As expenditure increases, they are evaluated on whether to allocate additional resources.

Sequential decisions are another case. Under uncertain situations, after preliminary evaluations, actual commitments are undertaken, the results are fed back to the next action, action is changed and better actions are implemented. This approach is used in the garment industry and the food industry, where initial investment is not large. This is one of the cases of double loop appraisal.

Summary

I. Evaluation of strategy
1. Evaluation of strategy is difficult, because the values concerned are various, and the estimation of long-term results is hard to do. Because strategy affects the promotion ladders of many people, information may be distorted. However, the evaluation is important because large amount of resources are invested into strategic projects, and they affect the overall performance of the company.
2. Long-term effects are important for Japanese corporations. "Break-even in the third year, all accumulated losses to be recovered by the fifth year" is a frequently used measurement for strategic decisions.
3. The discounted cash flow method is rarely used, but, rather, accounting methods for the rate of return and the payback period computation are used. The rating scales and merits-demerits counting are frequently used where a format cannot be applied.

   As to the evaluation criteria, intermediate measurements are used. This is a kind of simulation model. External consistency, competitive strength, feasibility, synergy and direct contribution to goals are items in popular use (see Table 10.2).
4. Strategic evaluation
   The group decision tends to be analytical, because enough information has to be provided. On the other hand group decisions can be risk-taking. Innovative and aggressive strategies

need unexperienced analysis, and cannot have definite forecasting of results. Thus, new ventures or new products will be considered as experiments launched by the faith and by the resolution of top management. During implementation, results will be fed back to the next decisions. These sort of sequential decisions are used wherever possible. The construction of information systems of the Yamato Transportation Co. is one of the cases.

B. Resource allocation

By allocating resources, a strategy can be implemented. Those who are promoting the strategy have to make efforts to obtain resources needed. Top management who wish to promote a strategy have to allocate resources to the strategy.

A pharmaceutical company with 1989 sales of 150 billion yen is spending about ten percent on new product development. The company believes that new product development, which takes about ten years, is a necessary condition for the survival of the company.

Kirin Brewery increased their share of the beer market from 30% to over 60% in 35 years, and one of the reasons for the increase of market share was the aggressive construction of production plants every other year.

On the other hand, one paper manufacturing company went bankrupt by the construction of a plant with too large a capacity. The top management did not analyze the demand for paper and did not estimate the risk. Many cases of bankruptcy show that capital investments without detailed analysis of future demand are the causes of failures. Resource allocation can be either a cause of growth, or a cause of bankruptcy.

Resources are money, personnel and knowledge, and are the common elements of functional resource structure, as is seen in Table 9.1. Money can be expended to materials and facilities. In this chapter, we will study the resource allocation for construction of capability structure, not the allocations of operating expenses.

Knowledge is different from other resources. It is a public goods, so the transfer of knowledge within the organization is costless. The allocation is done through personnel planning.

Resource allocation is conducted after the evaluation of strategy, but it is different from that evaluation. The resource allocation measures the efficiency of limited resources, and helps decide on the size of commitment.

Evaluation for resource allocation is conducted in the middle of development or in the later stages of development, where a large amount of resources are going to be invested. In the process of comprehensive long-range planning resources are actually allocated to each project in the course of medium-range planning. In this process, the efficiency of limited resources are measured, and the quantity of input to each project and priority for the project are decided. The contribution of the projects to corporate goals are measured not only by their profitability, but also by the growth of the company and contributions to the stability of the company. This means that more than one ratio, i. e. multiple criterias, are used for evaluation.

10.7 Total amount

Resource allocation has two steps. The first step is to decide on the total amount of money and personnel to be invested in the company as a whole, and the amount to be allocated to product divisions and to functional areas, such as research, marketing and production. This process is carried out by the head office.

The second step is to allocate resources to projects. This is done by head office and by concerned departments, which compute the output-input ratio.

The basic principle of deciding on the total amount should be based on the output-input ratio. The O-I ratio of inside investment is compared with the O-I ratio of outside investment: if the inside return is lower than the return of investment, then it can be invested outside. This computation is difficult, because long-term prediction are hard to make, but the basic logic remains. The future rate of return tends to be forecasted by the present average rate of return and thus a high rate of return company can attract more money and more people. In addition to enough reserved profit and depreciation, the company can also attract outside financial resources. The high return company can have more "slacks", and have more choice on strategic decisions. The reverse is opposite.

This principle has important implications. At the time when the company has enough slacks, the company should plan for future growth. In other words, while the company can be satisfied with present high profit, while it does not have a sense of crisis it has to forecast future crisis and has to prepare now for the future.

(a) Financial resources
In order to determine the total amount available for investment the comparison of marginal rate of return within the company and outside the company should be used, although the estimation of the future rate of return is difficult so some other approach is used:

The asset turnover approach. This approach assumes that if the normal asset turnover rate is observed, then the future rate of return on total assets will be normal.

> Future sales × normal turnover ratio = future total asset
> Increase of sales × normal turnover ratio = total net increase of total asset.
> Depreciation + net allowed increase = total gross investment

This method is also used for the allocation of resources to product departments. The growth product department can obtain more resources and declining department will receive less resources. The "star products" departments will receive more resource allocation than the "cow products" departments.

Debt ratio. The total amount of debt is also constrained by the debt ratio. This ratio sets limits to debt financing. The average debt ratio of Japanese corporations in 1988 was about 65%.

Times-interest-earned ratio sets limits to debt financing. This ratio is computed by

Profit before interest and after tax – interest paid = times-interest-earned.

(b) Human resources
The total number of human resources is computed by using a normal productivity of labour.

Sales – number of personnel = labour productivity

The average labour productivity of the industry is used frequently. This model assumes that the average number of this ratio of the industry is the optimum value.

Labour cost – sales = percentage of labour cost

This percentage tends to be constant over time, and almost the same among companies in the same industry. This formula assumes that the increase of wage level is in proportion to the increase of labour productivity.

These two ratios are also used to allocate resources to products and to product divisions.

10.8 Allocation of resources to projects

For this purpose, O-I ratios are used

Table 10.5 shows the results of a survey on measurement used for resource allocation. Estimated accumulated profit divided by invested financial resources (2.1.A) and estimated annual sales or annual value-added divided by financial resources invested (2.1.C) have a high frequency of use, although the computation of them is supposed to be difficult.

When personnel, rather than financial resources, are more scarce, then the number of personnel (or man-hours) rather than financial expenditure is used as a limiting factor. Estimated profit over the number of personnel employed and estimated annual sales or annual value added divided by invested (or accumulated) number of personnel are used to set the priorities of the projects. (See Table 10.5, 2.1.B and 2.1.D.)

Estimated profit or sales divided by manpower invested in development personnel is the measurement of limited resources. The efficiency of use of limited resources is useful (a) to determine the quantity of resources to be invested, (b) to determine whether resources should be invested or not and (c) to determine the priority of the projects.

In many cases the quantity of resources to be invested in one project is not a divisible amount, but a fixed amount. That is, if the resources invested are less than a certain amount, the effect will be zero, and if the quantity is over a certain amount then marginal efficiency drops. In this case, the problem is one or zero decision, whether

Table 10.5 Methods of resource allocation

Corporations with long range plans			249 co.
			12 (%)
ganizational process r allocation	A. Total amount is decided by top management and resources are allocated for each product		
	B. Top management decide the total amount but distribution is done following the request of responsible personnel		23
	C. By assessing the requests of responsible personnel		64
	1. By the ratio of estimated profit over invested resources	A. Estimated accumulated profit ÷ invested financial resources	29
		B. Estimated accumulated profit ÷ invested number of personnel	9
		C. EEstimated annual sales or annual value added ÷ financial resources invested	16
		D. Estimated annual sales or annual value added ÷ invested number of personnel	19
iciples of source allocation quently used		E. Others	7
	2. By qualitative method	A. By strategic goals and policy	66 *
		B. By the position in the product life cycle	4
		C. BBy the position in PPM matrix	5
		D. By evaluation of the future size of sales, growth rate and strength of the company	31
		E. Synergy with other products	9
		F. To accumulate management knowledge and technological knowledge or to build bridge head to invade into new market	11
		G. Clarity of goals and effects of projects	20
	A. Recruitment of personnel from other corporations		50
	B. Relocation of personnel		68
eans used to cope	C. Retraining		25
th the shortage	D. Increase in new recruits		61
human resources	E. Temporary dispatch from other companies		12
	F. By grouping with other company		16
	G. Acquisition of other company		2

otes) 1. Survey in 1989 2. Number indicates the percentage of responding companies 3. Asterisks (*) indicate successful companies in planning (subjective judgement, 146 co.) have higher frequency (< 5 %)

the project should be undertaken or rejected, and the amount of resources to be invested and ranking are decided on simultaneously. However, in other cases the amount of resources invested is a divisible and continuous amount. The amount of investment will be divided and the additional or incremental amount will have a different ranking, like the policy of zero base budgeting (Stonich, 1977).

Qualitative measurement

Strategic goals and policy are used in allocation, most frequently to allocate resources to projects as seen in Table 10.5. The reason for the use of this method is due to the difficulty of estimating future profit or future sales. This approach assumes (a) the priority of the strategy is high or acceptable , (b) a project contributes to the attainment of the strategy, (c) the amount of input of resources to a project is optimum.

Two factors, the attractiveness of the industry and the strength of the company are also used frequently. These measurements assumes that these factors are closely related with profitability.

Constructing a bridgehead (2.F item in Table 10.5) means that the purpose of a project is not to make a profit by itself but rather to accumulate knowledge by carrying out a new project, such as new entry into a new market. This measurement is used particularly in food products, machinery, transportation equipment industries and commerce. These industries have more opportunities to introduce new products.

10.9 The process of resource allocation

The decision process of resource allocation is the same as other decision processes.

This process shows a process of one department. For capital investment, the identification of needs starts from sales forecasting, and by using ratios, the turnover ratio for example, a department can find rough needs for capacity of facilities. Then the inventory of present capabilities, qualitative and qualitative, are made clear, gaps are identified and this becomes a request. Surplus facilities will be scrapped or switched to other use.

The cash flow from operations will be computed in the same manner through simple profit planning. The surplus money will be transferred from cow products to problem child products and star products. Distribution of surplus funds is completely controlled by head office even under the product division system with profit responsibility.

Personnel also has an internal market. The demand and supply of one department is estimated with macro computations and the shortage and surplus of skills are identified and transfers are planned. For Japanese corporations, these internal markets are particularly important. When growth products departments or project teams for development need competent personnel, they will be transferred from other departments. This could cause a conflict of interest.

Organizational process. There are three organizational processes for resource allocation: the top down approach (1.A), the interactive process (1.B), and the bottom up approach (1.C). The top down approach means that the demand and supply of resources for departments are computed by head office, and resources are allocated by head office. For large projects or important projects this method is used. The interactive process means that the policy or outline of amount allocated are delivered from head office to the departments and interactive negotiations are conducted. The bottom up approach means that the demand and supply are computed by departments, then allocations are requested from the finance department and the personnel department of head office. When guide lines or outline of the amount is not given to the departments beforehand, then the proposal tends to be inflated, and the reviewer in turn has to cut down the request. The bottom-up approach has the highest frequency, as shown in Table 10.5. It has the defect of producing inflated requests and cutting approaches. If little movements of resources are needed, under a stable environment or under a conservative strategy, the bottom-up approach may work. Where a drastic mobilization of resources is necessary, the top down or interactive process is necessary. An innovative company uses the top down approach or gives guidelines beforehand to departments.

10.10 Political behavior

Resource allocation involves a number of conflicts, and this affects their allocation. For example, (a) Departments want to have more facilities and more personnel with which to build their "castles", if the profit responsibility is not emphasized. The "hockey stick" type profit planning is used to obtain more men and facilities without having heavy responsibilities for profit in the short range.

A department manager may be a friend of the CEO, and then he will obtain more resources. A department manager who has a louder voice might obtain more resources.
(b) Departments do not want to spend resources which do not bring short range profit, if the profit responsibility is emphasized. For example, new product development or sales may not be welcome by the product division if the short range profit is not expected.
(c) Departments do not like to transfer their most competent personnel to other departments, or to project teams. The harvest products departments or profitable departments are requested to increase the profit further by making every effort to cut cost and to increase sales in order to help other infant products. These are the source of complaints. The growth of new infant departments will affect the promotion path of people in existing products departments.

These political behaviors are more or less seen in every organization, and corporate planners have to take into consideration these as a basis of behavior. (These problems are well analyzed by Allison's second and third mode, Allison, 1971). How to cope with these political behavior will be studied in the next chapter.

Summary

1. Resource allocation is one of the key factors of growth in the company. Aggressive capital investment and large amount of expenditures for research and development are the sources of growth, although it affects short range profit. At the same time, too fast an expansion is the cause of bankruptcy. The resource allocation has both effects on growth and risk of failure.
2. Profit is the source basis of resource acquisition and resource allocation. With high profits the company can stand the increased cost caused by investment. While the company is profitable and when the company does not feel the necessity for innovation, the company has to invest resources for future development. The company with many slacks can have more choices for new strategies.
3. To estimate the total amount required for investment, turn-over ratios and other macro ratios are used to estimate appropriate amounts. It is useful to use these computations to formulate guide-lines, before the bottom-up request is presented to head office.
4. To allocate resources to projects, the output-input ratio is used for evaluation and ranking. For output measurement, sales levels are frequently used, and for input, man-hours are used when personnel, particularly researchers, are the limiting factor.

   When the output-input ratio is hard to estimate, the strategic policy is used for ranking . This is more often used. In this case, it is assumed that the ranking of strategy is appropriate, and the amount invested to the project is also appropriate.
5. Concentrated allocation of resources on key strategies is usually more successful than scattered allocation to too many projects. The level of marginal productivity increases up to a certain amount of investment, allocation less than that is extremely unsatisfactory. This is the logic behind concentrated allocation.
6. In order to carry out a large scale transfer of resources or to conduct large investment, top down approaches or interactive approaches are needed. The authority of resource allocation is usually reserved for head office and top management.
7. Political factors are usually involved in resource allocation. Departments request more resources, but sometimes hesitate to commit themselves to new ventures because they reduce short-term profit and they have risks of failure. Departments are usually against the transfer of competent personnel to other growth products or to the development of new products.

Chapter 11 The integration of strategic decisions

The planning process is composed of many planning activities and by many departments with divergent goals and perceptions participate in it. The more divergent the components of the strategy are and the more divergent the participant are, the more creative the strategic plans may be; but at the same time the need for integration increases.

Integration is (a) to rank projects by priorities and allocate resources, (b) to complete plans, so that they are integrated 'wholes' of necessary elements, and to see whether there are no overlappings or not between the plans, (c) to construct a workable interface between organizations so that self-coordination is possible, (d) to identify sources of conflict and solve the conflict between organizations on specific issues.

11.1 Ranking of projects and co-ordination of planning activities

The following problems could happen in the strategic planning process.

There are too many projects in the plan. The resources are scattered and insufficient amounts are distributed to too many projects without any focus. Because of the considerations of human relations, unimportant projects are not pruned. Important projects cannot realize their intended effects because of shortages of resources.

The resources are allocated to managers who are influential, who have large voices, who have personal connections with top management.

Or the resources are allocated by "first in, first out" or as issues come up.

These problems arise between independent plans. Integration by the planning department or by the top management is needed to assign priority to projects and to focus the allocation of resources to important projects.

The second problem is concerned with plans involving complementary relations. Some projects are imperfect. The facilities plan is not accompanied by personnel plans as to who will operate machinery, is not supported by financial plans. After capital investment is carried out, the company experiences a financial difficulty.

The strategic long-range plan is not connected with the medium-range plan and the latter is not integrated into the short range budgeting. There are no consistencies between the three plans.

Table 11.1   Guidelines to departments

Year	1985	1989
Number of companies	384 co.	249 co.
(a) Format, schedule, items of the plan	38 %	32 %
(b) In addition to (a), overall goals and the directions of strategies are indicated	48 %	45 %
(c) In addition to (a) and (b) outlines of strategies of departments are indicated	31 %	35 % *
(d) In addition to (a) and (b), specific goals of departments, basic directions of strategies of basic departments and resources allocations to them are indicated	14 %	15 %

(note) * indicates that successful corporations (146 co.) have higher frequency (40 %) in 1989.

The integration of plans is an important function of comprehensive plans where all plans are compared and reviewed at the same time. Thus, piece-meal decisions are avoided and the first-in first-out decisions are averted. Integration is an important duty of corporate planners. The methods of integration used by the planners are the followings;

(a) Sharing of corporate philosophy, sharing of information, sharing of strategic goals
These planning assumptions are clearly formulated and distributed to departments before the departments build their plans.

The planning guides could include not only the overall goals of the corporation, but also the goals of the departments and strategic directions. The guide might allocate resources to departments. The detailed guidelines will make it easy for these departments to build a strategic plan, decrease the amount of bargaining over requests for large amount of resources from departments and the cut downs by the planning departments. However, detailed guide-lines have to be based on the right decision of the planning departments. (See Table 11.1 on the contents of guidelines.)

According to our survey, about one third of companies use guidelines which indicates the overall directions of each department, about 15 percent use detailed guidelines for departments. The successful companies in planning use directions to the departments. Diversified companies (many companies in chemistry & drugs, machines and the electrical equipment industry) use guidelines which state specific goals to divisions more frequently.

(b) Format and ratios
Formats and rules are generally used to integrate the plans. Formats detail the elements of planning to be filled and thus prevent departmental plans from errors of omission and overlapping. The formats used to be detailed, but they are becoming simpler.

The ratios are assumptions used for planning and there two kinds. One is assumptions on the environment, the other is on goals. They are useful for integration. The assumptions include such items as an exchange rate, estimated wage increase, general price level, prices of key resources. The goals are a rate of growth, sales amount, profitability and others.

The items of goals given to product divisions were surveyed and are shown in Table 11.2.

Important items are sales, profit, market share, new product development, number of personnel and amount of capital investment. We should notice that the amount of resources (personnel and capital investment) are used frequently for these guidelines. Optimum amounts can be computed by using a macro model, or by profit planning.

(c) The corporate functional staff departments organize the integration on functional plans such as personnel, capital investment, cash flow and information systems. These functional plans are a kind of threads going through departmental plans and project plans, thus assuring the appropriate allocation of resources.

Table 11.2 Goals for product division

(1) What goals are given to product divisions?

Number of corporations	21 co.
1.1 Sales	81 %
1.2 Values added	10
2 Growth rate of sales or value added	5
3.1 Profit amount	95
3.2 Profit/total asset	29
3.3 Profit/sales	52
3.4 Cost of production	24
4 Share of market	43
5 Sales/total sales	19
6 New product sales/total asset	14
7.1 Total number of personnel	38
7.2 Labour productivity	5
7.3 Total capital investment	43

(2) What kind of qualitative goals?

    (a) Functional goals
        Policies for development, production and marketing
        Cost reduction
        Percentage of products which are unique in the industry
    (b) Innovation goals
        New product development capability
        Marketing in foreign markets
        Internationalization
        Strengthening research
        Obtaining new customers
        Future vision of the divisions

(note) Mail questionnaire survey in 1982. 44 responses from 102 corporations, out of 44,
       21 corporations which have product division structures were analyzed

The corporate planning department conducts the integration of projects and departmental plans. It writes down the consolidated estimation of financial statements and summaries of total plans.

For ranking, the assessment of projects, which was studied in a previous chapter is used. Theoretically, the projects are ranked in order of the productivity value of limited resources, and they will be cut off where the marginal productivity is equal to the rate from outside use, or they will be cut off at the maximum available resources.

Goal attainment and resource deployment should have annual balances. For example, a situation where a huge loss exists in the first year and a large profit exists in the second year is not desirable for the survival of the corporation. This can be checked by having financial planning. Linear programming can be applied where estimations are possible.

The planning department also reviews whether the plan has every element and whether there is any overlap between the plans. If the corporate planner participates in the process of constructing the project plans and departmental plans, coordination can be done in the early stage of planning.

11.2 Interface between departments – conditions for self-co-ordination

The interface between research laboratories, production departments and marketing departments affects new product development. If the self-coordination is not carried out, the research laboratory might neglect the needs of consumers, and the cost of production might be higher. The share of market of Asahi Brewery continued to decline for 35 years, from 35 percent to 9 percent in 1985. One of the reasons for this decline was a misconception that the research laboratory knew the consumer, that it knew what was the best beer. Communication between the research laboratory and the marketing department was lacking and the needs of consumers could not be fed back to researchers. The movement to change the corporate culture started in 1982, in the long-range planning of 1983 and 1984, it was decided to change corporate culture and a project team to change CI (corporate identity) was formed, and the development of new beer was recommended. Marketing research by the marketing department was conducted and this was used as the basis for the development of new beer. With the basic concept on the new beer established, the research laboratory looked for new yeast, and the new beer was launched (a new draft beer in 1986, and new Super Dry in 1987). Both resulted in surprising success; share of the market had risen from 9 percent to 25 percent in 1989. Prior to this cooperative new product development, a new corporate creed was established in 1982, and this new creed placed emphasis on (a) making consumer-oriented products adapted for new life styles and (b) creating a free and open atmosphere which respects people in the company.

Following this new creed, TQC training was conducted in 1984, 600 managers of the company received 4-day retreat training. Through this training, communication gaps between research, production and the marketing departments were removed.

This case shows how the interface between the laboratory, the production department and the marketing department was improved by the enactment of corporate creed, by a CI movement and through the important communication by 4-day retreat training. The mobilization of members from different department or to the streets for sales campaigns of the new beer were also useful.

Generally speaking, the problem areas on the interface between departments were as follows:

"System products" are increasing and they need the cooperation of a number of product departments, between software development departments and hardware development departments, between electronics products departments and mechanical products departments. Because of the narrow demarcation of product divisions, cooperation is difficult.

There are discrepancies between the visions of top management and departmental managers.

The cooperation between the component manufacturing supplier and manufacturing department was not good, cooperation between the sales channel and production department were not smooth.

What are the means to improve the interface or to "thread the fish on a skewer" as it is called in Japanese corporations? We will concentrate on the interface between research and development departments, production or engineering departments and marketing or sales departments.

1. Movement of personnel

(1.1) Movement of researchers. At Hitachi Central Research Laboratory, researchers move to other departments in order to transfer technology. There are three patterns to this. (a) Researchers are sent temporarily to the factory to transfer developed technology. (b) Factory engineers go to the laboratory to absorb new technology. (c) A branch of a laboratory is located in the factory to transfer technology and researchers. (Kuwahara et al., Long Range Planning, 1989, June.)

(1.2) Formation of project teams. At Honda, to develop a new product, staff from manufacturing (or engineers who design the production system), from marketing department and staff in the development department form the "SED" team and work together to coordinate the development of a new car. The development of a new car needs many teams which develop engines, frames, bodies and wheels, and needs more than 100 or 150 engineers to do this. The SED team is actually an assembly of project leaders. Leader 'S' is dispatched from marketing or planning departments, leader 'E' comes from a department to manufacture production equipment. Ds are from the development department and are the project leaders of many development teams.

At Nihon Sanso (Oxygen products), when a stainless thermos bottle was developed, a team of ten members was formed, three were young girls who represented consumers, one member was from the marketing department, one member was from production, one from outside designers, and three from the development department. This product development resulted in a great success: sales of it reached more than ¥ 50 billion a year including OEM production.

These cases show that formation of a project team is one of the means to make possible the communication between a number of departments. There are two kinds of inter-departmental project teams.

(a) Formation of corporate level project teams. Large projects are studied by a corporate level project team under the corporate planning department or under top management. These sort of teams are frequently formed at Japanese corporations.

Assignment of strategic projects to line departments. Clear assignment of corporate level projects to several departments are used for projects which predominantly use the capabilities of one department, but need the cooperation of other departments. The projects are taken up by head office and assigned to several departments. This system is used at Taisei (construction) and at Nihon Sanso (oxygen products).

(b) Project teams in the development department which include members from sales and production departments. The case of Honda and Nihon Sanso are these kind of project teams.

2. Frequent communication as a corporate culture

At Hitachi Central Research Laboratory and Fujitsu Central Research Laboratory, research staff go to production departments and sales offices frequently. At Asahi Brewery, the communication between the research laboratory and marketing department was lacking. This was one of the causes of decline of their share of the market. For example, in 1968 the laboratory developed a beer without "bitterness". The researchers apparently forgot that bitterness is an inherent taste of beer. The relations were improved through retreat training and the CI (corporate identity) movement (Nakajo & Kono, 1989, Dec.).

3. Organizational setting

(3.1) Organizational location. When the laboratory is located in the plant, it is clear that the communication between the laboratory and the production department is good, but problems will arise about relationships with the marketing department. In the case of Japanese corporations, research laboratories are mostly under head office. They are centralized, and few laboratories are under product divisions. The product divisions themselves are not necessarily complete organizations; most of the marketing functions are in central office (Hitachi, Matsushita) and some production engineering functions are in the head office. Thus, the concentrated functions of research, marketing and production make communication easier.

Most of the product divisions, however, have a development department which is responsible for the improvement of present products. This makes the communication between laboratory and production departments easy.

At the diversified products company, new product development is conducted in centralized research laboratories, the improvement of present products is carried out at the product divisions or at the plants.

In the U.S. and U.K. most of the product divisions have laboratories in addition to one or two central, basic research, laboratories. This decentralized location aims at the improvement of the interface between three functions.

(3-2) Product groups. Several product divisions form a group. The group director will integrate the activities of product divisions. The group usually has staff who help the director. The group will build the strategic plans of the product division.

11.3 Conflict resolution

1. Concept and cases

A conflict is a situation in which there is a "condition of oppositions". (Frazer and Hipel, 1984.) When one party obstructs the behavior of the other party, there is a conflict. The causes of conflict are, (a) differences of values (b) differences of perception (c) limited resources. In order to resolve conflict these causes need to be removed.

When a conflict is on an issue or on a project, it is a one time conflict. When a conflict is between departments, or between the corporation and a department, it is a continuing conflict between departments. We will study here conflicts over projects. The conflict may be an issue between the corporation and the environment. This is a problem of social responsibility for the corporation.

The conflict may be constructive, or destructive. In the former case, through the conflict the issue is made clear, communication is improved and the organization is rather vitalized. Where a conflict is destructive, an antagonistic feeling is increased, communication is discontinued, perception on results is distorted and there is an escalation of conflict.

There are many cases of conflicts in strategic decision-making.

At the research laboratory, the subject a researcher wants to follow is not allowed, he has to join with a team to carry out research that is of strategic importance to the corporation. The more competent he is, the more he tends to stick to a subject he likes, but the corporation needs to obtain him for the team.

The transfer of resources from existing product departments to a new business may not be welcomed by former departments, because the departments will be requested to cut costs to raise more money for the development of new business and in addition the promotion of managers will be adversely affected.

The employees of a plant that is closing will be against the plan.

Using the PPM model, the managers in the losing dog products departments will manipulate information, claiming that in the future their product will become profitable.

The cash cow product departments are against the movement of personnel and
money to the problem child or to the star products departments.

To request resource allocation, managers will use a hockey stick style estimation
of profit and sales.

2. Prevention of conflicts

Prevention is a measure to be taken before the behavior of disturbance occurs. It is
more important than the solution after the conflict has already started. However, the
methods of prevention and solutions are almost the same.

One important difference is in personnel management systems and organizational
settings. Conflict tends to occur in certain situations. When remuneration is based on
the performance of present business, the division will be reluctant to accept the introduction of new products with attached risks. The evaluation system should separate
the reviewing of the operation of present business and the assessing of the performance of future business.

The separation of organization is an another step. New products are brought up in incubator divisions which have loose profit responsibility but have successful growth
as a major goal. This goal is different from the profit responsibility of the product di-

Table 11.3 Five Types of conflict resolution

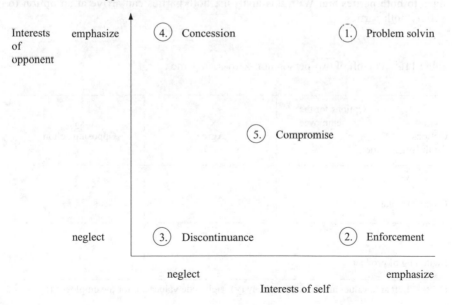

visions of existing products. The resistance to bring up new products in existing departments are thus avoided.

The following steps are used for both preventing and solving conflict.

3. Solutions

There are five types of solutions to conflicts, as is shown in Table 11.3. When the interest of this party can be emphasized and the interest of the other party neglected, it is (2) an enforcement. If this party has more resources and more power, this is made possible. The opposite case is (4) a concession. In between them there is a (5) compromise. If resources and powers are in balance, or when a hurried stoppage is necessary, this option tends to be taken. (1) The problem solving type is to find out a solution which satisfies both parties.

We will study here only the "problem solving" type, because other types are not real solutions. In the problem solving type, a solution which satisfies both parties are found out.

A. Sharing goals and information – understanding interests of other parties

In order to arrive at an option which satisfies the both parties, it is necessary to collect information to clarify the facts – facts about the values of both parties and the effects of actions on the values of both sides. Take an example like Table 11.4. Both parties can clarify the payoffs with each party, what the benefits and damages to both parties are. With this analysis, both parties can arrive at an option to satisfy both parties.

Table 11.4   Pay-off of two-person non-zero-sum game

Options for the organization \ Options for the employee	x_1 Agree	x_2 Opposing action
y_1 Closing of plant	6. −1	2. −3
y_2 Switching of product	7. 3	3. 1

(Note)   Left side values are for the company (y), right side values are for the employee (x)

Table 11.5   What methods are effective to arrive at the consensus in the new product development

number of corporations	173 (high performer)
1.1 Top management commitment	56 co.
1.2 Decisions by the management committee	38
1.3 Decisions by the meeting of department heads	9
2.1 Listen to top management opinions and explain ideas	13
2.2 Clear goals and policies, sharing of goals and strategies	5
2.3 Enough information, forecast of future market, deliberate planning	18
3.1 Free discussion among members of related departments committee	21
3.2 Decision by development committee or planning committee	17
3.3 Searching and planning by project teams	17
4.1 "Nemawashi", or communication with related departments (to marketing department in particular)	15
4.2 Decisions on formal planning are made public	14

note (1) Survey on new product development in 1985.
 (2) Free answer survey
 (3) Number indicates the number of responses, not the percentage.
   Responses from high performing corporations are analyzed.

We conducted a survey on the process of arriving at consensus on new product development (see Table 11.5).

In this response, (1.1) top management commitment, and (1.2) decisions by top management committee are important, because they show the importance of the issue for the corporation or the payoff to the corporation. (2.3) Enough information clarifies the effects of the issue for both parties. (3.1) Free discussion makes clear the value of the issue to related departments.

When the Sumitomo Metal Mining Company wanted to close an old copper mine, those employed there opposed the attempt. The company allowed then to invest another one billion yen to continue searching for a new copper vein, for one or two years. After trial digging, it became clear that there was no hope of such a find, and employees could recognize that the mine had to be closed.

Many conflicts start by different perceptions, misunderstandings. Mutual perception of the other parties' values are important, and common estimation of the future results are more necessary. The above cases show that both parties could arrive at the same forecasting on future results.

B. Working together to find out a plan which could satisfy both parties

In table 11.4, the solution $x_1 y_1$, $x_2 y_1$ are not satisfactory. The $x_2 y_2$ has the least difference of pay-off, but $x_1 y_2$ dominates other solutions for both parties. This solution is stable because other options are not profitable for both parties. For example, if the issue is the closing down of a factory, the switching of products produced in the factory to other products, and their continuation of operation could be studied. If the case is a discontinuance of unprofitable products, instead of sudden stoppage of production, several steps of improvement can be taken - cost may be reduced by decreases in the number of brands, by automation or by concentration of production. If it involves the closing of a factory, new jobs at other places will be provided to the employees and the cost of moving the residence will be born by the company. This is a "side payment" in the terms of game theory, by which pay-offs to the both sides are equalized.

According to the survey in Table 11.5, again (3-2) decisions by conference, (3-3) searching by project team are important because they will lead to better alternatives. These responses mean that the solutions of participation, or solutions from many people who have information are important.

C. Persuasion

A persuasion means to inform others that the plan is important for the survival of the organization, or the plan has great merit to the organization, or the plan will be eventually beneficial to the individuals concerned.

By persuasion, both parties try to change the value system or the estimation of results, so that an agreement can be arrived at. Conflict exists when values are different and the forecasting of results is different. Persuasion aims to reduce the differences.

Through the second phase in finding out an option which could satisfy both parties, efforts of persuasion are conducted, but there remain some differences. The majority of people concerned cannot attend negotiations, so explanations are necessary. Some factions of employees may be for the plan but others may be against the plan. Here a change process of unfreeze, change, refreeze can be used. According to the survey in Table 11.5, (4.1) "Nemawashi" or explanation and persuasion to the departments concerned is considered as important. Also, (4-2) formal planning is useful for persuasion.

D. Top management commitment

For all processes mentioned above, top management commitment is important to prevent and solve conflict. It is shown in Table 11.5. Top management commitment states that the plan is important to the organization, that the solution should be worked out by serious consideration. It is also a useful means for persuasion.

NKK (one of the largest steel manufacturers in Japan) declared "A New Birth of NKK", tried to change the product mix from steel to other products, because steel was not a growth business. NKK wants to enter into a city development, electronics and biotechnology. These product lines have potentials for NKK. NKK has analyzed that it has competitive strength in these areas. For example, NKK has large areas of unused land, which could be used for the city development. It expects that these three product lines will account for half of the sales in 2000. Since they should be developed by internal growth, about one third of research expenditure will be allocated to the development of these new lines.

The recognition and expectations of the company by the employees was surveyed, it was found that the employees perceived the future was not very hopeful. It was necessary to orient the mind of employees to the new direction, and to prevent the opposition of the steel departments. In order to arrive at the consensus, a new corporate creed and a new company song was formally decided, the name of the company was changed from Nippon Steel Pipe to NKK. The top management was on the front to appeal to employees that the "new birth" was necessary to the company. The president visited the steel mills, sales offices, and talked with the employees. The video tapes which explain the new creed, the new birth campaign, the new business, and the speech of the president were distributed to every place. The long-range planning to implement the new strategy was built. The planning of the new businesses were written by a project team (afterwards by three teams) assisted by the planning department. New divisions of three businesses were established. The long-range planning and the new organizations had the effect of refreezing the change. (References for conflict resolution: Deutsch, 1972; Kriesberg, 1973; Neuman and Morgenstern, 1953; Ruce and Raiffa, 1957; Robins, 1974; Fraser and Hipel, 1984.)

Summary

1. Integration is necessary because a diversity of knowledge is mobilized to build and implement strategic plans. The more diversified the capabilities of participants, the more outstanding the plan may be, but the more difficult integration becomes.

    Integration aims to (a) put priority to projects to allocate limited resources, (b) complete the elements of a project so that key elements are not lacking, overlapping of elements do not exist, overlapping of projects among different departments are not seen. It aims to complete the plan with respect to components, quantity, timing and place.
2. The integration of operational activities are mostly done by organizational structure and rules, but the integration of strategic activities are done by planning, particularly by comprehensive planning. The planning department plays an important role in this. Without comprehensive planning, decisions will be taken by the first-in first-out method and the implementation will be delayed by defective composition of parts.
3. Integration can be done by the planning department and top management, by the initiators themselves. In both instances, the sharing of goals and the sharing of information are important means. When a corporate philosophy and basic strategies are clearly stated, goal integration can be achieved.

    The guidelines of long-range planning are used to integrate the planning process. In the guideline, the new directions of strategy of the corporation as a whole and of the divisions are indicated, and also the amount of resources (personnel and capital investment) are directed. The survey shows that the goals to divisions include the goals for innovation, such as the percentage of new products. The appropriate amount of resources can be computed by the use of macro analysis.

    Detailed guidelines to division may kill the initiatives of the divisions, but it can prevent large amount of requests and severely cut down the allocation of resources. Rather, clear goals can stimulate initiatives. This can be found even in the research laboratory.
4. Self integration or coordination by the initiators of plans are feasible under certain conditions. The interface between departments, particularly the interface between research and development, production and marketing is important. Interface can be improved by (a) the moving of personnel, (b) frequent communication as a corporate culture, (c) closer location of departments concerned or the centralization of locations.
5. Conflict is a situation in which one party obstructs the behavior of other parties. Conflict arises when the values of two parties are different, when perception is not the same, when resources are limited. The real solution of conflict aims to arrive at the option which satisfies both parties. The solution process is similar to the integration process. (a) Sharing of goals is the starting point. This means to recognize the value of other parties. (b) Sharing information aims to have common perception of results. The difference of estimation is often the cause of conflict. (c) Searching for the options which satisfies both parties. This is possible by participation or negotiations and bargaining. (d) Persuasion is the last phase. Some people will not agree with the solution, and some part of the solution will not be satisfactory, so persuasion becomes necessary. (e) Throughout the process, the commitment of top management is important.

    The above processes are not only useful for the solution of conflict after it has occurred, but also for the prevention of conflict. The prevention of conflict is more important than solving is. The planner who is insensitive to others feelings, or who thinks that the best thing for the company should be acceptable to everybody will not be successful in strategic planning.

Chapter 12 Long-range profit planning

12.1 Concept and types

1. Systems of profit planning

The long-range (or medium-range) profit plan is the financial expression of the long-range plan. It has the following systems:

```
┌ Quantitative plan
└ Profit plan     ─┌ Project profit plan
                   └ Period profit plan of each product ─┌ consolidated profit
                                                         └ plan
```

The quantitative plan, such as production plan and personnel plans, is sometimes called the profit plan, but here we are concerned with only the financial profit plan.

The project profit plan is the estimation of the effects of capital investment, or of large research projects. The schedule of investment, the schedule of revenue and expense, and the computation of the rate of return (by either the accounting method or by the discounted cash flow method) or the net present value are the major contents. The project profit plan is the important ingredient of the period profit plan. It makes clear what amount of resources are required for specific projects, and what are the financial effects of projects. Thus, the ranking of projects and the smoothing of fluctuation in resource allocation are made possible. Without excellent project planning, the period profit plan cannot attain outstanding financial goals.

The period profit plan aims to estimate (a) the profit and loss statement, (b) the balance sheet, (c) the cash flow statement and (d) the financial ratio analysis. Models of these profit plans are exhibited as Table 12.1, 12.2, 12.3 (The division assets plan and the corporate balance sheet plan are omitted.).

The period profit plan for each product is mostly computed on the existing products. If new products are at the stage of producing the sales and profit during the planning period, the profit plan is formulated.

The consolidated overall corporate profit plan is an overview of the financial performance of the company. The consolidation of future profit plans are not necessarily easy, so rough estimations of consolidated corporate profit plans are formed. Many companies do not consolidate the plans of foreign subsidiaries because of the difficulty of estimation, for example, the estimation of foreign exchange rates.

Table 12.1   Profit and Loss Statement Plan

Year \ Item	Actual		This year	Planned		
	−2	−1		1	2	3
External sales						
Internal sales						
Total						
Cost of goods sold						
Variable cost (external)						
Variable cost (internal)						
Fixed cost						
Total						
Gross profit						
Marketing expenses						
Research & development						
General administrative						
Marginal profit						
Operating profit						
Decrease of price						
Decrease of cost						
Revised operating profit						
Other income & expense						
Interest expense						
Net profit						
Net profit & interest						
Total asset						
Return on investment						
Return on sales						
Sales ÷ total asset						

Table 12.2   Cash Flow Plan

Item \ Year	Actual		This year	Planned		
	−2	−1		1	2	3
Cash from operating activities						
Net profit						
Increase of receivables & inventories						
Increase of accounts payables						
Depreciation						
Income tax						
Net cash from operation						
Investing activities						
Increase of fixed assets						
Increase of securities						
Net cash from investment						
Financing activities						
Increase of short-term debt						
Increase of long-term debt						
Increase of stock issue						
Cash dividend payment						
Net cash from financing activities						
Net increase of cash & deposit						

2. Types of profit planning

There are three types of profit planning: (a) forecastive (b) goal type and (c) forecast after the issues are solved.

The forecastive type is the estimation of future financial performance of the corporation when the present strategy mix is continued, when the value of parameters (e.g. rate of material cost on sales) and the value of policy cost (e.g. research expense) are not changed. This type is used to find out the gaps of performance in the future, at an earlier stage of planning.

The goal type profit plan aims to describe the desired level of financial ratios and thus construct the three financial plans. The values of parameters (e.g. ratios of expense to sales) are artificially set and the policy variables are artificially determined

Table 12.3   Financial Ratio Plan

Item	Year	Actual		This year	Planned		
		−2	−1		1	2	3
Growth	Sales Growth rate						
Profitability	Return on total investment (Before interest and tax) Profit ÷ sales Sales ÷ total assets						
Stability	Return on equity (After interest and tax) Net worth ÷ total assets Current asset ÷ current liabilities						
Productivity	Capacity utilization Employee Sales ÷ employee						
Investment for future	R & D ÷ sales New product ÷ sales						

(e.g. the sales amount is increased and the turnover of assets is decreased), so that the gaps of goals will not exist in the future. If gaps still remain, then new projects are studied to close the gap. This plan shows the desired level of efforts, but it could be misunderstood so that problems are already solved.

The "forecast after the issues are solved type" uses estimated parameter values, practical policy variables and the gaps are closed by the new projects and efforts of the profit improvement plan. This is used in the later stages of long-range planning.

By the process of computation, profit planning can be classified into (a) the macro approach and (b) the micro, or build-up, approach.

The macro approach uses the percentages of sales and the standard ratios as the value of parameters. Sales amounts are the most important independent variables. This approach is applied in the earlier stage of long-range planning.

The micro model uses the intermediate variable as the independent variables. For example, the production plan, the material consumption rate and the prices of material are the elements of material cost. The capital investment plan is fixed before the profit plan. This approach is used in later stage of planning.

The relations between these two sorts of types tend to be the following:

(a) forecastive ┐
(b) goal type ┘ ────▶ (a) macro approach
(c) forecast after the issues are solved ────▶ (b) micro approach

The detailed explanation of these two approaches is stated below in Section 3 of this chapter.

12.2 Purposes and limitations

1. The Purpose of long-range profit planning

The purposes are the followings:

(a) To attain financial goals. By forecasting future profit and cash flow, the company can find out the issues, and can plan the strategy and financial efforts required to attain balanced financial performances. The bankruptcy of the Van Jacket Company is one of the illustrations of this point; the company grew rapidly by successful sales of suits for young males. The president was, however, an artist, he was not interested in profit planning.

(b) To make clear required resources. The period profit plan makes clear what amount of human resources, materials, capital investment, research expenditure and cash are required and when. The acquisition of resources takes time, so the company can make better preparations for it.

(c) To coordinate project planning. By profit planning, the yearly fluctuations of resource requirements are disclosed, the leveling of resource allocation can be made possible. The ranking of projects and the cut-off of projects by the amount of resources available are carried out.

(d) To formulate guidelines for budgets. Long-range profit planning, particularly on first year figures becomes an important part of the guidelines of the annual budget. Since profit plans have financial expressions, it is easy to connect the long-range plan and the annual budget. However, the figures of long-range planning and the annual budget are not identical, because of the timing of planning and because of the detailness of planning.

2. Limitations of Long-Range Profit Planning

(a) If excellent strategies and outstanding projects are not planned in advance, the profit plan is only a set of vain numbers. The profit plan cannot be attained only by the pressure from top management. According to a survey on profit planning by the Japan Productivity Center (1982), one of the problems of profit planning is the discrepancy of opinions between top-management and division management (26% of responding companies). This shows that the projects to close the gaps of the future are lacking.

(b) Involvement of line managers in profit planning. If line managers do not consider the plan as their own plan, the plan is only a set of abstract numbers. The same JPC survey stated that for the successful implementation of the plan, it has to be trusted by the line departments (30% of responding companies). (JPC, 1983; A survey on profit planning, 267 responses) (Similar findings are in, Hofstede, 1967.)

(c) Uncertainty. Future estimation has uncertainties and errors. The long-range profit plan is based on many assumptions which could change. In addition to uncertainty over present products, there is a larger uncertainty on new products and new businesses. For this reason, the long-range profit plan is most useful to find out gaps, and to indicate future goals. The attainment of goals needs to be supported by outstanding projects. What we should do today is more important than future numbers. The JPC survey tells that, to be successful, it is necessary to adapt to the change of environment (59%), and to reduce errors of estimation (48% of responding companies) (JPC, 1983).

12.3 Process of profit planning

1. Location of profit planning in the total planning process

Different kinds of profit planning are conducted in the process of long-range planning. (See Table 12.4.)

The first kind of profit planning is to estimate the future gaps when the present strategies and some sorts of improvements are carried out. At this stage the profit planning is of a forecasting type and a macro model is used.

When the projects to close the gap are studied, the project profit plannings are computed on large scale research projects and on capital investment projects. The return on investment, or the net present value or the payout period are computed for ranking and for cutting off the projects.

The third kind of profit planning is to estimate the financial effects of future strategies, so that the financial balance is attained. Mostly the macro approach is used at this stage. The allocation of resources is the most important aim at this stage.

The financial guidelines for the medium range profit plan of each products are determined at this stage. This guideline is the summary of goals, such as the sales,

Table 12.4   Location of Profit Planning in the process of Long-range Planning

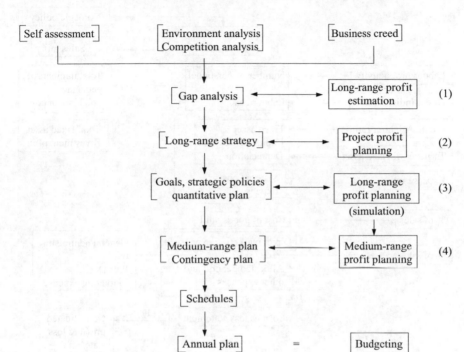

profit rate, asset turnover and labour productivity. The guidelines also includes key assumptions on the environment such as the growth rate of the economy, wage increase, general price level and estimation of exchange rate.

The fourth profit planning is the financial expression of the medium-range plan. The micro and build-up approach is used. The profit plan becomes realizable goals.

2. Macro approach

The macro approach is explained in Table 12.5.

(1) Product Divisions and Projects

Sales are estimated by demand forecasting in each products. The quantity is forecasted first and then it is converted to money values. The sales by fixed price is used as the independent variable for the equations to compute other variables. The price

Table   12.5 Macro Approach

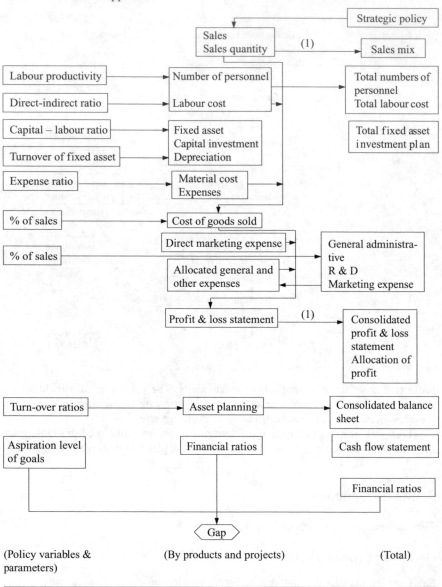

(Policy variables   (By products and projects)   (Total)
parameters)

Note: (1) intersegment transfer elimination.

index will then change the fixed price sales to the current price sales. The transfer sales to other departments are computed by a ratio of the buying department.

The number of personnel is computed by the target labour productivity. It is multiplied by the estimated wage rate.

The fixed asset is computed by the capital-labour ratio, or by the turnover ratio of the fixed asset. The increase of the fixed asset plus depreciation makes the allowed amount of capital investment. It is compared with the total of capital investment projects.

The relationship between labour productivity, wage rate and capital-labour ratio is explained in the "note" to Section 6 of Chapter 9.

Other expenses are computed as percentages of sales, or by econometric models arrived at by regression analysis.

The administrative, marketing and research expenses are allocated from head office.

Thus, the profit and loss statement, the asset table and the financial ratio are estimated.

(2) Corporate profit planning

(a) Head Office Departments

The number of personnel, personnel cost, fixed assets and other expenses of the staff departments, the sales department and the research and development departments are computed as percentage of sales.

(b) Total Company

The total sum of sales of each products makes the total sales of the company. All expenses are also added. The intersegment transfer sales and the corresponding cost are eliminated. The corporate profit and loss statement is thus computed. The asset plans of each products and head office departments are added, and after the cash flow plan, the balance sheet and the financial ratio plan are estimated.

If the financial ratio does not satisfy the desired level of goals, and gaps are forecasted, then this is fed back to the strategic policy and to the value of parameters and policy cost.

If new projects are not planned, and the value of parameters and policy variables are estimated ones, the plan is a forecastive type. If the sales, parameters and policy costs are modified so that gaps are closed, the plan is a goal type. If the new strategies are planned to close the gaps, the plan becomes the forecast after the issues are solved type.

3. Micro or build-up model

The profit planning by this model is computed at the final stage of long-range or medium-range planning. It assumes that the sales amount , price, production plan, personnel plan, capital investment plan and sales activities are all determined in ad-

Table 12. 6   Micro Approach

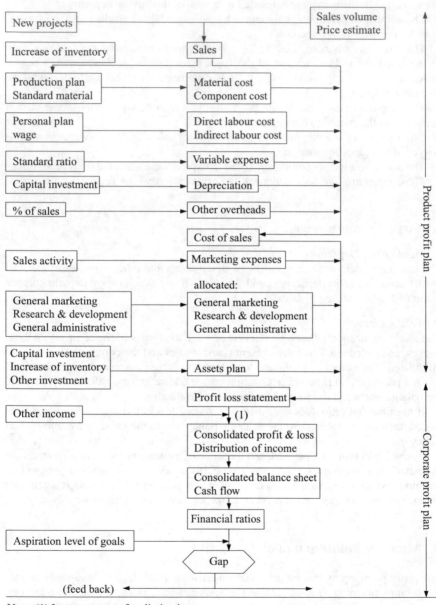

Note: (1) Intersecter transfer elimination.

vance, and the plan is the monetary expression of these preceding plans. The specific areas of decision in this plan are the to decisions on the cash flow plan and the evaluation of the estimated financial ratios.

4. Determination of the value of parameters and policy variables

(1) Percent of sales

The percent of sales is frequently used for macro approach and also for the micro approach. Past average values or industry averages are used. This method is based on the following assumptions:
(a) The value of percentages is the optimum value.
(b) There is no economy of size.
(c) The increase of productivity is offset by the increase of price (e.g. wages).
(d) If the element cost (e.g. material cost) declines (or increases), the price of products declines (or increases), and the percentage of the element in sales stays the same.
(e) There is no interrelationship (e.g. if the price declines, the demand will increase) between the variables.

(2) Regression Analysis

Past data is collected and parameters are determined by regression analysis. If we use the linear model,

$$Y = a + b X \qquad \text{where } X = \text{sales, } Y = \text{expenditure,}$$
$$\text{and a, b} = \text{parameters.}$$

The values of a and b are determined by past data.
For example:

$$\frac{S}{L} = a + b \frac{K}{L} \qquad \text{where,}$$

S = sales, L = number of personnel,

$$\frac{K}{L} = c + dW \qquad$$

K = fixed assets,

W = wages,

The assumptions of regression analysis are the following:
(a) The values of parameters are the optimum values, (b) there are no interrelationships between the variables.

(3) Time series analysis

The time series trends are used for estimation. For example, the consumption of coke per ton of steel was 900 kg in 1950, but it is almost one third of that now. The time trend of material consumption and the price of materials are forecasted by time series analysis. These values are assumed to be the optimum values.

(4) Determination of policy cost

The policy costs means the marketing cost, research and development cost, the welfare cost and the expenditures for education. These costs are controllable, and if the amounts are reduced, sales will decrease. The effects of these costs stay for long term periods and are hard to measure. There are the following approaches however;
(a) Marginal analysis
(b) Percentage of sales
(c) Competitive approach
(d) Amount required to attain the goals
(e) Maximum amount leaving the appropriate level of profit.

The explanation of these methods and the proof of them are beyond the scope of this book. (See, for reference, Kono, 1975.)

12.4 Profit planning and simulation

Computer simulation usage the is widely used in profit planning. The basic concept of simulation is described by the following model.

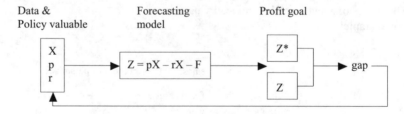

In this model, X, p and r are independent variables. They are either given data or controllable variables. Models are used to forecast dependent variables when the independent variable changes. We can know the value of dependent variables when X or p or r change individually or collectively. When the distributions of values of X, p and r are assumed, then the distribution of profit (Z) can be estimated by a Monte Carlo Simulation. By sensitivity analysis, we can find out what independent variables affect profit (Z) greatly and thus we can find out what data variables and policy variables are important.

The above model uses only one equation and a linear equation. If the relationship between demand and price is found out, then $X = a - bp$ is added, and the equation becomes a non-linear model.

When a company has several product divisions, and when the models are constructed for each product or parameters are differentiated from product to product, then the number of equations may easily exceed one thousand. If the values of parameters are updated every year, the computation is easily conducted with the use of computer.

By the use of computer simulation models, many cases or many scenarios can be computed easily and the planner can identify what changes are important. The planner is relieved from the burden of computation, and can spend more time on strategic policy decisions.

The limitations of the simulation are that qualitative effects cannot be analyzed. For example the quantitative effects of the improvement of quality of products and of the improved information system can hardly be estimated.

12.5 Profit improvement plan

Profit improvement is studied in all the processes of long-range planning. Profit planning discovers whether the plan is satisfactory or not. When the forecasted profit is not satisfactory, three kinds of measures are taken. (a) It will be fed back to the total process of planning. (b) A special profit improvement plan will be worked out. (c) A project team will be formed, and a drastic profit improvement plan, such as the decrease of employees and the closing down of factories will be worked out.

In all three measures, we need to know what are the areas and means to improve the profit, and what are the principles of project improvement.

1. Areas of profit improvement

The rate of return is a comprehensive measurement of profit. It is composed of the following components:

$$\frac{\text{Sales} - \text{cost of sales}}{\text{Sales}} \times \frac{\text{sales}}{\text{total assets}}$$

Thus, there are three areas: increase of sales, decrease of cost and increase of turnover of assets. The increase of sales improves both the profit rate by economy of scales and the turnover of assets. This is a positive strategy. The successful development of new products and increase of the share of the market are important strategies. Many cases are illustrated in Table 12.7.

Cost reduction is the second area. This is a rather negative approach. Divestment of unprofitable products and centralization of production facilities are examples.

The third area aims to increase the turnover of assets by the decrease of investment. The centralization of facilities, closing of an old plant and decrease of inventories by the computerized information system, by the just-in-time system are examples of this increase.

2. Principles of profit improvement

There are three principles of profit improvement. Table 12.7 shows the cases of three principles. These cases were derived from a number of actual cases.

The first principle is innovation. It aims to undergo discontinuous change of the product-market strategy and the production system. New product development, starting a new business and the construction of a new plant are such cases. The long-term effects of these innovations tend to be the largest.

The second principle is economies of scale or economy of scope. It aims to concentrate activities and to mass produce products and other service activities. Mass production enables the specialization of operations and the higher level of mechanization and automation, which reduces the cost and improves quality.

The third principle is standardization. It aims to find the best method and to set standard methods. Value analysis, and quality control are examples of this. Standardization aims to accumulate small improvements. The effects of this principle are not small, but they decrease as improvements progress and reach the limit. Then, innovative changes becomes necessary.

Innovation and mass production are mostly planned in long-range planning, whilst standardization is largely planned in the short-range planning. Long-range planning enables the planning and implementation of the innovation.

From another view point, profit improvement can be classified into positive measures and passive measures. The positive measures are easily accepted by the members of the organization, whilst the passive measures tend to receive resistance of members, having a gloomy tone. Positive measures means the expansion of activities, new product development and the increase of market share. The increase of activities will result in mass production and thus it could enhance the productivity of resources.

Passive measures have repercussive effects. The decrease of sales promotion expenses and decrease of R & D expenditures will decrease future profit. People do not like the reduction of costs, so they will resist the closing of the plant, decrease of personnel and discontinuance of the old product. If these plans are implemented without enough understanding, they will result in decreased morale and the loss of competent personnel.

However, in slow economic growth and under severe world-wide competition, the decrease of man-hours per unit, the decrease of unit fuel cost and other passive measures have also to be planned for.

Table 12.7   System of Profit Improvement

Areas of improvement	Subject of Planning	Cases of profit improvement	Innovation	Economy of scale	Standardization	By long-range planning	By short-range planning
1. Increase of sales	A	New business, new product	O			O	
		Change of product mix	O			O	
		Multi-national management	O			O	
	B	Expansion by capital investment		O		O	
		Strengthening of sales channels		O		O	
	C	Sales promotion		O			O
		Price cutting prevention, price rising			O		O
2. Cost reduction	A	Divestment of unprofitable products, separate company		O		O	
		Vertical integration, disintegration	O			O	
	B	Alliance	O			O	
		Horizontal merger		O		O	
		Mechanization, automation		O		O	
		Concentration of production		O		O	
		Improvement of logistics		O		O	
		Innovation of organization & systems	O			O	
		Computerization		O		O	
		Decrease of employee, temporary lay-offs, transfer to subsidiaries		O		O	
	C	Improvement of product design			O		O
		Change of production system			O		O
		Value analysis			O		O
		Quality control			O		O
		Standardization			O		O
		Improvement of sales promotion		O			O
3. Increase of Turnover of asset	A	Decrease of product lines	O			O	
	B	Centralization of production		O		O	
		Divestment of unused assets		O		O	
	C	Just-in-time system		O			O
		Increase of shift	O				O
		Decrease of account receivable		O			O

Note: A --   product-market strategy,   B --   structure,   C --   Operation

12.6 Financial ratios

Financial ratios are based on the hierarchy of goals of the company. The items of financial ratios are described in Table 12.3. They are the financial expression of basic goals and basic strategies. The company has three basic goals.

1. Growth of the company – Sales amount and growth rate of sales.
2. Profitability – Return on total investment. This is divided into two parts – profit on sales and turnover of total assets.
3. Stability – Stability of the company is measured by how the company has what the chances of incurring deficit and of having shortages of money. It is expressed by rate of return on net worth and equity ratio. When both ratios are high, there is little chance of having such deficit. The equity ratio and the current ratio show the probability of falling short of this case.
4. The productivity of resources – They are the factors to enhance the profitability. The turnover of total assets, the capacity utilization and the productivity of labour are the most important factors here.
5. Seeds for future growth – Research and development expenditure is the key seed for future growth, and the new product development is an intervening variable for future growth and profitability. (For discussion of goals, see also Chapter Seven.)

Summary

1. Long-range or medium-range profit planning aims to plan the future profit and loss statement, balance sheet, flow of funds and financial ratios. It is a financial "period plan" .

    There are three types: a forecastive, a goal type and a forecast after issues are solved type. These three types are used consecutively as planning proceeds.

    There are two approaches: a macro approach and a micro or build-up approach. The former approach is used in many cases, but in the later stage of planning, the build-up approach is used.

2. The purpose of profit planning are to attain the balances achievement of financial performance and to make clear the amount of required resources. Thus, it is used to coordinate research costs and capital investment and other large projects. It is a means of resource allocation.

    The long-range profit plan has three limitations.

    (a) If innovative projects are not planned in advance, it cannot improve profit. (b) If the planning is not participated in and does not involve line departments it cannot become the goals of the corporation and cannot provide effective budget guidelines. (c) The long-term profit estimation is based on many assumptions, and includes uncertain elements. The errors are large. The character of the plan tends to be a sort of set of goals.

3. A macro approach to planning is used for long-range strategic planning, but a micro approach is used for medium-range planning.

4. Computerized simulation is widely used in long-range profit planning, particularly for macro models. By using simulation, many alternatives of strategy mix can be tried, by using 'what-if' trials.

5. Profit improvement plans cover not only the cost reduction plan, but also many areas of positive planning, such as expansion of sales. It is based on three principles: (a) innovations, such as the introduction of new products, foreign direct investment, (b) concentration and economies of scale and (c) standardization.
6. The financial ratio plan is the final conclusion of the plan. This is the financial expression of the hierarchy of goals of the corporation.

(References: Aoki, 1977; Kono, 1973; Nishizawa, 1978; AMA, 1960; Anthony & Welsch, 1981; Caplan, 1971; Hofstede, 1967; NAA, 1964)

Chapter 13 Decision making under uncertainty

The difficulty of forecasting the future environment and the future result of action taken is the most serious problem in long-range planning. Yet companies have to make large investment in both research and facilities based on long-term anticipation. Since the lead time is long, a company cannot avoid uncertainty. If a company tried to avoid every uncertainty, it cannot make a profit. On the other hand, if it ignores risk, it might go bankrupt. It has to try to enter a growth business or to introduce a new product earlier than a competitor. It has to try to "get a tiger child in the tiger hole." It will forecast the risks involved and will take into account these risks. It will prepare for every contigency. It can reduce the risk by minimizing the adverse effects in the worst case.

Some authors define uncertainty as the difficulty of prediction by the lack of information, and risk as a range of forecasting. However, we do not distinguish the two. We use both words for the same meaning, but we recognize the level of uncertainty varies from situation to situation.

When the decision have to be made under uncertain conditions, there are several alternative methods of coping. Table 13.1 shows the alternatives, which are arranged in order of uncertainty or in order of scarity of information.

13.1 Increase of information (1.1)

Most bankrupt companies did not collect information which could have been collected and did not forecast the future which could have been predicted. Many bankruptcies happened by avoidable risks. Good companies collect enough information on the environment, look for many alternative ideas and select the best one from amongst many alternatives. In so doing, they can have better standard strategy and can prepare for the worst of situations.

In order to increase the amount of information, C company has a planning department which collects strategic information regularly. It is classified by classification code of the company. Summaries are put into cards and stored in a computer, so necessary information can be retrieved immediately. The staff in foreign offices gather information on the overseas environment, staff departments collect functional information and the research laboratories collect technical information.

The increase of information makes it possible for the company to not only produce better predictions of the future, but also to increase the number of alternatives.

Table 13.1   Coping with uncertainty
What is done when the forecasting is uncertain? (Please tick as many as necessary)

Corporations with long-range plan	1979 327 co.	1985 384 co.	1989 249 co.
(1-1) Increase of information in proportion to the importance of effects	18 (%)	17 (%)	17 (%) *
(1-2) Range forecasting, including the worst case	36	30	44 — *
(2) Sequential decision	39	41	51
(3-1) Early warning system	8	16	16
(3-2) Contingency plans	8	6	8
(3-3) Frequent revision of plans	–	14	15
(4-1) Flexibility by diversification or by holding reserves	4	5	8
(4-2-1) Streng competitive power	15	9	12
(4-2-2) Basic strength, e.g. improvement of net worth (equity), or employee morale	17	19	19

Note (1) The number indicates the responding companies
     (2) The asterisks (*) indicate successful companies in planning (subjective judgement, 146 co.) have higher frequency (< 5 %)

Suppose a company is considering building a plant in a foreign country. If the country risk is forecast, then the company can consider not only the construction of a plant but also licensing or exporting as alternatives. If the risk is not predicted, then the decision may be taken on only the size of the market and its competitiveness.

13.2 Range forecasting (1.2)

Range forecasting predicts a range of sales or profit, usually on three points: maximum, probable and minimum. One Japanese film company take into consideration optimistic and pessimistic cases for total national sales, two cases for a share of imported brands and two cases for the share of their own company among Japanese brands. Two levels of three factors make fifteen combinations, but these are reduced to three points. The most probable case is the standard assumption which is used for the standard plan.

What the probability should be of the pessimistic case and the optimistic case, is a problem. It is practical to assume that the most probable value is not just the mean value but also covers the probability of two thirds. In other words, pessimistic values and optimistic values are plus or minus one standard deviation from the most probable value.

The merits of range forecasting are various. Firstly, the most probable value is used to build the standard strategy and standard long-range planning. It should be noted, however, that three point forecasting does not mean that a company should construct three kinds of long-range plans.

Secondly, the planner can recognize the real meaning of the expected value of estimation and can avoid building a comprehensive plan on too pessimistic or too optimistic assumption.

Thirdly, it helps to increase the number of strategic options. The company has to be prepared for the pessimistic assumptions, for example.

Fourth, the causes of minimum values are identified beforehand. Thus it becomes possible to have an early warning system or to have contigency plans to prevent performance from going below the expected average. About one third of Japanese companies use range forecasting.

13.3 Sequential decisions (2)

Sequential decision-making involves making a partial commitment, collecting information through it and then making a larger commitment. For example, a new product is sold in a small city as an experiment, and if successful, large scale production is carried out. It can also mean making a flexible decision first, waiting until enough accurate information is available and then making detailed decisions later.

One does not run under a solid plan, but instead proceeds some distance and then, after looking around, proceeds to more distant place. This approach is used when uncertainty is high, without knowing the probable value nor the range of prediction. This approach can be applied to the situation where negotiation with a partner is necessary because there is high uncertainty about the conclusion. Lindbolm mentions that most political decisions are taken by "muddling through", and this approach is similar to sequential decisions (Lindbolm, 1959).

There are two kinds of sequential decisions. The first one is to make a flexible decison tentatively, and then, after the elapse of time during which more information is collected and situation become clearer, make a large scale decision. For example;

Driving a train by following the diagram schedule as a general plan, but looking at the signals and deciding whether to go ahead.

Introducing a new product as a second entry, but carrying out the research beforehand.

Constructing a plant, by first procuring a lot and constructing a part of the plant. Then, on sufficient land area, increasing the capacity of the plant as the demand increases.

Carrying out important research and development by more than two teams in parallel. Then, in the course of time, selecting one approach.

Having long-range planning comprised of a long-range strategy and a medium range plan.

The second kind of sequential decision-making is to make a partial commitment and, after carrying out a small scale project, adding more information and revising predictions, then taking out a larger commitment. This is a more important approach.

Selling a new product in a small city. If this experiment is successful, then enlarging the production capacity and selling the product to the whole market of the country.

Women's suits are subject to a rapid change of fashion. Small lots of new suits are sold first; the company gets quick feedback on sales, and if sales are increasing the sales are expanded.

Constructing a plant for home electric appliances in a foreign country, building a small plant first to produce the batteries. Collecting much information, then expanding items and quantity of production.

Implement a cost reduction plan, by exercising a small scale trial in an experimental unit. After reviewing the effects on cost and the reaction of workers, applying the method to all of the plant, if it is successful.

Updating long-range planning every year.

These kinds of sequential decisions are widely used. A sequential decision assumes that a decision and its implementation can be incremental and divided. If this is difficult, as in the construction of chemical plant or the development of new model of car or the development of completely new drugs, this method is rarely applied.

13.4 Early-warning system (3.1)

An early-warning system makes it possible for an organization to adapt itself to changes in the environment at an early stage by identifying the necessity of change.

An early-warning system involves finding unfavorable events and their preceding events. Some person is assigned to monitor preceding events. For example:

A Japanese company is selling textbooks and other educational material for high school and middle schools. The preceding event for a change of textbook is a change of policy by the Ministry of Education, which is decided at a certain meeting. The company therefore keeps an eye on the Ministry's meeting.

For pharmaceutical companies, change in regulation for public medical insurance have a tremendous impact on the demand and price of products, so this factor is monitored.

The change of exchange rate is predicted by monitoring the inflation in one country and its trade balance.

To predict political change in a host country, movements of major political parties are monitored.

Manufacturing of air conditioners pay attention to long-term weather forecasting.

Emergence of new products by competition are watched by collecting information on purchase orders addressed to material suppliers.

Table 13.2 Contingency plan and decision tree

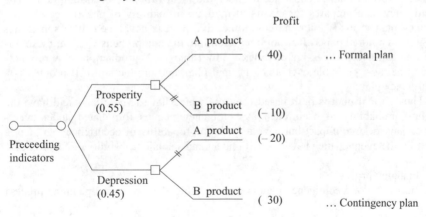

(Notes) 1. ⊣⊢ This shows that this path will not be taken. Indicates that plan is not implemented
2. Formal plan is formulated by selecting the plan with the largest profit under the event with highest probability, that is, A product is produced in prosperity
3. Contingency plan is built by choosing the plan with the largest profit under the events with medium probability, that is, B product are planned in depression

By watching these preceding indicators, the company can adapt to a change of situation quickly. This approach can be applied even when the direction of change is not predictable. However, the plan is built after preceding events occur, so adaptation might be too late. Contigency planning involves preparing a plan in advance, in addition to this early warning system.

13.5 Contigency plan

A contigency plan is actually used in daily operations. For example, every company has an emergency plan for fires. Recently, strategic contigency plans have come to attract attention, and these are a new development for Japanese corporations.

A contigency plan is also called an "emergency plan", "shadow plan", "road map plan" or "alternative plan". "There is no worry where there is a good safeguard" is Japanese proverb. It is different from flexible budgeting and different from alternative plans under the same assumptions.

A contigency planning system is shown by a decision tree (see Table 13.2). A company can make a better choice by having a contigency plan to produce a product B in a depression, in addition to a formal plan to produce product A in a period of prosperity. Such a performance is better than only producing A or B. Thus, a contigency plan has to have an adaptive planning system. It is an "all weather strategic plan". However, it is impossible to have multiple comprehensive plans, so the standard formal plan is constructed under the most probable of assumptions. The contigency plan prepares for events of medium probability of occurrence. A contigency plan is made after the comprehensive plan is developed. It is sometimes written on colored paper. It is not integrated into the comprehensive plan, by so doing one can avoid excessive complexity. In Table 13.2, production of A products under the most probable events is a normal plan, and production of B product is a contigency plan.

Thus, formal plan is built based o events which have large effects and have the highest probability of occurrence. A contigency plan is formulated under events which have a large impact but have a medium probability of occurrence. No plan is built for the events which have a small impact and a small probability of occurrence.

(1) Planning process
An illustration of a contigency plan is seen in Table 13.3. A typical planning process occurs as follows.

(1) Identification of an important environmental event
Any event which has a great impact on company performance is identified. Every company predicts the growth rate of the economy and demand of products. Other key events, discontinuous events in particular, which have a great impact on the company are identified. This could be carried out by the brain-storming of a panel consisting of

Table 13.3   Example of a contingency plan for a new product

1. What if ...?

If competitor Y introduce new product Y, before our company introduce new product

2. Probability of occurrence

20 %

3. Financial impact

If any measures are not taken, the sales amount of new product X will decrease by one billion yen in the first year and also profit will decrease by 0.2 billion yen.

4. Signaling indicators, trigger points and individuals responsible for 'tracking'

Signaling indicators	Responsible for watching
New contract for new materials for new product Y is presented from Y company to A company or B company befor June 1.	Director, materials department

5. Contingency plan and its financial effect

Contingency plan	Effects on sales amount and profit
(1) Actions to neutralize the effect. Development of new product. "Super X" is developed in parallel with the development of product "X" and it is completed befor June 1. (2) Actions. To decrease the introduction of new product "X". Promote development of new product "Super X". Sales campaign for "Super X" is implemented instead of the campaign for new product "X". (3) Effects. The decrease of sales by early introduction of new product "Y" is avoided by 80%. (The number on the right side indicate the increase of the amount by the implementation of contingency plan.)	Sales 0.8 billion yen Profit 0.16 billion yen

approximately ten persons from several departments who have a variety of information at their disposal.

These key events are classified into three parts: the secondary environment (economy in general, society, political environment, technology, international environment and natural environment), the primary environment (market), and the international situation.

Sometimes the future performances is included in the key events of a contigency plan. The contigency plan become a means of control or means for enforcement in this case, because with this sort of contigency plan, managers have to attain goals by any means possible.

(2) Prediction of probability of occurrence
Events with a high probability are used as assumption under a formal plans. Assumptions with medium probability are used for contigency plans. Assumptions with medium probability are used for contigency plans.

(3) Prediction on the impact of financial performance
The impact of events on sales and profit is analyzed. This is used to show a goal which the contigency plan has to recover.

(4) Trigger points and responsible person for watching
Preceding events are discovered. In the case of Table 13.3, the competitor will issue an order for procuring components to introduce a new product. Preceding events can be found by analyzing time series casual relations.

A trigger point is a certain level of preceding events which has large impact on company. It decides when the contigency plan will be implemented.

A responsible person to watch events is selected from personnel who have the best access to the preceding events. He does not necessarily belong to operating units.

The trigger point could cause an overreaction, or too late reaction, depending the timing. The timing is set, so that the impact is large, and the situation will not reverse.

(5) Contigency plan and its financial impact
By having a contigency plan beforehand, damages caused by anticipated events can be alleviated.

When a preparatory action is necessary before a contigency plan, it is clearly stated. However, preparatory actions, in addition to a contigency plan, are more expensive to carry out than a simple contigency plan. The cost of preparatory action may be offset by a decrease in damage.

Actions under a contigency plan should be immediately carried out and should have a quick impact. This is the reason why action is named 'emergency action'.

The effects of the actions of contigency plans are made clear. This can show the importance of the actions.

Types of contigency plan

The following are types of contigency plans.

(A) Opportunity catching or threat avoidance. Opportunity catching is important. But in many cases, it is used as a safeguard.

(B) Contigency plan in a comprehensive strategic plan, in a project plan and in a short-range annual plan. Up to the present time contigency plans were used in short-range plans of the repetitive activities of production and sales. However, the importance of it is increasing in strategic planning.

(C) Contigency plans to cope with uncontrollable external events and contigency plans applied to changes in performance. Change in performance is caused by external events and internal efforts. If the change in performance is used as a trigger point, a contigency plan can be used for control purposes. In this case, the manager is requested to reach the goal by any means.

13.6 Revision of the plan (3.3)

A strategic plan can adapt and take advantage of a change in the environment by revising the plan promptly when the situation changes. Updating of the plan resembles a sequential decisions. However, a sequential decision makes a temporary decision first and then makes detailed decision afterwards. Updating builds a formal plan and then it is revised. Many companies revises the long-range plan once a year, some revise it more than once a year.

When the demand goes down with a time-lag behind the change of indices of business cycle, a change of strategy can be on time by revision of the plan, if no contigency plan is prepared beforehand. Also when it is hard to predict a change of technology or the behavior of a competitor, a plan has to be revised after events occur.

Many American corporations which make use of long-range planning, such as General Electric, revises the long-range plan several times a year. On the other hand, GE does not revise the parts of plan which are important for two years. This means that GE is selective in revision in order to concentrate on strategic project planning.

Many Japanese companies use a similar approach in that they do not revise the plan every year; they are selective in revision to save effort and to make the plan more strategic.

13.7 Diversification and flexibility of business (4.1)

The flexibility of business aims to maintain profit in the worst case. It aims to improve the profit in the most pessimistic case, even if the average profit is made lower.

For example, as is seen in in Table 13.2, A product can get a profit of 40 in prosperity but it brings (–) 20 profit in depression; on the other hand, B product is sold to public organization so it yields (–) 10 profit in prosperity, while it yields 30 profit in depression. When two products are produced with the ratio of A as 0.4 and B as 0.6, then this mixture of products brings a profit of 10 at any time. This product-mix results in a remarkable improvement of the profit in the worst case, compared with the situation when only A product is produced or only B product is sold. We should notice that both A and B are a risky product because the loss is large in the worst case, but the movement of profit is in the opposite direction.

There are many means to improve the profit in the worst situation by having flexibility.

To use general purpose equipment rather than to use specialized equipment, flexible manufacturing system (FMS), for example.

To reduce man power by introducing an automated machine and to make it possible to produce profit even if the capacity is utilized only at 50 percent level. (We should recognize that in Japan reduction of man power is hard because of the life time employment system.)

To switch materials into ones which can be obtained all the time to avoid the effect of shortage of key resources.

Variation of profits in a variety of products should have a negative correlationship or should have a zero correlationship.

Diversification of customers.

By multinational management, market and production centers are diversified. The performance of a company can be stabilized if the changes of the situation in several countries are mutually independent.

13.8 Relative competitiveness and strengthening of resource capabilities

A man could be infected by a disease, but the damage is small if his body is strong and sound. On the other hand, a man will be shocked by a slight disease if his body is weak and less resistant. Similarly, if the resource capability of a company is strong, it will not go bankrupt if it suffers from a temporary loss.

Strengthening of corporate resource capability means changing the utility value of the loss. The following are the methods used to strengthen it.

To increase the equity ratio. If the company suffer a loss it can be made good with equity.

To keep enough current assets and unused assets. To have a strong relationship with main banks. To form an alliance with other corporation to help each other.

To enhance the loyalty of employee, thus preventing them from quitting in cases when a company is struggling for a turnaround.

To enhance the trust of customers.

To ensure that their products have strong competitiveness and that the company will be last to go bankrupt among other companies.

To have a high share of market.

To rationalize and to reduce the cost for preparation of a change of exchange rate.

To separate money-losing departments.

What kind of means to cope with uncertainty are practically used? These are surveyed as shown in Table 13.1: increase of information (1.1), range forecasting (1.2) sequential decisions are most frequently used (2), early warning systems (3.1) are used with some frequency, but contigency plans (3.2) are used less frequently. They are rather used for project planning. relative competitiveness (4.2.1) and strengthening of resource capabilities (4.2.2) are also considered as important.

There are some differences in practices among industries. Industries in severe competition, such as machinery, electrical machinery and transportation equipment use increase of information (1.1), range forecasting (1.2) and sequential decision-making (2).

Industries with heavy capital investment, such as those in chemicals, oil refining, iron and steel, electricity and gas supply use range forecasting (1.2) and early warning systems (3.1) frequently.

The successful companies in planning (subjective judgment, 146 companies) use (1.1) increase of information and (1.2) range forecasting more frequently.

13.9 The relationship between four approaches

What are the relationships between the four approaches (in detail, eight approaches)? We will consider them by using the decision tree of Table 13.2.

An increase in information is needed when most of the data in Table 13.2 is lacking. One cannot tell what kind of events ar there, what kind of products can be produced, and what kind of effects there will be for each combination of events and strategy. In this situation, we try to increase the amount of information on the events and on the options of strategies to find out better strategies.

Range forecasting tries to determine the higher value and lower value of sales or profit under prosperity and under depression respectively, to discover better alternatives.

Sequential decision-making means that the events in the table are not clear, and the company will try to experiment with the sales of A products. If there is a profit, then the company will expand the production and sales of product A. Sequential decisions assume that a decision and its implementation can be incremental and divisible.

Early warning system and contigency plans try to select A product or B product depending upon forecasted events. There are more than two plans to produce A or B.

Revision of a plan means that whilst A products are being produced, the depression appears, then the A product may be switched to B product, or when some other events happen, then a new product C, may be introduced. When new ideas (for example C product) are discovered and when it is more profitable, then the plan is revised.

Diversification means that when product A produces 40% sales, and B produces 60%, then the company can maintain a profit of 10 all the time. This assumes that the cost is the same at any capacity utilization, and also that the movement of profit of A is in the opposite direction.

Basic strength is attained by constructing a strong physical body for the corporation by improvement of net worth or by alliance with other companies, so that the company can stand the loss of minus 10 (B product in prosperity), minus 20 (A product in depression) in the worst cases. This alleviate the damage of loss in the worst cases or it changes the utility value of the loss.

Chapter 14 Implementation and control

14.1 Models of implementation and control

Implementation and control of a plan means to formulate an action program, to allocate resources and to carry out the plan, to see the results. The process is, action program – do – see.

There are three errors in the implementation and control of a strategic plan.

(a) No implementation. The implementation of a strategic plan is different from that of an operational plan. The organization cannot survive without operations, so the operational plan has to be implemented under some sort of cybernetic system. However the strategic plan can be postponed, so it may happen that the plan is completely ignored. At B University, a long-range plan was formed by a committee of deans of departments, key staffs and the president. They met once a week and after spending long hours, they completed a plan. The contents of the plan were innovative, but it was completely ignored. The president retired and almost all deans were changed. No formal explanation was made, the extent of participation of the staff was very narrow.

(b) An error of running away without control. A strategic plan is formed by one department and is authorized by head office, and when it is beneficial to the department for some reasons or another, it is implemented although it is not profitable to the company as a whole. For example, a capital investment plan may be implemented, whilst the labour force reduction plan is not implemented.

Ataka Trading Company was a large company with sales of ¥ 2000 billion in 1975, a history of 70 years, but went bankrupt in 1976, because of the improper follow up of a strategic plan. The company could not collect an accounts receivable of 100 billion yen from NRC in Canada. NRC was established in 1973 to refine oil. NRC was not a well established company, but a precarious company. Ataka hastily made contracts to be the sole agency of importing oil for NRC. Ataka did not conduct enough investigation on the management of the company. After the oil crisis, the price of crude oil soared, NRC encountered financial difficulties and payments were delayed. From October, 1974 until November, 1975 the amount of delayed payment reached to ¥ 100 billion in a year. This information was not delivered to the head office, and no action was taken for one year. No follow-up was carried out. The reason for no action was that a director, Takagi, in the head office wanted to hide his failure, because he was a promoter of the contract whilst he was the president of the Ataka American Company. Another reason was that the top management of the company were weak because they were controlled by the family of the founder. The control and auditing functions were also weak and the use of computers for controlling was much below the standard of other trading companies. Thus, defective follow-up of a strategy lead to the bankruptcy of a huge trading company.

(c) Error of overcontrol. Some new projects tried to accumulate knowledge, not just to get profit. For example, an early stage of research, and an early stage of new product development are in the process of learning and the plan should be revised from time to time. If the original plan is forced, the best path to arrive at the final destination will not be explored.

In order to avoid the above errors, and to get the best approach to control, the following different models need to be selected to match with different situations.

(a) Construction project model. Once the construction project has been started, large investment is committed continuously. In this case, implementation should follow the plan, and it is costly to revise the plan. The detailed plan before the construction should be studied thoroughly, so that no revision is required after construction starts.

Follow up aims to review the actual results on progress and cost-performance and to compare them against the plan. Reviewing is also done by estimating the results upon completion against the plan. This model is applied to a large investment project when the situation is relatively stable.

(b) Learning or adaptive model. When a project contains many unknown elements, sequential decisions need to be applied. Implementation is necessary, but the plan itself is explored. Learning rather than implementation, or learning through running is the feature of this model. In the basic research project, or in the early stage of new product development, this model is applied.

(c) Periodic reviewing model. The comprehensive strategic plans and numerical plans are reviewed at certain intervals. The deviation from the plan is measured and corrective action is studied. If the deviation is very large, the plan is revised, or it is switched to the contingency plan.

Thus, three models are applied to different situations. The construction project model is applied to the later stage of large investment projects, or to large product development stages, the learning model to an early stage of development under uncertain situations, the periodic reviewing model to a comprehensive plan.

14.2 Promotion of implementation

A strategic plan is not implemented automatically, rather it is not necessarily welcomed by a number of people. For the person who is assigned to implement the plan, it is an unexperienced new job, it involves uncertainty and it contains a risk of failure. For the person who is not in charge of implementation, it will change their promotion ladder and location of authority. These facts raise strong resistance to the plan.

2.1 Reasons for no implementation

These are many cases where long-range plans are not implemented, where they are "stored in the document case". According to our survey, there are three main reasons for this neglect of long-range plans.

(a) Lack of involvement. The department which should be responsible to carry out the plan does not accept that the plan is their own plan. (Table 14.1.b at the end of this chapter.)

This lack of understanding and support from operating departments comes from no participation of the operating units in the process of planning. Also, where the communication is defective, operating units do not understand the needs of new strategy.

Incomplete organization for implementation (C item of Table 14.1) is another organizational problem. A plan is not assigned to an appropriate department, or it is not studied by a project team. In these instances, nobody feels that it is his own plan.

(b) The plan is incomplete. When a strategic plan is only a policy or an outline and is not supported by detailed action programmes, it is not carried out (See D item in Table 14.1.b). This is one type of incompleteness of a plan.

When the plan is unrealistic, it is not implemented. (See Table 14.1.b, F item). Premises may be mistaken because of errors of forecasting or because of changes of environment. Goals are too high or too low. Important components are lacking, for example, financial resources are not allocated adequately. These problems arise when the change of environment is fast and the plan is not revised properly. The use of contingency plans is one way to cope with this situation, but the contingency plan cannot cover every case. The original plan needs to be revised and updated to match with the changed situation. If this is not done, the plan becomes unrealistic.

When the responsibility to execute the plan is not clear, when there is no action programme, the plan cannot be implemented. This is another aspect of the imperfectness of the plan. (D item of Table 14.1.b.)

(c) No follow-up, no performance evaluation (Item E of Table 14.1.b)
This happens when the plan is delegated to one or two departments, and the management does not do the follow up of the plan. One company revised their long-range plan occasionally, but the new plan was built on actual results, no analysis was done on the deviation of results from the plan. The plan was simply reshuffled. The operating departments were not interested in the implementation.

Warren details the testing of the plan viewed from the operating department (Warren, 1966). One of the tests to judge whether the plan is worthy of implementation is

Table 14.1   Factors affecting the implementation of strategy

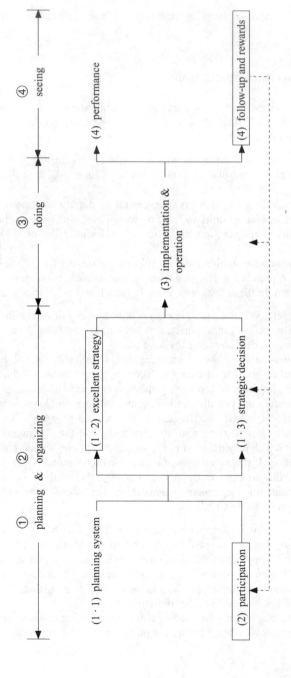

(Note)   (1)   This chart is essentially the same as Table 1.2.
         (2)   The process follows planning, organizing, doing and seeing.
         (3)   Three important factors are participation, strategy is excellent and appropriate follow-up and rewards.
         (4)   The follow-up and rewards system are feed back to willingness for participation, strategic decision and willingness for implemen-
               tation.

to see whether top management is committed to the long-range plan. If they are not, people understand that the plan is not important and the performance evaluation on the implementation will not be serious.

Factors which impede the implementation are the same as their factors which promote the implementation. Theoretically, these factors can be explained in two ways. One is by the management process, the other is by the motivation theory. The latter approach will be explained in the next paragraph.

The Table 14.1 follows the management process: planning, organizing, doing and seeing.

(1) The planning system, or information processing system, affects the contents of strategy and also strategic decision-making styles. The contents of strategy affect the implementation of the strategic plan.

(2) The participation or the organizational process affects the contents of long-range plan and strategic decision styles and also directly affects the motivation to implement the plan.

(3) Follow-up and rewards are fed back into the process, and they affect the motivation to participate, seriousness on strategic decision-making and implementation, in the next planning cycle. However, usually the planners and operating units can anticipate future follow-up and rewards by the commitment of top management. If past experience is lacking, this commitment can evoke the above anticipation.

The reasons why these factors affect the implementation is explained by the motivation theory in the next paragraph.

2.2 Promoting implementation

The factors to promote the implementation of a long-range can be explained by a general theory of motivation. According to expectancy theory, the reasons why people take actions and co-operate to attain the goals of an organization depends on the following three items: (1) the value of behavior itself, (2) the probability of success and the value placed in the success, and (3), the probability of obtaining the rewards and the value of the rewards. If this is shown by an equation the following model can be used (Staw, 1976).

> Strength of motivation (M) = intrinsic value of behavior (Ia) + probability of achieving (Pb) × value of internal satisfaction coming from achieving a job (Ib) + probability of obtaining extrinsic rewards (Qi) × the value of extrinsic rewards (Ei)
> This means; $M = Ia + Pb\ Ib + \sum Qi\ Ei$

Intrinsic satisfaction originating in behavior itself is the satisfaction over the planning of strategy itself and with its implementation.

Internal motivation coming from achievement is a feeling of satisfaction originating from the full implementation of plan. This satisfaction cannot be obtained when the plan becomes a failure.

Extrinsic rewards are promotion, increases in salary and bonuses. If these extrinsic rewards have a high probability of being obtained when a strategy is accomplished, then motivation is high. There are many extrinsic rewards and the aggregation of them becomes necessary.

This model put emphasis on self-realization needs and on intrinsic rewards. Thus (1) the behavior itself can be a source of satisfaction. For example, it is challenging to be engaged in new product development; (2) there are two intrinsic rewards (Ia and Ib) and extrinsic rewards (Ei); and (3) the value of rewards varies from person to person, but generally speaking, the value of internal rewards or intrinsic rewards are more important than external rewards or extrinsic rewards. Particularly for Japanese employees, the job itself is more stimulating than money.

We conducted a survey on the practices used for promoting implementation. (See Table 14.2.b at the end of this chapter.)

The factors for trouble are similar to the factors of success. This success factors are as follows.

(2.2.1) To perceive that the plan is his own plan, it is worth challenging

To increase a sense of ownership, participation is most important (item C of Table 14.2.b). When the implementation department does not participate in the formulation process, the plan has to be explained well (item D), and preferably, the top management should participate in the explanation of the plan from time to time, for example, in the new year's message or in the company news letter. A slogan or a nickname is frequently used (item E) to appeal to the feelings of employees.

(2.2.2) Plan is complete

The plan is relatively (not absolutely) complete with respect to assumptions, rankings and combinations, resource allocations (item L and M). The plan has action programmes, is integrated into MBO (management by objectives) programmes, is linked with annual budget. (item F, G, H, I)

Linking with the annual budget is considered as the most important. In the budget guideline, the contents of long-range plan should be included.

The annual budget can be devised into two parts. One is operating budget, another part is strategic budget. The latter contains capital investment, expenditure for research and development, establishment of a foreign factory and so forth. These expenditure tends to decrease the present profit, so the budget should be held in the corporate head office or assigned separately to divisions (Yavitz, 1988, Rowe, 1985) .

(2.2.3) To review actual performance

Reviewing by the top management is important (item B), because it symbolizes the value of plan. Reviewing is important (item N), because it confirms the importance of achievement, and suggests that implementation will be reflected on the external reward by some of the means.

(2.2.4) Top management involvement

Top management makes possible the above three elements be installed and communicates the possibility of sanction based on the implementation of the plan.

The relationship between these means with a theory of motivation is as follows.

(a)   His own plan to be challenged ——— Increase of internal value (Ia)
(b)   Plan is complete ——— Increase in internal value (Ia) to increase the probability of success (Pb)
(c)   To review actual performance ——— This increases the internal satisfaction coming from the achievement of jobs (Ib), and also increases extrinsic rewards (Qi Ei)

(2.3) Promotion of plan from the side of the initiator.

The promotion of a plan seen from the bottom or from the initiator has some different aspects. From observation on many cases, we find that the following process is necessary.

(1) Mobilization of the power center. A large project and a large system of comprehensive plans cannot be implemented by a single planner alone. The planner has to obtain resources allocation, and has to have the cooperation of many people. To acquire these resources and cooperation, the planner needs access to the power center, such as the president, one of the members of the management committee, the head of the department to which he belongs, or the head of the finance department, each of whom can have the power to allocate resources. In the case of the development of Walkman at Sony, the power centers who cooperated in the final decision was that of the president and CEO Morita. There were many opposing opinions among the marketing department, because the price of Walkmans were about three times higher than the ordinary tape recorders.

(2) The support of a couple of powerful middle managers. In the above case of Walkman, the head of the marketing department of the Audio division, Shirokura, was a supporter. The middle manager is helpful in formulating a group of cooperators on the middle management level.

(3) Force field analysis. Those who are for the plan and who are against the plan are analyzed. How they are influential and to what degree they can agree with or oppose each other are made clear. The power of opposers multiplied by the degree of opposition determines the strength of opposing force. To the opposing group, the model of conflict resolution can be used. The opposers could be changed to neutrals or to supporters.

The power of supporters multiplied by the degree of support makes the strength of supporting force. Powerful supporters are organized to form the supporting power, and let them move to persuade the opposers and neutrals. This makes the implementation possible.

(4) Obtaining the resources. To implement an plan, the money and personnel are essential. The budget of the project has to be approved and has to be integrated into the annual budget. (On these processes see, Kanter, 1973; Galbraith, 1984; Hersey & Blanchard, 1977.)

It is a fallacy to think that a good plan in the company will be supported by everybody. It is a fallacy to think that a good plan will be implemented without any political action.

14.3 Action programmes

(3.1) Different action programmes

The detail of action programmes varies depending upon whether the plan is a construction project type or a learning by practice type. In the former case a programme is detailed, but in the latter case a programme is only a rough schedule, and the programme is revised frequently. It is not possible to draw a detailed PERT chart.

(3.2) Elements of action programme

Elements of action programmes generally consist of 5 W 1 H, and are arranged in order of importance, (1) who is responsible (who), (2) the schedule (when), (3) plan of action (what, where, how), (4) expected results (why), and the reporting system. An example of action programmes used in MBO is exhibited in Table 14.2. This case illustrate the above elements.

Table 14.2 An example of management by objective systems for carrying out the long-range plan

Department _____   Year _____

Priority	Name of the plan	Goals (Objective and quantity, contribution to the performance of the company)	Elements of the plan (Individuals responsible, contents of research, production, sales, productivity)	Conditions assumed for the plan (Resource allocation, responsible department, team, department to co-operate with the project)	Schedule (Upper line : Plan, Lower line : Implementation and performance) Year						Evaluation of the implementation
					First quarter	Second quarter	Third quarter	Fourth quarter	First quarter	Second quarter	

(3.3) Location of action programmes

The implementation plan of the long-range plan has a variety of forms. They can be classified into three patterns. The first one is to include in the long-range plan a detailed implementation plan. About 50 percent of Japanese corporations have this sort of implementation plan. (Table 14.3.b, 2A, 2B.)

The second pattern is to let responsible departments or project teams construct implementation plans. In Table 14.5, examples of this pattern include: the department responsible for implementation building an implementation plan for one or two years and receiving approval (2C); the responsible department building an implementation plan for its own use (2D), in this case resources are already allocated. The implementation plan in "the management by objective plan" for half year or one year (2E) is another case. A simple illustration of "management by objectives" to implement long-range plan is shown in Table 14.4. In the case of management by objectives, the results are reviewed mostly by the implementing department. In practice, there is little difference between (2C) and (2E).

The third pattern is to have the budget considered as an implementation plan (in Table 14.3.b, (2F) and (2G) belong to this type). A plan for capital investment and the personnel plan in the budget should be based on a long-range plan. If the planning department is responsible for both budgeting and the long-range plan, the budget as an implementation plan functions well. If this is not the case, the budget should have a detailed description and schedules of the long-range plan. Otherwise, the strategic plan will be buried in the numbers of the budget. Research and development, new product development, new business development and production plans in foreign countries, for example, should be planned in a strategic budget.

The practice of successful companies in planning (subjective judgment) and unsuccessful companies are compared and we find that successful companies tend to build detailed implementation plans in the long-range plan (b), or have MBO plans as an implementation plan (E).

14.4 Follow-up

In Japan, the follow up of a plan tends to be delegated to operating departments, for the reason that senior managers at higher level tend to trust lower level managers because of lifetime employment and because remuneration do not necessarily reflect short range performance.

The long-range plan is followed up by a variety of methods (see Table 14.4.b). For example, in the case of B company, the finance department construct the medium-range plan, it is integrated into budget and followed up by that department. The finance department reviews the performance and progress of medium-range plans once a year. On the other hand, project plans have schedules and they are reviewed at every milestone by the planning department and by the top management.

In the case of H company, the planning department in each product divisions prepares the long-range plan and also the annual budget plan, so that the long-range plan is integrated into the budget. The performance of the long-range plan is reported to the president (CEO) once a year by the directors of the product divisions. Sometimes it happens that losing dog products are not divested because of the decentralized style of decision-making of the company.

E company (pharmaceutical products) has been using a long-range plan for many years and it is well implemented. The long-range plan is distributed to every manager above the section chief with serial number to be kept confidential. Thus every manager knows the detailed contents of long-range plan and the plan is well implemented.

At this company, the long-range plan is followed up every month. Important projects are viewed at check points or milestone, but the comprehensive plan is thoroughly reviewed every month by the management committee. If there is a deviation of action from the plan, the reasons for it have to be explained.

The actual performance is compared both with the plan and the past performance, and is indicated by point numbers. This point number reflects not only short range performance measures such as sales and profit but also the performance of the strategic plan, such as the progress of new product development and its success, the rate of increase of sales and rate of decrease of terms of collection of account receivables. They are compared with the plan. The performance is also compared with the results of the previous year, so that the time series improvement is taken into account to prevent the formulation of an easy plan.

Point numbers are related to pay and promotion in the marketing department, but in the other departments it is not related to pay. The point number itself can be a source of motivation to implement the plan.

Computation of point number based on the execution of the plan is done by computer, but it takes time and has a certain cost. This company has a slogan "planning is implementing" and considers cost of follow-up worth the effort.

E company has a policy that there is a gap between the results and the plan, this gap has to be filled by some other plan. The company sympathizes with the planners over the gap, but they are not excused. This means that goals have to be attained by any means, in many cases by alternative plans. This is another side of the principle that planning is implemented.

(4.1) The level of reviewer

There are various levels of follow-up: self-control, follow-up by the planning department and follow up by top management. In E company, follow-up is done by the management committee. In other companies , top management will go to divisions or to the operating units to conduct the follow-up of long-range plans four times a year. TDK and Matsushita Electric Products Company send top management to each department to conduct follow-ups. This results in strong motivation to implement the strategic plan. The follow-up by top management is the most effective means of assuring implementation.

(4.2) Follow-up of projects

There are two kinds of follow-up subjects. One is the follow-up of projects in progress and the accumulated expenses compared with the plan. The other one is on a periodic plan or on a comprehensive plan. It is mostly a follow-up on numbers, such as the sales of a new product, the actual expenditure for research and development, activities of training, amount of capital investment and decrease of personnel.

The follow-up on the milestones of a project is practiced extensively. As shown in Table 14.4.b, it is done several times a year. Table 14.3 shows a follow-up of a large construction project. The dotted line shows the earliest and latest physical progress of the construction. Line 1 shows the actual physical progress. The physical progress is measured by square meters, by inputted standard man-days, etc.

The actual cost of construction is shown by line 2 and 3. Line 2 shows the cost which has already been contracted. Line 3 shows the cost which was already paid out. By adding the remaining cost of reserve expense, plus the remaining cost of construction to the actual expense, the total cost of construction is predicted (Line 5). For such control of progress and cost, a reporting system has to be established.

In this table, progress is indicated by numbers, but in other projects, the progress can be measured by stages of project. For example, in the case of the construction of building, stages are divided into concept designing, detailed designing, estimation of construction, order for contract for construction, purchase order for procurement of material, procurement of equipment, land 'formation', manufacturing of parts and construction. These are shown by a bar chart or by PERT, and progress is followed up by the use of these methods.

In Table 14.3 we can find two kinds of follow-up, one is on actual results, the other one is on future results. The former is a control by past results, the latter is a control by estimation or a 'feed-forward' process. By the latter method, a quick corrective action can be taken.

(4.3) Follow-up of periodical plan and quantitative plan

Areas of follow-up can be divided into the following: (a) follow-up of basic goals such as sales, profit and capital structure, (b) product-market strategy such as product-mix, change of the position on PPM chart, ratio of new product on sales, amount of export, (c) structure plans such as investment for research and development, capital expenditure, number of personnel, and (d) productivity plans such as labour productivity and turnover of assets. Achievements on these items are compared with the plan.

Table 14.3   Control of the progress of construction

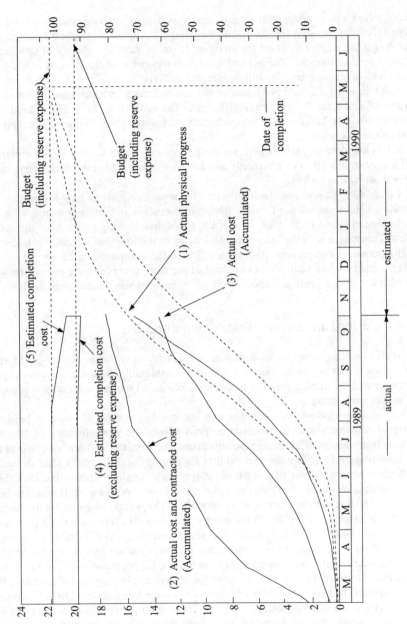

These follow-ups overlap with internal analysis. Unlike internal analysis, however, these follow-up focus on the change of the company, capital investment for example, and do not put an emphasis on the analysis of status, such as capacity of production or the age of equipment. The achievement is compared with the plan, it is not compared with other companies as it is in internal analysis.

The follow up of actual performance is indicated either as a variance amount or as a ratio of actual result over planned figures. The ratio is easier to understand. The variance could be broken down into volume variance and price (home market and exchange rate) variance.

When the trend of performance for the past several years is reviewed, the plan itself can be evaluated as to whether it was too easy or not. This time-series analysis is carried out by E company.

Table 14.4.b shows how the follow-up of quantitative parts of long-range plan are conducted. In about 80% of cases, the actual result is directly compared with the long-range plan and in another 40% of the cases (overlapping responses), the actual result is compared with the budget which integrates the long-range plan. With respect to the period of comparison, about one third of the companies compare the results with the plan for one year, about one third of the companies compare the results with the plan for several years and about one third companies use a time-series analysis.

(4.4) Performance evaluation of departments

The performance evaluation of departments is different from the follow-up of strategic plans in that (a) the evaluation takes into consideration both the operational performance and the implementation of strategic plans, (b) the department or a group is the unit of assessment.

At Texas Instrument, the operating unit is requested to wear two hats, to hold operational responsibility and strategic responsibility. The performances of line departments are assessed by two responsibilities. The profit is divided into two parts, the operating profit before the expenditure for strategy and the profit after deducting strategic expenses. A case of a Japanese corporation is exhibited in Table 14.4. This is a case of assessment of product divisions at T Company in Japan. It assesses both the operational results and strategic performance. The weight of items for evaluation vary by the stage of life cycle. At the early stage of, or for, "question mark products" of PPM (or GSM or BCG) model, the share and progress of strategy has more weight, at the final stage, or for, "cash cow products", profit has the largest weight. The assessment item is composed of (1) final goals, (2) product-market strategic performance (3) efforts to improve the resource structure, (4) progress of projects. The standard of evaluation, absolute level, time series improvement, level of achievement of budget and overall evaluation are used. These multiple standards will encourage the unit to build good plans and to implement them. If only the result is compared with the plan, the manager will tend to build easy plans.

Table 14.4 Assessment of departments at Company T

criteria	standards weight	absolute level	time series improvement	achievement of budget	overall evaluation	weight for products in early stage of life cycle
		34 %	26 %	42 %	24 %	
(1) profitability	40					0
(2) market share	5					30
(3-1) technological competence	10					20
(3-2) production technology	10					15
(3-3) marketing competence	15					15
(3-4) personnel management	10					10
(4) progress of strategic projects	10					10
Total	100					100

(1) Levels of evaluation are A ~ B.
(2) Results are reflected on the amount of bonus of units, on evaluation of manager of units. This is applied to production and sales units.
(3) Self assessment + planning department assessment are brought to the management committee.

14.5 Rewards for implementation

Rewards for implementation are necessary in motivating people who are responsible for implementation or in promoting the activities for long-range planning. The theory of motivation in this respect was already explained. Intrinsic rewards originating in the action itself and coming from the achievement of goals are important on the one hand, and extrinsic rewards such as financial rewards and promotion are important on the other hand. We are here concerned with only the extrinsic rewards.

Extrinsic rewards have both promoting effects and distorting effects. If the rewards are too large, then the planners will take an easy road, they will build easy-to-attain levels of plans and thus they will try to secure the rewards. A hockey stick style is a typical case.

If there are no rewards, the planners will not be interested in planning and implementation. They will become more interested in operational issues, in particular the short-range profit which is usually related with the rewards. Grescham's Law on decision is the result.

The effective way is in between the above two extremes. Problems are on what results the rewards should be based. There are some principles for this;

(a) If both the contents of plans and their performances are reviewed, the departments will try to build good plans.

If only the results are compared with the plan, the units will tend to formulate plans that are easy to complete.

In order to evaluate the plan effectively, the time series results of performance are reviewed, and the time series comparisons of plans are reviewed. (See Table 14.4.b, 2B4.)

(b) If the performance of present operation and of strategy implementations are both reviewed, then Grescham's Law on decision will be avoided. The weighting of reviewing varies depending on the following.
(1) Completely new products (or projects).
(2) Products at the early stage of life cycle ("question mark products" and "star products").
(3) Products at the end of the life cycle ("cash cow products")
   For new projects, progress should be reviewed. For early stage products, increase of market share and technological competence are considered. For the later stage products, profit is emphasized. Thus it is necessary to see both the strategy implementation and operation, by changing the weight of evaluation items. (See Table 14.4. Many books on the product portfolio state similar ideas.)

(c) If both short-term performances and efforts for long-term performances are reviewed, then the preparation for future growth will be emphasized. This means that not only the profit or sales, but efforts to improve technological research efforts, to modernize equipment and to train people should be emphasized. (See Table 14.4.)

(d) If the rewards are given on the long-term basis or continuously, then managers will make continuous efforts every year.

If the rewards are given slowly and cumulatively, based on efforts to attain long-term results, a long-term efforts can be expected. In Japan, the long-term cumulative evaluation is reflected in the promotion of the job class ladder and of the status ladder, rather than the bonus. This needs a long-term evaluation, and the promotion results in eventually wage increases.

The survey shows that financial rewards are increasing (Table 14.4.b), probably because of the enhanced importance of long-range planning and corporate strategy.

We compared the successful companies in planning (subjective judgment) and unsuccessful companies in all industries. The successful companies use financial rewards more frequently than unsuccessful ones. For reviewing, the successful ones use time-series analysis more often than the unsuccessful ones.

Financial rewards are emphasized in such industries as food products, textiles and electrical appliances. In these industries, the execution of the long-range plan depends a great deal upon efforts of line departments. These industries also pay attention to the time-series analysis of performance.

Summary

Unlike daily operations, strategy is not necessarily implemented, because it does not affect short-term survival, because it rather decreases short-term profit.
(1) Reasons for no implementation are similar to factors for promotion. There are three factors. The three factors can be explained by the management process: planning, organizing, doing and controlling.

In the planning process, the plan needs to be realistic and worth challenging. The plan should be followed by detailed action programmes.

In the organizing process, participation for planning is important. But planners are not necessarily the doers, then full explanation are essential to make them feel that the strategic plan is their own plan.

In the controlling process, the plan needs to be followed up at milestones or periodically, and the accomplishment of the plan needs to be confirmed. (See Table 14.1.)

The top management commitment in planning, promotion and reviewing supports the above three factors.
(2) The promotion viewed from the initiator has some different aspects from the above. The promoter should make access to power centers and should get the support of middle managers. Force field analysis becomes necessary. Eventually, it has to obtain resource allocation for implementation.
(3) Action programmes are either located in the long-range planning documents, or they are formulated by each department, sometimes as a management-by-objective system or integrated into the budget. The action programme is the first step towards implementation. In many cases, the action programme is written in long-range planning documents.
(4) There are three styles of follow-up. One is a construction project style. The plan has to be implemented, and the revision of the plan is costly. Another one is the learning process model. The plan itself should be revised. The research projects, or projects in the early

stage of development belongs to this style. The above two styles should be applied differently.

The third style is periodical reviewing, which is applied to the comprehensive plan and to the numerical plan.

(5) In order to prevent the formulation of easy-to-accomplish plans, or the hockey-stick style plan, the reviewing should compare the present plan with the previous plan and should consider the time-series improvement of performance. If simply the result is compared with the plan, the operating units will build an easy plan.

(6) The performance evaluation of a department should see both the profit from operation of present products and implementation of new strategies. The department with "question mark products" have more emphasis on the increase of market share or on technological development. The assessment of two hats is necessary.

(7) The balance of short-term performance and preparation for future 'fruit' should be evaluated. Even for present products, the replacement of equipment, the training of employees and technological development are necessary to prepare for the future. As Likert says, the intervening variables needs to be recognized. (R. Likert, 1967).

(8) Not only the intrinsic rewards, but also extrinsic rewards are necessary to motivate the implementation. If the rewards are given slowly and on a cumulative basis, such as by promotion rather than by bonus, long-term efforts can be expected. This is possible in Japanese corporations, in which a life-time employment system is used.

Table 14.1.b Causes of trouble of implementation

			1979	1985	1989
		Corporations with long-range plans	327 co.	384 co.	249 co.
(1) How the plan is implemented		A. Implemented over-all	42 (%)	48 (%)	61
		B. Implemented partially	53	47	31
		C. Not well implemented	4	4	2
		D. Not implemented	0	0	0
(2) Causes of troubles of implementation		A. Lack of understanding and support from top management	5	— 7	
		B. Lack of understanding and support from operating departments	17	— 18	
		C. Incomplete organization for implementation	20	— 12	
		D. Incomplete implementation plan	27	— 27	
		E. Not used for evaluation of performance	15	— 13	
		F. Incomplete plan	21	— 22	
(Cases of B, C, D)		a. Premises were mistaken	8	3	
		b. Errors in demand forecasting and competitive analysis	3	5	
		c. Goals were too high or too low	7	8	
		d. Decisions were defective	2	3	
		e. Lack of important components	7	12	

(Notes) Number indicates the number of responding companies.

Table 14.2.b Promoting the implementation of long range-plans

		Companies with long-range plan	249 co. (%)
(1) How the long-range plan is implemented		A. Implemented over-all	60
		B. Implemented partially	31
		C. Not well implemented	2
		D. Not implemented	0
(2) To promote the implementation what kind of means were were actually active?	Top management committment	A. Top management spends many hours for planning and reviewing	27
	Participation	B. Top management and directors will go to each department or to field of operation to review the implementation.	22
		C. Participation in planning of line departments	60
		D. When the plan is completed, the meeting with each department to explain the contents of the plan is frequently held	29
		E. Slogan or nickname is attached to the long-range plan	25
	Planning system	F. Construct action programme	47 *
		G. Integrated into management-by-objective systems of departments	42 *
		H. Relationship with the long-range plan is stated in various plans	27 *
		I. The long-range plan is linked with the annual budget	55 *
		J. Profit of the division is divided into two-operating profit and profit after the strategic expense	3
		K. Organizations to implement the strategy are separated from other department	8
		L. Human and financial resources are allocated well for the implementation of the long-range plan	14
		M. Priorities are put to projects	15
	Follow-up	N. Detailed follow-up	39 *
		O. Public recognition and praise	5
		P. Implementation is linked with promotion and saraly increases	2

(Note) 1. Survey in 1989
2. Number indicates the percentage of responding companies
3. Asterisks (*) indicate that the sucessfull companies in planning (146 companies) (subjective judgement) have higher frequencies of these items

Table 14.3.b Implementation plan of the long-range plan

		1985	1989
	Corporations with long-range plan	384 co.	249 co.
(1) Do you have implementation plans?	A. Yes, I have.	87 (%)	87 (%)
	B. No, I haven't. Budgeting is different from long-range plan.	12	9
	A. In the long-range plan, there is schedule of each projects.	29	31
	B. In the long-range plan, implementation are cescribed in detail.	11	16 *
	(Responsible individuals, schedules, allocation of resources are specified)		
(2) Where do you have implementation plans, how is it described?	C. Department responsible for implementation (and project team) will build implementation plan for one or two years, in additior to long-range plan, and it is approved by the top management.	17	29
	D. Responsible department wil build implementation plans for their own use.	14	19
	E. Implementation plan is described in "the management by objective" plan for half a year or one year of the responsible department to carry out the long-range plan.	29	29 *
	F. Strategic projects are included in the budget expenditures and revenues of the project and progress of the schedule are stated in the budget; they are followed up as independent items of the total budget.	5	5
	G. Budget is an implementation plan, there is no implementation plan other than budget.	24	18

(Notes) 1. Implementation plan means the following: detailed plans; individuals responsible for carrying out; schedules; resource allocations; expected effects
2. Survey in 1985 and in 1989
3. The number indicates the percentage of responding companies
4. Asterisks (*) indicate that the successful companies in planning (subjective judgement) has much higher frequency than the unsuccessful companies in planning.

Table 14.4.b   Follow up of the long-range plan (or medium range plan)

		1979 327 co. (%)	1985 384 co. (%)	1989 249 co. (%)
	Corporations with long-range plans	73	79	65 *
(1) Follow up of the progress of projects	A. Is progress of projects reviewed by head office? — Yes			
	1. Several times a year	31	44	39 *
	2. Once a year	40	33	35
	B. Is performance, such as benefits over investment ratio, in addition to progress, reviewed by head office? — Yes	42	16	23
	C. Progress is not reviewed	15	13	9
	A. Is actual performance against quantitative parts of the long-range plan reviewed by head office? — No, but	41	38	41
(2) Follow up of quantitative parts of plan	1. Performance against budget is reviewed	37	38	40 Δ
	2. No follow up at all	1	1	1
	B. Is actual performace against quantitative parts of long-range plan reviewed by head office? — Yes, and	70	73	75
	1. For one year	33	26	23
	2. Cumulative values of performance for several years are compared	13	11	10
	3. For several years each	23	21	20
	4. Time series performance for several years are reviewed	5	27	22 *
(3) Is progress and performance related to some kind of economic rewards of managers (bonus or stock option)?	A. Not at all	57	48	34
	B. To some extent	36	46	62 *
	C. To a great extent	1	2	4

note (1) Asterisks (*) indicate the successful companies in planning (subjective judgement) has higher frequency.
(2) Triangle (Δ) indicates the successfuls have less frequency.

Chapter 15 Problems and success factors

15.1 Framework of analysis

The analysis of success factors needs to find out what are the cause-effect relationships. The basic framework of the analysis is presented in Table 15.1. It can be stated simply.

controllable variables $\rightarrow$ intervening variables $\rightarrow$ performance variables
(cause variables)   (end-results variables)

Controllable variables are planning systems and organizational planning prœesses. Intervening variables are strategic decision-making style and change of corporate culture, strategy contents, implementation of strategy and business operations. Performance variables or end-results variables, are growth, profit and employee satisfaction.

The analysis of effects or purposes of long-range planning system is the same as the analysis of success factors. In the analysis of effects, causes are fixed and intervening variables and performance variables are found. For example, "the long-range planning that puts emphasis on the key strategies improves the strategic decisions and makes the company environment-oriented". This is an effect on an intervening variable. In the analysis of success factors, on the other hand, the end-result variables are fixed, intervening variables and cause variables are searched. For example, "So that the long-range planning can contribute to the growth of the company, the top management should make clear the future vision of the company." An interesting thing is that the intervening variables are sometimes viewed as the effect of planning and in other times they are seen as the causes of performance. The problem is whether they can be controllable (or semi-controllable) or not. In this chapter we treat them as controllable.

The analysis of cause-effect relationship has many difficulties. To identify the causes, we have to identify the differences of end- results variables.

A types of planning $\rightarrow$ A' end-results
B types of planning $\rightarrow$ B' end-results

If end-results A' is better than end-results B' then A type of planning is better, and could be successful. The difference is important, however this observation is not easy. The reasons are:

Table 15.1   Framework of analysis

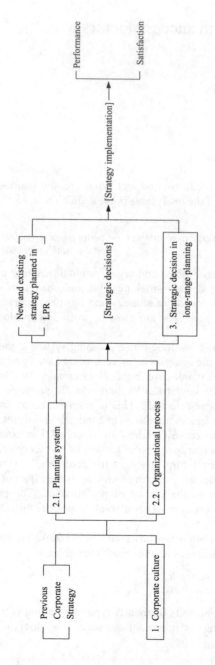

(note) (1) ☐ •••• Causes of success

(2) This chart is essentially the same as table 1.2, table 14.1 and table 15.2

There are time lags between the causes and the effects
The environment evolves, the assumption changes
The strategy and resources before the planning affect the performance.

Because of these difficulties, it is impossible to identify the success factors precisely. We have to use the subjective judgment to some extent.

There are many papers that analyze the effects of planning and thus to find out the success factors. In early times the performances between the companies that possess long-range planning and non-planners were compared (Thune and House, 1970), but now most of companies have somewhat long-range planning, so we have to find what sorts of planning process causes the satisfactory results.

Many papers try to find out the factors by using sophisticated statistical analysis such as canonical analysis, path analysis besides traditional correlation analysis, multiple regression analysis and others (i. e., Freeman, 1988). Most of these papers, however, use the subjective judgment as the data base, done by personal interviews or by mail questionnaires.

This chapter uses the subjective judgment of corporate plan to the cause-effect relationship. The data are mail questionnaires, interviews, discussions of the study groups of corporate planners and case studies.

Although these data are the results of subjective judgment, the number of responses is approximately over 300, covering several years. Interviews try to find out the facts in the depth of reality. (Some past research papers on the success factors are as follows: A. Rowe, 1982; G. Steiner, 1983; W. King, 1983; W. Blass, 1983; Lenz & Lyles, 1985; J. Robinson, 1986; Ramanujam and others, 1987; A. Langley, 1988; E. Freeman, 1989).

15.2 Problems

Problems or limitations of long-range planning are the factors that disturb the attainment of desirable results. The problem areas are very similar to the success factors, because the means to overcome the obstacles are also the factors of success. The problems are factors that are not easily controllable, although the planners know that they are success factors. The problems are surveyed, the free style answers are classified and exhibited in Table 15.1.b (at the end of this chapter).

(1) Inertia
People are more involved with daily operations. The corporate culture is not strategy oriented. The change of corporate culture is hard to carry out.

The top management is not concerned with the long-range planning, does not support the planning. There is no consensus among the top management.

In this situation, it is hard to build a good plan. One sugar company is making profit continuously because the import of sugar cane is controlled by the government. There is little competition. The company is satisfied to be "lying in a warm bathtub." One electric power company controlled by government regulation, allowed a regional monopoly, has been implementing long-range planning for many years, but concentrates on its capital investment plan. It has no plan to cope with the change of competition among energy suppliers.

(2.1) Planning system does not stimulate innovation

The plan is only a set of numbers. The plan lacks the details, is only a statement of basic strategy. The plan is only the aggregation of plans submitted from many departments, is forecastive, is full of too many minor projects. The planner is sometimes interested in computation, in having consistent numbers among the different plans. The number is, however, the result, and the road to the number is more important.

Too many projects, or "too many flowers" in Japanese, appears when the corporate planner or the top management cannot put appropriate priorities to the proposal by appropriate assessment. This is caused by human relations. Even though, resources are limited, enough resource allocation to key projects makes the innovation possible.

(2.2) Not willing to participate

Although people recognize the needs for innovation, and the company is innovation oriented, the line departments are too busy for daily operation, and have no time to participate in formulating the future strategy. This situation happens in the growth industry. The operating units do not recognize that plans have to be built when there are much resources available.

To avert this problem, the corporate culture should be changed, or the strategic planning function should be separated from the operating function, and be reinforced.

3.1 Difficulty in forecasting

The planner has to solve the dilemma that the more changing the environment is, the more difficult the forecasting becomes. As a result, the company has to make strategy changes. There are more opportunities in uncertain environment. The company can make use of the uncertainty. However, difficulty in forecasting is one large problem and limitation of long-range planning. There are two approaches to cope with this problem; one is to collect information, and the other is to use many means to deal with uncertainty (See Chapter 13).

3.2 Wrong goals and poor ideas

It is difficult to set the basic direction of strategies because of uncertainty and lack of wide range of search by top management. Excellent ideas are not automatically generated from the information, they are borne by a somewhat discontinuous ideas or by jumping ideas. M shipbuilding company was aggressive in new product development and diversification, the long-range planning well established, but profits dropped sharply during the declining demand for oil and subsequent fall of prices. It became clear that the diversified products were mostly related with oils – plant engineering, large engines, steel fabrications besides shipbuilding. This is the result of narrow range of search, a lack of large visions and an insufficient number of options.

3.3 Difficulty in coordination

Due to conflict of interests between departments, it is difficult to do appropriate evaluations, to drop inefficient new projects and select and put priority to projects. Top management needs to be courageous to prune undesirable projects.

In the diversified company that is producing highly technological products, the corporate planner and top management cannot understand the meaning of strategy. This is one reason why proper ranking of projects is difficult.

3.4 Implementation

(1) The long-range plan is not implemented if there is no involvement of top management. The line department is not interested in implementation if it is not well informed with the plan, if it does not participate in planning.

The line department is not able to implement the plan if the department is too much occupied with the daily operation.

(2) The plan is not implemented by the unrealistic nature of the plan. The environment has changed drastically after the formulation of plan, and the plan is not updated.

(3) Lack of resources. Not the shortage of money, but the shortage of engineers is the problem. Japanese universities, public and private, can supply a large number of graduates in natural science, engineering in particular, but because of rapid increase of demands in high technology goods, such as computers, automated machines and home electric appliances there is shortage of engineers. The large companies tend to attract and monopolize those university graduates, because of life time employment, other medium sized companies or new companies that are going into high technology areas have difficulty in recruiting high caliber engineers.

(4) Incomplete follow-ups. The follow-up and sanctions for implementation have feed back effect to willingness for participation and implementation.

All these problems have been studied in the preceding chapters, can be mostly solved. Also, these problems will be studied in the following paragraphs. There are many papers which deal with the limitations of analytical approach and over-emphasize the limitation of long-range planning, but the experiences of Japanese corporations show that analytical approach is a factor for success of business management. (Literatures emphasizing the limitations of long-range planning. B.J. Loasby, 1967, Lindblom, 1959; Allison, 1971; Peters & Waterman, 1982; Quinn, 1980.)

15.3 Meaning of success

The evaluation of any business system is to be done by comparing with the goal of organization. In private corporations, financial goals and non-financial goals such as satisfaction of employees should be used. However, there are long time lags between the planning and performance. In addition, environmental changes and other factors affect the performance, it is difficult to isolate the effect of planning. We have to use the intervening variables. We use subjective judgments in two areas: (a) whether the innovative strategies were formulated, (b) whether the long-range plan was implemented.

Many other research papers use the similar variables. For example, (1) Improvement of decision-making style (Freeman, 1989; King, 1983), (2) Improvement of strategy (Freeman, 1989; Ramanujam, 1987; King, 1983; (3) Improvement of capabilities (Freeman, 1989; Ramanujam, 1987), (4) Performance (Ramanujam, 1987); (5) Morale of employee (Freeman, 1989).

15.4 Success factors

Subjective judgments by corporate planners based on the experience were surveyed. The success is measured by (a) whether the plan is innovative, (b) whether the plan is implemented. The results are presented at the end of this chapter in Table 15.2.b.

The framework of success factors is the same as the framework of problems in Table 15.1. The responses are structured responses and arranged by the theoretical framework.

15.4.1 Strategy oriented culture

The corporate culture affects the success of long-range planning. If it is inertia oriented not innovation oriented, the internal environment is not favorable for formulating and implementing the innovative long-range planning. To be successful, the need for new strategy, the need for environment orientedness has to be recognized first. At Nissan Motor Company, the long-range planning did not work prior to 1987 due to top management and union leaders' concentration of power. For example, the president intervened in the details of car designing. The next president Ishihara wanted to normalize the labour-management relationship, and then the implicit conflict between the two arose. For these reasons, along other reasons, the corporate culture was stagnant. At these times, the real innovative long-range planning could not be formed, was not considered as important means of management. The president of the company and the long reigned union leader retired, the new president Kume started to change the corporate culture. He said, "do not look up your boss, but rather think by yourself". He set new corporate creed, emphasizing the customer orientedness; emphasizing the feeling of the customer. With many other measures, the corporate culture has changed completely, the long-range planning was used to institutionalize the change, to "refreeze" the change.

On the other hand, the long-range planning has the effect to change the corporate culture. The formal assessment of the future gap of corporate performance, the regular scanning of the environment, the regular revision of the competitive strategy and other process remind people the need for innovation. Once started, it can change the corporate culture.

However, at the start, people are more inclined to perform the daily operation, aiming at the short term results. The corporate planner or top management should start to let people recognize the need of long-range planning, new strategy, and long-term visions. As Table 15.3 shows, the creation of strategy oriented atmosphere is important for the success of long-range planning.

Why is it necessary? Because there is an inertia in the mind of people. As indicated in Table 15.2, the problem is that people are more involved with the daily operation. People are more inclined to the accustomed jobs rather than do new and risky things.

On the other hand, the new strategy has to be invented by many departments, by strategic planning departments in particular. New strategies need to be implemented by many departments, new action programmes have to be planned and carried out by many departments.

It is a fallacy to think that good things to the company should be good things to everybody. It is a fallacy to promote the long-range planning technically, applying the most sophisticated method, without paying attention to human relations, without conducting some sorts of the force field analysis.

How we can change the attitude of people has been studied in Chapter 4 (Also see Kono, 1988; Kilmann, 1986; Shein, 1985).

Unfreezing is the first step. Let people know the future gap of the company: the decline of sales, loss of market share, and decrease of future profits. Inform management the actual practices on long-range planning systems of other companies, in particular its competitors, and recognize how the company is behind the orientation of other competitors.

Second step is to change the culture. If the information approach is used, the effects of innovative long-range planning should be realized and the success story of other companies should be informed. The past success story of the company is also made public.

Some companies do not dare to build the innovative long-range plan, because there were a few of failures in the new product development. Here the causes of failure should be made clear. It should be recognized that the failure happens anyhow, in any company. The study of failure cases in new product development or in capital investment of other company is useful. A famous case is Canon' s failure in the development of the "Synchro-reader", somewhat disc recorder. The causes of this failure were made clear. The company tried to avoid the similar error, although it could not completely avoid the failure. The president did not blame any person here, thus the failure enhanced the spirit for innovation.

When the company is introducing the long-range planning for the first time, or when it is re-establishing the planning after suspension, and when the member is not very motivated for planning, we can use a learning process. At first, a simple long-range plan is installed and a long-range plan of the key strategies or a goal type long-range plan is formulated. The plan is improved year after year. This is an incremental approach (Quinn, 1980).

If we use the sanction approach, the personnel management system will be changed so that the positive attitude should be evaluated. The safety first attitude should be treated coldly. The commitment of top management symbolizes what are the values of the company, what are the bases of merit ratings of employees.

15.4.2 Planning system

(2.1.a) Clear visions

The clear visions on the future of the company are the first step to formulate the long-range plan. The future vision means the values of the company and the basic product-market strategy of the company. For example:

"The percentage of sales of the present product will be less than thirty percent of total sales in 1995."

"The production in foreign countries will account for thirty percent of total production of the company."

"From the partial factory automation to CIM (computer integrated manufacturing)."

These visions are based on the corporate philosophy. The corporate philosophy needs to be revised every five years, as the aspiration of stakeholder changes. The Nissan Motor changed the business creed from "Distinctive Technology" to "Feel the Beat" (meaning "feel the sentiment of the customer"). The car design was changed a great deal by this change of the corporate creed.

The new vision is formulated after the analysis of strategic issues of the company. The strategic issues include both the opportunity and threat outside and inside the company. After the analysis of strategic issues, the corporate visions are formulated.

Through the detailed planning, if the new opportunities are found, then the earlier visions could be revised. It can be a learning process.

The reason the vision is needed is that (a) the long-term vision orients the information and ideas to one direction. By limiting the direction for exploration, the efficiency and creativity of planning are enhanced. The clear "will of the corporation" makes possible the large change of direction, avoiding the inertia. There are too many information and ideas. (b) It is useful to coordinate the activities of many departments. It makes possible to integrate the thought of the corporation, to share the common values. (c) It motivates the people. The future of the company can expand the expectation of employees, and enrich the meaning of the present job. If it affects the situation of employees of some departments adversely, the company should prepare the rescue measures. In particular, it is necessary under life-time employment.

The practices of successful companies show that the goals are not decided by bargaining as Lindblom states (Lindblom, 1959). The future visions of the top management are decided after collection of many information and ideas, by the analysis of the strategic issues.

The successful strategies are not decided by incremental approach as Quinn states (Quinn, 1980), but strategies are stimulated by the future visions. However it is true that, sometimes at the starting of a project, or under uncertain situations, other approaches are tried. For example, a build up approach, a bottom-up approach is used for uncertain new projects or for small projects. We call this approach a sequential decision.

(2.1.b) Focus on key strategies

The key strategies are selected and are analyzed thoroughly, resources are allocated predominantly. For example, steel company wants to diversify into computer, biotechnology and real estate businesses. These new businesses have synergies with the present business. The company decided to pour one-third of research budget to these three areas.

Taisei (Construction) Corporation wants to diversify into a private home construction, hotels, recreation centers, resort centers, overseas construction. These projects were nominated as the head office projects. They are studied by head office project teams or allocated to functional divisions.

The number of key strategies should be less than ten, so that the attentions and resources are allocated with concentration. The opposite types of the concentration are: (a) the plan is a collection of a set of numbers, and (b) "too many flowers" type, or too many projects type. In Table 15.2, too quantitative, or too many projects are raised as problems. In Table 15.3, (2.1.b) focus on key strategic issues are suggested as success factors. The survey on the transition of planning system shows that the trend is toward greater concentration to the core strategic issues.

The reasons for the concentration are as follows: (1) The effectiveness of resource allocation is usually a convex curve. The marginal productivity of resources increases up to certain point and then decreases. A small amount of allocation of resources to a project is inefficient. (2) Large scale innovations are necessary to make use of new opportunities in the changing environment. Incremental innovations are not effective. For example, the development of a new drug requires an investment of about ten billion yen and ten years of time. The construction of a new factory in foreign country requires an investment of twenty or thirty billion yen. Amount varies depending the industry. (3) The concentration to a core strategy is also effective to change the mind of people, to change the corporate culture. (4) The cost saving of information processing. By concentrating into key strategies, the planning becomes simpler, less expensive. The smaller projects are planned in the medium range plan or in the annual budgeting.

The concentration does not mean that the small projects and incremental innovations are curtailed, but they are pooled, and planned in lower levels. This increases the flexibility of planning.

The actual system of applying this principle is the two plans system, the long-range strategy and medium-range plan. Also, the project emphasis with quantitative integration type follows this principle.

(2.2) Organizational process

(A) Top management commitment
This factor is repeatedly stated in every book. Our survey also shows that it is an important factor for success (2.1.a of Table 15.2.b). The meaning of commitment was also surveyed as Table 4.1 shows. It means the following: (1) To take many actions to change the corporate culture to be strategy-oriented. (2) To state future visions of the company, or be serious about the formulation of them. (3) To take symbolic actions, such as to state the contents of long-range plan in the new year speech; to talk on strategies with the staffs of departments; and to go to the front to observe the implementation. (4) To link the long-range plan to the annual budget, and review the implementation frequently in regular meetings of the management committee.

The reasons why the top management commitment is necessary are the following: (1) there are risks involved in an innovative strategy. People tend to be afraid of failures. The top management commitment shows implicitly that doing-nothing will be subject to punishment, and challenge to risks will be the basis of merit rating. (2) There are conflicts of interests among departments. The top management can persuade the opposing departments and can make decision to offer any type of side-payment. (3) The ideas of many departments are required to generate excellent strategies, and to mobilize the ideas of many departments. Top management leadership is necessary. The successful companies such as Canon and Bridgestone Tire have been having aggressive top management.

From the corporate planners' side, it is a mistake to build the plan without asking the opinion of top management. Since their intentions and powers are important.

There are some risks of the top management involvement. When top management sticks to misconceptions, to a wrong strategy without collecting enough information and ideas, they will mislead the planning process. President Oya of Teijin (synthetic fiber) was too autocratic during his final years of reign. He made many wrong decisions, such as much emphasis on unrelated diversifications, however, nobody could protest against him. Top management commitment means that the visions and directions should be based on enough collection of informations and ideas.

(B) Participation
The participation means that the ideas are presented following the basic goals and basic policies. Also the ideas are presented following the guidelines stipulated by the corporate planning department. There are three types of planning process: top down approach, bottom-up approach and interactive approach. Each participation varies depending upon the types of planning process. The trend was from top down – bottom-up – interative – interactive with strong top down leadership. The last approach is required to make innovative change of corporate strategy.

The planning system of Matsushita Electric Company followed similar stages: the stage that the founder, Matsushita, undertook strong leadership; then the stage that the product division structure was established and authority for strategic decisions were decentralized; then the stage where the "Action 61" plan was declared and the plan emphasized the top down strategic leadership to change the product-mix from focus on home appliances to information processing industrial products.

There are limitations in participation. The ideas presented from the operating divisions cannot go beyond the present business. The ideas that are against the interest of the divisions are not presented. The operating units tend to be too much involved with the daily operation.

To avoid these limitations, separation of strategic planning departments is a means. The other means is to use the detailed guidelines before the operating units formulate the plan.

The reasons for the needs of participation are clear. The sense of ownership of the plan is enhanced, the operating units think that the plan is their own.

Another reason is that the information and ideas of the departments have to be exploited to shape an excellent strategy particularly, to establish the strategy of the present product.

There are two fallacies for participation. One error is too much participation of operating units. The plan is only an assembly of the plans of each unit, only the forecasting of present operation, without any general corporate strategy. Another error is that the corporate planning department does planning too much extent without the participation of operating units. The implementation becomes a problem here.

15.4.3 Strategic decision in the long-range planning

A. Enough strategic information
The survey results show that (a) awareness of the key factors of change in the environment, (b) sharing information with the top management and departments, (c) awareness of the weakness of the company. (See Table 15.2.b, item 3.1)

There are great differences on the level of collection of strategic informations. Some companies do nothing while other companies collect many environmental information, having elaborate computer processing system or SIS (strategic information system).

Two approaches are used. One is to see the environment with some focus and collect information to find out the opportunities and threats (outside-in approach). Other approach is to collect information for a specific strategy. This is a problem oriented (or an inside-out) approach. The outside-in approach with focus is useful to find out the strategic issues, the inside-out approach is necessary to articulate the programme.

Nippon Plate Glass Company forecasted extensively the glass related industry, the future technology and the strength of its own technology, then the corporate planning office found out thirty possible areas to enter, and among them seven areas were selected.

This case explains that the information collection can (a) increase the strategic options, (b) improve the evaluation of alternatives.

The analysis of our survey shows that the successful companies on long-range planning collect more information with focus than the unsuccessful companies (See Table 5.1.b in Chapter 5).

There are limitations on information collection. (1) It is difficult to forecast the future. (2) There is too many information. It is expensive and time consuming to collect information. (3) If the jumping ideas or discontinuous imaginations are not added to the ideas derived from the collection of information, then the ideas tend to be the same as that of the competitor. It happens that many companies enter the same areas.

The analysis of weakness is often neglected because it is sometimes seen as the criticism against the present management. However, it is important to select better strategies and to improve the resource structures.

B. Clear long-term visions and distinctive strategies

After the analysis of information, the long-term goals and distinctive strategies need to be formed (See Table 15.3, item 3.2.a, 3.2.b). The visions and goals orient the information and idea, so that the analysis can be deep.

The distinctive visions and strategies have the following meanings. It is: (a) strategies aimed at the growth fields; (b) strategies that have competitive edge, a surprise to the competitor, making full use of the strength of the company, or by reinforcing the resource structure; (c) timing of preparation and implementation of the strategy is appropriate, generally earlier than the competitor finds out.

A case of JATCO (Japan Automatic Transmission Company) illustrates the above principle. JATCO has been using the long-range planning for strategic decisions for long years. The strategy contents have several characteristics, it put emphasis on exchange rather than secrecy, emphasis on cooperation. The company recognizes that the automatic transmission is a tremendous high growth product, and has a strong competitive edge as one of the largest producers. As a competition strategy, the company emphasizes exchange with the buying company than technology secrecy, emphasizes on cooperation than competition. The buyers of the automatic transmission are also the manufactures of the same products and thus they are competitors. The company selected the exchange of technology rather than secrecy. As the basis of competition, the company planned the drastic expansion of research laboratory, researchers were increased from thirty people to 300 in five years. Because of the success of the strategy, the sales increased from fifty billion yen in 1985 to ninety billion yen in 1989.

The above types of strategy is, however, one of the types; it is a strategy type of leader. The strategy types of the challenger, the follower and the nicher are different (For these types, see Kotler, 1980).

Miles and Snow also state three strategy types that are successful if there is good fit with other management systems (Miles and Snow, 1978). The three types are analyzer, prospector, defender (and reactor that is not successful).

3.3 Priorities

As is shown in Table 15.2.b (item 3-3), the strategies are assessed and ranked by priorities. The resources are allocated predominantly to the high priority projects.

The reason for this principle is almost the same as the principle (2.1.a), "focus on key strategies." The concentration of resources makes possible the effective uses of resources. Scattered allocation does not bring an innovative change.

The different principle is uniform percentage increase, say ten percent increase, of the past actual allocation of resources.

Another erroneous principle is that the long-range plan is only a compilation of many plans submitted from many departments, without integration of individual plans and without priorities.

So as to apply this principle, the guideline should be detailed. It is better to show the principle on policy on priority than to rank after the draft is presented. The success group uses this policy more frequently than the unsuccessful group.

The PPM model or the growth-share matrix model is an example of the concentration of resources allocation. By this concentration, the effectiveness of resources is supposed to be improved.

The application of this principle involves two difficulties. One is the difficulty of evaluation. The formulation of evaluation criteria is difficult. The forecasting of results is not easy.

The other reason comes from the human relations. It is hard to appraise a project as lower ranking when the head of the department who submitted the plan is influential, or is on intimate relation with the top management.

(3.4) Promotion of implementation

The survey results show that the promotion of implementation and the follow-up of the plan is important success factors (Table 15.3, item 3.4.a and 3.4.b). Implementation is one of the elements of success factors, so the forces for implementation have to be analyzed.

The formulation of the action programmes is the first prerequisite. The action programme contains the assignment of responsibility of a project, setting the schedule and articulating the detailed courses of action.

The action programme should be revised from time to time, there should be a learning process.

Table 15.2 Factors of success

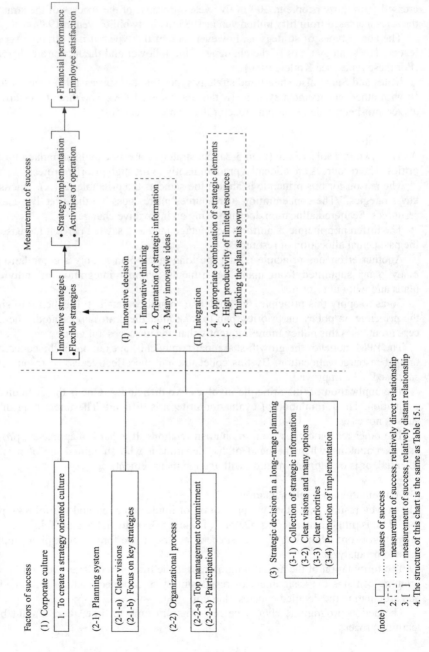

Factors of success

(1) Corporate culture

    1. To create a strategy oriented culture

(2-1) Planning system

    (2-1-a) Clear visions
    (2-1-b) Focus on key strategies

(2-2) Organizational process

    (2-2-a) Top management commitment
    (2-2-b) Participation

(3) Strategic decision in a long-range planning

    (3-1) Collection of strategic information
    (3-2) Clear visions and many options
    (3-3) Clear priorities
    (3-4) Promotion of implementation

Measurement of success

• Financial performance
• Employee satisfaction

• Strategy implementation
• Activities of operation

• Innovative strategies
• Flexible strategies

(I) Innovative decision

    1. Innovative thinking
    2. Orientation of strategic information
    3. Many innovative ideas

(II) Integration

    4. Appropriate combination of strategic elements
    5. High productivity of limited resources
    6. Thinking the plan as his own

(note)
1. ☐ ...... causes of success
2. ⌐ ¬ ...... measurement of success, relatively direct relationship
3. [ ] ...... measurement of success, relatively distant relationship
4. The structure of this chart is the same as Table 15.1

To motivate the implementation, the outline of the plan needs to be informed by some channels to all employees. Often, the president addresses all employees through the company newsletter or video tape. Top management commitment is the important factor for motivation.

Many companies put a nickname to the long-range plan to distribute the plan. For example, "Action 61", "Challenge 2000", "Heart and Action 555", "Toward Knowledge Intensive Industry".

The means of motivation for implementation have already been studied in Chapter 14. We will here state the most important three reasons for no implementation, even after the distribution.

(1) No participation. The department who should carry out the plan did not participate in formulation of the original strategy, or of the action programme. The style of participation varies depending on the top-down approach, the bottom-up approach or the interactive approach of the planning process. The participation does not mean the simple bottom-up approach.

(2) The plan is imperfect. If the plan is not innovative, is outdated because of the change of environment, is not refined, then the plan is not implemented. When the planner is not trusted by top management nor the manager of the line department, then the plan is subjectively understood as imperfect. The subjective judgments play important role in this case.

(3) Follow-up is not carried out. In some companies, the president goes to the field to observe the implementation of the plan. He hears about the progress and cost and the reasons of deviation. This motivates the implementation. In other cases, the implementation is not reviewed. Every year, the updating is done "from the start,"doing no analysis on the deviation. The plan will not be implemented if this pattern is repeated.

The reasons for success are summarized in Table 15.2.

15.5   Recent changes in the long-range planning systems

Recent changes of long-range planning practices were surveyed, they are shown in Table 15.3.b at the end of this chapter.

The change is related to success factors since most companies change their planning system to avoid pitfalls and succeed in planning. Therefore the change can be proof of the success factors we studied in the preceding sections. Items are grouped in:

1. Strategic orientation. In order to change the culture to strategy orientation, many companies tried to improve the cooperation of line departments by involvement and communication.

2. Change of planning system.
   Clear expression of long-term visions has become emphasized by many companies.

Many companies changed from emphasis on the financial aspect and quantitative aspect of planning, to greater concentration on core strategic issues. This is one of the key success factors.

2.2 Behavioral and Organizational Problems

A top down or interactive approach with the involvement and strong leadership of top management is necessary for the success of a long-range plan. Top management involvement is necessary because a long-range plan is a plan for innovation. It affects the overall performance, it involves risks, and it affects the promotion of people.

The cooperation of each division, and the involvement of product divisions, line departments or functional departments are necessary to make them understand the meaning of planning, and make them feel that long-range plans are their own plans.

Reinforcement of the organization for planning and implementation is practiced by many companies (b and c). So as to avoid Greshame' s law of decisions, strategic planning departments need to be strengthened.

3 Decision-Making Process

Information and forecasting. Uncertainty of forecasting is a great obstacle to long-range planning. Many companies try to improve the environmental forecasting and to increase information on the market and on the competition. Increase of information is considered important for success.

Many companies tried to develop the excellent strategies in the long range planning process. Many also tried to improve the capabilities of the company.

Introduction of two time span plans, revision of time span and change of methods of updating were introduced by many corporations. This is related with the emphasis on strategic issues.

Implementation. More follow-up on the long-range plan, and the introduction of an action plan to implement strategy is emphasized to carry out the long-range plan.

Summary

1. In order to find out the problems and success factors of long-range planning, it is necessary to clarify the framework on the cause-effect relationship. The analysis of effects of planning looks at the process from the up-stream that is determined first. The analysis of key success factors sees the process from the down-stream. The down-stream is fixed and looks for the conditions in the up-stream. The process of cause-effect relationship is seen in chart 15.1. The problems of long-range planning are the factors that disturb these relationships, factors that cannot be easily controlled. Areas of problems are almost the same as the factors of success, so will summarize on the key success factors.

    As the measurement of success, the eventual goals of the organization, such as the profit or the growth of sales should be used. However, due to time lags and many factors affecting performance, it is hard to use it as the measurement. We will use the intervening variables as the measurement of success. We will use the innovative strategic decisions, integration of strategic actions and resulting innovative strategies as a measurement of success.

The summary of our findings is shown in Table 15.2.

(1)   When the atmosphere or the corporate culture is strategy oriented, the number coop-
         erates to plan of innovative strategy, and is willing to implement the plan. The long-
         range planning can change the corporate culture, but the vital culture is necessary con-
         dition. In order to change the culture, three approaches are available – information ap-
         proach, experience approach and sanction approach.

(2.1.a) The clear visions improves the effectiveness of information collection and generates in-
         novative ideas. The visions are useful to change the inertia of thought, make clear the will
         of the company to change its direction. By sharing the common visions, integrated ac-
         tions are made possible. The visions are formulated after strategic issues are identified.

(2.1.b) Focus on key strategic projects and concentrated allocation of limited resources will en-
         hance the productivity of resources. Thus, they will increase the probability of success in
         the new strategies. Scattered allocation of resources to "too many flowers" will not be ef-
         fective. The PPM model (or Growth-share matrix model) is one of the models of con-
         centration of resource allocation. Projects for growth products need to have concentrated
         allocation. Generally speaking, large projects need full allocation of resources, because
         there is a law of increasing marginal productivity up to a certain point.

(2.2.a) The top management commitment and statement of clear visions will give stimulus to stra-
         tegic thinking and will suggest the basis of rewards and punishment. If the top man-
         agement does not have clear visions the planning will not succeed. If the corporate planner
         does not understand the intention of the top management, the planning will not succeed.

(2.2.b) The participation for planning of related departments will increase the information and
         ideas, thus enrich the strategic options. It will foster the sense of ownership of the plan,
         thus improve its implementation. However, simple application of a principle "the doer is
         the planner" has limitations. Before participation, the strategic planning departments
         should be reinforced, so that the strategies outside the existing product domain can be
         planned.

(3.1)   The intent of systematic collection of strategic information varies from company to
         company. The strategic information increases the strategic options and is useful to as-
         sess the options. When the environment is uncertain, it is difficult to foresee the future.
         However, the more uncertain the future is, the more opportunities lie in the future.
            It is an error to overemphasize the difficulty of forecasting. It is also an error to start
         the planning without enough analysis of the future environment.

(3.2.a) Clear visions and many options make possible the innovative change of strategy. With-
         out visions, the strategies will be collections of small ideas. The visions will stimulate
         and orient the innovative ideas, will generate many strategic options toward the visions.
            The workable visions are arrived at after the analysis of strategic issues, the analysis
         of niches and own competitive strength. Recently many companies have established a
         team of young managers to study the future visions of the company.

(3.3)   When the priorities of projects are clear, the resource are allocated predominantly to
         key projects, the productivity of resources will be enhanced. Although the satisficing
         principles are applied to small projects, the maximizing principle by proper ranking of
         projects is applied to strategic planning.

(3.4)   The promotion of implementation is made possible by communicating the planning to
         the departments, assigning the responsibility to project teams or some existing de-
         partments, and timely follow-ups of the plan.

Table 15.1.b   Problem of planning systems

		1979	1985	1989
		327 co.	384 co.	327 co.
	Corporations with long-range plans			
1. Inertia	a. Too much involvement in daily problems	28 (%)	2 co.	12 co.
	b. Management is indifferent to the plan and the postion of support	6	11	23
2-1. Planning system	a. Too quantitative, without strategic projects	36	9	3
	b. Broad policy, without detailed projects	19	4	4
	c. Too much build up, too many projects	34	10	11
	d. Problem identification only, without strategies to solve them	12	2	1
2-2. Organizational problems	a. Lack of recognition & co-operation from operating units	39	24	25
	b. Too much time in preparing and reviewing the plan	14	9	7
	c. Weak planning department	17	28	5
3-1. Forecasting	a. Difficulty in forecasting general environment (such as national policies and economy, international situation, etc.	62	67	46
	b. Difficulty in forecasting demands for existing products	33	44	15
	c. Difficulty in forecasting demands for new products	26	12	7
	d. Lack of data and information	—	15	7
	e. Difficulty in forecasting price of products, wages, cost of raw materials	24	10	1
	f. Difficulty in forecasting business fluctuations	26	21	3
	g. Difficulty in 'domestic' analysis	5	4	5

continued

Table 15.1.b Problem of planning systems (cont.)

		1979	1985	1989
	Corporations with long-range plans	327 co.	384 co.	249 co.
3-2. Goal setting and idea generation	a. Goal and policies are not clearly stated (lack of vision by top management)	11 (%)	16 co.	3 co.
	b. Setting goals is difficult	25	20	2
	c. Setting goal levels is difficult	49	17	2
	d. Difficulty in planning new product development	27	11	⎫
	e. Too quantitative and without project development	19	8	⎪
	f. Unexpected decisions (for instance, acquiring another company makes the plan unrealistic	4	2	⎬ 5
	g. Planning is repetitive and lacks new ideas	27	9	⎪
	h. Quality of plan is not reflected in performance evaluation	31	12	⎭
3. Co-ordination	a. Difficulty is co-ordinating division plans and project plans	31 (%)	30 co.	38
	b. Difficulty in evaluation	—	—	16
4. Implementation	(1a) Not implemented due to management indifference	1	3	⎫
	(1b) No involvement of operating units	7	5	⎪
	(1c) Not implemented because of priority given to current work	14	13	⎬ 30
	(1d) Plans are not well informed	2	43	⎭
	(2a) Hard to implement due to poor forecasting	16	39	2
	(2b) Implementation program is not well formulated	43	29	5
	(3a) Shortage of resources and difficulty of allocation of resources	—	39	14
	(4a) Inconsistent follow-up	44	25	13
	(4b) Implementation is not reflected in performance evaluation	24	26	12

(notes) 1. Survey in 1979 was by structured question and survey in 1985 and 1989 was by unstructed question, for this reason the frequency is different

2. Numbers in 1979 indicates percentage, but the numbers in 1985 and 1989 are the actual number of responding companies

Table 15.2.b Success factors in long-range planning

			year	1989
			Corporations with long-range plans	249 co.
Was the planning successful?		a. Very successful		19
		b. Relatively successful		40
		c. Not clear		33
What were the important factors for success? (Please cheque important 5 factors)	Corporate culture	(1-1)	To create strategy oriented atmosphere	38
		(1-2)	To clarify strategic issues	35
	Planning system	(2-1-a)	Top management states clearly the corporate philosophy and visions	59
		(2-1-b)	Focus on key strategic issues	22
	Organizational process	(2-2-a)	Communication between planners and top management	29
		(2-2-b)	Participation in planning with line departments and staff departments	37
	Strategic decision in long-range planning	(3-1-a)	Enough information collected on the general environment, the industry and available technology. Awareness of the key factors of change.	19
		(3-1-b)	Sharing of information with the top management and departments	16
		(3-1-c)	Awareness of the weakness of the company	24
		(3-1-d)	Have plans to cope with uncertainty, forecasting of the worst possible scenarios	5
		(3-2-a)	Clear long-term visions and goals	54
		(3-2-b)	Sufficient analysis and elaborate distinctive strategies	12
		(3-3-a)	Integration of the plans of units, priorities are appropriately given, resource allocation are concentrated to key strategies	28
	Implementation	(3-4-a)	Implementation is promoted, action programmes are formed and long-range plans are integrated into a variety of plans The long-range plans permeates every management area.	31
		(3-4-b)	Follow-up of the long-range plan to analyse the results against the plan is carried out	28

(note) Asterisks (*) indicate (a) very successful and (b) relatively successful planning companies (146 co.) who responded with higher frequency (significance level 5 %). Responses on other items were less or the same.

Table 15.3.b Changes of planning systems

		1979 327 co.	1985 384 co.	1989 249 co.
	Corporations with long-range plans			
(1) Strategic orientation	a. Involvement and cooperation of division or line departments. (Improvement of communications)	18 co.	24 co.	19 co.
(2-1) Planning system				
(2-1-1) Clear visions	a. Clear expression of corporate objective. (Revision of goals and policies by establishing long-range visions)	14	62	33
(2-1-2) Concentration	b. Greater concentration on the core strategic issues. (Less emphasis on the financial aspect of planning. From extended budgeting to project planning)	23	37	14
	c. From 'too many issues' core project planning	17	24	5
(2-2) Organizational process				
(2-2-1) Top management involvement	a. Strong leadership by top down approach. (Greater involvement of top management)	16	25	14
(2-2-2) Participation	a. More participation of many departments, planning by the bottom-up approach	17	29	12
	b. Clear responsibilities of departments for planning implementation. Establish committees responsible for planning and control of implementation	7	29	4
	c. Strengthening of the function of corporate planning departments, project teams and departmental planning sections.	15	26	13

continued

Table 15.3.b Changes of planning systems (cont.)

Corporations with long-range plans	1979 327 co.	1985 384 co.	1989 249 co.
(3) Decision-making process			
(3-1) Information and forecasting			
a. Strengthening of environmental forecasting. (More analysis of competition and market)	29 co.	25 co.	11 co.
b. Better review of strenghs and weaknesses	–	8	4
(3-2) Development of excellent strategy			
a. Clear expression of departmental goals	10	6	8
b. Development of excellent projects (corporate strategy, new product development agressive strategy etc.)	32	24	4
c. Improvement of capabilities of the company	–	21	5
d. Introduction of contingency plans (or early warning systems)	15	5	1
e. Use of simulation. Use of computer.	25	17	5
f. Change of planning system. (Introduced BCG model, operation research model, use of consultants)	25	14	4
g. Change of time horizon; introduction of two time span plans, choice of rolling plans or fixed time plans	19	62	17
h. Integration of plans by subsidiaries	5	8	7
(3-3) Coordination			
a. Coordination of project planning and departmental planning	5	12	12
(3-4) Implementation			
a. More follow up	36	33	12
b. Rewarding the quality of plans and its implementation	19	8	5
c. Building implementation plans. (Better linkage between long-range plans and short-range plans)	31	25	21

References (All Chapters)

References on corporate culture – at the end of chapter 6
References on the product-market strategy – at the end of chapter 8
References on the resource structure planning – at the end of chapter 9

In Japanese

Aoki, S., (1977), Kigyo no Yosanseido (Business Budgeting), Diamond-sha, Tokyo.

Aonuma, Y., (1965), Nihon no Keieiso (Japanese Top Management), Nihon Keizai Shimbun Sha, Tokyo.

Ishikawa, J., (1987), Asahi Beer no Chosen (Challenge of Asahi Breweries, Ltd.), Japan Management Association, Tokyo.

Japan Productivity Center, (1982), Kigyo Yosan no Jisho Kenkyu (Survey on Budgetary Control), Tokyo.

Kagono, T., (1988), Kigyo Paradigm no Henkaku (Change of Corporate Paradigm), Kodan-sha, Tokyo.

Kansai Productivity Center, (1976), Keiei Soshiki no Shindoko (New Trends on Business Organizations), Kansai Productivity Center, Tokyo

Kansai Productivity Center, (1986), Keiei Soshiki no Shintenkai (New Trends of Management), Kansai Productivity Center, Osaka.

Kono, T., (1956), Keiei Keikaku no Riron (Theory of Business Planning), Diamond-sha, Tokyo.

Kono, T., (1968), Kigyo Seicho no Bunseki (Analysis of Corporate Growth), Maruzen, Tokyo.

Kono, T., (1973), Keiei Simulation (Business Simulation), Maruzen, Tokyo.

Kono, T., (1974), Keiei Senryaku no Kaimei (Analysis of Corporate Strategy), Diamond-sha, Tokyo.

Kono, T., (1975), Choki Keieikeikaku no Tankyu (Analysis of Long-range Planning), Diamond-sha, Tokyo.

Kono, T., (1978), Choki Keieikeikaku no Jitsurei (New Cases of Long-range Planning), Dobunkan, Tokyo.

Kono, T., (1980), Senryaku Keieikeikaku no Tatekata (Introduction to Strategic Planning), Diamond-sha, Tokyo.

Kono, T., (1985), Gendai no Keiei Senryaku (Modern Corporate Strategy), Diamond-sha, Tokyo.

Kono, T., (1987), Keieigaku Genri (Principles of Management), Hakuto-shobo, Tokyo.

Kono, T., (1987), Shinseihin Kaihatsu Senryaku (New Product Development Strategy), Diamond-sha, Tokyo.

Kono, T., (1988), Henkaku no Kigyo Bunka (Change of Corporate Culture), Kodan-sha, Tokyo.

Kono, T., (1988), Keieigaku Genri (Principles of Management), Dobunkan, Tokyo.

Kono, T. & Watanabe, F., (1975), Juyoyosoku (Demand Forecasting), Diamond-sha, Tokyo.

Matsuura, K., (1984), Shafu no Kenkyu (Study of Corporate Culture), PHP, Tokyo.

MITI, 1973-80, (1986), 1987, Keiei Ryoku Hyoka (Measurement of Corporate Capability), MITI, Tokyo.

MITI, (1987), Keiei Ryoku Hyoka (Evaluation of Management Capability), Ministry of International Trade and Industry, Tokyo.

Morita, T. et al., (1989), Senryaku Joho System (Strategic Information Systems), Kodan-sha, Tokyo.

Nishizawa, O., (1978), Ricki Keikaku Nyumon (Introduction to Profit Planning), Zeimukeiri, Tokyo.

Okamoto, K., (1982), Kanri-kaikei no Kisochishiki (Introduction to Managment Accounting), Chuokeizai-sha, Tokyo.

Okochi, A., (1979), Keiei Kosoryoku (Strategic Competition), Tokyo Daigaku Shuppan, Tokyo.

Okumura, A., (1981), Nihon no Top Management (Japanese Top Management), Diamond-sha, Tokyo.

Tsugumo, N. & Matsumoto, J., (1972), Wagakuni no Kigyo Yosan (Japanese Business Budgeting), Japan Productivity Center, Tokyo.

Umezawa, T., (1983), Soshiki Bunka no Shiten kara (View-points on Corporate Culture), Gyosei, Tokyo.

Umezawa, T., (1986), Kigyo Bunka no Sozo (Creation of Corporate Culture), Yuhikaku, Tokyo.

Urabe, K., (1975), Shin Keieisha Ron (New Top Management), Diamond-sha, Tokyo.

In English

Aaker, D. A., (1984), Developing Business Strategies, John Wiley & Sons , New York.

Abernathy, W. J. & Hayes, R. H., (1980), Managing Our Way to Economic Decline, Harvard Business Review, July–August.

Ackoff, R. L., (1970), A Concept of Corporate Planning, Wiley Interscience, New York.

Aguilar, F. J., (1967), Scanning the Business Environment, Macmillan, New York.

Al-Bazzaz, S. and Grinyer, P.H., (1980), 'How Planning Works in Practice – A Survey of 48 UK Companies', Long-Range Planning, August.

Allen, T. J., (1977), Managing the Flow of Technology, M.I.T. Press, Cambridge, Mass.

Allison, G. T., (1969), 'Conceptual Models and The Cuban Missile Crisis', in: American Political Science Review, September.

Allison, G. T., (1971), Essence of Decision; Explaining the Cuban Missile Crisis, Little, Brown, Boston.

AMA, (1960), Financial Planning for Greater Profits, AMA, N.Y.

Andrews, K., (1971), The Concept of Corporate Strategy, Dow Jones-Irwine, Homewood, Ill.

Ang, J. S. and Chua, J.H., (1979), 'Long-Range Planning in Large US Corporations – A Survey', Long-Range Planning, April.

Ansoff, H. I., (1965), Corporate Strategy: an Analytical Approach to Business Policy for Growth and Expansion, McGraw-Hill, New York.

Ansoff, H. I., Roger P. Declerck, and Robert L. Hayes, Editors, (1976), From Strategic Planning to Strategic Management, Wiley, New York.

Anthony, R. N., (1965), Planning and Control Systems: A Framework for Analysis, Harvard Business School, Boston.

Anthony, R. N. & Welsch, G.A., (1981), Fundamentals of Management Accounting, Irwin, Ill.

Argyris, C., (1964), Integrating the Individual and the Organization, John Wiley & Sons , New York.

Argyris, C., (1977), "Double Loop Learning in Organizations", Harvard Business Review, September–October, 115–125.

Barnard, C. I., (1938), The Functions of the Executive, Harvard University Press, Cambridge, Mass.

Berle, A. A. and Means, G. C., (1967), The Modern Corporation and Private Property, 1932–1967, Harcourt, Brace & World, New York.

Blass, W. P., (1983), Ten Years of Business Planners, no. 3, Long-Range Planning.

Burgleman, R. A. & Maidique, M. A., (1988), The Strategic Management of Technology and Innovation, Irwin, Ill.

Burns, T. and Stalker, G. M., (1961), The Management of Innovation, Tavistock, London.

Buzzell, R. D., Gale, B. T. & Sultan, R. G. M., (1975), "Market Share – A Key to Profitability", Harvard Business Review, January–February, 97–106.

Camilus, J. C., (1986), Strategic Planning and Management Control, Lexington, Mass.

Caplan, E. H., (1971), Management Accounting and Behavioral Science, Addison-Wesley, Mass.

Carpenter, M. A., (1986), Planning versus Strategy, Which Will Win, Long-Range Planning, December.

Chandler, A. D., Jr., (1962), Strategy and Structure: Chapters in the History of the American Industrial Enterprise, M.I.T. Press, Cambridge, Mass.

Channon, D. F., (1973), The Strategy and Structure of British Enterprise, Macmillan, London.

Clark III, R. D., (1971), 'Group-induced Shift Toward Risk, A Critical Appraisal', vol.76, no.4, Psycological Bulletin.

Comerford, R. A. & Callaghan, D. W., (1985), Strategic Management, Kent Publishing Co., CA.

Cyert, R. & March, J., (1963), A Behavioral Theory of the Firm, Prentice-Hall, N.J.

Davies, A.H.T., (1981), Strategic planning in the Thomas Cook Group, Long-Range Planning, October.

Davies, S. M., (1984), Managing Corporate Culture, Ballinger Pub. Mass.

Davies, S. M., (1986), Managing Corporate Culture, Harper & Row, New York.

Deal & Kennedy, (1984), Corporate Culture, Addison-Wesley, Mass.

Deutsch, M., (1969), 'Conflict, Productivity and Unproductivity', in: Zaltman et al., Editor, 1972, Creating Social Change.

Diesing P., (1955), 'Non-economic Decision-Making' in: Rowe, Mason & Dickel, Editors, Strategic Management & Business Policy, 1982, Addison-Wesley, Mass.

Dore, R. P., (1973), British Factory, Japanese Factory, University of California Press, Berkeley.

Drucker, P. F., (1954), The Practice of Management, Harper and Row, New York.

Drucker, P. F., (1974), Management: Tasks, Responsibilities, Practices, Harper & Row, New York.

Fildes, R., Jalland, M. and Wood, D., (1978), 'Forecasting in Conditions of Uncertainty', Long-Range Planning, August.

Fraser, N. M. & Hipel, K. W., (1984), Conflict Analysis, Models and Resolutions, North-Holland, N. Y.

Freeman, E., (1989), Effectiveness of Strategic Planning: A Paper Presented at the Annual Meeting of the American Academy of Management, August.

Frost, P. J. et al, Editors, (1985), Organizational Culture, Sage Publishing, N. Y.

Galbraith, J. & Nathanson, D., (1978), Strategy Implementation: The Role of Structure and Process, West Publishing, St. Paul, Minn.

Galbraith, J. R., (1984), 'Designing the Innovative Organization', in: Lamb, R.B., Competitive Strategic Management, Prentice-Hall, New York.

Gilber, X. & Strebel, P., (1988), 'Developing Competitive Advantage', in: Quinn et al, 1988, The Strategy Process, Prentice-Hall, N. J.

Glueck, Kaufman & Walleck, (1980), Strategic Management for Competetive Advantage, Harvard Business Review, July–August.

Glueck, W., (1976), Business Policy, Strategy Formation and Management Action, McGraw-Hill, New York.

Glueck, W.F., (1980), Business Policy and Strategic Management, McGraw Hill, New York.

Glueck & Tauched., (1984), Business Policy and Strategic Management, McGraw-Hill, New York.

Godiwalla, Y. M., Meinhart, W.A., and Warde, W. D., (1978), Corporate Planning: a functional approach, Long-Range Planning, October.

Goldhar, J. and Jelink, M., (1983), Planning for Economics of Scope, Harvard Business Review, November–December.

Grant, J., Editor, (1987), Strategic Management Frontiers, JAI Press, Greenwich, Conn.

Greiner, L. E., (1972), Evolution and Revolution as Organizations Grow, Harvard Business Review, July–August.

Grinyer, P. H. & Spender, J.C., (1979), Turnaround: Managerial Recipes for Strategic Success, Associated Business Press, New York.

Harrigan, K. R., (1983), Strategies for Vertical Integration, P.C. Heath & Co. Mass.

Harris, S. G., (1989), A Schema-Based Perspective on Organizational Culture: a paper presented at the Annual Meeting of the Academy of Management, August.

Hayes, R. I. & Radosevich, R., (1974), Designing Information Systems for Strategic Decisions, Long-Range Planning, no. 4.

Hayes, R. H. & Abernathy, W. J., (1980), "Managing Our Way to Economic Decline", Harvard Business Review, July–August.

Henderson, B. D., (1970), The Product Portfolio, Boston Consulting Group, Boston.

Henry H. W., (1977), 'Formal Planning in Major U.S. Corporations', Long-Range Planning, October.

Hershey, P. & Blanchard, K.H., (1977), Management of Organizational Behavior, Prentice-Hall, New York.

Hofer, C. W. & Schendel, D., (1978), Strategy Formulation: Analytical Concepts, West Publishing, Minnesota.

Hofstede, G. H., (1967), The Game of Budget Control, Koninklijke Van Gorcem.

Hofsteade, G. H., (1980), Culture's Consequences, 1980, Sage Publishing, N.Y.

Holden, P. E., Fish, L. S. and Smith, H. L., (1941), Top Management Organization and Control, Stanford University Press, CA.

Homans, G. C., (1974), Social Behavior: Its Elementary Forms, Harcourt Bruce Yavanovich Inc., New York.

Hussey, E. E., (1974), Corporate Planning, Theory and Practice, Pergamon Press, Oxford.

Johnson, G., Scholes, K. and Sexty, R. W., (1989), Exploring Strategic Management, Prentice-Hall, Canada Inc.

Kanter, R. M., (1973), The Change Masters, Simon & Schuster, New York.

Karger, D. W. and Malik, Z. A., (1975), 'Long-Range Planning and Organizational Performance', Long-Range Planning, December.

Katz, A., (1978), 'Planning in the IBM Corp.', Long-Range Planning, June

Katz, D. & Kahn, R. L., (1966), The Social Psychology of Organization, John Wiley & Sons, New York.

Kilmann, R. H., (1984), 'Five Steps for Closing Culture-gaps', in: Beyond The Quick Fix, (1984), Jossey Bass, CA.

Kilmann, R. H. et al, Editors., (1986), Gaining Control of the Corporate Culture, Jossey Bass, CA.

Kilmann, R. H. et al, Editors, (1988), Corporate Transformation, Jossey Bass, CA.

King, W.R., (1983), Evaluating Strategic Planning Systems, Strategic Management Journal, vol. 4.

Kono, T., (1976), 'Long-Range Planning-Japan-USA: A Comparative Study', Long-Range Planning, October.

Kono, T., (1984), The Strategy and Structure of Japanese Enterprises, Macmillan Press, London.

Koontz, H., (1967), The Board of Directors and Effective Management, McGraw-Hill, New York.

Kotler, P., (1980), Marketing Management, Prentice-Hall, New York.

Kriesberg, L., (1973), The Sociology of Social Conflicts, Prentice-Hall, New York.

Kudo, H. et al, (1988), 'How US and Japanese CEO's Spend Their Time', Long-Range Planning, December.

Kuwahara, Y. et al, (1989), Planning Research and Development at the Central Research Laboratory of Hitachi, Long-Range Planning, June.

Langley, A., 1988, 'The Roles of Formal Strategic Planning', Long-Range Planning, no. 3, April.

Lawrence, P. R. & Lorsch, J. W., (1967), Organization and Environment, Harvard University Press, Cambridge, Mass.

Lenz, R. T. & Lyles, M. A., (1981), 'Tackling the Human Problems in Planning', Long-Range Planning, April.

Lenz, R. T. & Lyles, M. A., 1985, 'Paralysis by Analysis: Is Your Planning System too Rational?', Long-Range Planning, no. 4, August.

Likert, R., (1967), The Human Organization, McGraw-Hill, New York.

Likert, R., (1969), New Patterns of Management, McGraw-Hill, New York.

Lindblom, C.E., (1959), The Science of Muddling Through, Public Administration Review, no. 2.

Litwin, G. H. & Stringer, R. A., Jr., (1968), Motivation and Organizational Climate, Harvard University, Mass.

Lagrange, P., (1980), Corporate Planning: An Executive Viewpoint, Englewood Cliffs, Prentice-Hall, N. J.

Lagrange, P. & Richard F. V., (1977), Strategic Planning Systems, Englewood Cliffs, Prentice-Hall, N. J.

Luce, R. & Raiffa, H., (1957), Games and Decision, John Wiley & Sons, Inc., N.Y.

Macmillan, I. C., (1978), Strategy Formulation: Political Concepts, West Publishing Company, St. Paul, New York.

Mann, C. W., (1978), 'The Use of a Model in Long-Term Planning – A Case History', Long-Range Planning, October.

March, J. G. & Simon, H. A., (1958), Organizations, John Wiley & Sons, Inc., New York.

McCaskey, M. B., (1982), The Executive Challenge, Pittman Publishing, N. C.

McGivering, I., Matthews, D. and Scott, W.H., (1960), Management in Britain, Liverpool University Press, Liverpool.

Merwe, A. & Merive, S., (1985), Strategic Leadership and Chief Executive, Long-Range Planning, February.

Miles, R. E. & Snow, C. C., (1978), Organizational Strategy, Structure, and Process, McGraw-Hill, New York.

Mintzberg, H., (1973a), Strategy-Making in Three Modes, California Management Review, Winter.

Mintzberg, H., (1973b), The Nature of Managerial Work, Harper & Row, New York.

Mintzberg, H., (1975), 'The Manager's Job: Folklore and Fact', Harvard Business Review, July–August.

Morris, G. C., 1982, Psychology: An Introduction, Prentice-Hall, N.J.

Murakami, T., (1978), 'Recent Changes in Long-Range Corporate Planning in Japan', Long-Range Planning, April.

NAA, (1964), Long-Range Profit Planning, NAA, New York.

NAA, (1967), Financial Analysis to Guide Capital Expenditure Decisions, NAA, New York.

Nakajo, T. & Kono, T., (1989), Success Through Culture Change in a Japanese Brewery, Long-Range Planning, December.

Naor, J., (1978), 'A New Approach to Corporate Planning', Long-Range Planning, April.

Nazel, A., (1981), 'Strategy Formulation for Smaller Firms', Long-Range Planning, August.

Neumann, J. & Morgenstern, O., (1944), Theory of Games and Economic Behavior, Princeton Univ. Press, N. J.

Organizational Science, (1983), Special Edition on Corporate Culture, vol. 17, no. 3, Tokyo.

Pascale, R. T. & Athos, A. G., (1981), The Art of Japanese Management, Simon and Schuster, New York.

Peters, T. J. & Waterman, R. H., (1982), In Search of Excellence: Lessons from America's Best Run Companies, Harper & Row, New York.

Pettigrew, A. M., (1973), The Politics of Organizational Decision-Making, Tavistock, London

Porter L. W. & Lawler E. E., (1968), Managerial Attitude and Performance, Homewood, Ill.

Porter, M. E., (1980), Competitive Strategy: Techniques for Analyzing Industries and Competitors, Free Press, New York.

Porter, M. E., (1985), Competitive Advantage: Creating and Sustaining Superior Performance, Free Press, New York.

Prahalad, C. K. & Hamel, G., (1989), Strategic Intent, Harvard Business Review, May-June.

Prahalad, C. K. & Hamel, G., (1990), The Core Competence of the Corporation, Harvard Business Review, May–June.

Pyhrr, P. A., (1973), Zero-Base Budgeting, John Wiley & Sons, Inc., New York.

Quinn, J. B., (1978), Strategic Change, Logical Incrementalism, Sloan Management Review, Fall.

Quinn, J. B., (1980), Strategies for Change; Logical Incrementalism, Richard Irwin, Ill.

Quinn, J. B., (1985), 'Managing Innovation: Controlled Chaos', Harvard Business Review, May–June.

Quinn, J. B., Mintzberg, H. & James, R.M., (1988), The Strategy Process, Prentice-Hall, N. J.

Ramanujam, V. and Venkatraman, N., (1987), Planning System Characteristics and Planning Effectiveness, Strategic Management Journal, vol. 8.

Richards, M. D., (1978), Organizational Goal Structures, West Publishing, St. Paul, Minn.

Riggs, H. E., (1983), Managing High-Technology Companies, Wadsworth, CA.

Robbins, S. R., (1974), Managing Organizational Conflict, Prentice-Hall, N. J.

Robinson, J., (1986), Paradoxes in Planning, Long-Range Planning, December.

Roethlisberger F. J. & Dickson W. J., (1939), Management and the Worker, Harvard University Press, Mass.
Rothschild, W. E., (1976), Putting it all Together, AMACOM, New York.
Rothschild, W. E., (1979), Strategic Alternatives: Selection, Development and Implementation, AMACOM, New York.
Rowe, A. J., (1982), 'What is an Effective decision?', in: Rowe, Mason and Dickel, Editors, (1982), Strategic Management and Business Policy, Addison-Wesley, CA.
Rowe, Mason & Dickel, (1982), Strategic Management and Business Policy, Addison-Wesley, CA.
Rowe, Mason & Dickel, (1985), Strategic Management and Business Policy, Addison-Wesley, CA.
Ruce and Raiffa, (1957), Games and Decisions, John Wiley and Sons, N. Y.
Rumelt, R. P., (1974), Strategy, Structure and Economic Performance, Harvard University Press, Mass.
Rumelt, R. P., (1979), 'Evaluation of Strategy: Theory and Models', in: Schendel, D. E. & Hofer, C. W., Editors, (1979), Strategic Management: A New View of Business Policy and Planning, Little Brown, Boston.
Rumelt, R. P., (1976), 'The Evaluation of Business Strategy', in: Glueck, W. F., (1980), Strategic Management and Business Policy, McGraw-Hill, New York.
Shein, E. H., (1961), Management Development as a Process of Influence, Sloan Management Review, May.
Shein, E. H., (1985), Organizational Culture and Leadership, Jossey Bass, San Francisco.
Shein, E. H., (1986), 'How Culture Forms, Develops, and Changes', in: Kilmann et al, Editors, Gaining Control of the Corporate Culture, Jossey Bass, CA.
Simon, H. A., (1957), Administrative Behavior, Macmillan, New York.
Simon, H. A., (1977), The New Science of Management Decision, Prentice-Hall, N. J.
Staw, B. M., (1976), Intrinsic and Extrinsic Motivation, General Learning Press, N. J.
Steiner, G. A., (1969), Top Management Planning, Macmillan, New York.
Steiner, G. A., (1979), Strategic Planning: What Every Manager Must Know. A step-by-step Guide, Free Press, New York
Steiner, G., (1983), Formal Strategic Planning in the U.S., Long-Range Planning, no. 3.
Steiner, G. A. & Miner, J. B., (1977), Management Policy and Strategy: Text, Readings and Cases, Macmillan, New York.
Stonich, P. J., (1977), Zero-Base Planning and Budgeting, Richard Irwin, Ill.
Sutton, Harris, Kaysen and Tobin, (1956), The American Business Creed.
Taylor, B., (1975), 'Strategy for Planning', Long-Range Planning, August.
Taylor, B., (1986), Corporate Planning for the 1990s: The New Frontiers, Long-Range Planning, December.
Taylor, B. & Hawkins, K., Editors, (1972), Handbook of Strategic Planning, Longman, London.
Taylor, F. W., (1911), The Principles of Scientific Management, Harper & Brothers, New York.
The Conference Board, 1972, Planning and the Chief Executive, The Conference Board, New York.
The Conference Board, 1974, Planning and the Corporate Planning Director, The Conference Board, New York.
The Conference Board, 1976, Corporate Guides to Long-Range Planning, The Conference Board, New York.

The Conference Board, 1978, Planning Under Uncertainty: Multiple Scenarios and Contingency Planning, The Conference Board, New York.

Thompson, J. D., (1967), Organizations in Action, McGraw-Hill, New York.

Thune, S. & House, R., (1970), 'Where Long-Range Planning Pays off', Business Horizons, August.

Tilles, S., (1963), How To Evaluate Corporate Strategy, Harvard Business Review, no. 4.

Tönnies, F., (1887), Gemeinschaft und Gesellschaft.

Topfer, A., (1978), 'Corporate Planning and Control in German Industry', Long-Range Planning, February.

Vogel, E., (1979), Japan as Number One, Harvard University Press, Cambridge, Mass.

Warren, E. K., (1966), Long-Range Planning, Prentice-Hall, New York.

Weick, K. E., (1969), The Social Psychology of Organizing, Addision-Wesley Publishing Co., Mass.

Wilkins, A. L. & Ouchi, W.G.: Efficient Cultures, (1983), Administrative Science Quarterly, September

Williamson, O. E., (1975), Markets and Hierarchies: Analysis and Antitrust Implications, Free Press, New York.

Wrapp, H. E., (1970), 'Good Managers Don't Make Policy Decisions', Harvard Business Review.

Yavitz, B. & Newman, W. H., (1988), Strategy in Action, Free Press, New York.

Yoshino, M., (1968), Japan's Managerial System, MITI Press, Cambridge, Mass.

Yoshino, Y., (1969), Japan's Managerial System: Tradition and Innovation, MITI Press, Cambridge, Mass.

Yoshino, M. Y., (1975), Japan's Managerial System: Tradition and Innovation, MITI Press, Cambridge, Mass.

Appendix: Sources of data

1. The findings of this book are based upon a variety of data sources. These included the following:

1.1 Two kind of monthly meetings between the author (acting as co-ordinator) and relevant corporate planners.

1.2 Published case-study books on the corporations, a great number of which are available in Japan.

1.3 Company visits and interviews with corporate planners.

1.4 General published literature from corporations, with particular attention to historical data.

1.5 Published articles on corporations, usually in business periodicals.

1.6 Mail questionnaire surveys (see below).

2. The mail survey method incorporated the following steps:

2.1 Historical surveys on long-range planning practises, conducted, since 1963, in Japan (eight times), the U.S.A. (once) and the U.K. (once). The two most recent surveys are described below.

2.2 In June, 1985 and July, 1989 questionnaires were distributed to relevant corporations. In the former study a response rate of 25.1% was achieved (384 valid replies from a distribution list of 1,673) and in the latter study this fell slightly to 21% (249 from 1,200).

2.3 The distribution of respondents by industry is recorded in Table A1, and by sales in Table A2, both of which are detailed below.

2.4 The *Japan Productivity Center (Tokyo)* assisted in the distribution and collection of survey mail.

Table A. 1 Distribution of Respondents by Industry

Industry \ Year	1985	1989
(1) Mining and Construction	37 co.	23 co.
(2) Food and Fisheries	17	8
(3) Fibre, Pulp and Paper	21	9
(4) Chemicals	44	32
(5) Petroleum, Rubber, Soil & Stone	20	15
(6) Iron, Steel & Non-ferrous metals	29	15
(7) Machinery	29	13
(8) Electrical appliances & Precision Machinery	58	35
(9) Transportation Equipment & Machinery	27	13
Sub-total:	282	163
(10) Finance & Insurance	39	33
(11) Commerce, Service, Real Estat	54	43
(12) Communication, Warehousing & Transportation		
(13) Electricity, Gas & Coal	9	10
Sub-total:	102	86
Total:	384 co.	249 co.

Table A. 2 Distribution of Respondents by Sales

Sales \ Year	1985	1989
$ over 20,000 million	12 co.	18 co.
$ 2,000 ~ 20,000 million	90	67
$ 800 ~ 2,000 million	89	67
$ 200 ~ 800 million	109	69
$ 70 ~ 200 million	63	18
$ 20 ~ 20 million	19	3
Less than 20 million	1	0
NA	1	7
Total:	384 co.	249 co.

(Note) Exchange rate: ¥ 150 = $ 1

Index